Hands-On Azure fo Developers

Implement rich Azure PaaS ecosystems using containers, serverless services, and storage solutions

Kamil Mrzygłód

BIRMINGHAM - MUMBAI

Hands-On Azure for Developers

Commissioning Editor: Gebin George
Acquisition Editor: Shrilekha Inani
Content Development Editor: Deepti Thore, Dattatraya More
Technical Editor: Sayali Thanekar
Copy Editor: Safis Editing
Project Coordinator: Jagdish Prabhu
Proofreader: Safis Editing
Indexer: Rekha Nair
Graphics: Jisha Chirayil
Production Coordinator: Shraddha Falebhai

First published: November 2018

Production reference: 1291118

Published by Packt Publishing Ltd.
Livery Place
35 Livery Street
Birmingham
B3 2PB, UK.

ISBN 978-1-78934-062-4

www.packtpub.com

For Klaudia, who inspires me to develop myself every day.
— Kamil Mrzygłód

`mapt.io`

Mapt is an online digital library that gives you full access to over 5,000 books and videos, as well as industry leading tools to help you plan your personal development and advance your career. For more information, please visit our website.

Why subscribe?

- Spend less time learning and more time coding with practical eBooks and Videos from over 4,000 industry professionals

- Improve your learning with Skill Plans built especially for you

- Get a free eBook or video every month

- Mapt is fully searchable

- Copy and paste, print, and bookmark content

Packt.com

Did you know that Packt offers eBook versions of every book published, with PDF and ePub files available? You can upgrade to the eBook version at `www.packt.com` and as a print book customer, you are entitled to a discount on the eBook copy. Get in touch with us at `customercare@packtpub.com` for more details.

At `www.packt.com`, you can also read a collection of free technical articles, sign up for a range of free newsletters, and receive exclusive discounts and offers on Packt books and eBooks.

Contributors

About the author

Kamil Mrzygłód is a skilled software developer, architect, and Microsoft Azure MVP. He is focused on delivering fast, reliable, and flexible cloud solutions based on the Microsoft Azure platform. He has spoken at multiple conferences and meetups, working on **open source software** (**OSS**) projects and driving workshops for different people and companies. Over recent years, he has developed an interest in Azure serverless architectures, data analysis, and big data components. Currently, he works at Demant Technology Center in Warsaw. His current goal is to make the world of cloud computing as accessible as it can be so that it's possible to lower the learning curve of this technology and help others start using it.

I would like to thank my editor, Dattatraya More, for his helpful insights and valuable guidance, which helped me a lot while writing this book. I would also like to thank Shrilekha Inani, who gave me the opportunity to become an author and assisted me in all the formal aspects of doing so. Last, but by no means least, I would like to thank my reviewers—you really made this book worth reading by carefully examining whether each chapter made sense.

About the reviewers

Kasam Shaikh, a Microsoft Azure enthusiast, is a seasoned professional with a can-do attitude and 10 years of industry experience working as a cloud architect with one of the leading IT companies in Mumbai, India. He is a certified Azure architect, recognized as an MVP by a leading online community, as well as a global AI speaker, and has authored books on Azure Cognitive, Azure Bots, and Microsoft Bot frameworks. He is head of the **Azure INDIA (az-INDIA)** community, the fastest growing online community for learning Azure.

Praveen Kumar Sreeram works as an Azure architect at MNC. He has 12 years of experience in the field of development, analysis, design, and delivery of applications of various technologies, including custom web development using ASP.NET and MVC to building mobile apps using the cross-platform technology Xamarin for domains such as insurance, telecoms, and wireless expense management. He has been awarded two times as the Most Valuable Professional CSharpCorner. You can also follow him on Twitter at @PrawinSreeram. His current focus is on analyzing business problems and providing technical solutions for various projects related to Microsoft Azure and .NET Core. He is also an author of a book call *Azure Serverless computing cookbook*.

Packt is searching for authors like you

If you're interested in becoming an author for Packt, please visit authors.packtpub.com and apply today. We have worked with thousands of developers and tech professionals, just like you, to help them share their insight with the global tech community. You can make a general application, apply for a specific hot topic that we are recruiting an author for, or submit your own idea.

Table of Contents

Preface   1

Chapter 1: Azure App Service   7
  Technical requirements   7
  Creating and deploying Azure App Service   8
    Creating Azure App Service using the Azure Portal   8
      Selecting Azure Web App from available services   8
      Configuring an Azure web app   10
        Creating an App Service Plan   11
    Creating an Azure App Service using Visual Studio   15
    Deploying Azure App Service using FTP   22
      Deploying Azure App Service with user-level credentials   22
      Deploying Azure App Service using app-level credentials   27
        Downloading app-level credentials from the Azure Portal   28
        Configuring WebDeploy in Visual Studio   29
    Creating Azure App Services using Visual Studio Code   30
  Working with different operating systems and platforms   33
    Selecting an operating system   34
    Selecting different platforms   35
  Different App Service Plans and features   37
    Dev/Test App Service Plans   38
    Production App Service Plans   39
    Isolated App Service Plans   40
  Securing App Services using different security providers   41
    Configuring authentication/authorization in the Azure Portal   41
      Using Azure Active Directory to secure App Services   42
      Using other authentication providers   46
  Diagnostics and monitoring of App Services   46
    The Overview blade   47
    Metrics   47
    Monitoring   48
  Summary   49
  Questions   49
  Further reading   50

Chapter 2: Azure WebJobs   51
  Technical requirements   51
  Creating WebJobs   51
    Creating and deploying WebJobs in Azure Portal   52
      Creating an application in Visual Studio   52
      Deploying a WebJob in the Azure Portal   53

Deploying WebJobs from Visual Studio 57
Working with the WebJobs SDK 60
Calling a job manually 63
Automatic triggers in WebJobs 64
Publish a job 66
Azure WebJobs limitations 67
Using different file types for WebJobs 68
Creating and deploying a Node.js application as a WebJob 68
Deploying a Node.js Azure WebJob from Visual Studio Code 69
Summary 71
Questions 71
Further reading 71

Chapter 3: Deploying Web Applications as Containers 73
Technical requirements 73
Working with AKS 74
Preparing an application 74
Container Registry and Kubernetes clusters 76
Pushing a Docker image to Azure Container Registry 77
Creating a Kubernetes cluster using AKS 80
Running, scaling, and updating an application in AKS 82
Solving problems with authentication 84
Scaling a cluster 86
Updating an application 86
Azure Container Instances 87
Creating and deploying an application and container 87
Pushing an image to Azure Container Registry 89
Deploying an application to ACI 89
Web App for Containers 92
Creating a web app hosted in a container 92
Deploying a custom application 96
Summary 98
Questions 99
Further reading 99

Chapter 4: Distributed Applications and Microservices with Service Fabric 101
Technical requirements 102
Understanding microservices 102
Monolith versus microservices 102
Microservice approach 103
Using different languages and frameworks 103
Scaling and updating services individually 104
Using well-designed interfaces and protocols 105
Dealing with state 105
Diagnosing and monitoring microservices 106
Containers, services, and actors in SF 107

Containers	107
Creating a cluster	107
Deploying a container	111
Packaging a service	113
Reliable services	114
Creating a SF application	114
Deploying an application to the cloud	119
Reliable actors	124
Creating a project with actors	125
Creating an actor's client	128
Communication between services	129
Creating a communication channel	130
Clusters in SF	133
Cluster security	134
Node-to-node security	134
Client-to-node security	135
Scaling	136
Scaling a cluster up or down	136
Monitoring and diagnostics	137
Application monitoring	137
Cluster monitoring	138
Health monitoring	138
Summary	139
Questions	140
Further reading	140
Chapter 5: Using Azure Search	141
Technical requirements	141
Creating an Azure Search service	141
Using Azure Portal	142
Full-text search in Azure Search	146
Sending a request	146
Linguistic analysis in full-text search	150
Analyzers in Azure Search	150
Analyzer selection	153
Indexing in Azure Search	154
Importing more data	154
Push model	154
Pull model	156
Cognitive search – adding AI to the indexing workload	157
Configuring Cognitive Search	158
Summary	160
Questions	160
Further reading	161
Chapter 6: Mobile Notifications with Notification Hub	163

Technical requirements 163
Reasons to use Notification Hub 164
  Challenges for application design 164
Push notification architecture 166
  Direct connection 166
  Queued communication 167
  Triggered communication 168
Registering devices in Notification Hub 169
  Notification Hub device registration 169
    Creating a Notification Hub 170
    Registering in an application 171
    Checking available registrations 173
    Using installations 174
Sending a notification 175
  Sending a test notification 175
    Test notification in Azure Portal 175
    Test notification in the SDK 177
  Using the SDK to send a notification 177
Rich content notifications 180
  Creating and sending a rich content notification 180
Summary 181
Questions 181
Further reading 182

Chapter 7: Serverless and Azure Functions 183
Technical requirements 184
Understanding Azure Functions 184
  Being "serverless" 184
    Responsibilities of cloud vendors 184
    Pricing model 185
  Azure Functions concepts 187
    Function app 187
    Functions 189
    Triggers and bindings 190
    Pricing models 191
  Scaling 192
    Scaling in the consumption model 192
    Scaling in the App Service model 193
Configuring the local environment for developing Azure Functions 193
  Starting with Azure Functions locally 193
Creating a function 198
  Using Visual Studio 198
  Using Azure Portal 201
Azure Functions features 205
  Platform features 205
  Security 207

Monitor 209
Host.json 211
Publish 212
Workflow in Azure Functions – Durable Functions 213
Orchestrations and activities 214
Orchestration client 215
Orchestration history 216
Timers 217
External events 218
Integrating functions with other services 219
Function file 219
Input/output bindings 221
Custom bindings 222
Summary 223
Questions 223
Further reading 224

Chapter 8: Integrating Different Components with Logic Apps 225
Technical requirements 225
What is Azure Logic Apps? 226
Azure Logic Apps – how it works 226
Azure Logic Apps – advantages 228
Connectors for Logic Apps 230
Connector types 230
Built-in connectors 230
Managed API connectors 231
On-premises connectors 232
Integration account connectors and enterprise connectors 232
Creating Logic Apps and integrating services 233
Creating Logic Apps in Azure Portal 233
Working with Azure Logic Apps in Visual Studio 239
B2B integration 241
Starting B2B integration in Azure Logic Apps 241
Summary 243
Questions 244
Further reading 244

Chapter 9: Swiss Army Knife - Azure Cosmos DB 245
Technical requirements 246
Understanding Cosmos DB 246
Creating a Cosmos DB instance in the portal 246
Using Azure Cosmos DB in Visual Studio 251
Pricing in Azure Cosmos DB 255
Partitioning, throughput, and consistency 256
Partitions in Azure Cosmos DB 256

Throughput in Azure Cosmos DB 258
Consistency in Azure Cosmos DB 258
CosmosDB data models and APIs 260
SQL 261
MongoDB 261
Graph 262
Table 262
Cassandra 263
Different features of CosmosDB 263
Account level throughput 264
Database level throughput 265
Firewall and virtual networks 265
Azure Functions 266
Stored procedures 267
User-defined functions and triggers 268
Summary 269
Questions 270
Further reading 270

Chapter 10: Reactive Architecture with Event Grid 271
Technical requirements 271
Azure Event Grid and reactive architecture 272
Reactive architecture 272
Topics and event subscriptions 274
Event sources 274
Event handlers 275
Topics and subscriptions 276
Connecting services through Azure Event Grid 278
Creating Azure Event Grid in Azure Portal 278
Azure Event Grid security 281
Creating a subscription 282
Publishing custom events to Azure Event Grid 286
Event gateway concept 287
Handling a custom event 288
Integrating Azure Functions with Azure Event Grid 292
EventGridTrigger in Azure Functions 292
Testing Azure Event Grid and Azure Functions 297
Summary 298
Questions 298
Further reading 298

Chapter 11: Using Azure Storage - Tables, Queues, Files, and Blobs 299
Technical requirements 299
Using Azure Storage in a solution 300
Different Azure Storage services 300

Different types of storage account 300
Securing Azure Storage 301
Replication 302
Storing data with Azure Storage Tables 303
Creating an Azure Storage service 303
Managing Table Storage 306
Storing data in Table Storage 308
PartitionKey 309
RowKey 309
Timestamp 309
General rules for entities 309
Querying data in Table Storage 310
Table API in Azure Cosmos DB 313
Implementing fully managed file shares with Azure Files 313
Azure Files concepts 314
Working with Azure Files 314
Blob Storage versus Azure Files 317
Queues in Azure Queue Storage 318
Queue Storage features 318
Developing an application using Queue Storage 318
Object storage solution – Azure Storage Blobs 320
Blob Storage concepts 320
Inserting data into Blob Storage 322
Containers and permissions 324
Blob Storage: additional features 328
Summary 329
Questions 329
Further reading 330
Chapter 12: Big Data Pipeline - Azure Event Hub 331
Technical requirements 331
Azure Event Hub service and concepts 332
Azure Event Hub concepts 332
Azure Event Hub durability 335
Working with Azure Event Hub 336
Creating an Azure Event Hub in the Azure portal 336
Working with Azure Event Hub in the portal 338
Developing applications with Azure Event Hub 342
Azure Event Hub security 350
Event publishers 350
IP filters 352
Azure Event Hub Capture feature 353
How Azure Event Hub Capture works 354
Enabling Event Hub Capture 355
Summary 358

Questions	359
Further reading	359
Chapter 13: Real-Time Data Analysis - Azure Stream Analytics	361
Technical requirements	361
Azure Stream Analytics introduction	362
Stream ingestions versus stream analysis	362
Azure Stream Analytics concepts	364
Input and output types	365
Create Azure Stream Analytics in Azure portal	366
Adding an input	368
Adding an output	370
Azure Stream Analytics query language	373
Writing a query	373
Event ordering, checkpoints, and replays	377
Event ordering	377
Checkpoints and replays	379
Summary	380
Questions	380
Further reading	380
Chapter 14: Enterprise Integration - Azure Service Bus	381
Technical requirements	382
Azure Service Bus fundamentals	382
Azure Service Bus versus other messaging services	382
Azure Service Bus and Azure Storage Queues	383
Azure Service Bus in Azure portal	384
Queues, topics, and relays	389
Queues	389
Topics	390
Relays	390
Azure Service Bus design patterns	391
Developing solutions with Azure Service Bus SDK	391
Azure Service Bus security	394
Managed Service Identity	394
RBAC	395
Advanced features of Azure Service Bus	396
Dead lettering	396
Sessions	397
Transactions	398
Handling outages and disasters	399
Disaster recovery	399
Handling outages	401
Summary	403
Questions	403

Further reading 404
Chapter 15: Using Application Insights to Monitor Your Applications 405
  Technical requirements 405
  Using the Application Insights service 406
    Logging data in the cloud 406
    Azure Application Insights fundamentals 408
    Creating Azure Application Insights in the portal 409
  Monitoring different platforms 411
    .NET 412
    Node.js 414
    Azure Functions 415
  Analytics module 418
    Accessing the Analytics module 418
  Application Insights automation 422
    Alerts 423
  Summary 428
  Questions 429
  Further reading 429
Chapter 16: SQL in Azure - Azure SQL 431
  Technical requirements 431
  Differences between Microsoft SQL Server and Azure SQL 432
    Azure SQL fundamentals 432
    Advanced Azure SQL features 436
    SQL Server on VMs 437
  Creating and configuring Azure SQL 439
    Creating an Azure SQL instance 439
    Azure SQL features in the portal 444
  Security 450
    Firewall 451
    Advanced Threat Protection 453
    Auditing 456
    Dynamic Data Masking 458
  Scaling Azure SQL 460
    Single database 461
    Elastic pool 462
    Read scale-out 462
    Sharding 463
  Monitoring and tuning 464
    Monitoring 464
    Tuning 465
  Summary 467
  Questions 468
  Further reading 468

Chapter 17: Big Data Storage - Azure Data Lake   469
  Technical requirements   469
  Understanding Azure Data Lake Store   470
    Azure Data Lake Store fundamentals   470
    Creating an Azure Data Lake Store instance   472
  Storing data in Azure Data Lake Store   475
    Using the Azure portal to navigate   476
      Filter   477
      New folder   478
      Upload   478
      Access   480
      Files and folders   482
    Microsoft Azure Storage Explorer   482
    Using SDKs   483
  Security   484
    Authentication and authorization   484
      RBAC   485
      POSIX ACL   487
    Network isolation   488
  Best practices   489
    Performance   489
    Security   490
    Resiliency   490
    Data structure   491
  Summary   491
  Questions   491
  Further reading   492

Chapter 18: Scaling Azure Applications   493
  Technical requirements   493
  Autoscaling, scaling up, scaling out   493
    Autoscaling   494
    Scaling up and scaling out   495
  Scaling Azure App Services   497
    Manual scaling   497
    Autoscaling   499
  Scaling Azure Functions   502
    Scaling serverless applications   503
    Scaling Azure Functions   503
  Scaling Azure Service Fabric   505
    Scaling a cluster manually   506
    Using Azure SDK to scale your cluster   508
  Summary   510
  Questions   510
  Further reading   510

Chapter 19: Serving Static Content Using Azure CDN   511
  Technical requirements   511
  Azure CDN fundamentals   512
    Working with CDNs   512
    Creating an Azure CDN in the portal   514
  Optimization and caching   519
    Configuring the endpoint   519
      Compression   520
      Caching rules   521
      Geo-filtering   522
  Developing applications with Azure CDN   522
    Configuring Azure App Service with Azure CDN   523
  Summary   525
  Questions   526
  Further reading   526

Chapter 20: Distributing Load with Azure Traffic Manager   527
  Technical requirements   527
  Azure Traffic Manager fundamentals   527
    Functions of Azure Traffic Manager   528
    Creating Azure Traffic Manager in the Azure portal   530
      Routing method – performance   531
      Routing method – weighted   532
      Routing method – priority   533
      Routing method – geographic   533
      Routing method – MultiValue   534
      Routing method – subnet   534
    Working with Azure Traffic Manager in the Azure Portal   535
      Configuration   536
      Real user measurements   537
      Endpoints   538
  Monitoring   542
    Nslookup   542
    Traffic view   543
  Summary   544
  Questions   544
  Further reading   544

Chapter 21: Tips and Tricks for Azure   545
  Technical requirements   545
  The Azure CLI and Cloud Shell   546
    The Azure CLI   546
    Cloud Shell   548
  Locks   551
    Creating and managing locks   552
  Naming conventions   555

Finding the best naming convention   555
Resources in Azure   557
Azure Resource Explorer   557
Summary   561
Questions   561
Further reading   561

Assessments   563

Other Books You May Enjoy   575

Index   579

Preface

Cloud technology is currently one of the most popular trends within the IT industry. Every day, a new company embarks on its journey with cloud computing, distancing itself from traditional on-premise setups, which have a tendency to hinder quick development and impede scaling operations. As the modern world requires us to adjust rapidly to changing expectations and dynamic workloads, knowledge of how to develop applications in the cloud is becoming more and more valuable.

You are holding in your hands a book that will guide you through the different capabilities and services of one of the most popular cloud offerings around—Microsoft Azure. We will focus mostly on **Platform-as-a-Service (PaaS)** components, which allow you to skip the cumbersome process of provisioning the infrastructure and focus directly on configuring various features and deploying your code, so that your application will be scalable, highly available, and resilient. The goal of each chapter is to give you a better understanding of multiple cloud patterns, connections, and integrations, so you can quickly start your very own project with an understanding of which Azure service you should use in this particular architecture.

Who this book is for

This book is designed to act as a journey through different Azure PaaS offerings. It covers many basic and intermediate concepts of different services, an understanding of which is crucial when it comes to developing reliable and robust solutions based on the Microsoft cloud platform. The main audiences are developers and IT pros who have just started working with Azure, or who want to do so, and who are seeking a detailed guide to enable them to extend their cloud skills.

What this book covers

Chapter 1, *Azure App Services*, covers how to work with and develop web applications, monitoring, and diagnosis.

Chapter 2, *Azure WebJobs*, explains how to develop jobs co-hosted with Azure App Services.

Chapter 3, *Deploying Web Applications as Containers*, explains how to develop a web application and host it within a container using Azure App Services.

Chapter 4, *Distributed Applications and Microservices with Service Fabric,* is a basic introduction to a microservice platform called Azure Service Fabric.

Chapter 5, *Using Azure Search,* explains how to develop a search engine using Azure Search and utilize it in your application.

Chapter 6, *Mobile Notifications with Notification Hub,* covers the development of applications that leverage push notifications.

Chapter 7, *Serverless and Azure Functions,* outlines the building of applications based on the FaaS model.

Chapter 8, *Integrating Different Components with Logic Apps,* discusses the integration of different parts of your system using Azure Logic Apps.

Chapter 9, *Swiss Army Knife - Azure Cosmos DB,* covers the utilization of a modern storage solution with multiple APIs and a consistency model.

Chapter 10, *Reactive Architecture with Event Grid,* demonstrates how to reverse a control with another serverless Azure component called Azure Event Grid.

Chapter 11, *Using Azure Storage - Tables, Queues, Files, and Blobs,* covers a common Azure storage service with many different features.

Chapter 12, *Big Data Pipeline - Azure Event Hub,* explains how to create applications handling thousands of requests per second.

Chapter 13, *Real-Time Data Analysis - Azure Stream Analytics,* explains how to perform analyses on a stream of data.

Chapter 14, *Enterprise Integration - Azure Service Bus,* introduces an enterprise-class Azure service for messaging.

Chapter 15, *Using Application Insights to Monitor Your Applications,* explains how to use Azure Application Insights to log data from different Azure services as well as from your own applications.

Chapter 16, *SQL in Azure - Azure SQL,* introduces a relational database PaaS offering that is available in Azure.

Chapter 17, *Big Data Storage - Azure Data Lake,* introduces a limitless storage service for storing schemaless data.

Chapter 18, *Scaling Azure Applications,* covers more advanced topics on scaling applications and how scaling works in Azure.

Chapter 19, *Serving Static Content Using Azure CDN*, introduces your very own CDN hosted within Azure.

Chapter 20, *Distributing Load with Azure Traffic Manager*, explains how to achieve high availability and offload traffic using Azure Traffic Manager.

Chapter 21, *Tips and Tricks for Azure*, provides a bunch of tips for working with Azure and Azure resources.

To get the most out of this book

Activate your Azure subscription (whether a trial version, MSDN subscription feature, or a commercial one).

Since most of the examples are based on the .NET stack, some prior knowledge of this technology will make things easier for you, although, where possible, other technology stacks are also included, while a basic understanding of HTTP concepts (such as the protocol or communication model) will be an advantage. A basic understanding of container-related topics will also be beneficial. More advanced topics and detailed instructions will often be included in the *Further reading* sections. Make sure you cover them all after finishing exercises from this book.

Download the example code files

You can download the example code files for this book from your account at www.packt.com. If you purchased this book elsewhere, you can visit www.packt.com/support and register to have the files emailed directly to you.

You can download the code files by following these steps:

1. Log in or register at www.packt.com.
2. Select the **SUPPORT** tab.
3. Click on **Code Downloads & Errata**.
4. Enter the name of the book in the **Search** box and follow the onscreen instructions.

Once the file is downloaded, please make sure that you unzip or extract the folder using the latest version of:

- WinRAR/7-Zip for Windows
- Zipeg/iZip/UnRarX for Mac
- 7-Zip/PeaZip for Linux

The code bundle for the book is also hosted on GitHub at `https://github.com/PacktPublishing/Hands-On-Azure-for-Developers`. In case there's an update to the code, it will be updated on the existing GitHub repository.

We also have other code bundles from our rich catalog of books and videos available at `https://github.com/PacktPublishing/`. Check them out!

Download the color images

We also provide a PDF file that has color images of the screenshots/diagrams used in this book. You can download it here: `https://www.packtpub.com/sites/default/files/downloads/9781789340624_ColorImages.pdf`.

Conventions used

There are a number of text conventions used throughout this book.

`CodeInText`: Indicates code words in text, database table names, folder names, filenames, file extensions, pathnames, dummy URLs, user input, and Twitter handles. Here is an example: "In the `Main()` method of your application, add the following code."

A block of code is set as follows:

```
using System;

namespace MyFirstWebJob
{
    class Program
    {
```

When we wish to draw your attention to a particular part of a code block, the relevant lines or items are set in bold:

```
var config = new JobHostConfiguration();
config.UseTimers();

var host = new JobHost(config);
```

Any command-line input or output is written as follows:

```
docker images
```

Bold: Indicates a new term, an important word, or words that you see on screen. For example, words in menus or dialog boxes appear in the text like this. Here is an example: "To do so, you have to right-click on the **WebJobs** section of your Azure App Service and select **Open in Portal**."

Warnings or important notes appear like this.

Tips and tricks appear like this.

Get in touch

Feedback from our readers is always welcome.

General feedback: If you have questions about any aspect of this book, mention the book title in the subject of your message and email us at customercare@packtpub.com.

Errata: Although we have taken every care to ensure the accuracy of our content, mistakes do happen. If you have found a mistake in this book, we would be grateful if you would report this to us. Please visit www.packt.com/submit-errata, selecting your book, clicking on the Errata Submission Form link, and entering the details.

Piracy: If you come across any illegal copies of our works in any form on the internet, we would be grateful if you would provide us with the location address or website name. Please contact us at copyright@packt.com with a link to the material.

If you are interested in becoming an author: If there is a topic that you have expertise in, and you are interested in either writing or contributing to a book, please visit authors.packtpub.com.

Reviews

Please leave a review. Once you have read and used this book, why not leave a review on the site that you purchased it from? Potential readers can then see and use your unbiased opinion to make purchase decisions, we at Packt can understand what you think about our products, and our authors can see your feedback on their book. Thank you!

For more information about Packt, please visit `packt.com`.

Azure App Service

Azure App Service is one of the biggest and most commonly used services available in the Azure cloud. It allows for easy development of web applications with multiple features available (such as support for different platforms, including .NET, PHP, and Java), manual and automated scaling, and different performance options. It's a general platform and runtime that fuels other services, such as WebJobs and Azure Functions.

In this chapter, you will learn about the following:

- Creating and deploying Azure App Service
- Working with different operating systems and platforms
- Choosing the right App Service Plan and what their features are
- Securing App Service using different security providers
- Diagnosing and monitoring your applications

Technical requirements

To perform the exercises in this chapter, you will need the following:

- Access to an Azure subscription
- Visual Studio 2017 with Azure development workload installed
- Visual Studio Code installed (available at `https://code.visualstudio.com/`)

Creating and deploying Azure App Service

To get started with Azure App Service, you have to learn how to create that service and deploy your code. You will see how Azure provides many different ways for doing so, and each path can be easier or harder, depending on your current needs and the specification of your application. However, the strength of a cloud and **Platform as a Service (PaaS)** offering lies in the straightforward and intuitive process of provisioning new components of your system.

Creating Azure App Service using the Azure Portal

To begin with App Service, I will show you how you can create your very first web app using the Azure Portal. In fact, all you need is your mouse and keyboard (because each application has to have a name)—neither external hardware nor detailed configuration information is required here, because Azure will do everything for you.

Selecting Azure Web App from available services

To create Azure App Service in the Azure Portal, you first have to find it in the list of available services. The easiest way to do so is to click on **+ Create a resource** button and search for `Web App`:

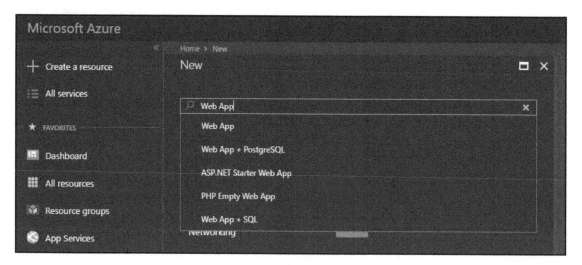

Instead of using the **+ Create a resource** button, you can click on **App Services**—it will forward you to a different view, where you can create an App Service by clicking on the **+ Add** button. This is true for all of the most popular Azure services, such as SQL databases, virtual machines, and storage accounts.

As you can see, the Azure Portal tries to help you find the service most relevant to the search string. When you click on the **Web App** item, you will see another screen containing multiple similar items, all related in some way to the one you are searching for:

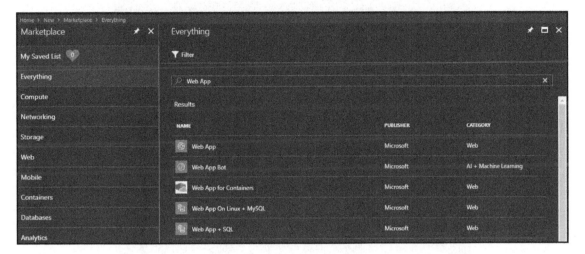

For the purpose of this exercise, select **Web App**, and then click on the **Create** button at the right bottom of the screen.

In the beginning, it is always easier to select the most generic option when it comes to choosing a service. When you gain more experience and become more familiar with available services, you will see that Azure offers many useful preconfigured setups (such as an integrated Web App and SQL database), which can be used to shorten development and configure all services in one place.

Configuring an Azure web app

When you click on the **Create** button, you will see a screen where you can enter all the information needed to create a web app. All required fields are marked using an * (asterisk) symbol:

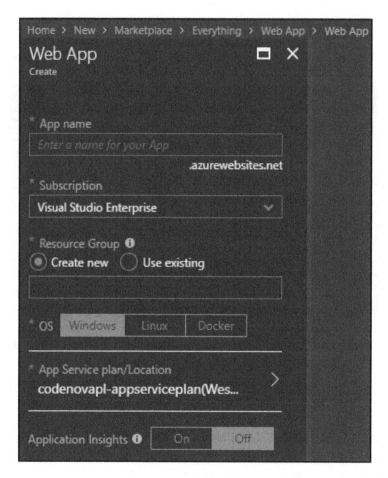

As you can see, when creating a web app, we have to fill almost all fields (with a little exception regarding the **Application Insights** radio button, which we will cover in the next chapters). Let's focus on each field separately, so we have a better understanding of how they work:

- **App name**: This field represents the domain name of your application. It is important to select both a unique and valid name, as it cannot be changed later on. Please note that you can easily attach your own custom domain if needed.

- **Subscription**: If you have access to more than one subscription, you will be given an opportunity to select the right one for this particular resource. Thanks to that, you will be able to differentiate the cost between, for example, different projects.
- **Resource Group**: In Azure, each resource has to be a part of a logic container, called a resource group. This does not imply any additional cost by itself, so you do not have to worry about creating multiple resource groups.
- **OS**: Currently in Azure, you can create a web app using the different operating systems of **Windows**, **Linux**, or **Docker** containers. This choice can impact both cost and performance, so make sure you have chosen the right operating system for your needs.
- **App Service plan/Location**: App Services in Azure are directly linked to App Service Plans, which provide different features and performance depending on the option you choose.

It is always a good practice to leverage resource groups and separate your resources using a specific filter, such as the lifetime of resources, or the given environment (that is, production, staging, or testing). Resource groups gives you better control over deployed services and allows for more granular control over who can access a resource.

Since you are just starting with Azure, you probably do not have any App Service Plans created. As we cannot create an App Service without an App Service Plan, we will sort this now.

Creating an App Service Plan

When you click on **App Service plan/Location**, you will see a screen with the **+ Create new** button, allowing for the creation of a new App Service Plan. It should look like this:

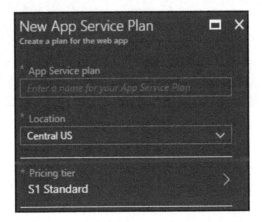

As you can see, we have to enter three fields:

- **App Service plan**: This is the name of your App Service Plan, which has to be unique within a resource group.
- **Location**: Thanks to this setting, we can locate our App Service Plan in a specific region. This sometimes implies different features are available.
- **Pricing tier**: When you click on this item, you will see another screen presenting available features for different available tiers. This choice is really important feature-wise, and will depend in most cases on the environmental characteristics you are planning (such as **Dev / Test** environments, **Production** applications, whether you need deployment slots or not, and so on):

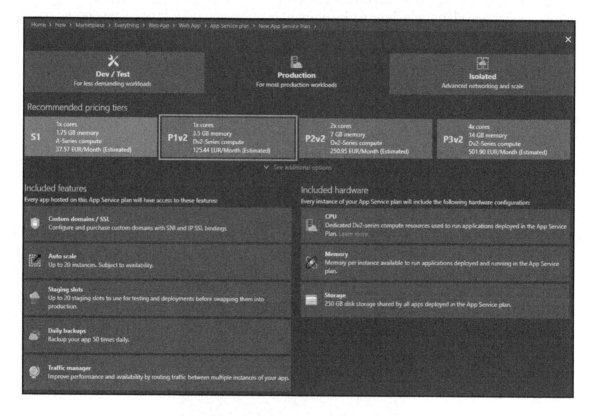

As you can see in the preceding screenshot, we have three categories of App Service Plans:

- **Dev / Test**: This one contains F, D, and B tiers (which stand for free, shared, and basic). They are designed for simple dev/test scenarios and lightweight web applications that do not need features such as autoscaling or backups.
- **Production**: This offers powerful machines and advanced features that are useful in many realistic scenarios, such as APIs, e-commerce, and popular portals.
- **Isolated**: This uses the same hardware as the **Production** tier, but with even more features and possibilities to isolate your web apps from external access. This is the most expensive category, but can be helpful when creating systems that cannot be made available publicly.

 It is important to remember that tiers F and D have a limited amount of computing time per day. That means that once you exceed the limit (60 minutes for the F tier, and 240 minutes for the D tier) of your processing time, your application will become unavailable and be suspended until the next day.

For the purpose of this exercise, I would recommend selecting any tier from the **Dev / Test** category. Once you are satisfied with the option you've selected, you can click the **Apply** button. My configuration, for example, looks like this:

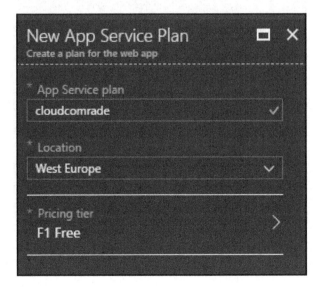

Remember that you can always upgrade (or scale up) the instance of your App Service Plan, for example, when you need a specific feature or the popularity of your application has grown. This is one of the biggest advantages of cloud over on-premises, where you would have to buy and set up new machines on your own.

Now, you can click **OK**, and you will return to the **Web App** blade, where you can enter missing fields. Here, you can see the whole configuration of my web app:

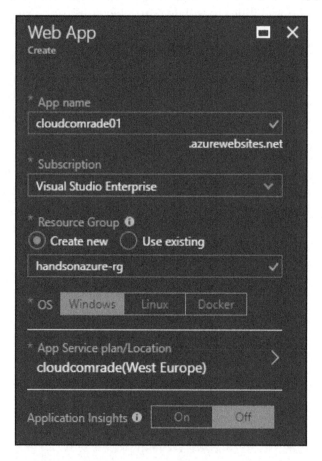

Now the only thing left is to click on the **Create** button and wait several seconds for the creation of a new resource. During this time, Azure will validate the template and parameters, and orchestrate multiple underlying controllers to create a service. Once a new resource is created, you should see a notification and be able to see in your resources. To quickly validate this, click on the **All resources** button on the left and filter all of them using, for example, the name of the App Service you have created:

Creating an Azure App Service using Visual Studio

If you do not want to create your web apps using the Azure Portal, you can use Microsoft Visual Studio, which has built-in integration for many different Azure services.

This exercise was created using Microsoft Visual Studio 2017 (15.6.4) with Azure workloads installed. If you want to configure your instance and ensure everything is set up correctly, please follow the short tutorial available at `https://docs.microsoft.com/en-us/dotnet/azure/dotnet-tools?view=azure-dotnettabs=windows`.

In Visual Studio, click on **File | New Project**. This will display a **New Project** window, where you can find plenty of different templates for starting with a new application. Because we are interested in cloud projects, let's start with the **Cloud** category:

Since we are working with App Services in this chapter, the template we are interested in is **ASP.NET Web Application (.NET Framework)**. The other valid option here is also **ASP.NET Core Web Application**—feel free to use it if you feel confident enough to work with the latest .NET releases, as we will cover both scenarios. When you are satisfied with your choice, click **OK**.

The next step is the selection of the proper template. Here, you have multiple options, such as the following:

- **Empty**: The most simple option, which lets you have full control over installed packages and overall structure
- **Web Forms**: The oldest available framework for building web applications, using many built-in controls with data access
- **MVC**: A well-known **model-view-controller** (**MVC**) architecture, which took the place of **Web Forms**
- **Web API**: A template for creating RESTful HTTP services using the .NET programming stack
- **Single Page Application**: This template comes with plenty of additional tools for building client-side interactions

All the preceding options should be more or less familiar to you. However, thanks to installing the Azure toolset, you should have access to two additional templates:

- **Azure API App**: This offers additional integrations with different Azure services such as Azure AD, API Management, and Logic apps
- **Azure Mobile App**: A template for building mobile backends

However, we will cover those two in the next sections of this chapter. For now, to proceed, let's select **MVC**, as this is the most common and simplest of all templates listed here. Use the default options for this template and click **OK**.

 You have probably noticed an additional button, which I have not described, **Change Authentication**. It allows for selecting the method used for authenticating access to your web application. We will cover that feature in the section describing the security of web apps in Azure.

After several seconds, Visual Studio should generate a project based on the selected template. I believe it should look familiar to you, as it is not that different to a traditional web application created from an MVC template. I am sure you cannot wait to see whether it works—do not wait any longer, and press *F5* to start the application.

You should see a screen similar to mine:

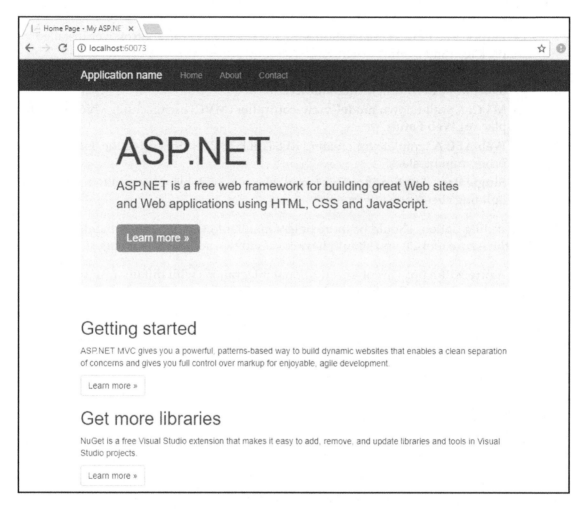

As you can see, it is the same generic template that you would see when starting with a traditional project. The question is, how can we deploy it to Azure to have our website working in the cloud?

Let's stop our website running locally and go back to Visual Studio for a moment. When you right-click on a project icon, you will see a context menu. There, between multiple different options, you can click on **Publish...**:

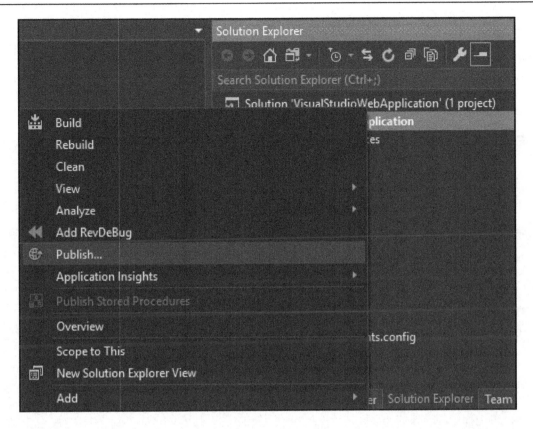

Since this is a cloud project, you will see additional options besides **IIS**, **FTP**, and **Folder**:

- **App Service**: This is for deploying your application to a PaaS service
- **Azure Virtual Machines**: This is for deploying your application to a virtual machine that you have configured

 Because the topic of this book is PaaS services, we will not cover deploying a web app to a virtual machine. However, if you are interested in doing so, proper instructions are available at `https://github.com/aspnet/Tooling/blob/AspNetVMs/docs/create-asp-net-vm-with-webdeploy.md`.

For now, let's select **App Service**. You should see two different options:

- **Create new**: For deploying an application to a freshly created App Service
- **Select existing**: This option is only useful if you have already deployed your site

Because we are just starting, the option we are interested in is **Create new**. After clicking on **Publish...**, you will see another screen, where you can enter all the required parameters. If you read the previous section about creating an App Service using the Azure Portal, some fields should look familiar—in fact, you are doing the very same thing as you would do in the portal. If you skipped this section, I strongly recommend that you go back and read the descriptions. After configuring my web app, my screen looks like this:

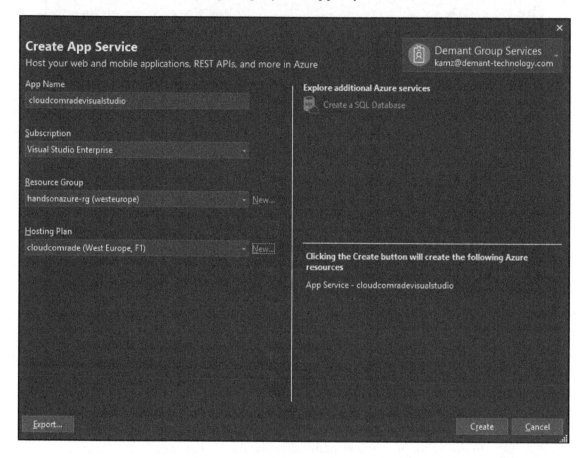

Remember that you can create both resource groups and App Service Plans directly from the preceding screen. If you do not like the options listed there, you can click on the **New...** button, which will guide you through the process of creating a new resource. This is another advantage of tools such as Visual Studio, as you do not have to leave your programming environment to work with Azure.

If you are satisfied with the current configuration, the last thing left is to click on the **Create** button and wait a moment for the application deployment to complete. Additionally, Visual Studio will prepare a publish profile that you can reuse whenever you want to. We will have a look at it, as it will help us in the next section of this chapter. Once deployment is completed, you should see your web application open automatically in your default browser:

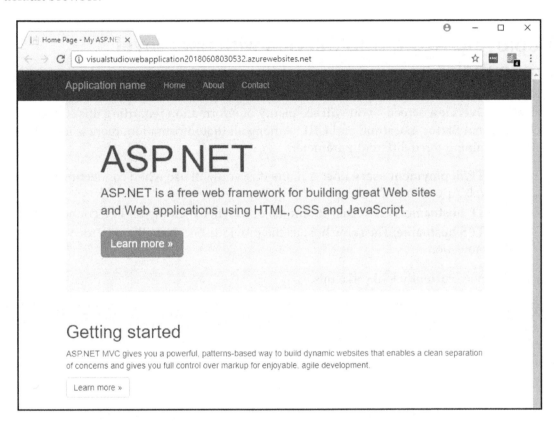

Congratulations! You have just created and deployed your very first App Service. If you take a look at the URL, you'll see that it contains the name you set in the Visual Studio wizard. All web apps in Azure can be accessed using the following URL format:

```
http(s)://{appservicename}.azurewebsites.net
```

This also explains why a name has to be unique: since, by default, all web applications hosted as Azure Web Apps are available publicly, you have to select a name that is not already in use in another URL. In the next section, we will try to use FTP to deploy our application, as an alternative to using Visual Studio.

Deploying Azure App Service using FTP

Using Visual Studio for deployments is a good idea for testing things and development, but for sure, it cannot be used for deploying production environments. The easiest option to upload files to App Service is FTP, which is already integrated with this particular Azure resource.

Deploying Azure App Service with user-level credentials

When you go to the Azure Portal and select the Web App you created previously, take a look at the **Overview** screen—you will see plenty of information regarding this service, such as current **Status**, **Location**, and **URL**. Among all that information, there is an FTP section containing three different parameters:

- **FTP/deployment username**: A name that you will use when connecting to your Web App using FTP client
- **FTP hostname**: A host that should be used when creating an FTP connection
- **FTPS hostname**: The same host as the previous one, but allowing for secure connection

My App Service currently looks like this:

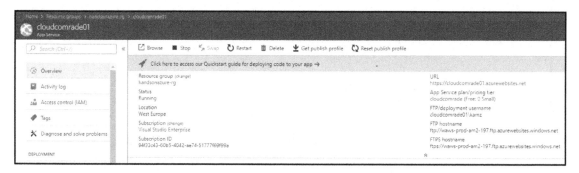

All FTP information can be found in the bottom-right corner of the whole section. What we need now is the FTP client that we will use to connect to the server. I do not have any particular recommendation when it comes to selecting such an application. Personally, I prefer using **FileZilla** for managing my FTP connections and file transfers. You can, however, use whichever client you like, as all are quite similar regarding functionality. Before we start uploading files to the server, we need one more thing, a password for the user. To generate a new password, go to the **Deployment credentials** blade, which can be found on the left in the **DEPLOYMENT** section of App Service features:

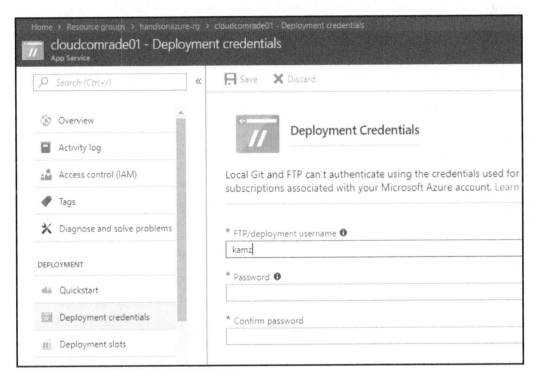

Here, you can set two fields:

- Username for FTP user
- Password for this particular user

You may wonder how this is connected to the previous username, which can be found on the **Overview** screen. The difference is quite simple: using **Deployment credentials**, you are creating a new user that will be used for all applications in all subscriptions associated with your Microsoft Azure account. This has the implication that you will be able to use the very same credentials for each App Service you deploy. This is not ideal for every scenario you will face, but for the purpose of this exercise, let's set a user and use it for deployment. In the next part of this section, I will show you how to retrieve credentials from a **Publish Profile** generated by Visual Studio. Once you enter a username and a password, press **Save**. Now, we can go to the FTP client and use these credentials for setting a connection. Here, you can see my configuration (note that your username has to be in the following format: `<appservicename>\<ftpusername>`):

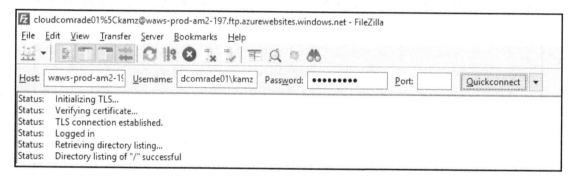

Once you connect to a server, you will see a list of available directories. The very first level contains the following:

- `LogFiles`: Files containing diagnostic information regarding running App Service
- `site`: Your Web App working files are stored here

We will cover `LogFiles` in the next sections of this chapter, describing monitoring and diagnosing an application. For now, we are interested in the `site` folder. When you enter it, you will see other directories: `deployments`, `locks`, and `wwwroot`. The last one should be familiar for those of you who have worked with IIS, as this is the most common name of the folder containing a web application. In fact, this is the working directory of your App Service, where all necessary files should be uploaded. Here, you have the full structure of an empty web app:

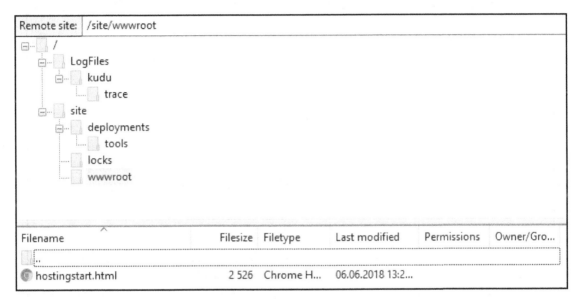

Now that you know how App Service is structured, you can deploy your files and see whether or not it works. If you want, you can reuse a project from the previous exercise, or upload a brand new website.

If you want to reuse files, you can publish a project once again, but this time, instead of publishing it directly to Azure, create a new **Publish Profile** and use a folder as the target. Once Visual Studio finishes creating the package, simply copy files from the output directory to the FTP location using your FTP client.

Here are the files from a previous project of mine uploaded to my FTP server:

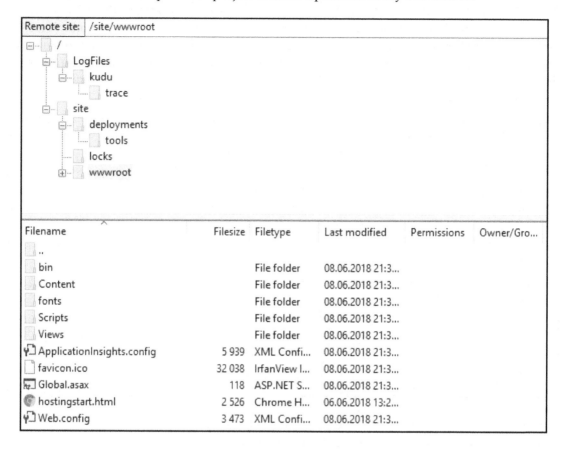

Now, when I go to the URL of my website, I will see a working application:

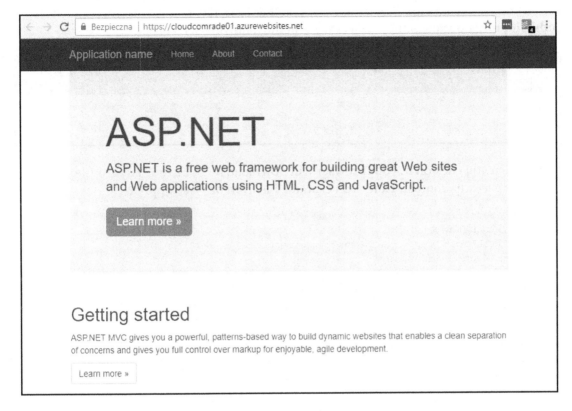

Great—you have just learned how to leverage the FTP feature of App Services to deploy an application from any location and environment. However, as I mentioned earlier, we are using user-level credentials, which will be the same for all web apps that you deploy within your subscription. How do we achieve the same result using an app-level username and password?

Deploying Azure App Service using app-level credentials

There are two ways to deploy an application using app-level credentials:

- Download them from the Azure Portal
- Configure WebDeploy in Visual Studio

Downloading app-level credentials from the Azure Portal

When you go to your App Service and click on the **Overview** blade, you will see the **Get publish profile** button at the top, as shown in the following screenshot:

Now, when you click on it, your browser will download a `.PublishProfile` file. Please open it to check its content. Here is an example file from my web app:

```xml
<?xml version="1.0" encoding="UTF-8"?>
 <publishData>
 <publishProfile profileName="cloudcomrade01 - Web Deploy"
publishMethod="MSDeploy"
publishUrl="cloudcomrade01.scm.azurewebsites.net:443"
msdeploySite="cloudcomrade01" userName="$cloudcomrade01"
userPWD="LEebknaDdg0KS6SgScLuXlwtzxvwYway7ssoKxCSkCLi6Gw0HRyt2iEGMLbP"
destinationAppUrl="http://cloudcomrade01.azurewebsites.net"
SQLServerDBConnectionString="" mySQLDBConnectionString=""
hostingProviderForumLink="" controlPanelLink="http://windows.azure.com"
webSystem="WebSites">
 <databases />
 </publishProfile>
 <publishProfile profileName="cloudcomrade01 - FTP" publishMethod="FTP"
publishUrl="ftp://waws-prod-am2-197.ftp.azurewebsites.windows.net/site/wwwr
oot" ftpPassiveMode="True" userName="cloudcomrade01\$cloudcomrade01"
userPWD="LEebknaDdg0KS6SgScLuXlwtzxvwYway7ssoKxCSkCLi6Gw0HRyt2iEGMLbP"
destinationAppUrl="http://cloudcomrade01.azurewebsites.net"
SQLServerDBConnectionString="" mySQLDBConnectionString=""
hostingProviderForumLink="" controlPanelLink="http://windows.azure.com"
webSystem="WebSites">
 <databases />
 </publishProfile>
 </publishData>
```

As you can see, it is a simple XML file containing plenty of useful information. What we are interested in currently is both the `userName` and `userPWD` properties. Those are what we have been searching for—app-level credentials automatically created on App Service creation. You can use these instead of the user-level ones that we created previously.

Configuring WebDeploy in Visual Studio

To check how to configure **WebDeploy** in Visual Studio, please go through all steps from the beginning of *Creating an Azure App Service using Visual Studio* section about publishing an application from this IDE. If you have done that, go once more to the **Publish** screen.

> If you want to import a publish profile from the previous section, then on the **Publish** screen, you can click on the **New Profile...** button and then select the **Import Profile...** option, which allows you to select a profile file generated previously.

When you click on the **Configure** button, you will see another window containing the whole configuration of your deployment:

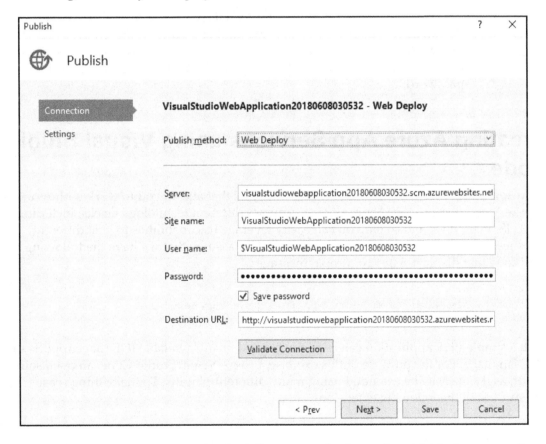

As you can see, it contains a completely different set of information, which does not reflect the user-level settings you have configured.

Please do remember the difference between user-level and app-level credentials. Note that multiple users with access to a given app can use their own user-level credentials individually. What is more, to be able to use app-level credentials, you have to have at least a **Contributor** role on a specific App Service. If you are only a **Reader**, you will not able to access those credentials.

The choice between app-level and user-level credentials depends solely on the process of delivering your application. In most cases, you don't need to check by checking and setting them, as tools such as Visual Studio or Azure DevOps (formerly Visual Studio Team Services) obtain and use them implicitly. App-level credentials are often only used when we are in need of manual deployment.

 You can always reset app-level credentials (for instance, if current ones should be revoked, because of some kind of security issue) from the **Overview** blade. Next to the **Get publish profile** button, you can find the **Reset publish profile** option, which will set a new username and password.

Creating Azure App Services using Visual Studio Code

Microsoft Visual Studio is not the only available IDE that allows you to work with Azure App Services. Because this Azure service supports different technology stacks, including .NET, JS, PHP, Java, and so on, you can easily leverage its capabilities to host different websites using different runtimes. For instance, let's assume that we have the following PHP code that displays a `Hello World` message:

```php
<?php
echo('Hello world from Azure App Service - PHP here!');
?>
```

Such a simple PHP application can be easily created in any available IDE that supports the PHP language. For the purpose of this exercise, I chose Visual Studio Code, an open source editor, as it can easily be extended using many different plugins. To make things easier, you can install the following extensions:

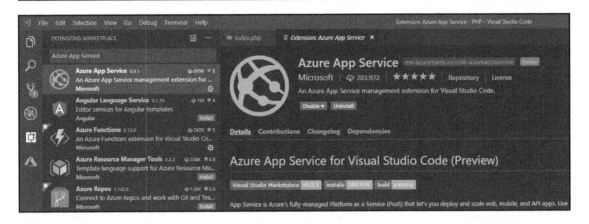

With this plugin installed, you will be able to easily deploy your applications from within the IDE, without the need to go to the portal or use other methods. To push the application to the cloud, you have to go to the **AZURE** tab and find the **APP SERVICE** section.

 Before the first use of these extensions, you may need to authenticate them. Follow the displayed instructions and Visual Studio Code will connect to your subscriptions.

Before we deploy our simple PHP application, we have to create an Azure App Service. To do so, you will have to click on the **Create New Web App...** button:

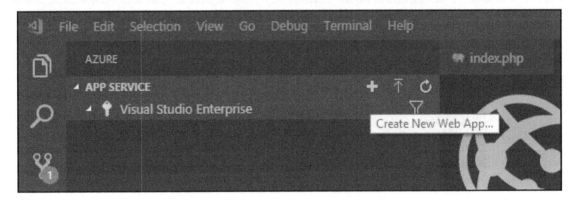

The wizard is a little bit different than in Microsoft Visual Studio, as it acts similarly to a command line, where you provide all fields and information one after another. In Visual Studio Code, you will have to enter the following:

- The Azure App Service name
- The operating system of your choice
- The runtime version

In this particular example, I specified the following:

- `handsonazure-euw-appservice`
- Linux
- PHP 7.2

Once the provisioning is complete, Visual Studio Code will ask you whether to deploy the application. Select **OK**, and then choose the folder to deploy to:

Once everything is set and ready, you will see a notification informing you that you are now able to browse the website:

When you click on the **Browse Website** button, you will be forwarded to the freshly deployed web application. Note that this extension allows you to directly manage the service from within the IDE, and gives you access to different features, including application settings, deployment slots, and Azure WebJobs (the latter of which is described in Chapter 2, *Azure WebJobs*). Here, you can see the working example hosted within Azure:

The important thing here is that by using the same path, you will be able to host a variety of different runtimes inside different Azure App Services. It doesn't matter whether it is a Java application, a Python script, or a Node.js backend—they are all supported and can be easily developed using IDEs such as Visual Studio Code.

> When using Visual Studio Code with the presented extension, you might want to have more control over the creation of a resource. To enable **Advanced Creation**, go to the **File | Preferences | Settings** window, find the **Extensions** section, and then click on the **App Service: Advanced Creation** checkbox.

Working with different operating systems and platforms

Currently, App Services supports a couple of different configurations when it comes to selecting operating system, runtime, and a platform. The following are some of the possible options for running your website using App Services:

- **.NET Core**
- **.NET Framework**
- **Node.js**
- **PHP**
- **Java**
- **Python**
- **Static HTML website**

Additionally, you can select a platform (**32-bit** or **64-bit**), HTTP version (**1.1** or **2.0**), and underlying operating system (**Windows**, **Linux**, or **Container**). Let's start by selecting a proper operating system for our application.

Selecting an operating system

To select an operating system to run your web app, we have to create a new application in Azure. Currently, there is no possibility to change this setting after an App Service is created. To create a new website, go to the Azure Portal and click on **+ Create a resource**. On the new screen, search for `Web App` and select the first item displayed (or just return to the beginning of the *Selecting Azure Web App from available services* section and perform all the steps mentioned there).

On the **Web App - Create** screen, you have an **OS** field. You'll have three options:

- **Windows**: The most common option for .NET applications, suitable for running .NET Framework, Java, Node.js, or PHP sites.
- **Linux**: If you have an application written in .NET Core, you can leverage this operating system and its unique features. Additionally, you can run Java, Node.js, PHP, and Python applications as well.
- **Docker**: Offers Web App for Containers, which we'll cover later in this book. Besides running all of the previous platforms, it allows hosting applications written in languages not currently supported in App Services (such as Go, for example).

The choice is yours. Each operating system has different characteristics: **Linux** is perfect for running Python applications, as **Windows** has some performance issues regarding this language; on the other hand, you may have many websites written in .NET Framework, which are optimized for **Windows** systems. Each of the operating system options also has different pricing. Let's compare **Windows** and **Linux** here:

	BASIC	STANDARD	PREMIUM	ISOLATED
Price per hour (Linux)	$0.071	$0.095	$0.19	N/A
Price per hour (Windows)	$0.075	$0.10	$0.20	$0.40

As you can see, there are small differences between these two operating systems. More importantly, Linux does not currently support the **Free** and **Shared** tiers. The **Isolated** tier is currently in public preview, and should not be used for production workloads, but this, of course, can change in the future. When you have considered all the pros and cons, you can create an App Service powered by the operating system of your choice.

Selecting different platforms

In the previous section, you learned how to choose a proper operating system for your application. This is, of course, not everything needed to run a website—you have to also enable a specific language if you want to deploy, for example, PHP code. To do so, go to your App Service (you have many options by which to do this: either choose **App Services** from the Azure Portal menu on the left and select your **Web App**, or go to the resource group you created by choosing it from **Resource Groups** blade) and then select the **Application settings** blade:

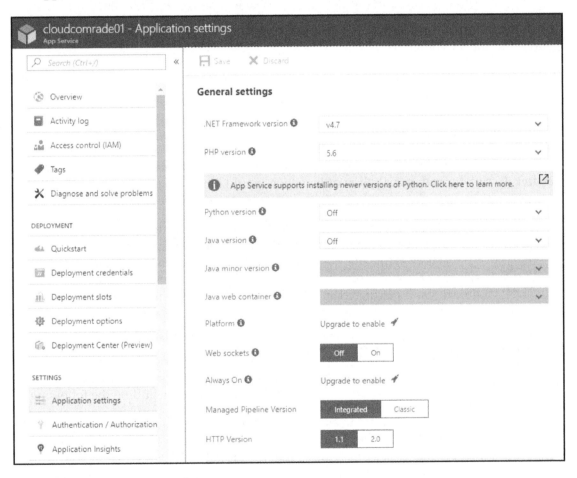

Initially, you could feel a bit overwhelmed by all those options available, but soon, as you gain more and more experience, all will become clear. You might have noticed the **Upgrade to enable** links here—some features, such as **Platform** or **Always On**, are only available from the **B1** tier upward.

Remember that the **Always On** feature could become crucial in some specific scenarios, as it defines whether your application is always running or not (so it can become idle when no one uses it). As you will learn in the coming sections, setting **Always On** to **On** is required when running, for example, continuous Web Jobs or Azure Functions.

Currently, we are interested in all options mentioning a programming language. These options include the following:

- **.NET Framework version**
- **PHP version**
- **Python version**
- **Java version**

By default, your App Service supports two languages: **.NET Framework version** and **PHP version**. To run, for instance, Python or Java, you would have to set an appropriate setting to a specific version such as enable Java support using Java version dropdown.

As mentioned earlier, always select the correct operating system powering your App Service, depending on the language that you chose for your application. While it is possible to run PHP or Python on Windows, selecting Linux, is recommended, could be recommended, as many libraries and packages can run only under this particular operating system.

Working with application settings

The **Application settings** blade offers more than simply enabling or disabling available features. When you scroll down, you will see additional sections, including the following:

- **Debugging**: If you want to enable remote debugging, you can toggle the **Remote debugging** option to **On**. This will allow you to set the Visual Studio version that you would like to use to debug your application locally.
- **Application settings**: This section contains settings used by your application while running.

- **Connection strings**: You can define a connection string for your website directly in the Azure Portal.
- **Default documents**: If you would like to have a custom default document (that is, the starting point of your application), you can set it in this section.
- **Handler mappings**: Sometimes, you need to specify a custom handler for a specific file extension or URL. Here, you can add the appropriate configuration to do so.
- **Virtual applications and directories**: If you need to have multiple applications in your App Service, you can map virtual paths to a physical path here.

Remember that **Application settings** for .NET applications are injected at runtime and will override existing settings stored in your `web.config`. When it comes to other platforms (.NET, Java, Node.js), settings from this section will be injected as environment variables, to which you can refer. This is also true for **Connection strings**.

Application settings in Azure are always encrypted when stored. What is more, you can easily secure them by disallowing all users from accessing them.

Connection strings for platforms other than .NET are always prefixed with appropriate connection type. There are four possibilities: `SQLCONNSTR_`, `MYSQLCONNSTR_`, `SQLAZURECONNSTR_`, and `CUSTOMCONNSTR_`.

Different App Service Plans and features

We touched on this topic at the beginning of this chapter, so you should have an idea of what we are going to cover now. As you remember, when App Service is created, you have to select (or create) an App Service Plan, which defines both available performance and additional features. Let's cover all three categories, this time focusing on the differences between each tier.

Dev/Test App Service Plans

App Service Plans designed for development and testing environments can be found in the **Dev / Test** category:

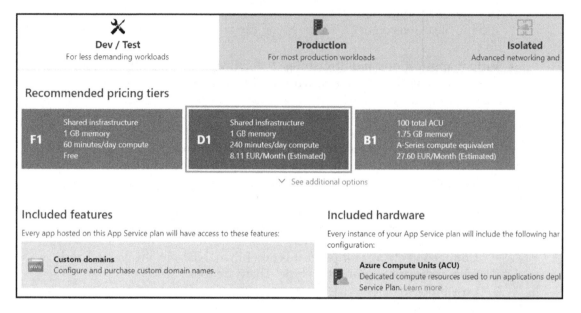

We have three different tiers available:

- **F1 (Free)**: The most basic option, with shared infrastructure, 1 GB of memory available, and 60 minutes of compute per day. When using shared tiers, some features of App Services are unavailable (such as **Always on**, or your selected platform). F1 is perfect for quick-testing or deploying an application for a presentation or demonstration. You will not be charged for using this App Service Plan.
- **D1 (Shared)**: Similar to **F1**, but this also allows for setting a custom domain for your App Service. What is more, you can run your application four times longer than when using the free tier. Still, this is shared infrastructure, so some features cannot be used.
- **B1**: The first tier recommended for running production workloads. It guarantees dedicated A-series machines, and more memory and storage. It is also the first tier that you can scale—although only manually. The **Basic** tier comes with additional versions (**B2** and **B3**), which provide more compute power.

If you are obligated to run your application in Azure in services defined by a **service level agreement (SLA)**, remember that you cannot use the **Free** or **Shared** tiers, as they do not support this.

Production App Service Plans

In this category, there are many more options when it comes to choosing different features available. Remember that, in terms of hardware, the **Basic** tier offers the very same performance as the **Standard** tier:

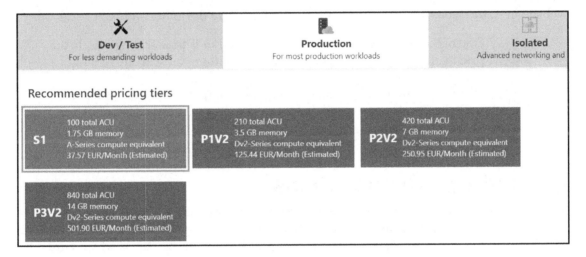

Here, we can choose between the following:

- **Standard (S1)**: The same A-series as **B1**. What we are getting here is autoscaling, staging slots, backups, and the possibility to use Traffic Manager (which will be described in coming chapters). This is the best tier for most production applications, as it supports blue-green deployment scenarios and can handle a bigger load (thanks to integration with Traffic Manager). If you need more compute power, you can choose either **S2** or **S3**.

- **Premium (P1v2)**: This is the new recommended option replacing **P1**, with new Dv2-series virtual machines underneath. It offers better performance and higher limits when it comes to scaling (a maximum of 20 instances, compared to 10 in **Standard**) and staging slots. You also have the option to choose **P2** or **P3**.

 Remember that the maximum amount of instances in particular tiers is subject to availability. In most cases, these are only soft limits that can be raised after contacting support.

In general, **Standard** should meet most requirements when it comes to performance, reliability, and automation possibilities. However, if you are going to run a very popular website in Azure, you may need Premium, as it offers more flexibility and better scalability.

 One of the most important things to remember is how scaling affects the pricing. In general, you have two options: either you scale up (changing tier to a higher one) or scale out (by deploying multiple instances of the same application). If you are paying, for example, $40 for an **S1** instance, when you scale out to 10 instances, you will pay $400 in total—$40 for each instance running.

Isolated App Service Plans

Sometimes you need even more than the **Premium** tier has to offer. Maybe you have to isolate your application from an external network. Maybe you would like to offer access only to some specific users. Maybe 20 instances are still not enough. This is why Azure introduced the **Isolated** category:

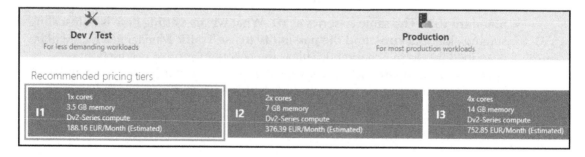

In this category, we have only one tier divided into three versions:

- **Isolated (I1/I2/I3)**: The same virtual machines as in the **Premium** tier (**Dv2**). Also includes huge storage to store your files (1 TB), private app access, an integrated virtual network (so you can access, for example, internal applications), and a more stable environment. This is the most expensive tier, but offers the most when it comes to functionality and the range of features provided.

In general, the **Isolated** tier is the most stable one when it comes to handling a huge load. While **Standard** or **Premium** tiers become unresponsive pretty quickly when utilization hits 100%, **Isolated** App Services need more time to return the `HTTP 503 Service Unavailable` response. Take this into account if you need a really reliable service that cannot be broken easily.

Securing App Services using different security providers

Most web applications have to be secured in some way, either by using your own security system or third-party identity providers, such as Facebook, Google, or Twitter. While working with the traditional application hosted on-premises, you often have to configure everything on your own. PaaS solutions, such as Azure App Services, already possess this functionality and make it easily accessible, thanks to the **Authentication / Authorization** feature. In this section, you will learn how to set it up so users will be prompted to log in.

Configuring authentication/authorization in the Azure Portal

As with most PaaS services, you can configure the features of App Services directly from the portal. Thanks to such an approach, you have all options in one place and can easily switch between them.

Using Azure Active Directory to secure App Services

Go to your App Service and the find **Authentication / Authorization** blade on the left, next to **Application settings** as mentioned previously. When you click on it, you will see a screen for configuration:

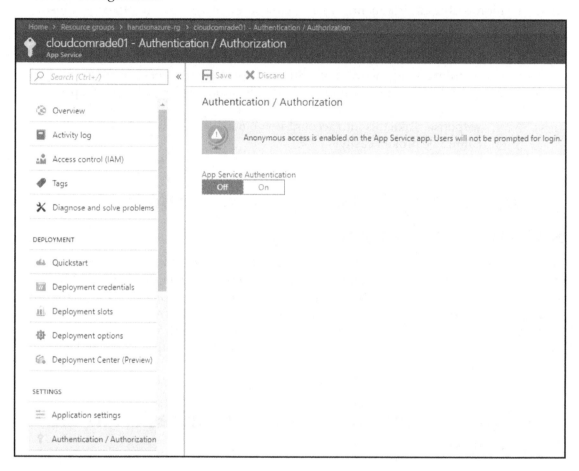

As you can see, it is currently disabled. When you toggle the **App Service Authentication** feature to **On**, you will see new options available, with which you can configure authentication for your web app:

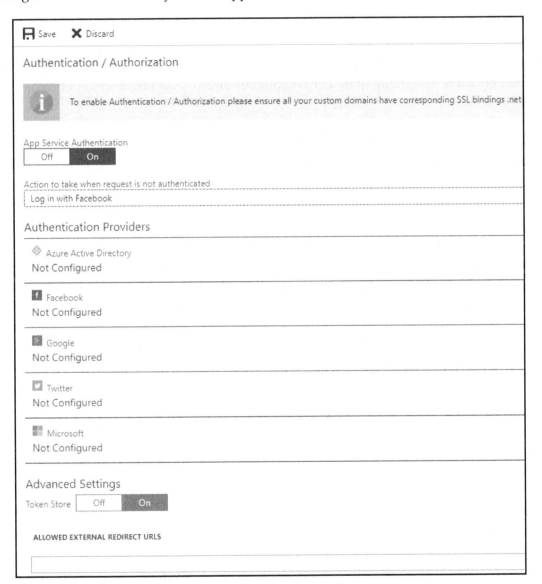

Change the **Action to take when request is not authenticated** field to any value available. The portal will display the following information:

```
To enable Authentication / Authorization please ensure all your custom
domains have corresponding SSL bindings .net version is configured to
"4.5" and manage pipeline mode is set to "Integrated".
```

Since we do not have a custom domain now, no action needs to be taken. The same applies to the .NET version and pipeline mode—if you have not changed the default parameters of your application, everything should be set correctly already. Let's now select one authentication provider and configure it—we will start with Azure Active Directory.

 You do not have to be an expert with Azure Active Directory to use it with App Service, especially now there is the possibility to let the Azure Portal configure it for you. However, if you would like to learn more about this service, the best place to start is its documentation: `https://docs.microsoft.com/en-us/azure/active-directory/active-directory-whatis`.

When you click on the **Azure Active Directory** option, you will see a new screen where you can configure integration. Firstly, you have to select the **Management Mode**:

- **Off**: Azure Active Directory authentication is disabled.
- **Express**: A quick way to configure authentication for your App Service using Azure AD. You will have to either select an already existing Azure Active Directory application or let the Azure Portal create a new one for you.
- **Advanced**: If **Express** is not enough for you, you can always enter all necessary parameters on your own. With this option, you will be able to configure integration by providing information about **Client ID**, **Issuer URL**, and optionally, **Client Secret**. All of these parameters can be found when browsing your Azure Active Directory application.

To start, I recommend using the **Express** option, as configuring applications in Azure Active Directory is beyond scope of this book. For now, you only need to provide a name for the application and click **OK**. You will go back to the previous screen, where you should be able to see that one authentication provider is already configured:

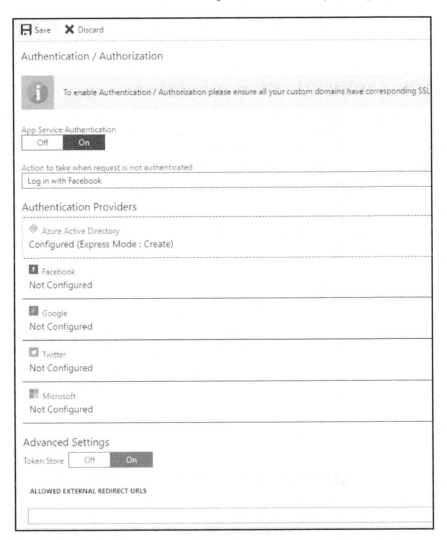

Now, let's click the **Save** button. After a moment, everything should be set and you can now access your application to see whether securing it works. Go to the **Overview** blade and click on the URL link, or enter it directly in your browser. When a default page is loaded, you will not see it, but rather will be redirected to the login page.

For this particular exercise, I have assumed that you have your application already deployed. If you have not, please go back to the previous sections and deploy your code with either Visual Studio or FTP.

Since we configured Azure Active Directory as our authentication provider, a user will be asked to give this particular application consent to access their information.

Using other authentication providers

As you can see, Azure Active Directory is not the only security provider available for App Services. We can select Facebook, Google, or even Twitter to handle authentication and authorization for us. This is especially helpful when you have a public application for people using different social media websites, as they can use their accounts from other applications and quickly sign in when entering your website. To use other authentication providers than Azure Active Directory, you have to create an application in one of the mentioned portals. In fact, there is no difference whether you select Facebook, Google, or Twitter—you will have to provide two fields:

- An **App ID** and **App Secret** for Facebook
- A **Client Id** and **Client Secret** for Google
- An **API Key** and **API Secret** for Twitter

We will not cover in this book how to create an application in other authentication providers. However, proper instructions can be found at `https://developers.facebook.com/docs/apps/register/`, `https://developers.google.com/identity/sign-in/web/sign-in`, `https://developer.twitter.com/en/docs/basics/authentication/guides/access-tokens.html`.

Diagnostics and monitoring of App Services

The last section of this chapter will show you how you can diagnose and monitor App Services that you've deployed. Those operations are crucial when you have a working application, as errors and performance issues always crop up, especially in popular services. Thanks to multiple integrated tools in Azure Web Apps, you can be sure that you'll always have enough information to find and fix a problem.

The Overview blade

The very first thing you probably already noticed is the charts visible in
the **Overview** blade:

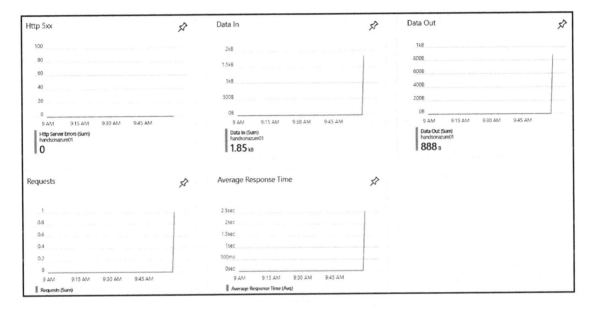

They provide basic insight into the behavior of your application, such as data transfer, the
number of requests, or HTTP 500 errors. Let's click on any of those charts—you will see
another important screen, which we will look at now.

Metrics

The **Metrics** blade gives you more detailed information and a better view of a specific
parameter. On the left, there are many different metrics to choose from. You create your
own chart by selecting more than only one parameter.

 Remember that you can only choose metrics of the same unit—there is no
possibility, for example, to connect the number of loaded assemblies and
average response time.

On this screen, you can also change the chart's time range. This is very useful when
searching for related issues (such as **Data In** and **Memory working set** to check how much
memory your application needs to handle incoming data).

Monitoring

Let's go back to the main screen of App Service. There, when you scroll down, you will see a **MONITORING** section containing even more useful features.

Click on the **Log stream** blade. You will see a black screen with the following information:

```
Application logs are switched off. You can turn them on using the
'Diagnostic logs' settings.
```

Apparently, we do not have this feature available for now. Let's go to the **Diagnostic log** blade. It offers some interesting features regarding logging, including the following:

- **Application logging (filesystem)**: Collects diagnostic traces
- **Application logging (blog)**: The same as the **filesystem** option, but this time logs are stored within the *Azure Storage* account
- **Web server logging**: Gathers diagnostics about a web server
- **Detailed error messages**: If you feel current messages are not sufficient, you can turn on this feature to get more information
- **Failed request tracing**: Gathers information about failed requests

Additionally, you can find the FTP location of all logs with user information to log in. Since we need **Application logging** for **Log stream**, let's turn this feature on. Now, we can go back to **Log stream** to see what kind of information we are gathering:

```
📖 Application logs   ⁝≡ Web server logs   ❚❚ Pause   ▶ Start   ✕ Clear

Application logs

Connecting...
2018-11-22T10:02:35  Welcome, you are now connected to log-streaming service.
#Software: Microsoft Internet Information Services 8.0
#Fields: date time s-sitename cs-method cs-uri-stem cs-uri-query s-port cs-username c-ip cs(User-Agent) cs(Cookie) cs(Re
win32-status sc-bytes cs-bytes time-taken
2018-11-22 10:02:27 HANDSONAZURE01 GET / X-ARR-LOG-ID=a1d487c8-fcde-4551-acb8-bc93f36c5cd6 443 - 83.31.147.112 Mozilla/5
Kit/537.36+(KHTML,+like+Gecko)+Chrome/70.0.3538.102+Safari/537.36 - https://portal.azure.com/ handsonazure01.azurewebsit
2018-11-22 10:02:40 HANDSONAZURE01 GET / X-ARR-LOG-ID=21853864-ab71-4ece-b614-ba6a076188e4 443 - 83.31.147.112 Mozilla/5
Kit/537.36+(KHTML,+like+Gecko)+Chrome/70.0.3538.102+Safari/537.36 ARRAffinity=351922e8227d230d303a550eebfd4ae42ceb4a65c5
re.com/ handsonazure01.azurewebsites.net 304 0 0 316 1353 15
2018-11-22T10:05:35  No new trace in the past 1 min(s).
2018-11-22T10:06:35  No new trace in the past 2 min(s).
```

If you do not see any information in **Log stream**, make sure you have set the correct level of logging. For all information possible, use **Verbose**.

Summary

In this chapter, you have learned what App Services are, and how to build and deploy a simple application that can easily be pushed to Azure. Learning the basics of this particular service is crucial for understanding other topics mentioned in this book, such as WebJobs or Azure Functions. Always remember that you can initially use the **Free** tier to avoid paying for an application when testing or developing, and then scale up when you need to do so. I strongly recommend you play around a little bit with Web Apps, as the cloud component has a lot more to it, and some other features are not that obvious initially. We will cover more advanced features such as integration with Traffic Manager, Azure SQL database, and scaling scenarios in the next chapters.

Questions

1. Do the terms "App Service" and "Web App" refer to the same Azure service?
2. How many categories of App Service Plans are there currently in Azure?
3. Why should **Free** and **Shared** tiers not be used for running production workloads?
4. How many authentication providers can you set up in App Services?
5. Is there any difference in hardware between the **Basic**, **Standard**, and **Premium** tiers?
6. What do you need to enable to see logs in the **Log stream**?
7. Can you attach a custom domain to each tier available in App Services?
8. Can you attach more than one App Service to an App Service Plan?
9. Which operating systems are available for App Services?
10. Can you change operating system after App Service creation?
11. Is it possible to deploy application files to App Services using FTPS? Where can you find the proper location address?
12. What is the difference between user-level and app-level credentials in App Services?
13. What is the difference between scaling up and scaling out?
14. Let's say that you pay $50 for one instance of App Service per month. How much will you pay if you scale up to 10 instances?
15. What is the purpose of using the **Isolated** tier in App Services?
16. Is it possible to run a Go application in App Services?

Further reading

- Azure App Service documentation: `https://docs.microsoft.com/en-us/azure/app-service/`
- Best practices for Azure App Service: `https://docs.microsoft.com/en-us/azure/app-service/app-service-best-practices`
- Reference architectures for Web Apps: `https://docs.microsoft.com/en-us/azure/architecture/reference-architectures/app-service-web-app/`
- Deployment slots: `https://docs.microsoft.com/en-us/azure/app-service/web-sites-staged-publishing`

2
Azure WebJobs

Azure WebJobs are one of the underlying features of Azure App Service. They allow for the easy running of so-called "jobs" using different intervals, or even running them infinitely. They are very flexible and provide a special SDK, so users can work with them efficiently and quickly.

The following topics will be covered in this chapter:

- How to create Azure WebJobs
- Working with different trigger types (continuous and triggered)
- Using different file types for WebJobs

Technical requirements

To perform exercises from this chapter, you will need the following:

- Access to an Azure subscription
- Visual Studio 2017 with Azure development workload installed

Creating WebJobs

Working with WebJobs is much simpler than working with App Services, as this is a much easier service to configure and use. In fact, there are two ways of working with them:

- Using Azure Portal and deploying a job manually
- Using Visual Studio to develop and deploy it manually

What is more, you can leverage the WebJobs SDK to prepare an application triggered by an external service. This will be covered at the end of this chapter, and will be an excellent introduction to Azure Functions, described later in this book.

Creating and deploying WebJobs in Azure Portal

The easiest and quickest way to start working with WebJobs is to create a custom console application, perform an action, and then deploy it using Azure Portal. Thanks to this exercise, you will understand the main concepts of jobs hosted within App Services.

Creating an application in Visual Studio

When you open Visual Studio, go to **File** | **New Project**. In the **New Project** window, select **Windows Classic Desktop** and then **Console App (.NET Framework)**. Give your application a name and click on **OK**:

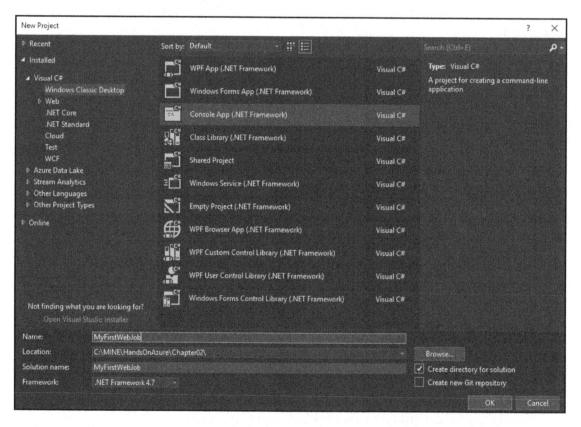

After a moment, you will see an empty project, which we can modify. We will try to trigger our job in intervals (let's say one minute), so we need to add code, which will finish within the given time.

For the very beginning, let's just display the current date. In the `Main()` method of your application, add the following code:

```
using System;

namespace MyFirstWebJob
{
    class Program
    {
        static void Main()
        {
            Console.WriteLine($"Current date and time is:
{DateTime.Now:yyyy-MM-d dddd HH:mm:ss}");
        }
    }
}
```

Now save and build your project—we will need the compiled version soon.

Deploying a WebJob in the Azure Portal

Now, when we have a code of our WebJob, we can try to put in the cloud. To do so we need App Service, which will host our code and execute it. You can either use one of your current Web Apps or create a new one:

1. Go to your App Service and find the **WebJobs** blade. (If you do not see it, scroll down a little bit—it can be found on the left in the **Settings** section.):

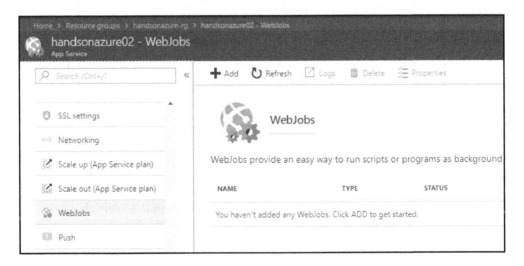

If you do not know how to create App Service or configure it, please take a look at `Chapter 1`, *Azure App Service*, where I describe the process of working with this Azure service in detail.

2. Since you currently do not have any jobs, click on the **+ Add** button. You will see a new screen, which allows you to configure a new WebJob:

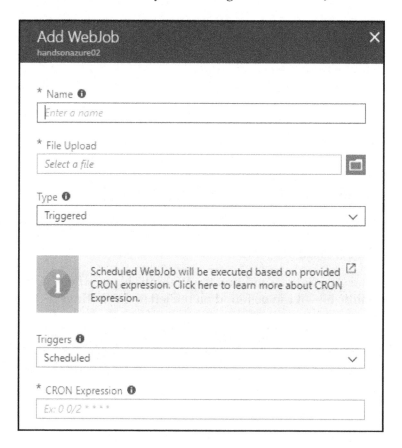

Available fields differ a bit depending on the selected **Type** field value. If you have selected **Triggered** job, you will see the following fields:

- **Triggers:** If you select **Scheduled**, one additional field (**CRON Expression**) will appear. The other option is **Manual**, which ensures that a WebJob can be triggered only manually.

- **CRON Expression**: A CRON valid expression, which defines an interval at which a job runs.

CRON expressions are a quite complicated topic themselves, and we will not focus on them in this book. If you have not heard about them yet, those two links should be useful for you to get started: `https://docs.microsoft.com/en-us/azure/azure-functions/functions-bindings-timer`.

Another option is to set the **Triggered** field to **Continuous**. In that scenario, only one extra field is displayed: **Scale.** Decide whether you want to always have a **Single Instance** of job or scale it across all instances of your App Service. This is helpful if you want, for instance, to implement a singleton pattern and never scale out a job. Note that you cannot change this option if you are using the **Free** or **Shared** tier as they do not support scaling.

3. For now, we will create a **Triggered** job to see how App Service executes it. Give it a name and attach an executable file of the console application you created in the previous section. Here, you can find my configuration:

4. I have decided to use the 0 */1 * * * * **CRON Expression** to run my job each minute. Once you are satisfied with your configuration, click **OK**. After a moment, you should see a new WebJob added to App Service and deployed:

 You do not have to deploy a single file as your WebJob. If your application has more files (such as additional dependencies or static files), you can archive them in a ZIP package and publish. After deployment, they will be unzipped and fully functional.

Now when you click on a job, new options will be available in the menu above. We would like to see the output—for that, please click on **Logs**. On the new screen, you will see the list of jobs available in this particular App Service. Click on the one you have just added—a list of recent runs should be displayed, which you can analyze. You can click on any of the positions available—you will be able to see a full log of the running job:

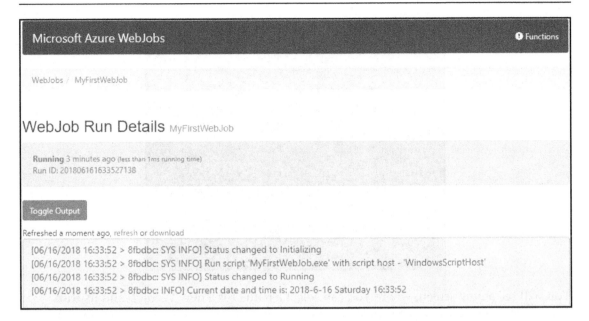

As you can see, a job was run and it displayed exactly what we have been expecting—the current date and time. Congratulations—you have just created and deployed your first WebJob!

 Remember that running continuous or triggered jobs require at least the **Basic** App Service Plan. If you use the **Free** or **Shared** tier, after some time, a WebJob will be cancelled and you will need to start it manually.

In the next section, you will learn how to deploy a WebJob directly from Visual Studio.

Deploying WebJobs from Visual Studio

In the previous part of this chapter, you saw how to create a simple WebJob and publish it from Azure Portal. Sometimes you would prefer not to leave your IDE and use it for deployments too. Fortunately, Visual Studio is integrated with Azure and makes such actions a piece of cake. Before, we started to create a brand new **Console Application** as we did in the beginning—this will be our starting point. You can add any code you would like to—I will use the one from the previous exercises, which will display the current date and time. Once you are satisfied with the provided functionality, right-click on your project icon.

From the context menu, click on **Publish as Azure WebJob...**:

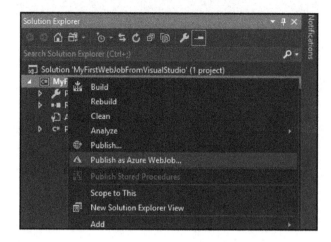

You will see a new screen, where you can select a name for a new WebJob and its **Run mode**. This time, I also decided on a continuous job, so I selected **Run continuously**. When you click **OK**, this wizard will install missing packages for your project and display the **Publish** screen:

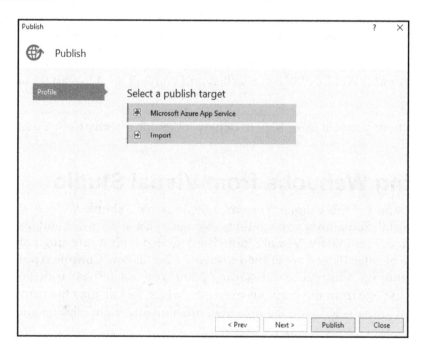

Here, you can create or import **Publish profile**, which is needed to deploy WebJob. We would like to publish our job to a specific location, and that is why we select **Microsoft Azure App Service**. On the next screen, you can select the appropriate App Service by filtering it using subscription and resource group fields. Select the one you are interested in and then click **OK**. Now you will be able to change different properties if you want and deploy configuration. I recommend leaving the default values for now and clicking on **Publish**. After several seconds, you should see a success message in the output window:

We can now check whether our job is available in Azure. Go to the **WebJobs** blade in your App Service. You should be able to see your job among others (I used the same Web App as in the previous section, that is why I have two WebJobs available):

It seems that everything is all right. I am sure you see one flaw of such an approach—we can define the **Run mode** of our job only as **Run on demand** or **Run continuously**. What we are missing here is running it on a schedule. In the next section, I will address this issue as we will start using the WebJobs SDK to have better control over our application.

In fact, it is possible to modify a continuous job to work in intervals. If you take a look at your project, you will see that now it contains a file called `webjob-publish-settings.json`. Its schema and description can be found here—http://schemastore.org/schemas/json/webjob-publish-settings.json.

Working with the WebJobs SDK

To simplify working with WebJobs in Azure and easily access their advanced features, you can use a framework called the WebJobs SDK. It is available out of the box in Visual Studio when an Azure workload is installed. To start, you can create a clean console application, or use the one used for the previous exercises—at this moment, it is up to you. You will need one more thing—the `Microsoft.Azure.WebJobs` package, which can be installed either using the command line or the NuGet package manager:

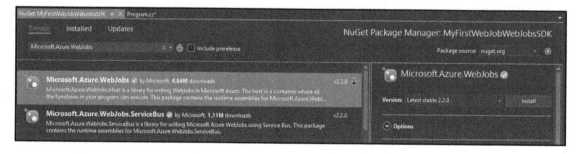

Please note that it is possible to develop .NET Core WebJob using the packages version 3.X. However, since they are still in the beta state, I will not cover them in this book.

When everything is set and ready, we can proceed and try to actually create a new application. Writing jobs using the WebJobs SDK is a bit different than creating them like we did in the previous exercises, but it gives you some interesting benefits:

- You have an available set of triggers integrated with other Azure services such as queues
- You have an integrated logging framework, which eases the process of monitoring a job
- It is a great start to developing Azure Functions, which will be covered later in this book

To get started you have to start a JobHost instance. It is a container for all of the jobs you will run within your application. (We can also call them functions, as described in the documentation.) The boilerplate code looks like this:

```
using Microsoft.Azure.WebJobs;

namespace MyFirstWebJobWebJobsSDK
{
    class Program
    {
        static void Main()
        {
            var config = new JobHostConfiguration();
            var host = new JobHost(config);
            host.RunAndBlock();
        }
    }
}
```

Those three lines are the actual host of your job application, which will handle its functionalities.

Try to compile and run—unfortunately, there is something missing, as you will see an exception thrown as follows:

It tells us that we have a missing Azure Storage account connection string. Because we have not covered this topic yet, you will have to perform one more exercise before continuing. Go to `Chapter 11`, *Using Azure Storage - Tables, Queues, Files, and Blobs,* and go through the very first section. It will guide you through the process of creating an Azure Storage account and tell where you can find the connection string to it. Once you have, we can proceed—add it to `App.config` as follows:

```xml
<?xml version="1.0" encoding="utf-8"?>
<configuration>
    <startup>
        <supportedRuntime version="v4.0" sku=".NETFramework,Version=v4.7"
/>
    </startup>
  <connectionStrings>
    <add name="AzureWebJobsDashboard"
connectionString="DefaultEndpointsProtocol=https;AccountName={NAME};Account
```

```
Key={KEY}" />
    <add name="AzureWebJobsStorage"
connectionString="DefaultEndpointsProtocol=https;AccountName={NAME};Account
Key={KEY}" />
  </connectionStrings>
</configuration>
```

As you can see, I already added two required connection strings—`AzureWebJobsDashboard` and `AzureWebJobsStorage`. Now, when you start the host, you should be able to see something similar to the following:

```
C:\MINE\HandsOnAzure\Chapter02\MyFirstWebJobWebJobsSDK\MyFirstWebJobWebJobsSDK\bin\Debug\MyFirstWebJobWebJobsSDK.exe    —    □    X
No job functions found. Try making your job classes and methods public. If you're using binding extensions (e.g. Service
Bus, Timers, etc.) make sure you've called the registration method for the extension(s) in your startup code (e.g. confi
g.UseServiceBus(), config.UseTimers(), etc.).
ServicePointManager.DefaultConnectionLimit is set to the default value of 2. This can limit the connection throughput to
 services like Azure Storage. For more information, see https://aka.ms/webjobs-connections.
Job host started
```

Since we have no jobs added yet, none is found and enabled. Let's try to add one and see how it works.

> **TIP**
>
> If you want, you can configure connection strings directly in your code by setting the `StorageConnectionString` and `DashboardConnectionString` properties of the `JobHostConfiguration` object manually.

Calling a job manually

If you would like to trigger a job manually, you can use the `[NoAutomaticTrigger]` attribute to tell a host that this particular function is not triggered automatically. Here, you have an example of the one I created and named `Manual.cs`:

```
using System.IO;
using Microsoft.Azure.WebJobs;

namespace MyFirstWebJobWebJobsSDK
{
    public class Manual
    {
        [NoAutomaticTrigger]
        public static void ManualFunction(
            TextWriter logger,
            string value)
        {
```

```
            logger.WriteLine($"Received message: {value}");
        }
    }
}
```

Now let's see what happens if you call it from the main point of your program:

```
using Microsoft.Azure.WebJobs;

namespace MyFirstWebJobWebJobsSDK
{
    class Program
    {
        static void Main()
        {
            var config = new JobHostConfiguration();
            var host = new JobHost(config);

            host.Call(typeof(Manual).GetMethod("ManualFunction"), new {
value = "Hello world!" });

            host.RunAndBlock();
        }
    }
}
```

You should be able to see the following result:

Automatic triggers in WebJobs

By default, the WebJobs SDK provides a limited set of triggers. Currently, it supports only the following ones:

- Blob storage
- Queue storage
- Table storage

All of these are connected to Azure Storage and will be covered in the chapter describing Azure Functions. Fortunately, we can install additional NuGet packages to extend the functionality of our host. For now, add the `Microsoft.Azure.WebJobs.Extensions` package so that we will be able to use `TimerTrigger`. When you have it, call the `UseTimers()` method on the `JobHostConfiguration` object:

```
using Microsoft.Azure.WebJobs;

namespace MyFirstWebJobWebJobsSDK
{
    class Program
    {
        static void Main()
        {
            var config = new JobHostConfiguration();
            config.UseTimers();

            var host = new JobHost(config);

            host.Call(typeof(Manual).GetMethod("ManualFunction"), new {
value = "Hello world!" });

            host.RunAndBlock();
        }
    }
}
```

Now we can create a new `Timer.cs` function, which will be triggered on schedule:

```
using System;
using System.IO;
using Microsoft.Azure.WebJobs;

namespace MyFirstWebJobWebJobsSDK
{
    public class Timer
    {
        public static void TimerFunction(
            [TimerTrigger("* */1 * * * *")] TimerInfo timer,
            TextWriter logger)
        {
            logger.WriteLine($"Message triggered at {DateTime.Now:yyyy-MM-
dd HH:mm:ss}");
        }
    }
}
```

When you start your project, `TimerFunction` should be discovered and called:

```
C:\MINE\HandsOnAzure\Chapter02\MyFirstWebJobWebJobsSDK\MyFirstWebJobWebJobsSDK\bin\Debug\MyFirstWebJobWebJobsSDK.exe           —    □    ×
Found the following functions:
MyFirstWebJobWebJobsSDK.Manual.ManualFunction
MyFirstWebJobWebJobsSDK.Timer.TimerFunction
ServicePointManager.DefaultConnectionLimit is set to the default value of 2. This can limit the connection throughput to
  services like Azure Storage. For more information, see https://aka.ms/webjobs-connections.
Executing 'Manual.ManualFunction' (Reason='This function was programmatically called via the host APIs.', Id=aef3a9ed-5f
44-4064-a92b-37efd0c3b220)
Received message: Hello world!
Executed 'Manual.ManualFunction' (Succeeded, Id=aef3a9ed-5f44-4064-a92b-37efd0c3b220)
The next 5 occurrences of the schedule will be:
17.06.2018 08:48:44
17.06.2018 08:48:45
17.06.2018 08:48:46
17.06.2018 08:48:47
17.06.2018 08:48:48
Job host started
Executing 'Timer.TimerFunction' (Reason='Timer fired at 2018-06-17T08:48:44.0109100+02:00', Id=a965d027-f64c-41fc-b0db-5
b1dd6915faa)
Message triggered at 2018-06-17 08:48:44
Executed 'Timer.TimerFunction' (Succeeded, Id=a965d027-f64c-41fc-b0db-5b1dd6915faa)
Executing 'Timer.TimerFunction' (Reason='Timer fired at 2018-06-17T08:48:45.0008161+02:00', Id=cd6eb912-05c0-40be-8d9f-e
90d69e93f29)
Message triggered at 2018-06-17 08:48:45
Executed 'Timer.TimerFunction' (Succeeded, Id=cd6eb912-05c0-40be-8d9f-e90d69e93f29)
```

You can install additional packages to leverage other bindings, such as `Http`, `Notification Hub`, or `SendGrid`. Search for packages with the `Microsoft.Azure.WebJobs.Extensions` prefix.

Publish a job

Publishing a job, which is written using the WebJobs SDK, is the same as in the previous exercises. Right-click on your project and click on **Publish as Azure WebJob**. You will be once more guided through the process of publishing a job package. At the end of it, you should be able to see a job available in your App Service:

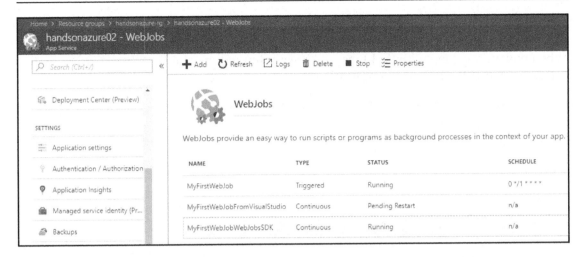

 If you find that your job has problems running, make sure the required connection strings are available in App Service. To do so, go to the **Application settings** blade and verify the contents of the **Connection strings** section. If something is missing, add it manually by adding a name and its value and set its type as **Custom**.

Azure WebJobs limitations

As Azure WebJobs are based on Azure App Services and, what is more, there is no way to host them individually (you can use an extra App Service Plan to power them, but this often means that you pay the double price for your service), you may find some of their limitations quite serious in your projects. When using this particular service, remember the following things:

- When co-hosting Web App and WebJobs, one may interfere with the performance of other. In other words, if your WebJob starts to utilize too much CPU/memory, it may affect your web application powered by the same App Service Plan.
- Azure WebJobs have a limited catalog of bindings that are offered—they are currently less popular than Azure Functions and are not so dynamically developed.
- There is no way to utilize the consumption model with Azure WebJobs; hence, you have to pay the full price, even if they do nothing 90% of the time.

Using different file types for WebJobs

When you are working with WebJobs, you are not limited to using EXE files. Currently, this service supports the following applications:

- Windows executables (`.exe`, `.bat`, and `.cmd`)
- Powershell (`.ps1`)
- Bash (`.sh`)
- Python (`.py`)
- PHP (`.php`)
- Node.js (`.js`)
- Java (`.jar`)

As you can see, the preceding list is quite similar to the supported languages in App Services. This should be understandable now, as you have learned that WebJobs are in fact an integral part of Web Apps in Azure. Let's try something practical—we will deploy a simple Node.js application, which will publish to Azure as a WebJob.

Creating and deploying a Node.js application as a WebJob

JavaScript is one of the most popular programming languages around the world. The strength of Azure lies in the fact that it does not block you from using other, non-native to Microsoft technologies. Before we start, you have to remember one important piece of information.

 The way in which the runtime executes WebJobs requires you to follow a specific convention. When searching for a job, the runtime will search for a file named `run.{job_type}`, where `job_type` is an extension representing a particular programming language (such as `.js` and `.py`). If that fails, it will try to find any file with a specific extension. If that also fails, a job will be skipped.

Here is a really simple code of my first WebJob written in JavaScript:

```
var myFirstWebJob = function() {
  console.log("Hello, this is my first WebJob in Node.js!");
};

myFirstWebJob();
```

To create it, you can use any kind of application supporting JavaScript (it can be, for instance, notepad or Visual Studio Code). Name your file `run.js` and publish it in Azure Portal as described previously. Here you can find the result:

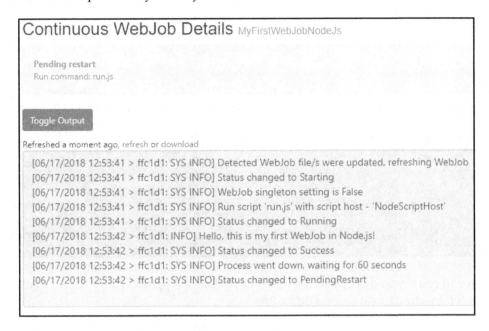

As you can see, it was discovered automatically—no additional configuration was required to run it using Node.js runtime. I strongly encourage you to take your time and test this feature a little bit using other file types.

 Remember that if your application needs additional files (such as extra packages for a Node.js job), you will have to archive them as a ZIP package and then deploy.

Deploying a Node.js Azure WebJob from Visual Studio Code

Unfortunately, it is not currently possible to deploy an Azure WebJob directly from Visual Studio Code. However, if you have the **Azure App Service** extension installed, you can quickly navigate from within the IDE to the portal and upload the code manually.

To do so, you have to right-click on the **WebJobs** section of your Azure App Service and select **Open in Portal**:

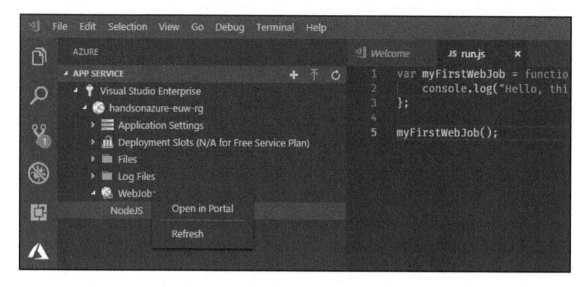

Doing so will route you directly to the instance of Azure App Service, where you can add a new WebJob by clicking on the **+ Add** button:

Summary

As you have seen, Azure WebJobs are a really helpful and useful feature of App Services that let you quickly develop jobs running either continuously or triggered on schedule. They start to shine when you have a working web app, which could be used to host them and execute many different actions asynchronously (such as generating a report or reading a queue, which will feed your application's database later). Thanks to the support of different programming languages, you do not have to limit yourself to only one particular platform. Last but not least, they are a great introduction to Azure Functions, which are one of the most popular services in Azure and extend the current possibilities of WebJobs even further. In `Chapter 3`, *Deploying Web Applications as Containers*, you will learn about deploying Web Apps as containers, what extends even more the capabilities of App Service when it comes to hosting web applications.

Questions

1. Can you run WebJobs using the **Free** or **Shared** tier?
2. What run modes does WebJobs currently supprt?
3. Can you run a Java application using WebJobs?
4. How can you ensure that runtime will find your job starting file?
5. Can you publish a WebJob containing more than only one file? If so, how can you do that?
6. How can you ensure that a WebJob will not be scaled out to multiple instances?
7. Can a WebJob access the application settings of the App Service that hosts it?

Further reading

- https://docs.microsoft.com/en-us/azure/app-service/webjobs-sdk-how-to

3
Deploying Web Applications as Containers

Containers are one of the hottest topics in the IT industry. They allow for deploying an application in "a box," so we don't have to worry about the OS it runs under or the installed services that are required for it. While containers are sometimes criticized for redundant abstraction over underlying resources, they guarantee a stabilized environment for both developing and hosting applications.

The following topics will be covered in this chapter:

- Understanding containers and their best use cases
- **Azure Kubernetes Service (AKS)** and hosting a Kubernetes environment using PaaS components
- Web App for containers for scalable applications
- Azure Container instances and how to manage a container without managing servers

Technical requirements

To start working with containers in Azure, you will need the following:

- A basic understanding of Docker concepts (`https://docs.docker.com/get-started/`)
- Docker development environment (depending on the OS you are using—`https://docs.docker.com/docker-for-mac/`, `https://docs.docker.com/docker-for-windows/`, or `https://docs.docker.com/install/`)
- A Docker Hub account
- The Azure CLI (`https://docs.microsoft.com/en-us/cli/azure/install-azure-cli?view=azure-cli-latest`)

- A basic understanding of Kubernetes (`https://kubernetes.io/docs/home/`)
- The Kubernetes CLI (`https://kubernetes.io/docs/tasks/tools/install-kubectl/`)

Working with AKS

AKS eases the process of deploying and managing containerized applications by eliminating the need to maintain or upgrade your resources on your own. It is a managed Kubernetes service hosted in Azure with many helpful features such as integrated logging and monitoring, identity and security management, and virtual network integration. In this section, we will create a simple application hosted in an AKS cluster, which we will scale and update.

Preparing an application

Let's start with a tutorial application proposed by the Docker documentation:

1. To begin, we need `Dockerfile`, which is a definition of how our container environment should look. It contains keywords such as `FROM` (defines an image that will be used for the container), `WORKDIR` (the working directory of the application), `ADD` (adds a directory to a container), `RUN` (runs a command), `EXPOSE` (exposes a given port in the container), `ENV` (adds an environment variable), and `CMD` (declares an entry point):

   ```
   FROM python:2.7-slim
   WORKDIR /app
   ADD . /app
   RUN pip install --trusted-host pypi.python.org -r
   requirements.txt
   EXPOSE 80
   ENV NAME HandsOnAzure
   CMD ["python", "app.py"]
   ```

2. We will need two more files:
   - `requirements.txt`: This one defines the external dependencies our application has to download
   - `app.py`: The main file of an application

If you are familiar with Docker, you can prepare your very own
`Dockerfile` and application; there is no need to follow everything in this
section as we are covering very basic topics.

3. Here, you can find the contents of `requirements.txt`:

```
Flask
Redis
```

4. And of course, `app.py`, which is the script we want to run. It is a simple Python
application that uses Flask to host a web app and defines the default route that
exposes an HTML web page. Note that it accesses
the `HandsOnAzure` environment variable defined in the Dockerfile:

```python
from flask import Flask
from redis import Redis, RedisError
import os
import socket

# Connect to Redis
redis = Redis(host="redis", db=0, socket_connect_timeout=2,
socket_timeout=2)

app = Flask(__name__)

@app.route("/")
def hello():
    try:
        visits = redis.incr("counter")
    except RedisError:
        visits = "<i>cannot connect to Redis, counter
disabled</i>"

    html = "<h3>Hello {name}!</h3>" \
            "<b>Hostname:</b> {hostname}<br/>" \
            "<b>Visits:</b> {visits}"
    return html.format(name=os.getenv("NAME", "HandsOnAzure"),
hostname=socket.gethostname(), visits=visits)

if __name__ == "__main__":
    app.run(host='0.0.0.0', port=80)
```

5. Now, you need two more things—to build an image and check whether it works.
To build an image, you will need the following command:

```
docker build -t {IMAGE_NAME} .
```

6. After Docker fetches all of the packages and builds an image, you can run it. I used the `4000` port but you can choose whichever works for you:

```
docker run -p 4000:80 {IMAGE_NAME}
```

7. If everything is correct, you should be able to see a running application:

In the next section, we will create a container registry and Kubernetes cluster to host an application.

Container Registry and Kubernetes clusters

To use a Docker image in Azure, we have to put it in a container registry. To do so, we can use **Azure Container Registry (ACR)**, which is a private registry for hosting container images. To get started, go to Azure Portal, click on **+ Create a resource**, and search for `Container Registry`. When you click **Create**, you will see a familiar screen containing multiple fields needed for service configuration. The following need clarification for now:

- **Admin user**: If you want to log in to your registry using the registry name and admin access key, you can turn on this feature. By default it is disabled.
- **SKU**: This defines the overall performance of the registry and available features. To start with, the **Basic** tier should be more than enough.

The following screenshot shows my current configuration:

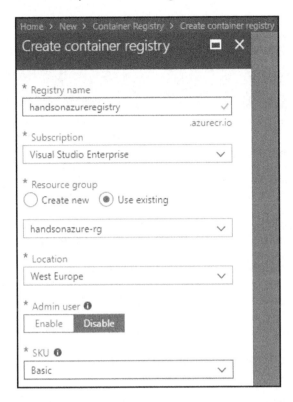

If you are satisfied with the configuration, you can click **OK**. Now we will push an image with an application to the registry to use it in Azure.

Pushing a Docker image to Azure Container Registry

To push an image to Azure Container Registry, we have to know the exact name of the image:

1. To list available images, use the following command:

```
docker images
```

2. The result of running the command is a list of all repositories available for Docker:

```
$ docker images
REPOSITORY          TAG         IMAGE ID        CREATED             SIZE
handsonazurehello   latest      455a5d8b2549    About an hour ago   132MB
python              2.7-slim    d0d1b97dd328    2 weeks ago         120MB
hello-world         latest      e38bc07ac18e    2 months ago        1.85kB
```

3. I want to push `handsonazurehello`, which I created previously, to Azure. To do so, I will need firstly to tag an image using the following command:

> **docker tag handsonazurehello**
> **{ACR_LOGIN_SERVER}/handsonazurehello:v1**

The reason for tagging is to both set a version for my container and give it the appropriate name that is required to push it to a private registry.

4. You can find **Login server** on the **Overview** blade:

> Login server
> handsonazureregistry.azurecr.io

5. Now you can try to push an image with the following command:

> **docker push**
> **handsonazureregistry.azurecr.io/handsonazurehello:v1**

6. Of course, you have to push your image name and registry server login. When you execute the preceding command, you will see the following result:

```
$ docker push
handsonazureregistry.azurecr.io/handsonazurehello:v1
The push refers to repository
[handsonazureregistry.azurecr.io/handsonazurehello]
bbdbf9d56e79: Preparing
128193523190: Preparing
f78e6f8eec4b: Preparing
20f93bdcee9c: Preparing
21b24882d499: Preparing
db9dabc5cfee: Waiting
d626a8ad97a1: Waiting
unauthorized: authentication required
```

7. Still there is something wrong—we are pushing a container to the correct registry, but we have not authenticated yet. To have access to Azure Container Registry, we have to use Azure CLI. Use two commands:

```
az login
az acr login --name {REGISTRY_NAME}
```

8. The first one is used to authenticate in Azure, the second one will let you work with your instance of Container Registry. After successfully authenticating, you can retry pushing an image—this time everything should work smoothly:

```
$ docker push
handsonazureregistry.azurecr.io/handsonazurehello:v1
The push refers to repository
[handsonazureregistry.azurecr.io/handsonazurehello]
bbdbf9d56e79: Pushed
128193523190: Pushed
f78e6f8eec4b: Pushed
20f93bdcee9c: Pushed
21b24882d499: Pushed
db9dabc5cfee: Pushed
d626a8ad97a1: Pushed
v1: digest:
sha256:2e689f437e1b31086b5d4493c8b4ef93c92640ad576f045062c81048
d8988aa6 size: 1787
```

9. You can verify it is available in the portal:

The next thing we need is a Kubernetes cluster—this is why we use AKS to provision a managed Kubernetes service.

Creating a Kubernetes cluster using AKS

To create a Kubernetes service, perform the following steps:

1. Go to the portal.
2. Click on the **+ Create a resource** button and search for AKS.
3. When you click **Create**, you should see the following screen:

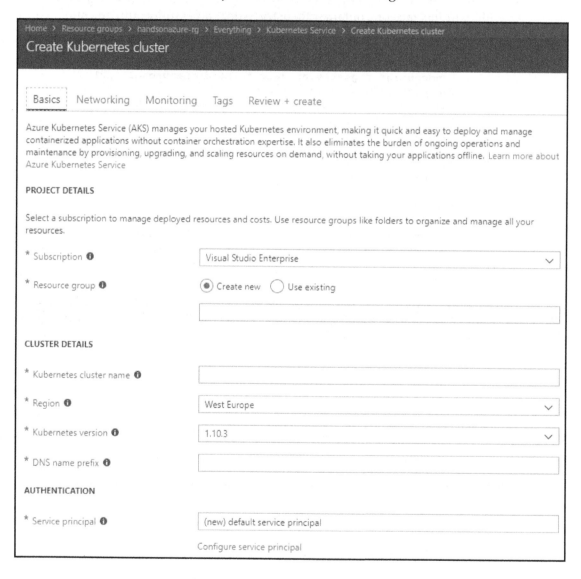

As you can see, we have plenty of different options and fields here. Some of them should be self-explanatory. Initially, I recommend using default values for most fields, such as **Kubernetes version** or **Service principal,** as they matter only if you have existing requirements regarding your application.

> To learn more about applications and service principal objects in Azure AD, you can read this short article from the documentation: `https://docs.microsoft.com/en-us/azure/active-directory/develop/active-directory-application-objects`.

You can go to different tabs such as **Networking** or **Monitoring** to see whether you want to change something—however, the current settings should be correct for the very first AKS cluster.

Once you have reviewed all fields, click on the **Review + create** button. The following screenshot shows my configuration:

Home > Resource groups > handsonazure-rg > Everything > Kubernetes Service > Create Kubernetes cluster

Create Kubernetes cluster

ℹ️ Validation passed

| Basics | Networking | Monitoring | Tags | Review + create |

BASICS

Subscription	Visual Studio Enterprise
Resource group	handsonazure-rg
Kubernetes cluster name	HandsOnCluster
Region	West Europe
Kubernetes version	1.10.3
DNS name prefix	HandsOnCluster
Node count	1
Node size	Standard_A1_v2

MONITORING

Enable container monitoring	Yes
Log Analytics workspace	(new) DefaultWorkspace-94f33c43-60b5-4042-ae74-51777f69f99a-WEU

NETWORKING

HTTP application routing	Yes
Network configuration	Basic

MONITORING

Enable container monitoring	Yes
Log Analytics workspace	(new) DefaultWorkspace-94f33c43-60b5-4042-ae74-51777f69f99a-WEU

When you click on **Create**, you will have to wait a moment until deployment is finished.

 Creating a cluster can take a while, especially when you select several machines to be deployed at once. Be patient!

Running, scaling, and updating an application in AKS

To run and deploy an application in AKS in Azure, we will need the Kubernetes manifest file, which will define how an image should be deployed. However, before we perform that part of the exercise, we have to configure Kubernetes locally, so it can connect with our cluster. To do so, perform the following steps:

1. Run the following command:

   ```
   kubectl get nodes
   ```

2. Initially, it will return the following result:

   ```
   Unable to connect to the server: dial tcp [::1]:8080:
   connectex: No connection could be made because the target
   machine actively refused it.
   ```

3. That means that we have not configured `kubectl` with the AKS cluster we just created. To do so, use the following Azure CLI command:

   ```
   az aks get-credentials --resource-group {RESSOURCE_GROUP} --
   name {AKS_CLUSTER_NAME}
   ```

   Running it should merge your cluster as a current context in your local configuration. Now, when you verify your connection, everything should be set and ready. We can go back to our manifest file—the initial version can be found in the *Chapter03* in the repository. In general, it is a simple YML file that defines and configures services and deployment.

4. Put the file in the directory for your application and use the following command to deploy it:

```
kubectl apply -f handsonazure.yml
```

5. After a moment, you should see the status of the process:

```
$ kubectl apply -f handsonazure.yml
deployment "handsonazurehello-back" created
service "handsonazurehello-back" created
deployment "handsonazurehello" configured
service "handsonazurehello" unchanged
```

6. Now, we need one more command to get the external IP of our service:

```
$ kubectl get service handsonazurehello --watch
NAME TYPE CLUSTER-IP EXTERNAL-IP PORT(S) AGE
handsonazurehello LoadBalancer 10.0.223.94 40.118.7.118
80:30910/TCP 4m
```

7. Initially, you could see the EXTERNAL-IP field as pending—it should change in a second. Now you can verify the installation of an application:

8. There is also one more method to get the status of the whole cluster. Try to run the following command:

```
az aks browse --resource-group {RESOURCE_GROUP} --name
{AKS_CLUSTER_NAME}
```

9. After a moment, you should see the whole Kubernetes dashboard available locally. Read all of the information carefully as it is really helpful when diagnosing possible issues with AKS:

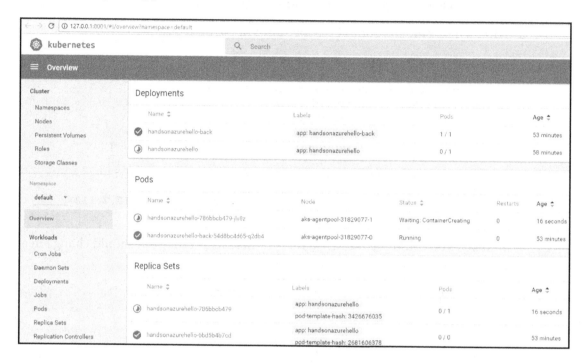

Solving problems with authentication

Sometimes AKS cannot access Azure Container Registry and needs the creation of a service principal, which can be used in pod deployment. To create it, you will need to perform the following script:

```
$ az acr show --name {REGISTRY_NAME} --query loginServer --output tsv
{YOUR_REGISTRY_NAME}

$ az acr show --name handsonazureregistry --query id --output tsv
/subscriptions/94f33c43-60b5-4042-
ae74-51777f69f99a/resourceGroups/handsonazure-
rg/providers/Microsoft.ContainerRegistry/registries/handsonazureregistry
{REGISTRY_ID}

$ az ad sp create-for-rbac --name acr-service-principal --role Reader --
scopes {REGISTRY_ID} --query password --output tsv
{PASSWORD}
```

```
$ az ad sp show --id http://acr-service-principal --query appId --output
tsv
{CLIENT_ID}

$ kubectl create secret docker-registry acr-auth --docker-server
{YOUR_REGISTRY_NAME} --docker-username {CLIENT_ID} --docker-password
{PASSWORD} --docker-email {DOCKER_ACCOUNT_EMAIL}
```

The full script can be also found in the source code for this chapter. Once the secret is created, you can modify the manifest file and add the `imagePullSecrets` line to it:

```
containers:
    - name: handsonazurehello
      image: handsonazureregistry.azurecr.io/handsonazurehello:v1
      ports:
      - containerPort: 80
      resources:
        requests:
          cpu: 250m
        limits:
          cpu: 500m
      env:
      - name: REDIS
        value: "handsonazurehello-back"
    imagePullSecrets:
    - name: acr-auth
```

Scaling a cluster

Scaling in AKS is one of the easiest things to do. All you need to do is go to Azure Portal, find your AKS instance, and click on the **Scale** blade:

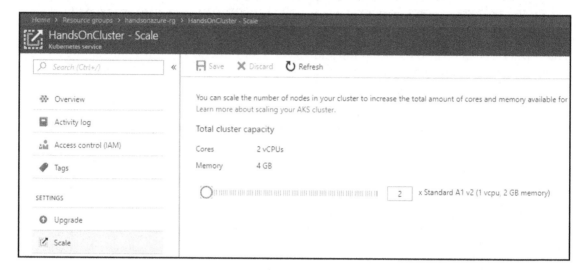

Once there, you can change the cluster capacity depending on your needs.

 Make sure you have the required number of nodes available for your application—such information can be found in the Kubernetes dashboard. If you don't have enough machines, some of your images might not be deployed.

Updating an application

Updating an application in AKS requires two things:

- Publishing a new image to Azure Container Registry
- Setting a new image as the actual one in AKS

When you make changes in your application, you need two commands to update it in a registry. First, change its version to a new one:

```
docker tag handsonazurehello {ACR_LOGIN_SERVER}/handsonazurehello:v2
```

Now what you need is to push this version to make it available in the cloud:

```
docker push
{ACR_LOGIN_SERVER}/handsonazurehello:v2
```

The final step to tell Kubernetes to update an image:

```
kubectl set image deployment handsonazurehello handsonazurehello=
{ACR_LOGIN_SERVER}/handsonazurehello:v2
```

> To ensure that your application is fully functional while updating, you
> have to scale it out to multiple pods. You can do it with the following
> command:
> ```
> kubectl scale --replicas=3 deployment/{YOUR_APPLICATION}
> ```

Azure Container Instances

While AKS is a complete orchestration solution, you might sometimes like to use a lightweight service instead that provides the most crucial features related to running containers. These features include no need to provision and manage virtual machines, security, and integrated public IP connectivity. If you want to run a containerized simple application such as a WebJob or website, **Azure Container Instances (ACI)** can be used to satisfy your requirements.

Creating and deploying an application and container

We will start our journey with ACI by creating an application that we will host in a container. In the previous section, we used a simple Python script—this time we will try to use Node.js.

> As always, you can find source files in the appropriate source file folder
> for this chapter.

The very first thing we need once more is `Dockerfile`. As you remember, it contains instructions on how an application should be run. The following is an example for this exercise:

```
FROM node:8.9.3-alpine
RUN mkdir -p /bin/
COPY ./app/ /bin/
WORKDIR /bin
RUN npm install
CMD node index.js
```

If you read it carefully, you will find it pretty easy—what it does (step-by-step) is as follows:

1. Installs the specific Node.js version (this time **alpine**, which is a smaller distribution well designed for running in containers)
2. Creates a new working directory
3. Copies files to it
4. Installs all dependencies with the `npm install` command
5. Starts an application by providing its starting point

Now we can create a container using the following command:

```
docker build ./ -t {CONTAINER_NAME}
```

After a moment, you should have a new image created and added. If you face any problems, make sure that you are in the correct directory and not doubling its name.

 Remember that you can always check what images are currently available for you and their names. To do so, you can use the following Docker command: `docker images`.

Now we can verify how our application works. To start it, use the following command:

```
docker run -d -p 8080:80 {CONTAINER_NAME}
```

You can go to `localhost:8080` and check whether your application is running. If everything is configured correctly, you should be able to see the `Welcome to Azure Container Instances!` message in the center of the screen.

Sometimes, you may face problems when working with some web applications and running them locally—for some reason, you cannot connect to them using the specified port. In such situations, it is always a good idea to reconfigure them and use different ports.

Now we will push an image to Azure so we can use it later in ACI.

Pushing an image to Azure Container Registry

You can find full instructions on how you can work with ACI in *Container Registry and Kubernetes clusters* section of this chapter. Now, the idea is the same as when working with AKS—we have to perform the following actions:

1. Log in to ACR
2. Tag an image
3. Push it to ACR

You will need the following three commands:

```
az acr login --name {ACR_NAME}
docker tag {CONTAINER_NAME} {ACR_LOGIN_SERVER}/{CONTAINER_NAME}:v1
docker push {ACR_LOGIN_SERVER}/{CONTAINER_NAME}:v1
```

After a successful push, we can deploy an application to ACI.

Deploying an application to ACI

The first thing we need is an instance of ACI. As usual, in Azure Portal click on **+ Create a resource** and search for Container Instances.

You should see a similar wizard to the following:

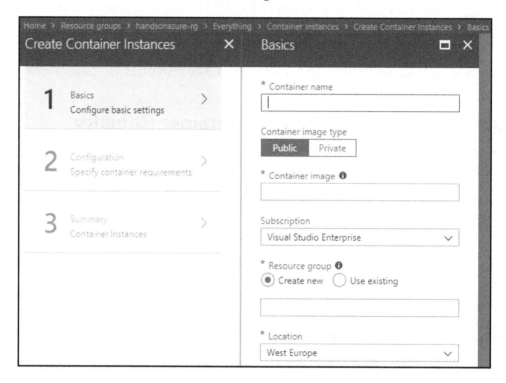

The important thing here is that you have to select **Private** when deciding on a **Container image type**. Choosing this option will display additional fields, which have to be filled in. When creating ACI, you will need to provide **Container image**. This is just the Docker tag you created when pushing an image to Container Registry. In my case it was `handsonazureregistry.azurecr.io/ handsonazure-aci`. The image registry login server is simply a login server for the registry (you can find it in the **Overview** blade of ACR). We need two more things—the registry username and password. While the username is simply the registry name, a password can be obtained using the following command:

```
az acr credential show --name {REGISTRY_NAME}--query "passwords[0].value"
```

 To obtain a password, admin credentials have to be enabled. To enable them from CMD, use the following command:
`az acr update -n {REGISTRY_NAME} --admin-enabled true`

Now we can go to the **Configuration** section:

This time, all of these fields should be self-explanatory and, in fact, I left the default values in force during this exercise. You can change them if you feel other values will meet your requirements (such as, for example, the OS or available memory). Once all is set, you can click **OK** and publish an instance of your container.

If you have problems deploying a container from the portal, you can always use the Azure CLI. Here is the full command to do the same as we did in Azure Portal:

```
az container create --resource-group {RG_NAME}--name
{ACI_NAME} --image {ACR_LOGIN_SERVER}/{CONTAINER_NAME}:v1
--cpu 1 --memory 1 --registry-login-server
{ACR_LOGIN_SERVER} --registry-username {REGISTRY_NAME} --
registry-password {REGISTRY_PASSWORD} --dns-name-label
{DNS_LABEL} --ports 80
```

When deployment is complete, go to your instance of ACI and check the **Overview** blade. Copy the value of the FQDN field and paste it into your browser. You should be able to see the very same screen you saw locally:

That is all! As you can see, using Azure Container Services is a really quick way to deploy your application in a container using a minimal set of features. In the next section, we will focus on leveraging containers in App Services.

Web App for Containers

You do not have to use AKS or ACI to leverage features of containers in Azure—currently, there is one more feature available that you can use to deploy web applications written in an unsupported language (such as Go). Web App for Containers is an extension to App Services that uses Linux under the hood with Docker to run a service built on a stack, which is not currently supported by Azure.

Creating a web app hosted in a container

To create an App Service running with a Docker instance, you have to follow the very same steps from Chapter 1, *Azure App Service*, when we were discussing the creation of a web app using Azure Portal.

Once you reach the web app creation blade, take a look at the **OS** field:

As you can see, the **Docker** option is available. When you click on it, two more fields will need to be set:

- **App Service plan/Location**: This is the same as with "traditional" App Services with one important note. When you select **Docker**, all App Service Plans you can choose from will be powered by the **Linux** operating system. This will impact both pricing and feature availability.
- **Configure container**: When you select this option, you will see another screen with many different options depending on container settings. Currently, we have three different options to choose from—**Single Container, Docker Compose**, and **Kubernetes**. The latest two are currently in preview, but we will also cover them. For now, select **Single Container** and use the **Quickstart** option.

Here you can find my configuration:

Now, after clicking on **Create**, Azure finishes provisioning new resources after several seconds. After creation, go to the freshly created App Service and take a look at the blades on the left. You will see that some of them are disabled:

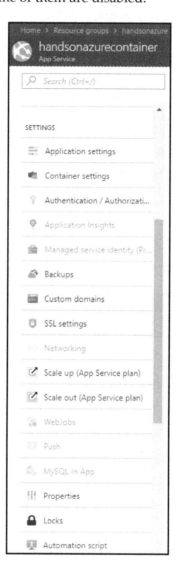

As you can see, using Web App for Containers doesn't allow us to use features such as **WebJobs** or **Application Insights**. Yet, we are still able to scale an application, attach a custom domain, or set a backup. Notice that one more blade is available—**Container settings**. When you click on it, you will see the same screen as during App Service creation:

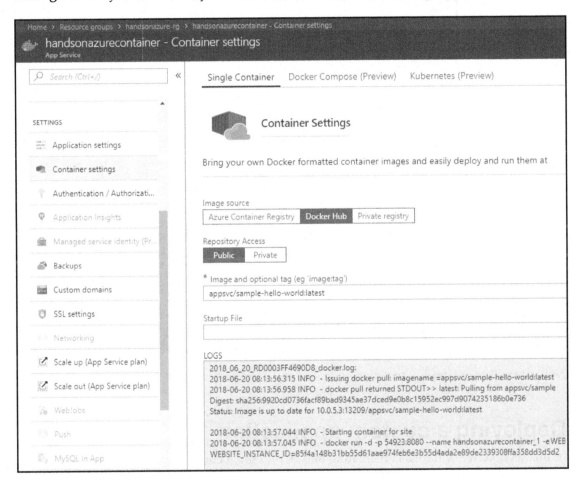

Let's see what happens when we change the image for our container. Change the **Image and optional tag (eg 'image:tag')** field to `appsvc/dotnetcore` and then click **Save**. After restarting an application, you should see a change in the visible logs:

Also, you should see a success message when browsing your web application:

Now we will try to deploy our own code and see whether it works.

Deploying a custom application

In this section, we will focus on creating and deploying a custom application to our Docker container in the web app. For the purpose of this exercise, we will reuse the container image from the previous part of this chapter where we were discussing ACI.

 If you would like to prepare a brand new application, go through the steps defined in the *Creating and deploying an application and container* section where we created a Docker image and pushed it to Azure Container Registry.

When you go once more to the **Container settings** blade, you can change **Image source** to three different options:

- **Azure Container Registry**: It allows you to select images pushed to your own instance of ACR
- **Docker Hub**: Provides access to all images available in this repository
- **Private registry**: You can also define a private repository from which to deploy your images

> Note that, if you use ACR, the two other sources will also point to ACR as it acts as your own private Docker Hub with your images.

Select the **Azure Container Registry** tab and fill in all required fields as suggested by the portal:

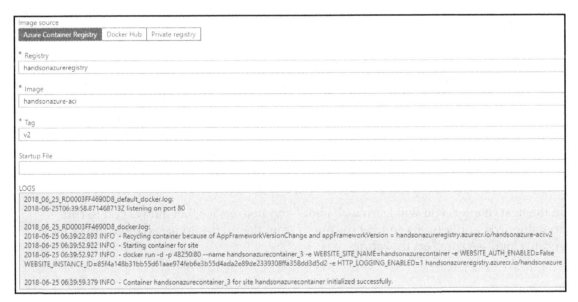

After a moment, a new image should be reloaded and working. If you browse to the URL of your application, you should be able to see changes:

As you can see, the very same container image I used while working with ACI is fully functional here in Web App for Containers.

Summary

As you saw, when working with containers in Azure you are able to focus on the delivery and shape of your application rather than configuration or maintenance. Of course, available features are not limited to those we covered in this chapter—you can also leverage functionalities such as continuous deployment, networking, or data volumes. What is available depends solely on the service you choose—Azure Container Instances and Web App for Containers are cloud components that are quite minimalistic and focus on running an application, while AKS delivers more advanced features. Nonetheless, containers are one of the most popular topics of recent months and it is quite possible that building and evolving that skill will help you in your future projects.

In the next chapter, you will learn a bit about another service that allows you to run containerized applications and get the out of from the microservice architecture in the Azure cloud—Azure Service Fabric.

Questions

1. What is Azure Container Registry?
2. What is the **Admin login** feature in AKS?
3. Which OS do you have to choose while creating an App Service to be able to run containers?
4. Can you use images from the public registry in Web App for Containers?
5. Can you scale AKS in the portal?
6. How you can lower your application's downtime in AKS when updating it?
7. What do you have to do if AKS cannot authenticate to your instance of Azure Container Registry?

Further reading

- https://docs.microsoft.com/en-us/azure/container-instances/container-instances-orchestrator-relationship
- https://docs.microsoft.com/en-us/azure/aks/networking-overview
- https://docs.microsoft.com/en-us/azure/monitoring/monitoring-container-health?toc=%2Fen-us%2Fazure%2Faks%2FTOC.jsonbc=%2Fen-us%2Fazure%2Fbread%2Ftoc.json

4
Distributed Applications and Microservices with Service Fabric

Service Fabric (SF) is a platform for distributed applications that greatly simplifies developing and deploying applications that are scalable and reliable. It's one of the best solutions for developing cloud-native apps and lets users focus on developing rather than on maintaining infrastructure and connections between particular components. It's a next-generation platform that is actively developed by Microsoft and has received much attention recently.

The following topics will be covered in this chapter:

- Microservice architecture and how to use it in the cloud with SF
- Basic concepts of SF, such as services or actors
- Communicating between services in SF
- Managing clusters in SF and securing them
- Monitoring services in SF and how to diagnose them

Technical requirements

To perform exercises in this chapter, you will need the following:

- Visual Studio 2017 with **Azure development** and **ASP.NET** and **web development** workloads
- Microsoft Azure SF SDK (`http://www.microsoft.com/web/handlers/webpi.ashx?command=getinstallerredirectappid=MicrosoftAzure-ServiceFabric-CoreSDK`)
- Node.js (`https://nodejs.org/en/`)

Understanding microservices

Probably you have heard about an architecture called **microservices**. There is no single definition that we could quote here, so the main purpose of this chapter will be to acquire a better insight into what we can call a microservice and how to develop an application in such a manner. This directly connects to SF, which is one of the biggest and most advanced services in Azure. If you aim at building a modular, loosely-coupled, and modern application, this particular cloud component is designed for you.

Monolith versus microservices

We will start our journey with microservices by comparing them with a traditional application, which is composed of multiple layers serving different purposes:

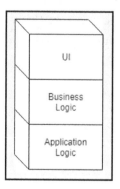

As you can see, we define such services as monolithic, where the whole code base is deployed as one application. This one application has multiple responsibilities:

- Serving the UI
- Running business logic
- Running additional processes (such as jobs)

We can also look at it differently—as a single module that handles features from different domains. Let's consider an e-shop, where we have the following:

- Payment logic
- Basket logic
- Order processing logic
- Discounts logic
- Many, many more different domains

Now the question arises—should our application run such logic in one instance or should we divide it into multiple independent modules, which have different lifetimes, run differently, and can be developed individually? Maybe we would also like to scale them separately depending on current workload or business requirements. The choice always depends on the requirements your application will have to face. However, if you would like to give try microservices, SF is the way to go, especially if you aim at using cloud-native components.

Microservice approach

You may wonder whether the microservice architecture is one you would like to choose and work with. In this section, I would like to focus on specific features this approach provides and how you can address them when writing an application and, in the end, using SF.

Using different languages and frameworks

Sometimes, we would like to address different problems resolved by our application by using different programming languages or tools. Maybe it is a good idea to write mainly in C# or Java and deliver more advanced features such as domain-specific calculations using a dedicated language. Maybe we have multiple teams working on different features and each one would like to use a different framework.

Maybe the whole work is so globally distributed that dividing it into multiple smaller packages (and finally services) is the way to go. All of these problems are possible to solve using a single application but, on a bigger scale, such an approach could become cumbersome and insufficient. By leveraging the capabilities of SF in Azure, we can organize multiple applications (containing multiple services each) as a single platform, which can be managed from one place and deployed individually, saving time and money.

Scaling and updating services individually

We have just talked about deploying each service individually. Thanks to such an approach, you do not have to push the whole code base at once. I am sure you have had at least one project that was so big that the whole process of delivering it to the production environment was difficult to automate and took really long to finish. In such a scenario, dividing the project into smaller modules can also be beneficial let's say that, in the last month, only one team delivered a new feature; you do not have to go through all your platform tests. What is more, if something is not right after deployment in a part of the system you have not modified, you do not have to bring in another team to investigate the problem. This confers the following advantages:

- The process of delivering a business value is shorter and simpler, and hence less vulnerable to mistakes
- You can focus on a particular module and changes in it often do not affect other modules

There is one more interesting feature of the microservices architecture—you can scale each component separately. This means that if, for example, there is a module responsible for processing payments and you have just had a big discount in your online shop, resulting in a rapid growth of incoming orders, you do not have to worry that they overwhelm it. What you can do in such a situation is simply scale it out, so you can process each order in parallel using as many instances of your module as you currently need. Later in this chapter, you will learn how you can achieve such scalability in SF using different approaches depending on the actual structure of your application. The following diagram describes the difference between scaling microservices and monolith application—while the former gives you the possibility to scale up each service individually, the latter has to be scaled as a single entity:

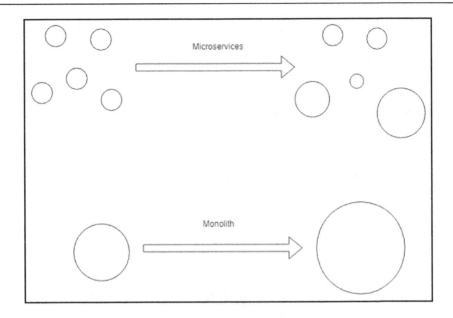

Using well-designed interfaces and protocols

You may ask, If we divide our application into, for instance, several smaller modules, how can we now ensure that communication between them will be smooth, seamless, and with the smallest latency possible? To satisfy such requirements, one has to refer to multiple communication patterns described by patterns for service-oriented architectures, which in fact are the very foundation of microservices. In general, you have to leverage well-known protocols such as HTTP or TCP, which are widely used in the IT industry and are understood by thousands of APIs, devices, and frameworks. Of course, you could think about designing a custom protocol or standard—while initially, it might be a good idea, sooner or later it may become an obstacle to expanding your application because it's not compatible with newer services. What is more, it is important to use popular serialization methods such as XML, JSON, or any binary format that is easily available and well documented. By following such guides, you can be sure that your microservice architecture will be easy to extend and integrate with.

Dealing with state

Nearly every application has some kind of state (of course, one can develop a stateless service, which does not have to store a state anywhere and just performs an action/returns a result; we will cover such services later in this chapter).

This state has to be managed and shared; in monolithic application handling, it is pretty straightforward and obvious—we have, for instance, a database, which holds all information from multiple parts of our system. In general, it is stored in one place (of course it can be scaled and shared, but we do not manage such features on our own), so we do not have to worry that we update it only partially (and if we do, there are always transactions). Of course, the state does not have to be stored in a database—we can use any kind of storage that holds data.

When using microservices, it turns out that each individual service has its own state and manages it independently. Problems arise where we have to query data from different modules or store data in more than one form of storage. To overcome such problems, one can use patterns such as eventual consistency. In SF, you can choose whether a state should be externalized or co-located. Additionally, SF takes care of making it highly available and durable.

Diagnosing and monitoring microservices

While the process of monitoring traditional applications is pretty straightforward and simple, when you have tens or hundreds of smaller services, making it right is not that obvious. This has also other implications such as: What is the actual impact if one module goes down? When you have a monolith, you are immediately aware of any issues as your application simply stops working properly. With microservices, you may find it difficult to react in time if your monitoring does not cover all areas of your system. In SF, you have multiple levels of monitoring, which you can define as follows:

- **Application monitoring**: This tracks how your application is used.
- **Cluster monitoring**: This allows you to monitor the whole SF cluster, so you can verify whether the whole service performs as expected.
- **Performance monitoring**: Sometimes, it is hard to understand how your application behaves if you do not monitor its performance. In SF, it is easier to track resource utilization and predict possible issues.
- **Health monitoring**: When working with microservices, it is crucial to know whether particular modules are healthy or not. In SF, you can leverage the Health API or health reports available in SF Explorer to gain a better insight into the current status of your application.

Containers, services, and actors in SF

To start with SF, we will cover three main topics, which allow you to divide an application logically and physically:

- **Containers**: Small, deployable components that are isolated from each other and enable you to virtualize the underlying operating system
- **Reliable services**: One of the programming models available in SD for writing and managing stateful and stateless services
- **Reliable actors**: Another programming model on top of Reliable services

Containers

For now, SF supports two types of container:

- **Docker** on Linux
- **Windows Server** containers on Windows Server 2016

When working with containers in SF, you can use any programming language or framework (as you probably expected), but the most important thing related to such a model is the fact that you do not have to stick to built-in programming models (Reliable actors and Reliable services). What is more, this approach is very similar to running so-called **guest executables**, where you deploy an existing executable to SF.

Creating a cluster

Before we start with containers, we will need to create an SF cluster. To do so, go to Azure Portal and click **+ Create a resource**. Search for `Service Fabric Cluster` and click **Create**. You will see a familiar screen, where you have to fill multiple fields with your cluster configuration. In SF, the process of creation is divided into four different steps, which we will cover one by one.

On the very first screen, you will have to enter basic information regarding the cluster:

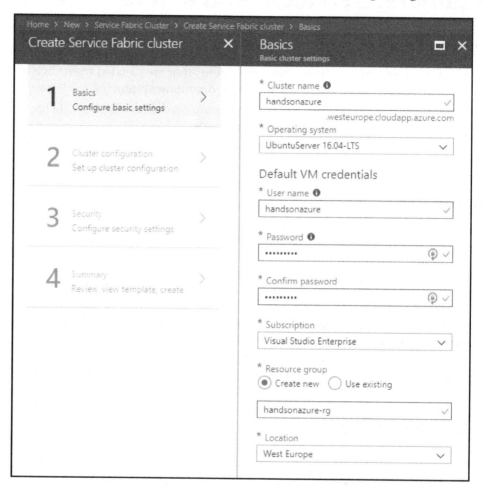

There is one field that probably requires a little bit of clarification, namely, **Operating system**. As mentioned in the beginning of this chapter, SF supports
both Windows and Linux containers, which you can select here. The choice affects both the pricing and available features, so you have to be sure which OS you're using.

Once you are satisfied with the setup, you can proceed to the next screen:

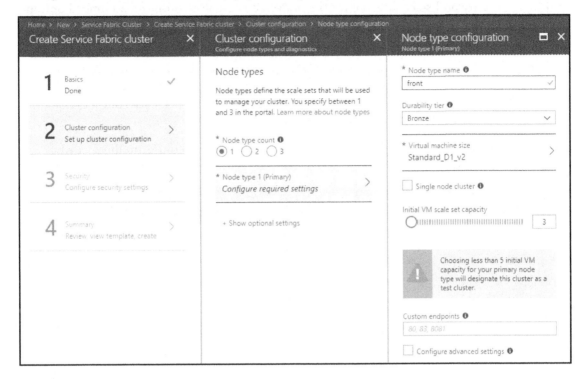

Now we begin with the actual cluster configuration. The first thing you have to do is select **Node type count**. To select the correct version, you have to understand what this actually means. This property defines the following:

- Virtual machine (VM) sizes
- The number of VMs
- Properties of VMs

So, to cut a long story short—if you need two different types of machine (because, for instance, you have a lightweight frontend and heavy backend), you will choose two different node types.

 Remember that you can always add or remove a node after cluster creation, but you will always need to have at least one.

On the **Node type configuration** blade, you will have to choose the size of virtual machines and their capacity and select a name for the node. You can also configure advanced options but, as we are just starting with SF, I would not recommend changing anything there.

 Using fewer than five virtual machines initially designates a cluster as a test cluster. The reason why SF requires you to run five or more VMs is to make sure that your solution is more resilient to simultaneous failures. You still can use a test cluster to run production workloads, but it is not recommended.

Now click **OK** to proceed. The last but one screen allows you to configure the security features of your cluster:

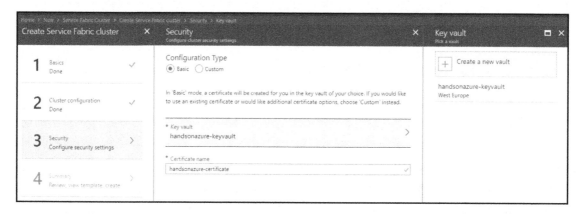

You can choose either the **Basic** or **Custom** configuration type—the difference between them is that, when using **Basic**, a certificate will be created for you and, when choosing **Custom**, you can enter certificate information on your own. Additionally, SF will require you to select a key vault (or create a new one) to store a certificate.

 We will not cover Azure key vaults in this book. If you would like to know more about this service, please take a look at the documentation—https://docs.microsoft.com/en-us/azure/key-vault/

When everything is set and ready, you can click **OK,** and you will see the final screen with a summary of the configuration of your cluster. Validate all of the information displayed there and, if you are ready to create the cluster, click on **Create**. When you go to the resource group you selected while creating the cluster, you should see a similar setup to mine:

NAME	TYPE	LOCATION
front	Virtual machine scale set	West Europe
handsonazure	Service Fabric cluster	West Europe
handsonazure-keyvault	Key vault	West Europe
LB-handsonazure-front	Load balancer	West Europe
LBIP-handsonazure-0	Public IP address	West Europe
sfdghandsonazure2006	Storage account	West Europe
sflogshandsonazure8980	Storage account	West Europe
VNet-handsonazure	Virtual network	West Europe

As you can see, it contains many different services already:

- **Virtual machine scale set**: To make sure you can easily scale out, SF uses the VMs scale set to automate the whole process
- **Service Fabric cluster**: The actual SF service
- **Load balancer**: To distribute the load between your machines
- **Public IP address**: So your application is available publicly
- **Storage account**: For storing data
- **Virtual network**: To secure and ease communication between machines, SF utilizes Azure Virtual Network to couple machines in the VMs scale set

Now that we have a cluster configured and running, we can proceed to deploy the Docker container.

Deploying a container

To use Docker images in SF, we will need a registry in Azure Container Registry. You can go back to Chapter 3, *Deploying Web Applications as Containers*, where I described in detail how to work with ACR and Docker.

Now we will try to deploy a simple Python application—to start, we will need Dockerfile, of course:

```
FROM python:2.7-slim
WORKDIR /app
ADD . /app
RUN pip install -r requirements.txt
EXPOSE 80
ENV NAME World
CMD ["python", "app.py"]
```

Additionally, let's create a Python application, which will display simple text:

```
from flask import Flask

app = Flask(__name__)

@app.route("/")
def hello():

    return 'This is my first Service Fabric app!'

if __name__ == "__main__":
    app.run(host='0.0.0.0', port=80)
```

Now, run the `docker build` command:

```
docker build -t handsonservicefabricapp .
```

We will be able to test and run it locally by typing the following:

```
docker run -d -p 4000:80 --name handsonsf handsonservicefabricapp
```

As you can see, all is working correctly—we can proceed by pushing an image and deploying it:

To push a container image, you will need of course a registry for it. If you want to use Azure Container Registry, please refer to the previous chapter for detailed instructions.

For now, you will need three Docker commands:

- docker login: To authenticate in ACR
- docker tag: To create an alias of an image and put it in the correct namespace
- docker push: To deploy an image to the registry

The following is the full syntax:

```
docker login handsonazureregistry.azurecr.io -u {USERNAME} -p {PASSWORD}
docker tag handsonservicefabricapp
handsonazureregistry.azurecr.io/sf/handsonservicefabricapp
docker push handsonazureregistry.azurecr.io/sf/handsonservicefabricapp
```

Packaging a service

To package our service, we will use Yeoman with the SF Yeoman container generator. To do so, you have to install them—in your command line, execute the following two commands:

```
npm install -g yo
npm install -g generator-azuresfcontainer
```

We will need one more thing—because the container image will be fetched from ACR, we have to configure its credentials in ApplicationManifest.xml. While the username can be traditionally found on the **Overview** blade of Container Registry, to find a password you have to run these two commands:

```
az acr login --name {REGISTRY_NAME}
az acr credential show -n {REGISTRY_NAME} --query passwords[0].value
```

Now, we will need to update the manifest generated by Yeoman so it uses our credentials:

```
<ServiceManifestImport>
  <ServiceManifestRef ServiceManifestName="HandsOnServicePkg"
ServiceManifestVersion="1.0.0" />
  <Policies>
    <ContainerHostPolicies CodePackageRef="Code">
      <PortBinding ContainerPort="80"
EndpointRef="HandsOnServiceEndpoint"/>
      <RepositoryCredentials AccountName="{LOGIN}" Password="{PASSWORD}"
PasswordEncrypted="false"/>
    </ContainerHostPolicies>
  </Policies>
</ServiceManifestImport>
```

Now, log in to your cluster using the following command:

```
sfctl cluster select --endpoint https://{ENDPOINT}:19000 --pem
{CERTIFICATE}.pem --no-verify
```

Finally, just run the `install.ps1` file Yeoman generated and wait a moment—your application image should be deployed to the SF cluster in the cloud and fully working.

> To get a certificate, you can download it from the **Certificates** blade in key vault.

Reliable services

In this section, we will try to create both stateless and stateful services using SF. This time, we will use Visual Studio to create a C# application and deploy it to our cluster. You can also start with Reliable services on Linux, but this will not be covered in this book. Refer to the *Further reading* section for links to the appropriate documentation.

Creating a SF application

When you open a Visual Studio instance, go to **File | New Project**. In the new window search for **Visual C# | Cloud** templates; you should be able to find the **Service Fabric Application** option:

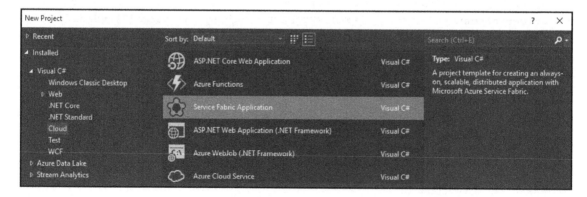

If you cannot find this option, make sure you have installed the SF SDK.

On the next screen, you will see many different options, most of which we will discuss later. For now, select **Stateless Service** and click **OK**:

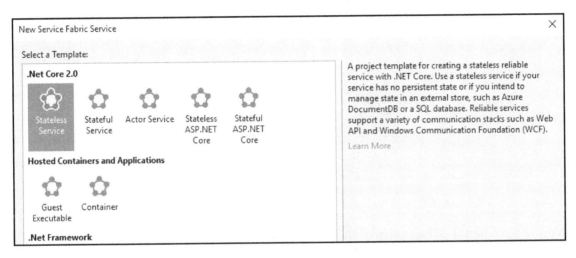

After a moment you should be able to see that a stateless service template has been built with SF. You can now press *F5* to see how it works with all the default values:

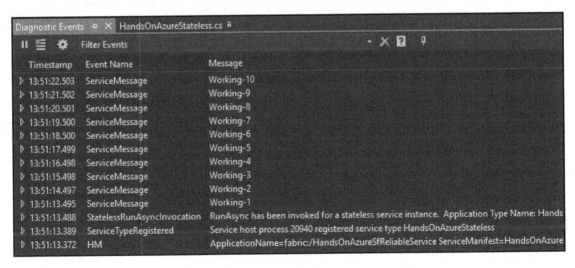

If you have trouble starting your local SF instance, make sure you have started Visual Studio as an administrator.

As you can see, each second a message—Working-{N}—is published. Take a look at the RunAsync() method:

```
protected override async Task RunAsync(CancellationToken cancellationToken)
{
  long iterations = 0;

  while (true)
  {
    cancellationToken.ThrowIfCancellationRequested();

    ServiceEventSource.Current.ServiceMessage(this.Context, "Working-{0}",
++iterations);

    await Task.Delay(TimeSpan.FromSeconds(1), cancellationToken);
  }
}
```

You will see that it is the source of those messages. In fact, it is the starting point of your service, which is called when it starts. It also accepts one parameter, cancellationToken, which is here to inform you about any of the following:

- There was a fatal error in your code and the service is currently in the invalid state
- There was a hardware outage in a cluster
- There is an ongoing upgrade
- The current instance of service is no longer required

Remember to honor that RunAsync() should return a task. The system will wait until the service finishes executing, so always try to do it as quickly as possible if you discover that cancellation was requested.

Let's now try to add also a stateful service—to do so, add a new **Service Fabric Application** project to the solution, but this time select **Stateful Service**:

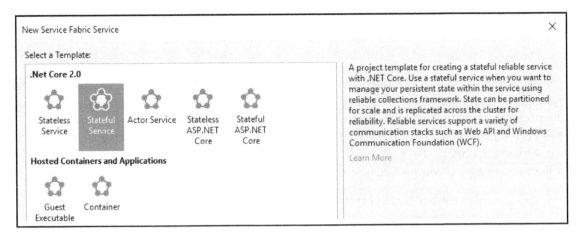

If you compare the stateless `RunAsync()` with the stateful one, you will see many differences:

```
protected override async Task RunAsync(CancellationToken cancellationToken)
{
  var myDictionary = await
this.StateManager.GetOrAddAsync<IReliableDictionary<string,
long>>("myDictionary");

  while (true)
  {
    cancellationToken.ThrowIfCancellationRequested();

    using (var tx = this.StateManager.CreateTransaction())
    {
      var result = await myDictionary.TryGetValueAsync(tx, "Counter");

      ServiceEventSource.Current.ServiceMessage(this.Context, "Current
Counter Value: {0}",
        result.HasValue ? result.Value.ToString() : "Value does not
exist.");

      await myDictionary.AddOrUpdateAsync(tx, "Counter", 0, (key, value) =>
++value);

      // If an exception is thrown before calling CommitAsync, the
transaction aborts, all changes are
```

```
    // discarded, and nothing is saved to the secondary replicas.
    await tx.CommitAsync();
}

    await Task.Delay(TimeSpan.FromSeconds(1), cancellationToken);
}
}
```

The most important one is a direct reference to state—in a stateful service, we have the state manager, which enables you to query state and execute actions within transactions. Here, in the previous example, we fetch a dictionary of the `IReliableDictionary<>` type from it—it is a reliable collection that stores data and replicates it to other machines. In fact, it is the same dictionary as, for example, `IDictionary<>`, but this time operations on a collection are asynchronous because data has to be persisted on disk.

 Remember that everything you store in the state manager has to be serializable.

When you start your application, you will see that both services are running at the same time:

Timestamp	Event Name	Message
14:41:13.718	ServiceMessage	Current Counter Value: 16
14:41:12.921	ServiceMessage	Working-24
14:41:12.713	ServiceMessage	Current Counter Value: 15
14:41:11.921	ServiceMessage	Working-23
14:41:11.709	ServiceMessage	Current Counter Value: 14
14:41:10.918	ServiceMessage	Working-22
14:41:10.703	ServiceMessage	Current Counter Value: 13
14:41:09.917	ServiceMessage	Working-21
14:41:09.684	ServiceMessage	Current Counter Value: 12
14:41:08.916	ServiceMessage	Working-20
14:41:08.678	ServiceMessage	Current Counter Value: 11
14:41:07.915	ServiceMessage	Working-19

Diagnostic Events — HandsOnAzureStateful2.cs — ApplicationManifest.xm — Filter Events

Now we would like to publish our simple application to Azure to see whether it really works.

Deploying an application to the cloud

If you take a look, you will see that our solution contains now three projects:

- Stateless service
- Stateful service
- SF project

Now right-click on the SF project and click the **Publish...** option:

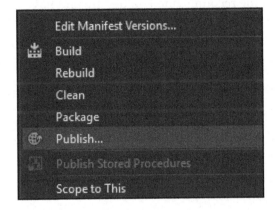

On the new screen, you can configure things such as **Target profile** or **Application Parameters File**, but the most interesting one is **Connection Endpoint**, which is empty now. In fact, you cannot proceed without selecting one option, so let's open the drop-down menu and see our options. Among the available options, you will have the following:

- **Local cluster**
- **Create New Cluster**
- **Use Trial Cluster**
- **Refresh**

While the local/new cluster option is self-explanatory, you might wonder what the **Trial** option is. When you select it, you will be given an option to sign-in to so-called **party clusters**. These are free-of-charge SF clusters, which you can use to play with this service a little bit and learn how it works. You do not need a subscription, but after an hour the cluster will be taken down. Because we are learning about services in Azure in this book, I will not use that option, but feel free to utilize it later if you decide you want to know much more about SF than this short chapter was able to provide.

When you select the **Create New Cluster** option, a new screen will appear with the whole SF cluster configuration. It is very similar to the one you can see in the portal—it has the same sections, such as **Cluster**, **Certificate**, and **VM Detail**.

 Creating an SF cluster from Visual Studio has one downside—you do not know what the recommended values are and have no direct reference to the documentation.

The following shows my configuration from the first tab:

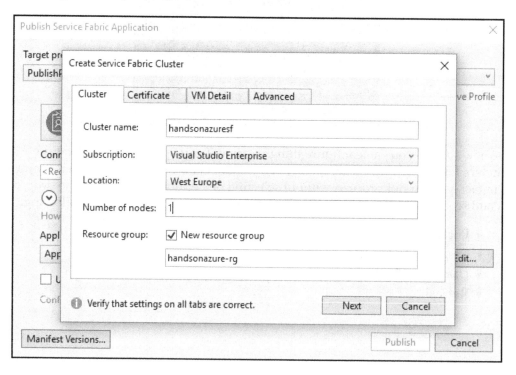

As you can see, I set the **Number of nodes** to 1—this is because I am not planning to deploy a production workload and do not need two different characteristics of virtual machines as both my services are more or less the same. When you click **Next**, you will see the second tab, where you will specify a certificate password. A certificate will be automatically created and imported if you leave the **Import certificate** option checked:

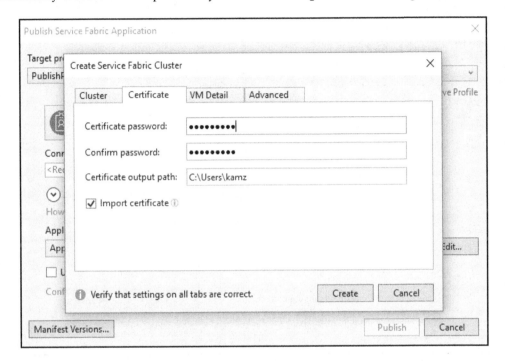

> Certificates in SF are a way to secure both node-to-node and client-to-node communication. These are X.509 certificates and, what is more, it is important to keep at least one valid—failing to do so can even make the cluster stop functioning.

The next tab is **VM Detail**, where you can specify details of machines running your cluster. After providing a **User name** and **Password**, you have to choose which operating system will be used to run SF and the size of each VM. After entering all the required information, you can click on **Create**:

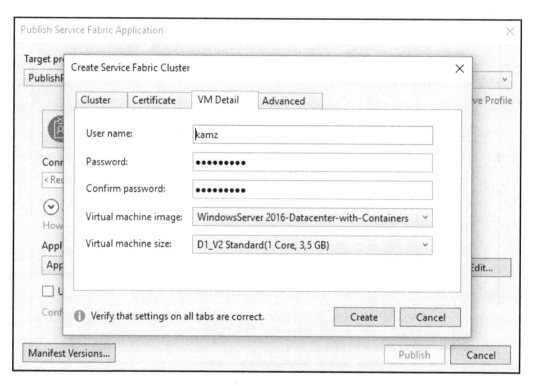

Deploying an SF cluster can take a while so be patient. Once it is finished, you can take a look at it in Azure Portal to see that all parts of the whole ecosystem are deployed. However, when you enter the SF cluster in Azure, you will see that it has both 0 applications and 0 nodes attached. This is because we just created it without deploying anything. This is why we have to go back to Visual Studio and click **Publish** once more, this time selecting a cluster we just created:

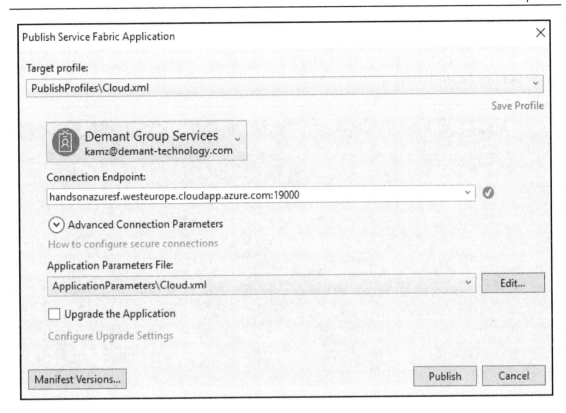

Now, let's go to Azure and explore our application. On the **Overview** blade of our SF instance, there is the **Explorer** button:

When you click on it, new windows will open in your browser and you will be asked to select a certificate, which will be used to secure a connection. Remember to select the one you created and exported during SF cluster creation. After accepting it, you should be able to see **Service Fabric Explorer**:

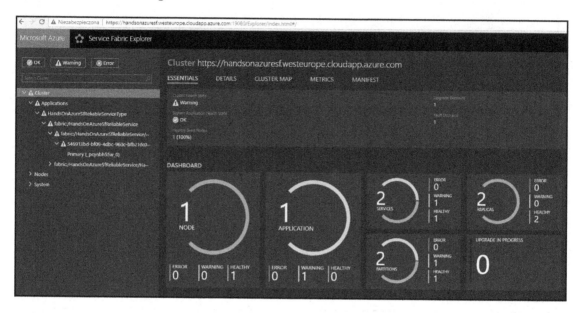

Congratulations—you have just created your very first microservice architecture using SF!

Reliable actors

In the previous section, we created an application that is made up of two services—a stateful and stateless one. In SF, there are many different frameworks to build your system—another one is Reliable actors. It is designed for creating a platform of distributed services that can work concurrently and independently—because each actor is isolated, an issue with one instance does not affect others working at the same moment. You may wonder when to choose **Reliable services** and when the best option is **Reliable Actors**? The rule of thumb could be defined as follows:

- If you require to divide your work among multiple workers (such as hundreds or thousands), choose **Reliable Actors**
- If you want to isolate your work and expect a single-threaded environment for simplicity, choose **Reliable Actors**

- If your business domain expects work to be performed in the transaction, choose **Reliable Services**
- If your service has to be reliable and highly available, choose **Reliable Services**

Of course, the aforementioned reasons do not cover all possible scenarios, but you should be able to understand the difference by now. In general, you cannot expect that actors will be very durable as the idea is to spawn new ones and forward the workload to them instead of ensuring that they can work indefinitely.

Creating a project with actors

We will start our journey with Reliable actors by creating a brand new project in Visual Studio—for this, click on **File | New project** and once more select an SF template. On the **New Service Fabric Service** screen, select the **Actor Service** template and click **OK**:

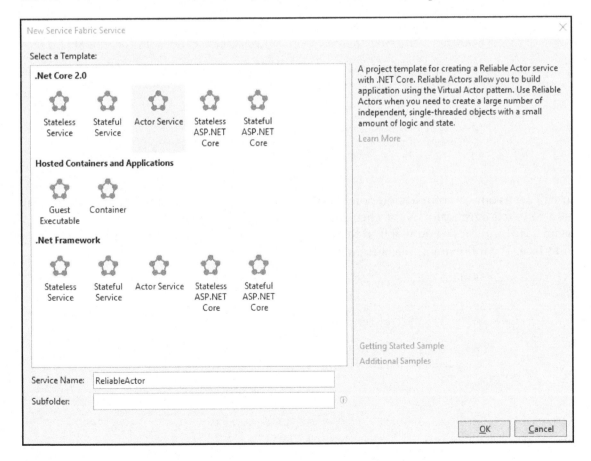

After your project is initialized, you will see that it is a bit different from the one for Reliable services—what is most important is that it now contains the `.Interfaces` project, which for now contains only one file with the following content:

```
[assembly: FabricTransportActorRemotingProvider(RemotingListener =
RemotingListener.V2Listener, RemotingClient = RemotingClient.V2Client)]
namespace ReliableActor.Interfaces
{
    /// <summary>
    /// This interface defines the methods exposed by an actor.
    /// Clients use this interface to interact with the actor that
implements it.
    /// </summary>
    public interface IReliableActor : IActor
    {
        /// <summary>
        /// TODO: Replace with your own actor method.
        /// </summary>
        /// <returns></returns>
        Task<int> GetCountAsync(CancellationToken cancellationToken);

        /// <summary>
        /// TODO: Replace with your own actor method.
        /// </summary>
        /// <param name="count"></param>
        /// <returns></returns>
        Task SetCountAsync(int count, CancellationToken cancellationToken);
    }
}
```

It will act as our communication point between the actor and its clients. You may think of it as a contracts aggregator. Now, check the main actor project (in my case it is `ReliableActor`)—you will find there the current implementation of the previous interface. The following is the current code:

```
namespace ReliableActor
{
    [StatePersistence(StatePersistence.Persisted)]
    internal class ReliableActor : Actor, IReliableActor
    {
        public ReliableActor(ActorService actorService, ActorId actorId)
            : base(actorService, actorId)
        {
        }

        protected override Task OnActivateAsync()
        {
```

```
            ActorEventSource.Current.ActorMessage(this, "Actor
activated.");
            return this.StateManager.TryAddStateAsync("count", 0);
        }

        Task<int> IReliableActor.GetCountAsync(CancellationToken
cancellationToken)
        {
            return this.StateManager.GetStateAsync<int>("count",
cancellationToken);
        }

        Task IReliableActor.SetCountAsync(int count, CancellationToken
cancellationToken)
        {
            return this.StateManager.AddOrUpdateStateAsync("count", count,
(key, value) => count > value ? count : value, cancellationToken);
        }
    }
}
```

Each actor implementation is decorated with the `[StatePersistence]` attribute. It has three different options:

- **Persisted**: Here the state is persisted to disk and replicated to replicas (three or more). It is the most durable option and prevents you from losing it even during a complete cluster failure.
- **Volatile**: Instead of persisting a state to disk, it is only replicated and held in memory on three or more replicas. This is the less durable option, similar to holding your data only in RAM memory, which will be lost once power is lost.
- **None**: If you do not need to persist in your state, you can use this option.

There is no best option here—it all depends on the requirements of your actors. Please note one more thing—an actor itself is not limited to some kind of "hard" contract; you define the code all by yourself and SF will do its best to replicate it, persist state (if needed), and scale out to meet your demands. Currently, we have only a worker—we also need a client to test our service.

Creating an actor's client

To create a client, we will use the most traditional **Console Application**. Once more, click on **File | New project** and search for it or just right-click on the solution and click on **Add | New project**. You will have to add two more things before we write some code:

- Add a reference to our .Interfaces project as we have to know which methods we would like to call
- Install the Microsoft.ServiceFabric.Actors package

We will write a simple application that calls our actor, fetches the current count value, and updates it. The following shows my example code:

```
using System;
using System.Threading;
using System.Threading.Tasks;
using Microsoft.ServiceFabric.Actors;
using Microsoft.ServiceFabric.Actors.Client;
using ReliableActor.Interfaces;

namespace ReliableActor.Client
{
    class Program
    {
        static void Main()
        {
            MainAsync().GetAwaiter().GetResult();
        }

        static async Task MainAsync()
        {
            IReliableActor actor =
ActorProxy.Create<IReliableActor>(ActorId.CreateRandom(), new
Uri("fabric:/ReliableActors/ReliableActorService"));
            while (true)
            {
                var count = await
actor.GetCountAsync(CancellationToken.None);
                Console.Write($"Current count is: {count}\r\n");
                await actor.SetCountAsync(++count, CancellationToken.None);

                Thread.Sleep(1000);
            }
        }
    }
}
```

As you can see, I am doing three things:

- I am getting a reference to my actor service by using the `fabric` protocol and a specific interface I created
- To obtain the count value, I am calling the `GetCountAsync()` method on my reference
- I am updating state by calling `SetCountAsync()`

The following shows the result of running both actor and client:

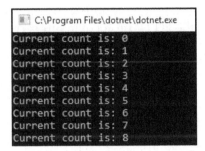

Great—all works as expected. You may wonder how actor instances are distributed in the SF cluster and how we achieve the distribution of hundreds of instances of them. Well, it is all handled by SF runtime by partitioning instances and attaching them to different nodes on a cluster. Thanks to that, you can expect that the workload will be balanced—what is more, you can reference an actor by its ID (as opposed to the presented method, `ActorId.CreateRandom()`), but it is not always recommended as you have to ensure you are not overloading one actor.

Communication between services

You currently know how to work with SF using Reliable services and Reliable actors. The next important topic refers to communication between each instance of a service. As we discussed at the beginning of this chapter, the best option when building your microservices is to create a platform that will be agnostic when it comes to choosing what is the best way to communicate and accept incoming requests. In SF, you do not have a single way to exchange messages—instead you are provided with a complete framework to do it your way. In this section, we will focus on building a simple communication channel for your services.

Creating a communication channel

To create a channel, you will need to implement the following interface:

```
public interface ICommunicationListener
{
    Task<string> OpenAsync(CancellationToken cancellationToken);
    Task CloseAsync(CancellationToken cancellationToken);
    void Abort();
}
```

As you can see, there is no information regarding technology or the framework used—it is up to you. We will try to open the HTTP protocol in our service. Since we cannot cover all types of service in this book, we will focus on the stateless service. If you open the project from the section about it, in the main file of your service, you can find the following method:

```
protected override IEnumerable<ServiceInstanceListener>
CreateServiceInstanceListeners()
{
    return new ServiceInstanceListener[0];
}
```

Currently, it returns an empty array—we would have to provide a custom implementation of `ServiceInstanceListener` and add it here. While it is, of course, possible to do so, it would take too much time to describe it in detail; instead, we use a NuGet package, which has the correct implementation of such a listener and is built using ASP.NET Core.

 Currently, it is possible to use Http Sys or Kestrel to resolve communication. Feel free to experiment as those technologies differ a little and are always a substitute for each other (for example, Http Sys is currently not designed for stateful services).

For this exercise, please install the following package: `Microsoft.ServiceFabric.AspNetCore.HttpSys`. Once you have it, you can modify the `CreateServiceInstanceListeners()` method as follows:

```
protected override IEnumerable<ServiceInstanceListener>
CreateServiceInstanceListeners()
{
  return new[]
  {
    new ServiceInstanceListener(serviceContext =>
      new HttpSysCommunicationListener(serviceContext, "ServiceEndpoint",
(url, listener) =>
        new WebHostBuilder()
```

```
            .UseHttpSys()
            .ConfigureServices(
              services => services
                .AddSingleton<StatelessServiceContext>(serviceContext))
            .UseContentRoot(Directory.GetCurrentDirectory())
            .UseServiceFabricIntegration(listener,
  ServiceFabricIntegrationOptions.None)
            .UseStartup<Startup>()
            .UseUrls(url)
            .Build()))
    };
  }
```

As you can see, it provided the full implementation of a listener and a pipeline for handling a request. You will also need to implement the Startup class, which will handle communication:

```
public class Startup
{
  public Startup(IHostingEnvironment env)
  {
  }

  public Startup(IApplicationBuilder appenv, IHostingEnvironment env,
  ILoggerFactory loggerFactory)
  {
  }

  public void ConfigureServices(IServiceCollection services)
  {
  }

  public void Configure(IApplicationBuilder app)
  {
    app.Run(context => {
      return context.Response.WriteAsync("Hello From Service Fabric!");
    });
  }
}
```

This may look familiar to you as this is a simple ASP.NET Core stack, which you would implement in the same manner, creating a web application not hosted in SF. Only one thing remains for now—we have to modify `ServiceManifest.xml` and specify that our endpoint is exposed by a service:

```
<Resources>
  <Endpoints>
    <Endpoint Name="ServiceEndpoint" Protocol="http" Port="80" />
  </Endpoints>
</Resources>
```

 Remember that the endpoint name must match the one you defined in your code.

Now, when you run your application, you should be able to call it by using the exposed endpoint, which can be found in **Service Fabric Explorer**:

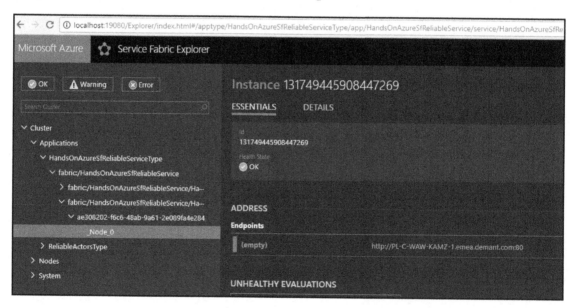

The following is the result of calling my service from the Postman application:

Now the question is: What you can do with such a feature? In fact, there are many possibilities—you can exchange messages between services, you can query a service for the status of a task currently performed, or you can change a state so a different path will be chosen when running a workload. This is a very powerful functionality and, in addition to all of the advantages that SF brings to distributed systems, you can be sure that your communication is reliable and fully under your control.

Clusters in SF

We have talked about clusters in SF, but how can you really understand such a concept in that service? You probably remember that, during the creation of a cluster, we had to choose both node types and their characteristics—the number of VMs and their type. If you choose to have three nodes with five machines in each one, you will end up with a cluster of fifteen machines in total. SF automatically balances it, so if you are changing its size, all services will be redeployed to achieve maximum utilization. In this chapter, we will talk a little about security, available features, and scalability.

The following is a conceptual diagram of a cluster organization:

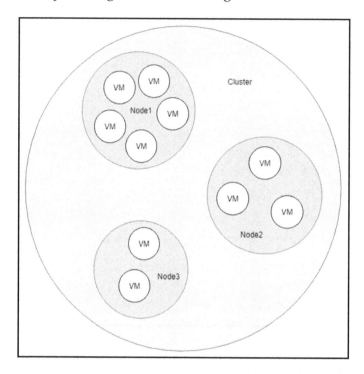

Cluster security

If you go back to the creation of a cluster, you will notice that we always had to create or import a certificate—without it, there was no way to proceed. You have to remember that it is your responsibility to secure your environment and prevent unauthorized access. As the documentation states, it is impossible to create an insecure cluster—this is, of course, true. However, if you expose your endpoint (especially in production workloads) publicly, there is always the possibility that somebody will figure it out and start abusing it.

Node-to-node security

Let's assume that you have three different nodes for different types of workload:

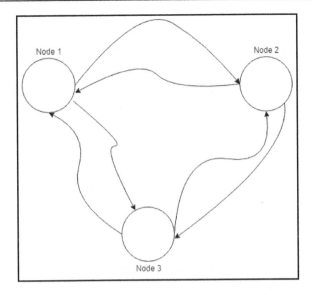

Those nodes could be exposed (or not exposed) to the external network. Now, you may wonder how SF ensures that communication is handled in a secure manner. In fact, there are two possibilities:

- **Certificate security**: In such a scenario, a client (node) attaches credentials to each request and signs a message with the private key
- **Windows security**: Based on the Kerberos protocol

The final solution depends on your actual needs.

Client-to-node security

Besides communicating within a cluster, you may need to allow authorized users to exchange messages with individual nodes. In fact, this is cover by similar security options as **node-to-node** security—here you can choose between certificates and **Active Directory (AD)** security. What is the advantage of using AD in that scenario? There is one very important aspect—in most cases, you do not want to share certificates with your client (this could also be cumbersome with a large number of them). AD security can be set in the ARM template by providing additional options:

```
"azureActiveDirectory": {
  "tenantId": "<guid>",
  "clusterApplication": "<guid>",
  "clientApplication": "<guid>"
}
```

Scaling

Scaling is one of the most important features of SF as the microservices architecture is all about being able to scale out when you need and preserving a stable environment while doing so. In most cases, you will need to scale horizontally (by getting more machines running your workloads) but, of course, it is also possible to scale vertically (so more powerful machines become available and, in some scenarios, it is a better option than scaling out). In general, the answer to whether you need to scale out or up depends on the work your code needs to do:

- If your work can be parallelized, choose to scale out
- If your work performs many calculations and is I/O-heavy and such actions cannot be distributed, choose to scale out

What is more, each node type in SF is a separate VM scale set. That means that you can scale your nodes independently, according to your needs. This is a very important feature—you probably would not appreciate, if only one part of your system requires more computing power, having to update the whole cluster.

In SF, each node has specific requirements when it comes to scaling, as it is important to keep the correct number of nodes running production workloads. Details can be found in the documentation; you can find a link to it in the *Further reading* section at the end of this chapter.

Scaling a cluster up or down

In general, it is not recommended to scale a cluster up or down, as it is a dangerous operation (especially if you would like to change the VM SKU of the primary node). If you wonder why, please consider the following operation—you are about to scale down a node. This is an infrastructure operation, which requires changing available hardware for your application. If you do not monitor and orchestrate all operations correctly, you may end up with your stateful services losing data (for example, you temporarily lost access to a database) and even stateless services may become unstable. In fact, to scale up or down in a secure fashion, you should first create a new node type, and then gradually reduce the instance count of the old one, so SF is able to distribute the workload correctly before the old node is shut down.

The SF documentation states that it is highly inadvisable to change the SKU of VMs running a primary node. However, it is, of course, possible when done carefully; you can find a link to instructions in the *Further reading* section at the end of this chapter.

Monitoring and diagnostics

In the final section of this chapter, we will cover some topics regarding monitoring and diagnosing your services in SF. As you probably remember, I noted such features as one of the most important in microservices, as you have to always be able to tell how each one works and perform the needed action (such as scale out, restart, or kill an instance) if required. In SF, there are a few levels of monitoring that we will briefly describe here.

Application monitoring

In most cases, you want to monitor how your application works, what the user traffic is, and how your services communicate with each other. While you are able to bring your own framework, you can also leverage **Application Insights (AI)** integration—this will ensure that you are getting all necessary logs and available diagnostic messages. You can set up AI integration while creating a cluster for SF:

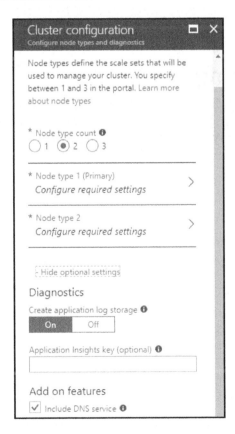

Cluster monitoring

While working, your cluster emits a variety of events, which map to one particular entity within it:

- Cluster
- Application
- Service
- Partition
- Replica
- Container

You can query these events by leveraging the `EventStore` service available in SF. It is possible to correlate them, so you can find out how one entity impacts others. The following is the example request to the API returning events from a specific time range:

```
http://{CLUSTER}:19080/EventsStore/Cluster/Events?api-version=6.2-preview&S
tartTimeUtc=2018-04-03T18:00:00Z&EndTimeUtc=2018-07-04T18:00:00Z
```

Health monitoring

Besides monitoring your application and cluster, you will also want to check how a particular service is working. To check its health, SF introduces **Service Fabric Explorer**, which you can access to verify the health of the following:

- Node
- Application
- Service
- Partition
- Replica

You can access the Explorer both locally and in the cloud. It presents a nice UI, which displays a lot of useful information that you can use to determine the current status of the whole system, notice possible problems, and get the necessary details to investigate an issue further:

Summary

In this chapter, we only took a brief look at SF and the microservices built with this Azure component. You have learned the basic concepts of SF, such as Reliable services and Reliable actors, and how to implement a communication protocol to exchange messages between services and clients. Remember that building an application based on microservices is not a trivial task and requires sticking to many important rules to avoid problems with dealing with state, monitoring, or scaling. Use SF as a framework for building distributed applications, which takes care of ensuring that they are reliable and highly available.

Last but not least: do not be discouraged if you have problems with SF or feel overwhelmed by its multiple options and configurations—this particular service has a pretty difficult learning curve, but after reading this whole chapter, you should be able to start writing your very own services without problems.

In Chapter 3, *Deploying Web Applications as Containers*, you will learn about another PaaS service available in Azure: Azure Search, which lets you start using your own search engine to index and query stored documents.

Questions

1. What is the difference between Reliable services and Reliable actors?
2. What is the difference between stateless and stateful services?
3. What one has to be implemented to introduce its very own communication channel in SF?
4. What is node type in SF?
5. Can you scale (up/out) node types individually?
6. Can you select a VM SKU when creating a cluster?
7. What are the two types of node security in SF?
8. What is the difference between cluster, application, service, partition, and replica?
9. Why does SF advocate creating a node with at least five VMs?
10. What is the reliability tier in SF?

Further reading

- https://docs.microsoft.com/en-us/azure/service-fabric/service-fabric-technical-overview
- https://docs.microsoft.com/en-us/azure/service-fabric/service-fabric-cluster-creation-via-arm
- https://docs.microsoft.com/en-us/azure/service-fabric/service-fabric-cluster-scaling
- https://docs.microsoft.com/en-us/azure/service-fabric/service-fabric-diagnostics-event-generation-operational
- https://docs.microsoft.com/en-us/azure/service-fabric/service-fabric-work-with-reliable-collections

Using Azure Search

5

When in need of using a search engine, it's always a good idea to use tested and well-known solutions that have been available on the market for a while. One of those solutions is Azure Search, which offers a search-as-a-service cloud solution with an API for developers, so users can focus on developing a working solution without the need to manage infrastructure or configuration. With the recent addition of the Cognitive Search API, we've been given an opportunity to enhance our search functionality with AI features, so it's possible to transform unstructured content into searchable content.

The following topics will be covered in this chapter:

- Using Azure Search in your projects
- Using full-text search for your needs
- Using linguistics analysis
- Using indexing, index definition, and indexers
- The new Cognitive Search API with indexing workloads supported by AI

Technical requirements

To perform exercises from this chapter, you will need the following:

- Access to an Azure subscription
- A tool for sending HTTP requests (cURL and Postman)

Creating an Azure Search service

Creating Azure Search is an easy task and should not take more than a few minutes. The important thing to remember here is that, if you have to recreate a service, there is no way to back up and restore data—if you make mistakes here, everything has to be done from scratch.

The reason to recreate would be changing the datatypes or other search attributes of the search index columns. While it will not be a problem during this exercise, have that in mind when creating a production workload.

Using Azure Portal

As with most services in Azure, we will start our journey by creating Azure Search in the portal. To do so, click on **+ Create a resource** and search for Azure Search. On the introduction screen, click on the **Create** button, which will take you to the configuration of this service:

As you can see, we have pretty standard options here, which should not be unclear to you by now. There is, however, an option to select a **Pricing tier**, where currently there are different options to choose from:

- **Free**: This is the most basic one without replicas available and shared resources.
- **Basic**: This comes with load balancing available, scaling, and dedicated resources.

- **Standard**: This is three different tiers with more compute power and partitions available.
- **High-density**: The same as **Standard** but with more indexes available (and fewer partitions). This particular tier is designed for SaaS developers specifically.

Before we proceed, you will have to understand what all of these concepts are:

- **Replica**: This is an individual instance of your search service, which hosts one copy of an index. If you have more than one replica, you can load balance your queries.
- **Index**: You can think of this as a table that contains multiple rows (or in other words, documents) with additional metadata used by a service.
- **Search unit (SU)**: This is a billing unit for Azure Search, which is a composition of the number of replicas and partitions (*SU = Replicas * Partitions*).
- **Partition**: Each partition provides storage and I/O for your instance of Azure Search, so scaling this unit will give more of those.

> The main difference between replicas and partitions is that, if you need more computational resources, you can increase partitions while, for larger query volumes, you need more replicas (so a query can be load balanced).

When you fill all fields and select a tier, click on the **Create** button and wait for a moment for service creation. Once it is created, click on it and go to the **Overview** blade. There, select **Import data**, so we can start with some samples before diving deeper into Azure Search:

On the next screen, you will see multiple options for importing records—you are able to select the data source and index and enable **Cognitive Search**, which we will cover in the next sections:

 Remember that it is possible to delete or change the fields used for indexing data, but such operations require re-indexing all documents. By re-indexing I mean that you have to delete, then recreate the index. However, it is possible to add new fields without re-indexing the documents—in that case, the values for the new columns will be null for the older ones.

Because we selected sample data, **Index** is already filled with some default values. When you click **Ok**, they will be validated and the **Indexer** screen will become available. You may wonder what indexer is exactly. Its definition is quite simple—it is a crawler that looks at your data source and extracts everything from it based on the mapping between an index and stored information. For example, if you selected a field named Status as a part of your index, the indexer will search for all records containing it and push it to your index.

 Indexers can be configured either to fetch data once or on schedule. We will cover scheduled indexers in the section regarding indexes and indexing documents.

If you are satisfied with import configuration, click on the **Ok** button and wait a moment until the data is imported and indexed. Now, we can test how our service works—on the **Overview** blade, you can find the **Search explorer** button. When you click on it, you will see the new screen, where you can enter your **Query string** and **Request URL**, which can be used in your application to get results:

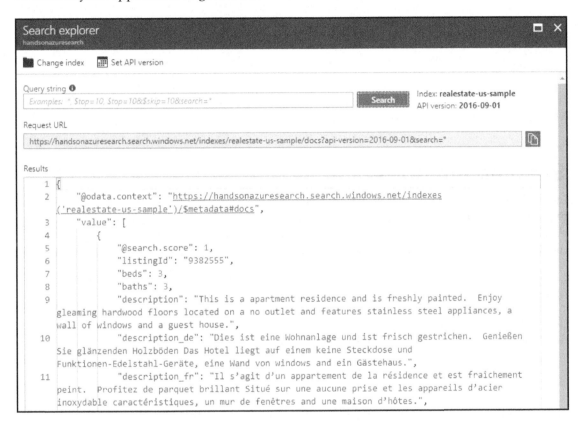

Full-text search in Azure Search

The power of Azure Search comes when you need to perform a full-text search to find relevant documents that will satisfy your query. This Azure service uses **Apache Lucene** under the hood, which is a well-known, high-performance search engine written in Java.

 You can find more information about Lucene here: `https://lucene.apache.org/core/`. It is an open source project available to download for everyone.

In this chapter, you will learn how to perform a full-text search, what is the syntax, and how to recognize potential issues.

Sending a request

In the first section of this chapter, you created your Azure Search instance and saw **Search explorer**, which enables you to send simple queries. Now, we will extend our requests, so you can select which fields should be used for query analysis, to filter results, and to order by a particular property. Here is the basic URL, which you will use for all of your requests:

```
https://handsonazuresearch.search.windows.net/indexes/realestate-us-sample/docs?api-version=2016-09-01&search=*
```

Of course, it will differ depending on the name of your Azure Search instance, the index name, and the version used. The URL template can be defined as follows:

```
https://[service name].search.windows.net/indexes/[index name]/docs?[query parameters]
```

As you can see, in this example I used *, which basically means that I am interested in all documents indexed. However, before we proceed, we need to do one more thing—as with most APIs, Azure Search is secured and requires a key to authorize a request. If you do not send it, you will get an `HTTP 403 response`. To obtain a key, go to Azure Portal and select the **Keys** blade:

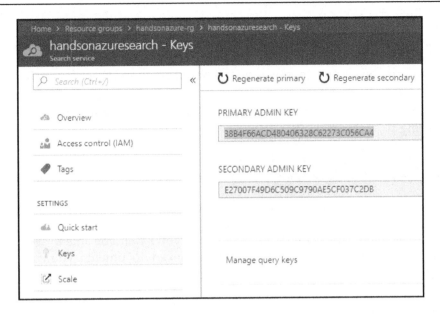

Now, with each request to your API, you will have to use the `api-key` header with the appropriate value. Here you can find an example:

```
GET /indexes/realestate-us-sample/docs?api-version=2016-09-01&search=*
HTTP/1.1
Host: handsonazuresearch.search.windows.net
api-key: 38B4F66ACD480406328C62273C056CA4
Cache-Control: no-cache
```

Nonetheless, in most cases, we are not interested in literally all documents available—we have specific parameters that we would like to use. Let's assume you would like to search for a specific city. In such a case, we have to use another endpoint and pass a valid payload, which will be used to build a query:

```
POST /indexes/realestate-us-sample/docs/search?api-version=2016-09-01
HTTP/1.1
Host: handsonazuresearch.search.windows.net
api-key: {API_KEY}
Content-Type: application/json
Cache-Control: no-cache

{
    "search": "Sammamish",
    "searchFields": "city"
}
```

As you can see, I changed the HTTP method to POST and used the /search endpoint for my request. The most important thing, however, is the body—for now, I used two fields:

- search: This is our query string, which we are using to tell Azure Search what we are interested in
- searchFields: Here we are passing fields, which should contain our query string

 Please remember that the fields passed in the request body are case-sensitive and you should follow camel case if there are multiple words.

If you run the preceding query on the sample index, you should be able to see some results returned. If you search for a city that is not in the indexed documents, you will see an empty result:

```
{
    "@odata.context":
"https://handsonazuresearch.search.windows.net/indexes('realestate-us-sampl
e')/$metadata#docs",
    "value": []
}
```

You may ask what are the rules for choosing a search field—the only requirement is that it has to be marked as Searchable. Take a look at what will happen if I use beds to search for records with a specific number of them:

```
{
    "error": {
        "code": "",
        "message": "The field 'beds' in the search field list is not
searchable.\r\nParameter name: searchFields"
    }
}
```

It seems we cannot use any field we would like to. You can check which fields can be used for searching in the index screen:

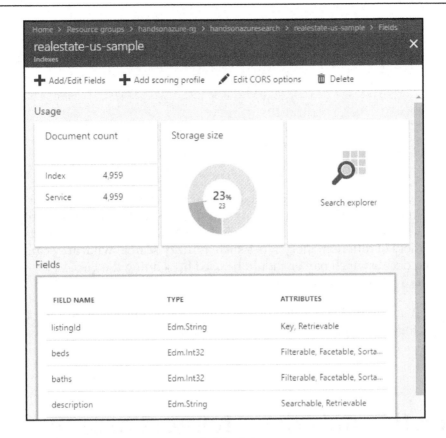

In fact, you cannot use any field of the `Edm.Int32` type as `Searchable`. There are some other types, which are also not supported (for example, `Edm.GeographyPoint`)—you can find information about them when building or modifying fields used in an index.

To overcome the aforementioned problem, you may use filters—these are expressions based on the OData syntax, which you can leverage to search for the entities you are interested in. The only requirement is to make a field you want to use into a filter using filterable. Here you can find all possible fields, which you can use in such an HTTP request:

```
{
    "count": true | false(default),
    "facets": ["facet_expression_1", "facet_expression_2", ...],
    "filter": "odata_filter_expression",
    "highlight": "highlight_field_1, highlight_field_2, ...",
    "highlightPreTag": "pre_tag",
    "highlightPostTag": "post_tag",
    "minimumCoverage": #( % of index that must be covered to declare query
```

```
successful; default 100),
   "orderby": "orderby_expression",
   "scoringParameters": ["scoring_parameter_1", "scoring_parameter_2", ...],
   "scoringProfile": "scoring_profile_name",
   "search": "simple_query_expression",
   "searchFields": "field_name_1, field_name_2, ...",
   "searchMode": "any" (default) | "all",
   "select": "field_name_1, field_name_2, ...",
   "skip": #(default 0),
   "top": #
}
```

We will not cover them all as this would take this whole chapter, however, we will focus a little more on the actual syntax of queries sent to Azure Search. As you probably remember, this service uses the Lucene search engine to index data and handle requests. Lucene supports a variety of different query types such as fuzzy search, wildcard search, and many more. You can decide which parser should be used by sending the `queryType` parameter with one of the available values—simple or full (Lucene).

 You can find supported query operations by Lucene by reading the following page: `https://docs.microsoft.com/pl-pl/rest/api/` `searchservice/lucene-query-syntax-in-azure-search`.

Linguistic analysis in full-text search

When using full-text search, you have to understand what are the rules for performing such operations. Search engines have to analyze search query lexically to be able to extract important information and pass it to a query tree. In this section, we will cover the most common lexical analysis, which is linguistic analysis, to help you understand how Azure Search works and how to perform correct queries.

Analyzers in Azure Search

To perform linguistic analysis, Azure Search supports a variety of different analyzers, which can be specified in the index definition. However, before we start defining one of those, you have to catch a glimpse of what we are talking about. When creating an index, each search service has to analyze all input documents and decide what will be important when performing a search procedure.

Additionally, each search query should be adjusted to some common rules, so the search engine can understand it. The necessary operations can be described as follows:

- All non-essential words should be removed (such as "the" in English)
- All words should be lowercase
- If a word contains multiple words in it (such as "up-front"), it should be divided into atomic ones

Now let's assume you are searching for an apartment using the following search query:

```
Spacious apartment with 4 and the Red Kitchen
```

Your analyzer will have to perform all of the preceding operations before passing the query to a search engine and, in fact, here you can find the result of such analysis:

```
{
    "@odata.context":
"https://handsonazuresearch.search.windows.net/$metadata#Microsoft.Azure.Se
arch.V2016_09_01.AnalyzeResult",
    "tokens": [
        {
            "token": "spacious",
            "startOffset": 0,
            "endOffset": 8,
            "position": 0
        },
        {
            "token": "apartment",
            "startOffset": 9,
            "endOffset": 18,
            "position": 1
        },
        {
            "token": "with",
            "startOffset": 19,
            "endOffset": 23,
            "position": 2
        },
        {
            "token": "4",
            "startOffset": 24,
            "endOffset": 25,
            "position": 3
        },
        {
            "token": "and",
            "startOffset": 26,
```

```
            "endOffset": 29,
            "position": 4
        },
        {

            "token": "the",
            "startOffset": 30,
            "endOffset": 33,
            "position": 5
        },
        {

            "token": "red",
            "startOffset": 34,
            "endOffset": 37,
            "position": 6
        },
        {

            "token": "kitchen",
            "startOffset": 38,
            "endOffset": 45,
            "position": 7
        }
    ]
}
```

As you can see, each word has its particular position and offset. To get a result similar to the previous one, you can send the following query:

```
POST /indexes/[index name]/analyze?api-version=2016-09-01 HTTP/1.1
Host: [service name].search.windows.net
api-key: [api key]
Content-Type: application/json
Cache-Control: no-cache

{
  "text": "Spacious apartment with 4 and the Red Kitchen",
  "analyzer": "standard"
}
```

In the request's body, you have to provide both texts to analyze and use the analyzer. Note that I used `standard` here, which means that the standard Lucene analyzer is used here.

 Azure Search supports several different analyzers for different languages—what is more, both Microsoft and Lucene versions are available. To get the full list, go to the documentation page: `https://docs.microsoft.com/pl-pl/rest/api/searchservice/language-support`.

If you are proficient in language analysis and syntax, you could create a custom analyzer that can be used for text analysis. Such analyzers can be defined during index creation, however, we will not cover that topic in this book as it is an advanced exercise and is out of our present scope. You will find a link to the tutorial in the *Further reading* section of this chapter.

Analyzer selection

You can select an analyzer for a specific field either during the creation of an index or while editing it. If you go to Azure Portal and to your Azure Search instance, you can click on an index and select the **Fields** section. It should display a list of all fields used in that index:

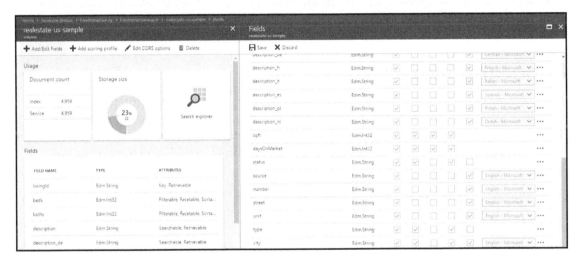

Now, when you scroll down, you will see that you are able to add a new field. If you would like to select an analyzer, you will need to do the following:

1. Select a checkbox **Analyzer** at the top of that blade
2. Select **Searchable** as an option of that field

Now you should see a drop-down list from which you are able to select a different analyzer than the custom one:

Note that selecting a different analyzer than the custom one is crucial when you have fields containing multiple languages. In such a scenario, you should select an analyzer appropriate for the language used.

Indexing in Azure Search

An index is one of the most important constructs in Azure Search. We defined it as a table that contains all imported documents with searchable data defined in it. At the beginning of this chapter, you learned how to create it and add or edit fields. In this section, you will learn a bit more about modifying it as an index is not a fixed being that cannot be altered and adjusted to your needs.

Importing more data

There is always a need to push more data to your index—your application grows, the storage of your documents becomes bigger and bigger, especially if you are creating a document repository, and you would like to be able to find what you are searching for even in the most recent documents. In fact, there are two options to add data to your index:

- The push model
- The pull model

We will cover both of them in the following sections.

Push model

The push model is the best solution for applications that have low-latency requirements. As opposed to the pull model, for this model, your document will be indexed immediately after pushing it using a RESTful API.

Currently, there is no other option to use a push model besides using a RESTful API or .NET SDK to perform an operation. In the pull model, it is also possible to get data using Azure Portal.

Here, you can find an example request for pushing a document:

```
POST /indexes/realestate-us-sample/docs/index?api-version=2016-09-01
HTTP/1.1
Host: [service name].search.windows.net
api-key: [api key]
Content-Type: application/json
Cache-Control: no-cache

{
  "value": [
    {
      "listingId": "12344234",
      "@search.action": "upload",
      "price": 250.0,
      "description": "The very apartment in Warsaw",
      "city": "Warsaw",
      "tags": ["pool", "view", "wifi", "gym"],
      "beds": 4,
      "location": { "type": "Point", "coordinates": [52.237049, 21.017532]
}
    }
  ]
}
```

If everything is correct, you should be able to see a successful result:

```
{
    "@odata.context":
"https://handsonazuresearch.search.windows.net/indexes('realestate-us-sampl
e')/$metadata#Collection(Microsoft.Azure.Search.V2016_09_01.IndexResult)",
    "value": [
        {
            "key": "12344234",
            "status": true,
            "errorMessage": null,
            "statusCode": 201
        }
    ]
}
```

Now, I would like to check whether my document is already indexed and available:

```
POST /indexes/realestate-us-sample/docs/search?api-version=2016-09-01
HTTP/1.1
Host: [service name].search.windows.net
api-key: [api key]
Content-Type: application/json
```

```
Cache-Control: no-cache

{
    "search": "Warsaw",
    "searchFields": "city"
}
```

The result should be a document that contains all of the fields we passed in the push request.

Pull model

A pull model is a bit different than a push model as it uses indexers to actually fetch the data. When using it, you are configuring both a data source and how frequently data should be pulled. As opposed to the push model, it can be configured and accessed when using Azure Portal.

> Please note one important difference between push and pull—when using push, you are able to use any data source you want. When using the pull model you are limited to Blob Storage, Table Storage, CosmosDB, and SQL Database (both on Azure and VMs).

Here, you can find an indexer configuration for pulling data when using Table Storage as a source:

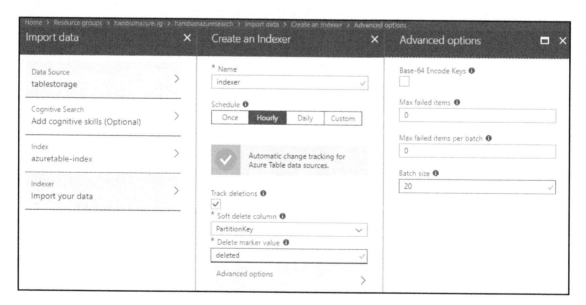

Please remember that you cannot configure a pull policy when using sample data.

What is more, you can access an indexer configuration and current status by clicking on the **Indexers** button on the **Overview** blade:

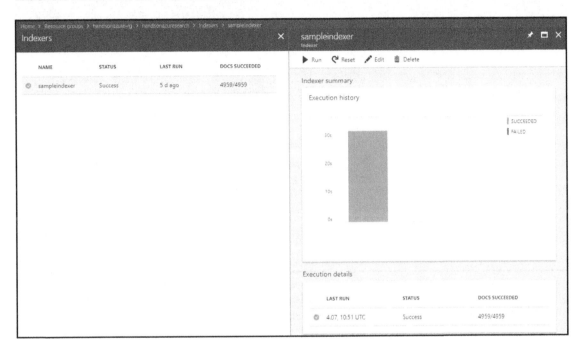

Cognitive search – adding AI to the indexing workload

When creating and managing an index, you always have to make sure that you have selected all required fields and marked them as searchable where needed. Additionally, we are limited to the current service functionalities, so we cannot use things such as image or natural language processing. Fortunately, Azure Service is about to start supporting the Cognitive Search feature, which adds AI to your indexing operations, allowing for richer analysis using more vectors. In this chapter, you will learn how to configure it, so you can start using it from the very beginning.

Configuring Cognitive Search

Cognitive Search can be configured when importing data for your service. When you click on the **Import data** button, you will see that one of the available sections is that feature exactly:

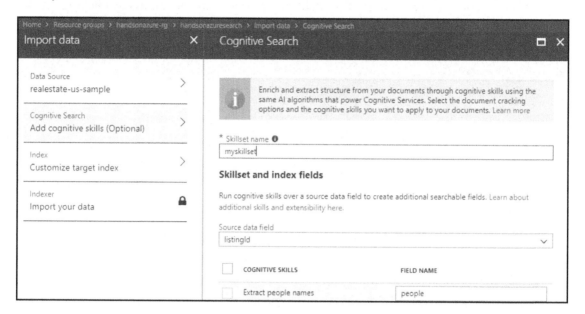

 At the time of writing, this feature is available only in the South Central US and Western Europe regions.

There is a list of Cognitive Skills that can be used for indexing your data. Whether you use one or not depends on your actual requirements—for the purpose of this exercise, I selected **Detect language**. You can customize the name of a field also; this could be crucial if your index will contain another one named the same, as it will be added to the result of a query. When you finish configuring your index, you can compare the previous one with the new one enriched by AI:

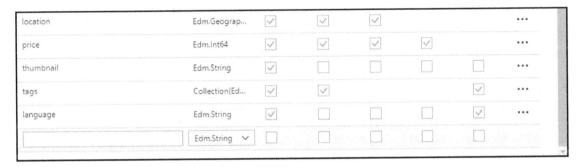

location	Edm.Geograp...	☑	☑	☑			•••
price	Edm.Int64	☑	☑	☑	☑		•••
thumbnail	Edm.String	☑	☐	☐	☐	☐	•••
tags	Collection(Ed...	☑	☑			☑	•••
	Edm.String ∨	☐	☐	☐	☐	☐	

As you can see, we are missing the **language** field here since we did not use it. Let's compare it with the newest index:

location	Edm.Geograp...	☑	☑	☑			•••
price	Edm.Int64	☑	☑	☑	☑		•••
thumbnail	Edm.String	☑	☐	☐	☐	☐	•••
tags	Collection(Ed...	☑	☑			☑	•••
language	Edm.String	☑	☐	☐	☐	☑	•••
	Edm.String ∨	☐	☐	☐	☐	☐	

Additionally, when I query a service using a newer index, I will get a result containing the **language** field filled:

```
{
(...)
"location": {
  "type": "Point",
  "coordinates": [
    -122.388,
    47.576
  ],
  "crs": {
    "type": "name",
    "properties": {
      "name": "EPSG:4326"
    }
  }
},
"price": 762048,
"thumbnail":
"https://searchdatasets.blob.core.windows.net/images/bd2bt2apt.jpg",
"tags": [
  "condominium",
  "dream home",
```

```
    "lake access",
    "no outlet",
    "miele appliances",
    "wall of windows",
    "guest room"
],
"language": "en"
}
```

Summary

Azure Search is a great service when you want to have your very own search solution and do not plan to maintain its infrastructure and configuration. With its flexibility and intuitiveness, you can quickly develop your application, leveraging features such as the push/pull model, scheduled indexing, or support for different kinds of data sources. Additionally, with the option to start from the free tier even for production workloads, you can gradually progress and scale your solution up adjusting costs based on real requirements. In Chapter 6, *Mobile Notifications with Notification Hub*, we will cover topics related to handling mobile and applications and push notification by using Azure Notification Hub.

Questions

1. What is an index?
2. What is the difference between the push and pull models?
3. Can an indexer be scheduled using a custom interval?
4. What analyzer does Azure Search use by default?
5. Can one implement a custom analyzer and use it in Azure Search?
6. What is the difference between partition and replica?
7. What is the name of a header used for authorizing requests to Azure Search?

Further reading

- Azure Search documentation: `https://docs.microsoft.com/en-us/azure/search/`
- Cognitive Skills for Azure Search: `https://docs.microsoft.com/en-us/azure/search/cognitive-search-predefined-skills`
- Apache Lucene documentation: `https://lucene.apache.org/core/`
- Filters in Azure Search: `https://docs.microsoft.com/en-us/rest/api/searchservice/odata-expression-syntax-for-azure-search`

6
Mobile Notifications with Notification Hub

Push notifications are one of the main features of many mobile apps. They facilitate informing a user about a wait for action, or maybe about a temporary discount that is available only for minutes within an application. While each mobile OS vendor has its own service for such notifications, it's always nice to configure such a feature in one place, so we don't have to worry about changes in the underlying API or the parameters required. Azure Notification Hub simplifies things greatly by providing a single service that acts as a single endpoint for our mobile applications, easing both development and testing.

The following topics will be covered in this chapter:

- Notification Hub and its benefits
- Notification architecture and the best patterns for sending a notification to mobile apps
- Registering a device within Notification Hub and maintaining registrations
- Sending notifications to multiple vendors
- Sending a rich content notification through Notification Hub

Technical requirements

To perform exercises from this chapter, you will need the following:

- An active Azure subscription
- Visual Studio 2017 with Tools for Universal Windows apps installed
- A Windows Store account

Reasons to use Notification Hub

If you have ever had a chance to develop an application that was integrated with any notifications system, you probably know the challenges that are faced when creating such a product. In this chapter, I will try to introduce you to some basic concepts such as PNS, push notifications, and device registrations. This will ensure that we can easily start developing applications leveraging Notification Hub features and focus on learning details and hidden functionalities.

Exercises from this chapter are written for **Universal Windows Platform (UWP)** applications—however, the concepts presented are true also for other platforms such as Android or iOS.

Challenges for application design

Let's assume you have the following architecture:

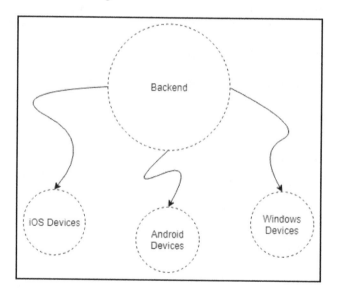

Here, we have a backend that sends some messages to three different platforms:

- iOS
- Android
- Windows

Now, if these messages are push notifications, our backend will have to communicate with three different services:

- **Apple Push Notification Service (APNS)**
- **Firebase Cloud Messaging (FCM)**
- **Windows Notification Service (WNS)**

Each of these services is called a **Platform Notification Service (PNS)**. Their responsibility is to accept a request to send a notification and send it to the appropriate device. They also handle registration of the devices that want to accept notifications (for instance, by tokens in APNS). The downside of such a solution is that none of these services has a common interface—we cannot introduce a simple wrapper in our backend to handle each request in the same fashion. The solution for that kind of trouble would be altering our architecture a little bit, so it contains a service that aggregates the logic for each PNS and is able to communicate with them:

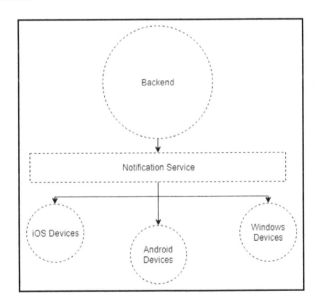

Notification Hub is such a service; it's an abstraction over different PNSes and is able to handle different device registration. We can consider two more problems—scaling and routing. It is important to know that, according do the PNSes guide, the device token must be refreshed with each app launch. Now, if it is your backend responsibility, you may end up with a solution that tries to handle refresh requests instead of focusing on your business logic.

Additionally, if you want to send a notification to a particular device, you have to store its identifier somewhere so you are able to route a message to it. All of these responsibilities can be moved to a notification service, so this whole overhead can be taken from the backend.

Push notification architecture

Creating a whole system that relies on push notification is not a trivial task. Besides ensuring that you are not focusing on handling each PNS logic individually and providing reliable device registration and routing systems, you have to introduce a pipeline for passing messages from one part of your system to the end device. In this section, we will focus on incorporating Notification Hub into a few reference architectures, which will help you understand its role and the connections between different cloud services.

Direct connection

The simplest architecture we could think of would be a direct connection between a backend and notification service:

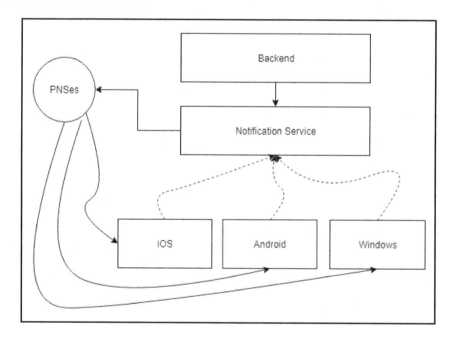

In such a scenario, each send notification request is handled by **Notification Service**, which communicate with different **PNSes**. Each PNS individually handles a request and sends a notification to a registered device. Device registration is handled by **Notification Service**—each device has to register in it to be able to receive a notification. Note that, even in that simple scenario, **Notification Service** (in our case—Notification Hub) takes responsibility for two important things:

- Providing a common interface for different PNSes
- Handling device registration and routing

Devices never communicate directly with the PNS itself—they only receive push notifications as a result of sending a request to **Notification Service**.

Queued communication

Sometimes exposing **Notification Service** to the backend is not the way to go—it could become unresponsive, have some performance issues, or just be overloaded. In such a situation, it is always good to have something that can cache messages and store them until all issues are resolved. Let's modify the previous architecture with one more service:

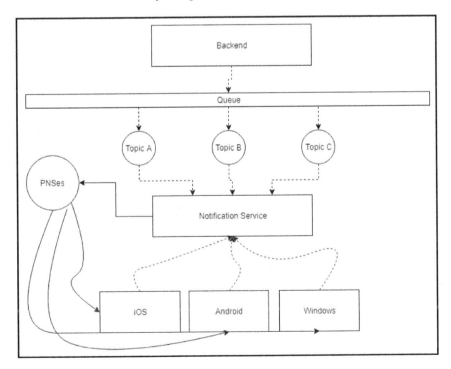

By introducing a **Queue** with readers, you can absolve the backend from handling communication with **Notification Service** and move the responsibility for delivering a message to them. Now **Backend** does not have to know how to handle undelivered messages and will not be aware of a storage for storing them. This solution can be also scaled much more easily than the previous one, as you do not have to worry about losing a message—a queue should be able to cache them as long as needed.

 Make sure that your caching mechanism makes sense in the business domain you are working with. Caching a notification request for a day, for example, and sending a notification after that time may not make any sense in scenarios such as geolocalization, a specific time, or a short-lived discount.

Triggered communication

Sometimes, you might like to send a notification based on some specific set of parameters or raising an event. Let's assume you would like to send it whenever a photo is uploaded to storage:

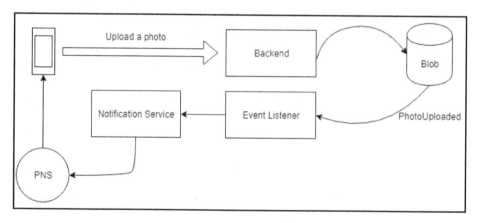

In this asynchronous scenario, you have an **Event Listener**, which listens to an event publication and performs an action based on the passed metadata. It sends a request to a **Notification Service**, which communicates with **PNS** to send a notification with the appropriate content (probable information regarding an upload status). Once more, we see the advantages of having a service acting as a proxy to PNSes—the whole communication can be made asynchronous and each component has its own responsibility.

Registering devices in Notification Hub

To be able to actually send a notification, you have to register a device in the PNS. Without using a service such as Notification Hub, you would have to know the individual logic of each PNS and storage device data somewhere. Such a challenge would be problematic in most cases, as usually you do not want to handle external dependencies by yourself; rather, your aim is to simplify the overall system logic. In this section, you will learn how device registration is handled in Notification Hub and how to monitor it.

Notification Hub device registration

When you register a device in Notification Hub, you are actually associating it with a template of a notification and tag. To create such a link, you need a PNS handle, which can be understood as an identifier of a specific vendor (such as a token or GCM registration ID). In fact, there are two ways to register a device:

- **Use registration**: Where you pass an identifier, tag, and template
- **Use installation**: An enhanced registration with an additional set of push-related properties

 Please note that, currently, if you want to use installation, there is no possibility to use a .NET SDK—you are limited to using the REST API of a service.

We have to also describe what tags and templates are to fully understand the process:

- **Tag**: This is a way to route a notification to a particular set of (or all) registered devices. It allows you to segment users, so you can easily decide who is an addressee of a message; you can use, for example, `version_Beta` to send a notification to a limited group of devices using a preview version of your application.
- **Template**: This is a particular schema of data designed to be sent to a client application. It differs depending on the PNS used and varies from JSON data to XML documents. By using Notification Hub, you can create a platform-agnostic template, which can be reused between different platforms.

Now we will try registering a device using both methods and understand the differences between them.

Creating a Notification Hub

Before we start sending notifications, we have to have a notification service provisioned and working. To create a Notification Hub instance, go to the portal and click on the **+ Create a resource** button. Search for **Notification Hub** and click **Create**. Here, you can see a completed configuration:

As you can see, there is nothing unexpected on that screen—the only things that need clarification are **Pricing tier** and **Namespace**:

- **Namespace**: You can have multiple Notification Hubs inside the same namespace. A namespace is a logical container for your hubs and holds the limit of available pushes for them.
- **Pricing tier**: Depending on the selected tier (**Free**, **Basic**, or **Standard**) you will have different features available and a different number of available pushes for your hubs. Additionally, it defines the price of extra pushes and the number of active devices. What is more, the **Standard** tier comes with handy enterprise features such as multi-tenancy or scheduled push.

For the purpose of this exercise, the **Free** tier will be more than enough. Once you are satisfied with your configuration, click on the **Create** button and wait a second for service creation. When it is created, you can go to its page where you will see an **Overview** blade:

There, you can click on the hub you created to see its features. We will cover them later in this chapter.

Registering in an application

In this section, we will try to perform a registration using a UWP application in Visual Studio. To get started, open the `HandsOnAzureApp` project from the source code for this chapter—you should see a blank UWP application with boilerplate code in it.

We will use a UWP application here because it is the easiest way to get started and work with Notification Hub. However, if you are a mobile developer, you can use any kind of project you want.

To get started with registration, you will have to install a package to work with Notification Hub—use the NuGet package manager and search for the `WindowsAzure.Messaging.Managed` package, which holds all of the components required for this particular exercise. In the `App.xaml.cs` file, you will have to add the following code:

```
private async void RegisterADevice()
{
    var channel = await
PushNotificationChannelManager.CreatePushNotificationChannelForApplicationA
sync();
    var hub = new NotificationHub("<hub-name>", "<connection-string>");
    var result = await hub.RegisterNativeAsync(channel.Uri);

    if (result.RegistrationId == null) return;

    var dialog = new MessageDialog("Registration successful: " +
result.RegistrationId);
    dialog.Commands.Add(new UICommand("OK"));
    await dialog.ShowAsync();
}
```

What we are doing here can be described as follows:

1. We are creating a notification channel to be used for a registration
2. We are defining a hub, which we will use to handle notifications and registrations
3. We are registering a device and displaying a dialog if an operation was successful

You may wonder how to obtain the connection string used for the communication; to get it, go to Azure Portal, select your Notification Hub namespace and click on the **Access Policies** blade—there you will see a policy named `RootManageSharedAccessKey`, from which you can copy a connection string.

I am using a root policy only for the purpose of this exercise. In a production environment, it is always good to create an individual policy for each application and select only those permissions that are required for it.

When you enter your hub name and paste a connection string, call
the `RegisterADevice()` method in `OnLaunched()`. Now, you can try to start an
application. If everything is successful, you should see a screen similar to mine:

Congratulations—you have just registered your very first device in Notification Hub!

Checking available registrations

Once you register a device, you need to make sure it is really available in Notification Hub.
The easiest way to do so is to check device registrations in a service itself using **Server
Explorer**, which can be accessed either by clicking on it in the **View** menu (**View | Server
Explorer**) or by using the *Ctrl + W + L* key combination:

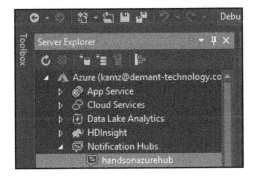

Now, when you double-click on an Notification Hub instance you would like to check, you
will see a new screen that contains two tabs—**Test Send** (which we will cover later)
and **Device Registrations**.

By clicking on the latter, you will able to verify all available registrations:

Using installations

Installations is a newer feature, which allows you to handle each device registration using a bit different syntax and tools. It has a few important advantages over registrations:

- While it is possible to duplicate registrations (by registering the same device twice), installations are idempotent. That means that sending the same installation multiple times will not result in the creation of more than one registration record.
- By using `HTTP PATCH`, you are able to update a specific parameter in an installation.
- It is easier to perform individual pushes, since each installation is automatically tagged using an installation identifier. In registrations, you would have to create such a tag by yourself and maintain it somehow to get the same functionality.

As I said in a previous part of this book, it is not currently possible to use installations with the .NET SDK on the client side—to check this functionality, we will have to use the Notification Hub RESTful API or use SDK for the backend. Here, you can find an example request for calling an API method:

```
PUT /<hub>/installations/12234?api-version=2015-01 HTTP/1.1
Host: <namespace>.servicebus.windows.net
Authorization: <authorization token>
Content-Type: application/json
Cache-Control: no-cache

{
    "installationId": "12234",
    "platform": "wns",
    "pushChannel": "<push channel>",
    "templates": {
        "myTemplate" : {
            "body" : '<toast><visual lang="en-US"><binding
template="ToastTest01"><text
id="1">$myTextProp1</text></binding></visual></tile>',
            "headers": { "X-WNS-Type": "wns/toast" },
            "tags": ["foo", "bar"]
            }
        }
}
```

 To generate an authorization token you will need to generate an SAS token. You can find a guide on how to generate it here `https://msdn.microsoft.com/library/azure/dn495627.aspx`.

Sending a notification

The main functionality of Notification Hub is to send a notification to a set of registered devices. You will see that, using its SDK and portal, you can easily start using that feature without knowing the internal logic of different PNSes. After this section, you should be able to use Notification Hub without problems and incorporate it into your applications.

Sending a test notification

While developing your application, you always need a way to test it. When using Notification Hub, you have two options when it comes to sending a test notification—either use the portal or its SDK. Both possibilities allow for similar results; however, using the SDK is a bit more flexible as it is easier to find all of the devices to which you would like to send a notification or add any kind of logic.

Test notification in Azure Portal

When you go to the hub you created, you will see that, at the top of the page, there is a **Test Send** button:

When you click on it, you will see a screen for the **Test Send** functionality. There are a few fields available and they all depend on the platform selected. In the following, you can find a sample request for the Windows platform:

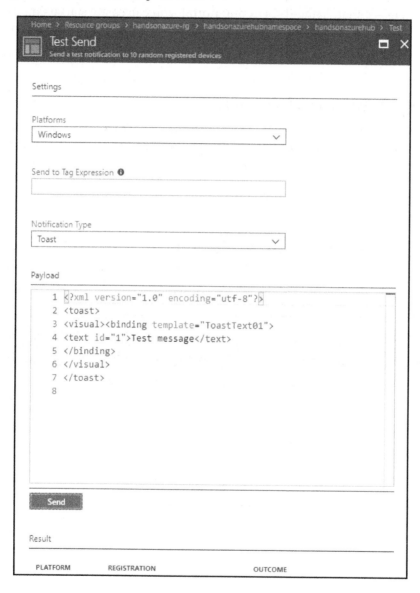

Now, if you click the **Send** button, Notification Hub will select ten different registered devices, which will receive a notification. If you want, you can change both the type and the payload sent. What is more, you can send a message to a specific set of devices by specifying the **Send to Tag Expression** option.

Test notification in the SDK

It is also possible to send a test notification using the Notification Hub SDK. To use it, you will need to install the following package: `Microsoft.Azure.NotificationHubs`. Consider the following example:

```
var hub = NotificationHubClient.CreateClientFromConnectionString(
            "<connection string>",
            "<hub>", true);
```

The last parameter enables sending a test notification. That means that, each time you send a notification using the SDK, it will be sent to a maximum of ten registered devices. Additionally, you will get the outcome of each operation (whether it succeeded or failed).

> Remember that, when test mode is enabled, each request to Notification Hub is throttled. That means that you will not be able to overload your communication channel as send operations will be queued and executed in a controlled manner.

You can check whether test send is enabled by checking a property on the `NotificationHubClient` object:

```
var hub = NotificationHubClient.CreateClientFromConnectionString(
            "<connection string>",
            "<hub>", true);
if (hub.EnableTestSend)
{
    // Do something....
}
```

Using the SDK to send a notification

The Notification Hub SDK brings many different methods for sending notifications, depending on the configuration and expected output. Here you can find all the methods available in the SDK:

```
hub.SendAdmNativeNotificationAsync();
hub.SendAppleNativeNotificationAsync();
```

```
hub.SendBaiduNativeNotificationAsync();
hub.SendDirectNotificationAsync();
hub.SendNotificationAsync();
hub.SendTemplateNotificationAsync();
hub.SendGcmNativeNotificationAsync();
hub.SendWindowsNativeNotificationAsync();
```

As you can see, we have two different categories:

- **Native notifications**: Methods for sending a notification to a specific platform only
- **Generic notifications**: A set of methods for sending a notification to a specific tag

I strongly encourage you to experiment and test different possibilities as each method is a bit different. Here you can find the result of calling `SendAppleNativeNotificationAsync()` and serializing the output:

```
var hub = NotificationHubClient.CreateClientFromConnectionString(
            "<connection string>",
            "<hub>", true);
hub.SendAppleNativeNotificationAsync("{\"aps\":{\"alert\":\"Notification
Hub test notification\"}}");
```

The result will be as follows in my case:

```
{
  "Result": {
    "Success": 8,
    "Failure": 0,
    "Results": [{
      "ApplicationPlatform": "apple",
      "PnsHandle": "<pns handle>",
      "RegistrationId": "1013412858828458675-3388525925469165319-3",
      "Outcome": "The Notification was successfully sent to the Push
Notification System"
    }, {
      "ApplicationPlatform": "apple",
      "PnsHandle": "<pns handle>",
      "RegistrationId": "4629243313258036270-2338090353657828558-2",
      "Outcome": "The Notification was successfully sent to the Push
Notification System"
    }, {
      "ApplicationPlatform": "apple",
      "PnsHandle": "<pns handle>",
      "RegistrationId": "5538320565569680693-6905916546981709583-3",
      "Outcome": "The Notification was successfully sent to the Push
Notification System"
```

```
    }, {
      "ApplicationPlatform": "apple",
      "PnsHandle": "<pns handle>",
      "RegistrationId": "5711668963446635284-8967913844749790004-1",
      "Outcome": "The Notification was successfully sent to the Push
Notification System"
    }, {
      "ApplicationPlatform": "apple",
      "PnsHandle": "<pns handle>",
      "RegistrationId": "5728263539515349341-3583197654290557965-2",
      "Outcome": "The Notification was successfully sent to the Push
Notification System"
    }, {
      "ApplicationPlatform": "apple",
      "PnsHandle": "<pns handle>",
      "RegistrationId": "6986970356553456728-8953287549645821249-1",
      "Outcome": "The Notification was successfully sent to the Push
Notification System"
    }, {
      "ApplicationPlatform": "apple",
      "PnsHandle": "<pns handle>",
      "RegistrationId": "7231787013272625417-8398074035919763615-3",
      "Outcome": "The Notification was successfully sent to the Push
Notification System"
    }, {
      "ApplicationPlatform": "apple",
      "PnsHandle": "<pns handle>",
      "RegistrationId": "8026985566358875763-8860727728212773916-1",
      "Outcome": "The Notification was successfully sent to the Push
Notification System"
    }]
  },
  "Id": 9,
  "Exception": null,
  "Status": 5,
  "IsCanceled": false,
  "IsCompleted": true,
  "CreationOptions": 0,
  "AsyncState": null,
  "IsFaulted": false
}
```

As you can see, we get the complete result of sending a notification to a set of registered devices. You can leverage that output to work with your application and, for instance, display the appropriate status or report.

Rich content notifications

In the last section of this chapter, we will talk a bit about another type of notification, which is called **rich content notification**. Sometimes you would like to send something more than plain text. In Notification Hub, it is possible to send, for example, an image to enhance the look and feel of an application.

 Please note that receiving rich content notifications requires making changes on the client side. We will not cover that in this chapter but, at the end of it, you will find a link where such an operation is described in detail.

Creating and sending a rich content notification

To create and send a rich content notification, you will need two things:

- A model of a notification
- The notification payload and content

The idea is to send it in a way that will enable a client application to fetch rich content and handle it on its side. In fact, the simplest way to do so would be to have an API that provides two operations:

- Send a notification
- Fetch notification data

In the following, you can find example code for both actions:

```
public class HubController : ApiController
{
  public static Lazy<NotificationHubClient> Hub = new
Lazy<NotificationHubClient>(() =>
    NotificationHubClient.CreateClientFromConnectionString("<connection
string>", "<hub>"));

  [HttpPost]
  public async Task<HttpResponseMessage> Send()
  {
    var notification = new Notification("Hey, check this out!");
    var fullNotification = "{\"aps\": {\"content-available\": 1,
\"sound\":\"\"}, \"richId\": \"" + notification.Id +
          "\", \"richMessage\": \"" + notification.Message + "\",
\"richType\": \"" +
          notification.RichType + "\"}";
```

```
    await Hub.Value.SendAppleNativeNotificationAsync(fullNotification,
"<tag>");
    return Request.CreateResponse(HttpStatusCode.OK);
  }

  public HttpResponseMessage Get(string id)
  {
    var image = Notification.ReadImage(id);
    var result = new HttpResponseMessage(HttpStatusCode.OK) {Content = new
StreamContent(image)};
    result.Content.Headers.ContentType = new
System.Net.Http.Headers.MediaTypeHeaderValue("image/{png}");

    return result;
  }
}
```

As you can see, the only thing we have to do is to keep the correct schema for sending a notification to a particular PNS. In the previous example, I used APNS but, of course, it is possible for other vendors (as long as their software supports receiving images or audio through push notifications). You can find the example in the source code for this chapter.

Summary

In this chapter, you have learned what Notification Hub is and how you can use it to incorporate push notifications into your applications. We covered some reference architectures and possible scenarios, which should help you understand what the purpose of this service is and how it solves problems when sending notifications to multiple PNSes and devices.

This chapter ends the first part of this book. In the next one, we will focus on serverless components and architectures.

Questions

1. What is PNS?
2. Do multiple platforms (iOS, Android, and Windows) have different PNSes?
3. What is the difference between registration and installation?
4. Can you register the same number of devices in the **Free** and **Basic** tiers?

5. What is the easiest way to check registered devices in Notification Hub?
6. How can you send a test notification?
7. What are rich content notifications?

Further reading

- **Azure Notification Hub documentation:** `https://docs.microsoft.com/en-us/azure/notification-hubs/`
- **IOS push notifications:** `https://docs.microsoft.com/en-us/azure/notification-hubs/notification-hubs-aspnet-backend-ios-apple-push-notification-service-apns-rich`
- **Registrations in Azure Notification Hub:** `https://docs.microsoft.com/en-us/azure/notification-hubs/notification-hubs-push-notification-registration-management`

Serverless and Azure Functions

Azure Functions are the main product of serverless architecture in Azure. They allow for executing small pieces of code within fully managed runtime, so we don't have to care about performance and scalability. They are open source, open for extensions, and built on top of App Services, so they provide a similar experience to WebJobs. Microsoft pays much attention to developing new features for Azure Functions and, with great support from the community, it's one of the best tools for quickly developing both simple and serious applications.

The following topics will be covered in this chapter:

- Understanding Azure Functions
- Configuring local environment for developing Azure Functions
- Creating a function
- Azure Functions features
- Workflow in Azure Functions—Durable Functions
- Integrating functions with other services

Technical requirements

To start using Azure Functions and to perform the exercises in this chapter, you will need the following:

- Visual Studio 2017 with Azure workload installed
- Azure Functions and the WebJobs tools extension for Visual Studio

Understanding Azure Functions

Azure Functions are a part of so-called serverless components that are available in the Azure cloud. Before you start learning about this particular service, you will have to understand what serverless really means. While, initially, you may think that this concept implies no servers at all, you will quickly re-evaluate your way of thinking (as, we are still quite far away from not using any kind of machine for our applications and workloads).

Being "serverless"

You can easily find many different articles describing the term serverless—to be honest, I would like to avoid promoting a one and only correct definition, as this topic is currently so fuzzy, it is hard to find the best description. My goal, however, is to give you some hints and best practices, which will let you understand it in a way that makes the most sense to you.

Responsibilities of cloud vendors

We will start with the following screenshot:

Model	IaaS	PaaS	Serverless
Data center	√	√	√
Network security	√	√	√
Operating systems	×	√	√
Dev tools	×	√	√
Application Host	×	×	√

In the preceding screenshot, you can see the comparison of two of the most popular cloud models with serverless architecture regarding vendor responsibility. I compared them using five different fields:

- **Data center**: DC infrastructure, security, maintenance, and staff
- **Network security**: Implementing correct and secure solutions regarding the network (firewalls, pen-tests, and anti-DDoS solutions)
- **Operating systems**: Updates, maintenance, and configuration
- **Dev tools**: Developing and delivering multiple features for programmers and administrators (such as extensions to IDE, management portal, and appropriate tools for managing services)
- **Application host**: The specific runtime that hosts and runs our application (such as App Service Plan)

As you can see, the only difference (at least when using the described characteristics) is the application host. When it comes to serverless components, the only thing that you deliver to your solution is your code (or some kind of configuration, which is needed to set up a service)—the rest is delivered and handled by your cloud vendor. Of course, this is not the only way to define this idea.

Pricing model

One of the most popular features of serverless services and architectures is the possibility to pay for the number of executions and used computing power. This pricing model is the exact opposite of the most common prepaid model, where you pay a fixed price depending on a set of configured fields such as the number of used VMs or the size of a cluster. Here, you can find a table describing pricing for Azure Functions:

Meter	Price	Free grant (per month)
Execution time	€0.000014/GB/s	400.000 GB/s
Total executions	€0.169 per million executions	1 million executions

Now, you may wonder how can you understand this so that you can calculate the estimated cost of your solution. There are two things you have to understand to make your calculation correct:

- **Execution**: This is a single function execution, which lasts N seconds
- **Consumption**: This defines how many resources (CPU and memory) your function consumes within a fixed time

Now, if you compare the preceding terms with the table, you will see that they differ slightly. This is because Azure Functions, pricing does not directly define the price for consumption but, rather, uses execution time.

 You have probably noticed the free grant column in the pricing table. Remember that it applies only to the consumption model—it will not work for the prepaid one.

Now, let's assume that you have estimated the following:

- You will need 10 million executions of your function per month
- Each execution lasts ~80 ms
- You are using 145 MB of memory per execution

To calculate the whole price for using Azure Functions, you can use the following formula:

$$(Rc \times €0.000014/GB - s) + (Te \times €0.169)$$

In the previous formula, the following is applicable:

- **Rc**: Resource consumption defined as a product of memory consumed and execution time (in GB/s)
- **Te:** Total executions number (in millions)

Now, if you enter the correct values and calculate the formula, you will get the following result:

$$((\frac{256}{1024}GB \times 1Ms) \times 0.000014/GB - s) + 10 \times 0.169)$$

This will give you the following cost: 5.19 EUR. However, you may find the previous formula a bit confusing—why did I use *256* (instead of 128) as the amount of memory consumed and *1 Ms* (instead of 800 Ks) as the execution time? Well, there is one important thing to remember when using the consumption plan: the minimum execution time is 100 ms and when it comes to resources consumption, it is always **rounded up** to the nearest 128 MBs.

 In fact, when it comes to function execution, you cannot go under 100 ms and 128 MBs of used memory. This is very important when calculating possible cost optimization as, often, you should not aim at optimizing functions and rather focus on overall algorithm changes (such as batching or better serialization methods).

Azure Functions concepts

Now that you are a bit familiar with what serverless architecture is, we can start learning something else about Azure Functions. To proceed, you will need to understand the difference between the following topics:

- Function apps
- Functions
- Triggers and bindings

Function app

The logical container for multiple functions is called a function app. A function app can host one or more functions, which will share configuration, settings, and runtime version. It is possible to run functions using multiple languages using the same function app.

Here, you can see what a single function app looks like, with several individual functions hosted within it:

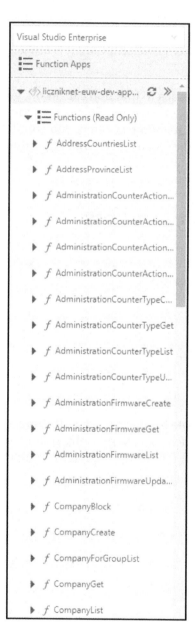

If you have the requirement to use both pricing plans (consumption and App Service), you will have to have two different functions apps, as a single one does not support such a scenario.

Functions

A single executable part of Azure Functions that hosts your code is called a **function**. Each function can execute code written in different supported languages (one can use C#, while another can leverage Python features). The currently supported languages are as follows:

- C#
- JavaScript
- F#

In the second version of runtime (v2), Java should also be available to use.

Please note that, at the time of writing this book, the v1 version is the only one that supports production workloads.

There is also the possibility of using a set of other languages (such as Powershell, PHP, or Batch), but they are in experimental mode and are not to be used in production. Here, you can find an example function with some boilerplate code:

```
[FunctionName("QueueTrigger")]
public static void Run(
  [QueueTrigger("myqueue-items")] string myQueueItem,
  TraceWriter log)
{
  log.Info($"C# function processed: {myQueueItem}");
}
```

Note that the previous code was generated using Visual Studio—the boilerplate generated in Azure Portal looks a little bit different.

As you can see, a function consists of the following components:

- **Function decorator**: `[FunctionName]`, which allows the runtime to find a function, and delivers the required metadata
- **Trigger**: `[QueueTrigger]`—each function requires a trigger to be configured correctly
- **Additional bindings**: `TraceWriter`, which will be injected during runtime
- **Function code:** The actual logic that will be executed each time the function is called

Of course, some parts of a function will differ depending on the features you use—in the previous example, we used a trigger for Azure Storage Queue, but there are also other possibilities (such as HTTP request, Azure Service Bus, or Azure CosmosDB); additionally, you can use other bindings and provide custom code each time. We will cover all of these topics in the following sections of this chapter.

Triggers and bindings

The power of Azure Functions comes when you consider all possible integrations, which can be used seamlessly and without much additional effort. In fact, the list of available triggers and bindings are quite impressive:

- Azure Storage
- Azure CosmosDB
- Azure Event Grid
- Azure Event Hub
- HTTP
- Microsoft Graph
- Azure Mobile Apps
- Azure Notification Hub
- Azure Service Bus
- Timer
- Twilio
- SendGrid

Additionally, you have access to some experimental triggers and bindings, which may not be officially supported, but can be used in your application if you decide to do so (such as external files and external tables).

 Remember that some experimental triggers and bindings will never reach GA status as there are specific recommendations (such as using Azure Logic Apps), which should be followed in most cases.

Of course, it is possible to introduce custom triggers and bindings since Azure Functions provides a full SDK, which can be used to extend runtime. However, this is an advanced topic that will be not covered in this book—you will find a reference to the appropriate tutorials in the *Further reading* section. Here, you can find an example of a custom binding, which I used for authorizing a user:

```
[FunctionName("UserState")]
0 references | Kamil Mrzygłód, 2 days ago | 1 author, 1 change
public static Task<HttpResponseMessage> UserState(
    [HttpTrigger(AuthorizationLevel.Anonymous, "get", Route = "state/user")] HttpRequestMessage req,
    [Table(TableName, PartitionKey, Connection = Constants.TableStorageConnectionName)] IQueryable<Us
    [Table(UserXCompanyEntity.TableName, Connection = Constants.TableStorageConnectionName)] IQueryab
    [Table(Company.Company.TableName, Connection = Constants.TableStorageConnectionName)] IQueryable<
    [Identity] UserIdentity identity,
    TraceWriter log)
{
    if (identity.IsAuthenticated() == false) return Task.FromResult(identity.Response);

    var user = users.Take(1).ToList().First();
    var userCompanies = usersXCompanies.Where(_ => _.PartitionKey == user.RowKey).ToList();
    var userMainCompanyId = userCompanies.First(_ => _.IsMain).RowKey;
```

Pricing models

In Azure Functions, there are two pricing models available:

- **Consumption model**: This was described in the previous sections, where you pay for the number of executions of your functions and the computing power used
- **App Service Plan model**: This is where you select an App Service Plan version, which has a fixed price, no matter how many times you execute your functions

Scaling

One of the most important features of serverless components and architectures is their ability to scale out as they are loaded more and more. While in traditional PaaS services, you often have to worry about available instances or scaling configuration. Serverless allows for the seamless handling of incoming requests, even if a service is hit by an unexpectedly high traffic. In this section, we will talk about the scaling capabilities of Azure Functions, with a focus on differences between consumption and App Service models.

Scaling in the consumption model

When you use the consumption model in Azure Functions, you are not defining any available instances for your service and are unable to configure auto-scaling settings. In fact, in this model, you are completely unaware of the number of machines running your workloads (however, if you integrate your functions with Azure Application Insights, you will be able to see how many instances have been created by taking a look at the **Live Stream** blade).

In the consumption model, you have a fixed limit when it comes to the memory available for each execution of your function—this is 1.536 MBs. Whether your functions will scale or not depends on the current utilization of both memory and CPU.

The advantage of this plan is the ability to easily scale to hundreds of functions while running the same code concurrently. Of course, it all depends on the actual trigger used in a function—while, with the HTTP trigger, you have to scale out to be able to handle multiple requests at once, using the event hub trigger, for instance, will automatically increase the number of working instances for each partition used. On the other hand, you cannot always rely on the consumption plan to be sure that you will not expect delays in responses or temporary unavailability—immediate scaling out is not guaranteed by any means, so this particular pricing plan is not always the best solution when your application has to face quick peaks of traffic.

Remember that the current maximum for scaling a function app is limited to 200. Also worth noting is the fact that the runtime will allocate new instances no often than every 10 seconds.

Scaling in the App Service model

Using the App Service model has its benefits, especially when it comes to covering some cases of scaling that are not covered in the consumption plan. As mentioned in the previous section, if you have to be sure that you are able to handle the incoming load, it is often a better idea to use this particular model, as it ensures that some fixed resources will be available for your function app. Additionally, you are 100% sure that the provided hardware is provisioned for your application—this is not always the case in the consumption model since you have no guarantees when it comes to delivered machines and their characteristics. What's more, you are sure that your runtime is always running—since, in the consumption model, when a function is not used, its resources will be de-allocated, you can face quite common issues such as cold starts.

Configuring the local environment for developing Azure Functions

To get started with Azure Functions, we will need an environment that will allow us to test our functions and start developing them quickly and seamlessly. Fortunately, this particular Azure service comes with multiple tools that help us during programming and running them locally. I will describe some extra applications as well, which should help you analyze and debug possible problems and test triggers before deploying to the cloud.

Starting with Azure Functions locally

If you have installed all of the required software mentioned at the beginning of this chapter, you should be able to start developing them without any additional configuration. To get started, we will create a simple function that we will try to run to make sure that everything is set and ready.

When you open your Visual Studio instance, click on **File** | **New Project**. In the new screen, search for the **Cloud** | **Azure Functions** template:

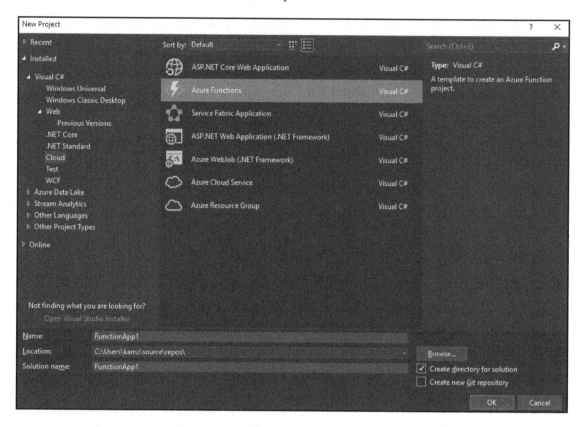

This is the first step that will ensure that everything on your side is configured correctly. When you click **OK**, you will see another screen that lets you select a few different things:

- **Runtime version**: You can choose between **v1** and **v2**. In this book, we will focus on **v1** as **v2** is still in preview.
- **Trigger type**: Depending on the SDK version you have, you will have different options available. Of course, this is not the full list of available triggers for Azure Functions.
- **Storage Account**: Most functions require a storage account to work. Fortunately, you can use **Storage Emulator** locally, which is a simple database running under the LocalDB instance that's installed on your computer.

A new version of SDK for Azure should install **Storage Emulator** automatically. If, for some reason, you are missing it, go to the following page and install the missing component: `https://docs.microsoft.com/en-us/azure/storage/common/storage-use-emulator#get-the-storage-emulator`.

For the purpose of this exercise, I chose **Http trigger** and left all of the fields with their default values:

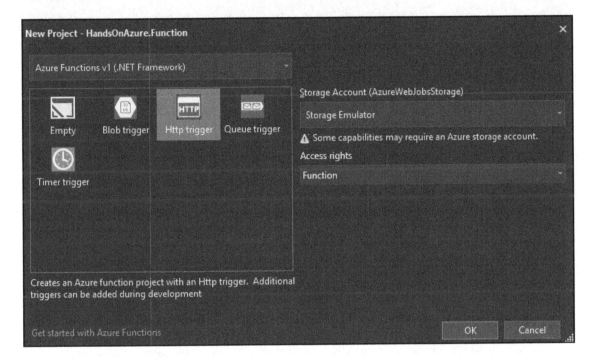

When you click **OK** and wait for a second, you will see that a new function file has been created with some boilerplate code already inserted. Since I will explain both creating a function and its features in the next section, I will not explain this in detail at this moment. To make sure that everything is working correctly, press *F5* and wait until the project is compiled. You will notice two things:

- **Storage Emulator** will be started in the background to handle function requests
- A new window with the console application will open, displaying some diagnostic messages regarding Azure Functions

The former is the actual Azure Functions runtime, which handles the whole work when you communicate with your functions. Here, you can see how it looks on my computer:

It's important to notice a few things:

- It displays under which port the runtime listens to incoming requests
- It tells you from which location the configuration file is fetched and loaded
- It notifies you about loaded custom extensions (as I said, it is possible to introduce custom bindings, which will be loaded in the runtime)
- It displays the names (and URLs, in the case of HTTP triggers) of all found functions

When you scroll down, you should be able to see an endpoint to the function you have just created:

```
Http Functions:

        Function1: http://localhost:7071/api/Function1

[21.07.2018 15:55:00] Host started (2389ms)
[21.07.2018 15:55:00] Job host started
[21.07.2018 15:55:01] Host lock lease acquired by instance ID '00000000000000000000000016B02F0D'.
Debugger listening on [::]:5858
```

Now, we will try to call it to see whether it works (I am using Postman, but you can use any kind of tool you are familiar with):

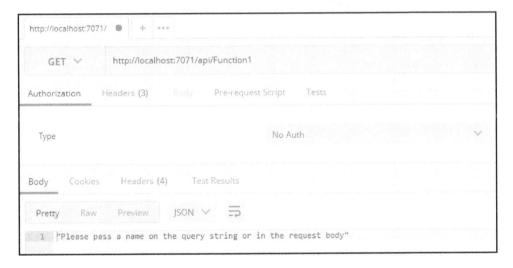

As you can see, it works—it returned a result (though the result itself is not a success—we are missing a required field, but that is not an issue right now). If you send the same request, you should be able to see the same result. If, for some reason, you are unable to do so, do the following:

- Make sure that your function's host is still working and that it displays no error
- Make sure that the port under which the runtime listens for incoming requests is open
- Make sure that the Azure Functions CLI is not blocked by your firewall
- Make sure that you are calling the correct endpoint

In the next section, I will describe the function's structure in detail so that you will be able to proceed with more advanced scenarios and features.

Creating a function

We discussed the overall serverless approach and went through local configuration to make sure that we have some basic understanding of what Azure Functions are and how we can start working with them. In the following of this chapter, I will show you what exactly this service offers and how to work with it on daily basis. This will help you start developing full projects with Functions—from the simplest to the most advanced ones.

Using Visual Studio

In the previous section, you created a function using a wizard in Visual Studio. If you go back to this particular project and open its file, you will see some common code, which is always created with this particular template. Here, you can find the same code but without the custom code introduced by it:

```
using System.Net.Http;
using System.Threading.Tasks;
using Microsoft.Azure.WebJobs;
using Microsoft.Azure.WebJobs.Extensions.Http;
using Microsoft.Azure.WebJobs.Host;

namespace HandsOnAzure.Function
{
    public static class Function1
    {
        [FunctionName("Function1")]
        public static async Task<HttpResponseMessage> Run(
            [HttpTrigger(AuthorizationLevel.Function, "get", "post", Route
= null)]
            HttpRequestMessage req, TraceWriter log)
        {
        }
    }
}
```

As you can see, I deleted the whole function body—this is the only part that is not a part of the service (remember our IaaS versus PaaS versus serverless comparison?). We can see some attributes, which decorate both a C# method and its parameters—they all are a part of the runtime that runs your functions. Let's compare it with a function that is triggered by Azure Storage Queue:

```
using Microsoft.Azure.WebJobs;
using Microsoft.Azure.WebJobs.Host;
```

```
namespace HandsOnAzure.Function
{
    public static class Function2
    {
        [FunctionName("Function2")]
        public static void Run([QueueTrigger("myqueue-items", Connection =
"connection-string")]
            string myQueueItem, TraceWriter log)
        {
        }
    }
}
```

Here, you can see that still we have the [FunctionName] attribute and some kind of trigger attribute. What differs is, in fact, the type of trigger parameter—in HTTP, we had HttpRequestMessage, while in Queue, we have a simple string parameter. This parameter (and its type) directly define the type of message delivered to a function. In general, it is pretty clear—each HTTP request is deserialized and delivered as HttpRequestMessage (as in Web API, for example), and each in-queue service and each message is a string. However, how about the following signature:

```
using System.Net.Http;
using Microsoft.Azure.WebJobs;
using Microsoft.Azure.WebJobs.Extensions.Http;
using Microsoft.Azure.WebJobs.Host;

namespace HandsOnAzure.Function
{
    public static class Function3
    {
        [FunctionName("Function3")]
        public static HttpResponseMessage Run(
            [HttpTrigger(AuthorizationLevel.Function, "get", "post", Route
= "Function3/name/{name}")]
            HttpRequestMessage req, string name, TraceWriter log)
        {
        }
    }
}
```

As you can see, the preceding example introduced one more parameter—name, which is a string, though the whole function is triggered by an HTTP request. This particular parameter will be used during the binding procedure, which will find that this function's route contains it in its URL template. This is the very same model as in traditional MVC/Web API frameworks, which provide the same feature.

The binding procedure itself is quite complicated and mostly depends on the type of used trigger. Unfortunately, it is out of the scope of this book, so I will not cover it in detail—fortunately, Azure Functions are OSS, so you can check how the host works directly in the code.

If you want to quickly add a new function to your project, perform the following steps:

1. Right-click on your project in Visual Studio and search for the **Add | New Azure Function...** menu item.
2. This will display a screen where you can enter new function name.
3. When you click **Add**, you will see another screen, which allows you to select a function type with far more options than we initially saw:

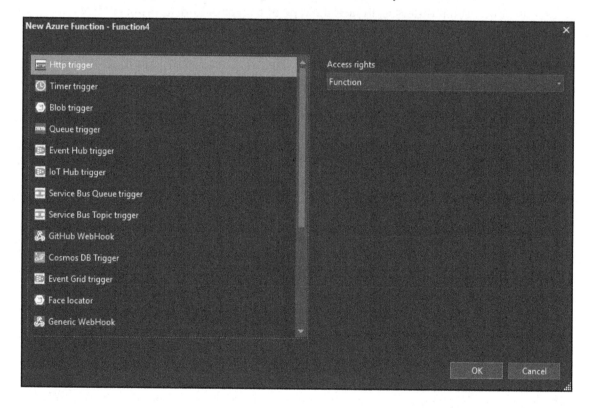

Using Azure Portal

As with all other Azure services, it is also possible to create a function app instance by creating it directly in Azure Portal:

1. When you log in, click on **+ Create a resource** and search for **Function App.**

2. When you click **Create**, you will see a screen with a couple of fields that need to be filled in before processing occurs:

As you can see, the preceding form is familiar to the one we used when creating an App Service instance. This is because, under the hood, Azure Functions is powered by this particular service and multiple available features are shared between them. As you can see, you are able to select **OS**, which defines the runtime you will be able to use.

If you are interested in using .NET Core, you can start working with Linux as your OS. This is currently in preview, but allows for using the v2 version of the runtime. It has many enhancements and uses the newest .NET stack so, in many cases, it can be quicker than v1.

In the **Hosting Plan** drop-down menu, you are able to select whether you want to use the **Consumption Plan** or **App Service** model for pricing. We discussed the differences between these in the previous part of this chapter, so you should be able to decide on which one to use by yourself. Remember that you will have to select the **B1** tier at least.

Azure Portal disallows you from using **Shared** or **Free** tiers as Azure Functions requires the **Always On** feature to be enabled—you probably remember that it is available only for **Basic** and higher tiers. While it is possible to create a function app with, for example, **Free** tier (using, for instance, ARM templates), it will not work correctly.

This wizard also gives you the possibility to enable **Application Insights** integration. Since we have not discussed this particular service yet, I will skip it in this chapter. However, if you are interested in monitoring your functions, it is a much better option than the integrated **Monitor** feature—it gives you much more detail and is much more intuitive in daily work.

Enabling **Application Insights** for your function app can drastically change the overall price of the whole service as, initially, each function produces many different traces and logs. For production, it is always a good idea to the lower logged severity of messages—you can find more information about configuration at: `https://docs.microsoft.com/en-us/azure/azure-functions/functions-monitoring`.

When you are satisfied with your settings, you can click **Create**. Azure Portal will validate all of the fields and initiate the service provisioning procedure. After several seconds, your function app should be ready for work. When you go to it, you will see the dashboard, which is the starting point for accessing all of the features of Azure Functions:

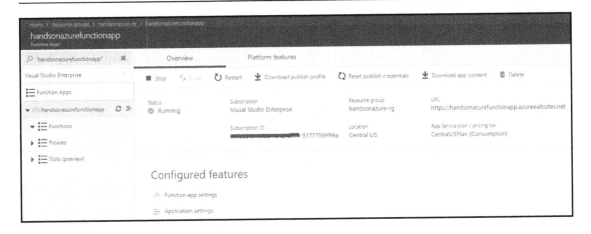

Now, if you want to create a function, move your mouse cursor over the **Functions** section and click on the plus sign (**+**). It will display a new wizard screen, where you can choose to either start with a premade function or create a custom one. For the purpose of this exercise, I decided to go with a timer function written in JavaScript:

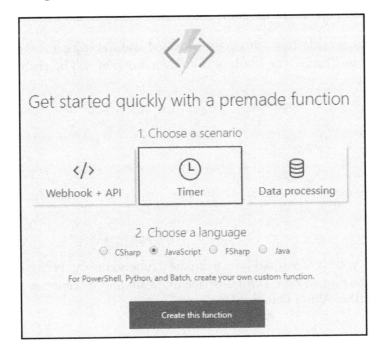

After clicking on the **Create this function** button, you will see that some function code has been generated. Azure Portal allows also you to edit a function directly in your browser window, so if you want to try out some custom code, there is nothing preventing you from doing so:

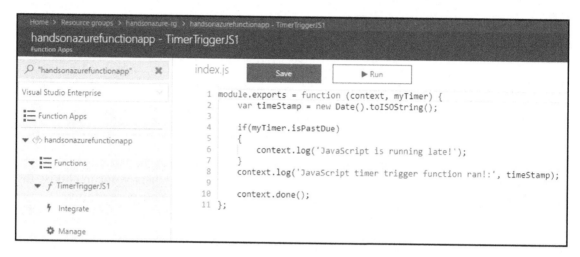

Additionally, you can click **Run**—this is the so-called **manual trigger** and enables you to start a function immediately. The result of running a function will be visible in the **Logs** window:

```
2018-07-22T09:15:36  Welcome, you are now connected to log-streaming
service.
2018-07-22T09:15:57.252 [Info] Function started (Id=63d9f8ff-
b807-4805-8b24-5f90edfc0134)
2018-07-22T09:15:57.377 [Info] JavaScript timer trigger function ran!:
2018-07-22T09:15:57.377Z
2018-07-22T09:15:57.377 [Info] Function completed (Success, Id=63d9f8ff-
b807-4805-8b24-5f90edfc0134, Duration=128ms)
2018-07-22T09:17:36  No new trace in the past 1 min(s).
2018-07-22T09:18:36  No new trace in the past 2 min(s).
```

Congratulations—you have learned how to create a function using both Visual Studio and Azure Portal. In the next section, I will describe more advanced scenarios and will focus on understanding further Azure Functions features.

Azure Functions features

Azure Functions is not only about providing executable code, which will be handled by the runtime. It allows for even more advanced scenarios, which make this service an excellent choice when you want to start developing quickly and with minimal configuration required. In this section, I will show you how to leverage more advanced features of functions and how to progress with your skill in using this Azure component.

Platform features

As you may remember, Azure Functions is built on top App Service, which allows you to use multiple already known features, such as **Custom domains**, **Application settings**, and **Authentication/Authorization**. To access all available **Platform features**, go to your function app in Azure Portal and click on the appropriate tab:

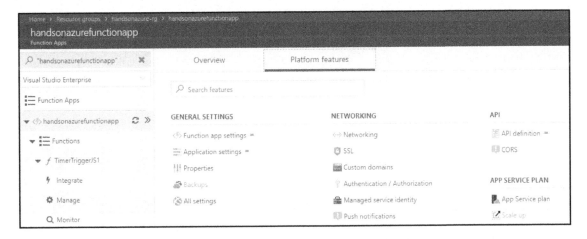

As you can see, we have a variety of different features available—what you are interested in depends solely on your specific requirements. There is, however, one function-specific feature that I would like to describe: **Function app settings**.

When you click on this link, a new tab will open, with some crucial options that can be set:

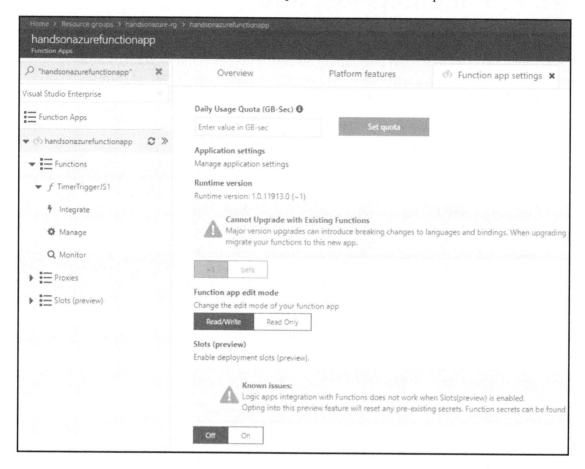

In the preceding screenshot, you can see that most of the features are either not enabled or unavailable. This depends on the state of your function app—by design, all problematic functionalities are opt-out, so they will not interfere with your functions. Anyway, I will describe them here so that you can decide whether you need them or not:

- **Daily Usage Quota (GB-Sec)**: If you want to set a hard limit for function app usage, you can set it here. Thanks to this, you can ensure that it will not exceed some predefined quota you are aiming at.
- **Runtime version**: This setting defines the current runtime version your function app uses. Note that it is not possible to change v1 to beta (v2, in this case), as it is possible that the newer version introduces some changes that would break your application.

- **Function app edit mode**: If you decide to deploy your functions with any kind of CI/CD pipeline, this setting will be automatically set to **Read Only**. This ensures that it is not possible to introduce changes while in runtime without going through the automated process.
- **Slots (preview)**: If you want to perform blue/green deployment (to perform a rapid rollback if something goes wrong), this enables you to deploy a new version as a new instance and immediately swap it with the existing one.

Security

We have not covered another important topic yet—Azure Function security. While it is possible to use, for example, Azure Active Directory or social providers as identity sources (and—as a result—add authentication to a function app), by default, functions are secured by their keys. You can check the available keys when you click on the **Manage** tab:

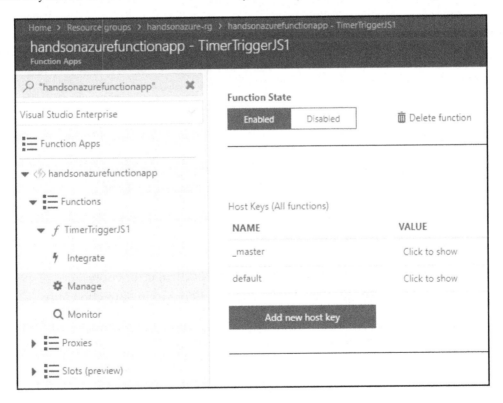

Depending on the way a function is triggered, different options may be available. Here, you can see what another function app looks like when it is triggered by an HTTP trigger instead of a timer:

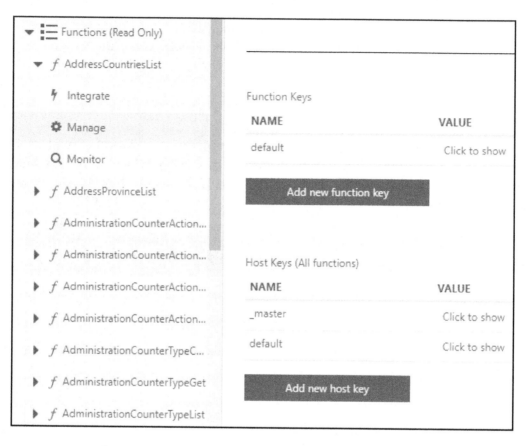

As you can see, we have two types of keys available:

- **Function Keys**: These are designed for this particular function
- **Host Keys**: These allow for calling any function within a function app

You can use keys as an easy way to implement authorization in your function app. You can generate a new one for each client, revoke them, and set a particular value.

Note that function keys are designed for functions that are triggered by HTTP requests—there is no possibility to use them for other kinds of triggers.

There are two ways of using function keys to authorize a request. You can put them in the query string:

```
https://handsonazurefunctionapp.azurewebsites.net/api/HttpTriggerJS1?code=a
wKhkdPqyQvYUwzn6zle6V4hqk460YwOBs9RyaQUthX/AWGBMjtRIA==
```

Or you can use headers and introduce the x-functions-key header, which will contain a key inside it:

```
GET /api/HttpTriggerJS1 HTTP/1.1
Host: handsonazurefunctionapp.azurewebsites.net
Content-Type: application/json
x-functions-key: awKhkdPqyQvYUwzn6zle6V4hqk460YwOBs9RyaQUthX/AWGBMjtRIA==
Cache-Control: no-cache
```

Monitor

Each call and each execution of a function is monitored and saved. When you click on the **Monitor** tab, you will see a screen that contains the next execution with some diagnostics data.

 If you do not see a list, you will probably be asked to enable the **Application Insights** integration. To access standard view, click on the **Switch to classic view** button.

Here, you can see the log of executions of my function, triggered by a timer:

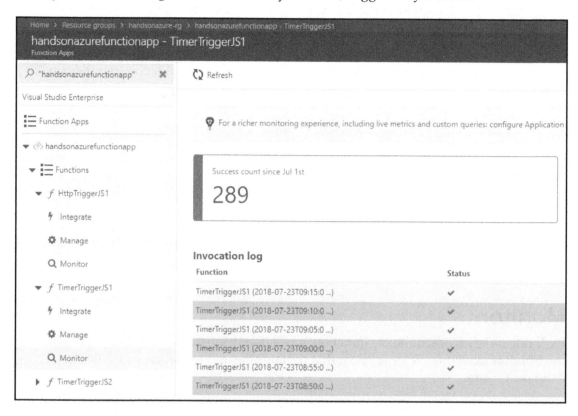

As you can see, it contains information about each particular execution, the success and error count, and invocation details. When you select a specific item, you will also see all of the logs from a function.

The **Monitor** feature is quite useful for quickly analyzing issues. For more detailed errors and logs, you will have to enable **Application Insights** and use its features.

Host.json

When you create a function, you will see that a host.json file is automatically created. While initially empty, it is a global configuration file that defines how triggers and function will behave. Here, you can find an example file with most features, such as bindings' configuration and generic features, available:

```json
{
    "aggregator": {
        "batchSize": 1000,
        "flushTimeout": "00:00:30"
    },
    "applicationInsights": {
        "sampling": {
          "isEnabled": true,
          "maxTelemetryItemsPerSecond" : 5
        }
    },
    "eventHub": {
      "maxBatchSize": 64,
      "prefetchCount": 256,
      "batchCheckpointFrequency": 1
    },
    "functions": [ "QueueProcessor", "GitHubWebHook" ],
    "functionTimeout": "00:05:00",
    "healthMonitor": {
        "enabled": true,
        "healthCheckInterval": "00:00:10",
        "healthCheckWindow": "00:02:00",
        "healthCheckThreshold": 6,
        "counterThreshold": 0.80
    },
    "http": {
        "routePrefix": "api",
        "maxOutstandingRequests": 20,
        "maxConcurrentRequests": 10,
        "dynamicThrottlesEnabled": false
    },
    "id": "9f4ea53c5136457d883d685e57164f08",
    "logger": {
        "categoryFilter": {
            "defaultLevel": "Information",
            "categoryLevels": {
                "Host": "Error",
                "Function": "Error",
                "Host.Aggregator": "Information"
            }
```

```
        }
      },
      "queues": {
        "maxPollingInterval": 2000,
        "visibilityTimeout" : "00:00:30",
        "batchSize": 16,
        "maxDequeueCount": 5,
        "newBatchThreshold": 8
      },
      "serviceBus": {
        "maxConcurrentCalls": 16,
        "prefetchCount": 100,
        "autoRenewTimeout": "00:05:00"
      },
      "singleton": {
        "lockPeriod": "00:00:15",
        "listenerLockPeriod": "00:01:00",
        "listenerLockRecoveryPollingInterval": "00:01:00",
        "lockAcquisitionTimeout": "00:01:00",
        "lockAcquisitionPollingInterval": "00:00:03"
      },
      "tracing": {
        "consoleLevel": "verbose",
        "fileLoggingMode": "debugOnly"
      },
      "watchDirectories": [ "Shared" ],
    }
```

As you can see, it contains things such as logger settings, function timeout value, and particular triggers configuration. In the *Further reading* section, you will find a link where each section of the host.json file is described in detail.

Publish

Azure Functions are published the very same way as App Service, since they share many common parts. If you right-click on your functions project in Visual Studio and select **Publish**, you will see a screen that's similar to the one we saw when working with App Services:

Traditionally, you have the possibility to select to either create a new function app or use an existing one. When you use the existing one and click on the **Publish** button, you will be able to find a function app in a specific **Resource Group**:

Now, when you click **OK**, a new publish profile will be created and the whole application will be deployed.

Workflow in Azure Functions – Durable Functions

In most cases, the best idea for working with functions is to keep them stateless. This makes things much easier as you do not have to worry about sharing resources and storing state. However, there are cases where you will like to access it and distribute between different instances of your functions. In such scenarios (such as orchestrating a workflow or scheduling a task to be done), a better option to start with would be to leverage the capabilities of Durable Functions, an extension to the main runtime, which changes the way you work a little bit.

It changes the way Azure Functions works as it lets you resume from where the execution was paused or stopped and introduces the possibility to take the output of one function and pass it as input. We will not cover this in detail, as this book is not only about Azure Functions, but you will get a glimpse of this feature, which will help you start it on your own.

To get started, you don't need any extra extensions—the only thing you will need is an additional NuGet package named `Microsoft.Azure.WebJobs.Extensions.DurableTask`.

Orchestrations and activities

The main elements of Durable Functions are orchestrations and activities. There are some significant differences between them:

- `Orchestrations`: These are designed to orchestrate different activities. They should be single-threaded and idempotent, and they can use only a very limited set of asynchronous methods. They are scaled based on the number of internal queues. What's more, they control the flow of one or more activities.
- `Activities`: These should contain most of the logic of your application. They work as typical functions (without the limits of orchestrations). They are scaled to multiple VMs.

Here, you can find the code for both types of functions:

```
[FunctionName("Orchestration")]
public static async Task Orchestration_Start([OrchestrationTrigger]
DurableOrchestrationContext context)
{
  var payload = context.GetInput<string>();
  await context.CallActivityAsync(nameof(Activity), payload);
}

[FunctionName("Activity")]
public static string Activity([ActivityTrigger] DurableActivityContext
context)
{
  var payload = context.GetInput<string>();
  return $"Current payload is {payload}!";
}
```

As you can see, they are both decorated with the [FunctionName] attribute as a typical function—the difference comes from the trigger that's used.

Orchestration client

To get started with an orchestration, you need a host for it. In Durable Functions, that host is the orchestration client, which enables you to perform the following actions on an orchestration:

- Start it
- Terminate it
- Get its status
- Raise an event and pass it to an orchestration

The basic code for a client is pretty simple:

```
[FunctionName("Orchestration_Client")]
public static async Task<string> Orchestration_Client(
   [HttpTrigger(AuthorizationLevel.Anonymous, "post", Route = "start")]
HttpRequestMessage input,
   [OrchestrationClient] DurableOrchestrationClient starter)
{
   return await starter.StartNewAsync("Orchestration", await
input.Content.ReadAsStringAsync());
}
```

As you can see from the preceding code, we started an orchestration by providing its name and passing some payload, which will be deserialized and decoded. Here, you can find an example of a client that has been hosted to terminate an instance by passing its identifier:

```
[FunctionName("Terminate")]
public static async Task Terminate(
   [HttpTrigger(AuthorizationLevel.Anonymous, "post", Route =
"terminate/{id}")] HttpRequestMessage input,
   string id,
   [OrchestrationClient] DurableOrchestrationClient client)
{
   var reason = "Manual termination";
   await client.TerminateAsync(id, reason);
}
```

Orchestration history

The way Durable Functions work ensures that, if any activity is replayed, its result will not be evaluated again (this is why orchestrations have to be idempotent). Here, you can find a diagram that shows how the framework works in detail:

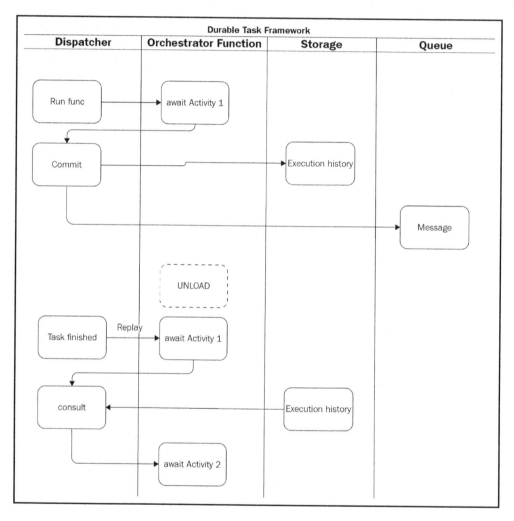

To make a long story short, I divided the process into four parts:

- **Dispatcher**: This is the internal part of the framework, which is responsible for calling orchestrations, performing replays, and saving the state
- **Orchestrator function**: This is an orchestration that calls activities

- **Storage**: This is a place where the orchestration history is stored
- **Queue**: This is an internal queue (implemented using Azure Storage Queues), which is used to control the flow of execution of an orchestration

The way Durable Functions works is as follows:

1. Dispatchers run an orchestration, which calls `Activity1` and awaits its result
2. The control is returned to a dispatcher, which commits the state in the orchestration history and pushes a message to a queue
3. In the meantime, orchestration is deallocated, saving memory and processor
4. After fetching a message from a queue and finishing a task, the dispatcher recreates an orchestration and replays all activities
5. If it finds that this particular activity has been finished, it gets only its result and proceeds to another activity

The preceding process lasts until all of the activities are processed. Information about execution history can be found in a table called `DurableFunctionsHubHistory`, which you can find inside the Azure Table Storage used by your function app.

Timers

Sometimes, you might want to schedule work after a specific delay. While using traditional functions, you have to create a custom solution that will somehow trigger a workflow at a specific time. In Durable Functions, it is as easy as writing one line of code. Consider the following example:

```
[FunctionName("Orchestration_Client")]
public static async Task<string> Orchestration_Client(
  [HttpTrigger(AuthorizationLevel.Anonymous, "post", Route = "start")]
HttpRequestMessage input,
  [OrchestrationClient] DurableOrchestrationClient starter)
{
  return await starter.StartNewAsync("Orchestration", null);
}

[FunctionName("Orchestration")]
public static async Task Orchestration_Start([OrchestrationTrigger]
DurableOrchestrationContext context, TraceWriter log)
{
  log.Info($"Scheduled at {context.CurrentUtcDateTime}");

  await context.CreateTimer(context.CurrentUtcDateTime.AddHours(1),
CancellationToken.None);
```

```
    await context.CallActivityAsync(nameof(Activity),
context.CurrentUtcDateTime);
}

[FunctionName("Activity")]
public static void Activity([ActivityTrigger] DurableActivityContext
context, TraceWriter log)
{
  var date = context.GetInput<DateTime>();
  log.Info($"Executed at {date}");
}
```

In the preceding example, I used the `context.CreateTimer()` method, which allows for creating a delay in function execution. If the previous orchestration is executed, it will return control to the dispatcher after awaiting a timer. Thanks to this, you will not be charged for this particular function execution as it will be deallocated and recreated later, after waiting for a specific interval.

External events

In Durable Functions, it is possible to wait for an external event before proceeding with a workflow. This is especially helpful if you want to create an interactive flow, where you initiate a process in one place and have a requirement to wait for someone's decision. To raise an event, you can use the following function:

```
[FunctionName("Orchestration_Raise")]
public static async Task Orchestration_Raise(
  [HttpTrigger(AuthorizationLevel.Anonymous, "post", Route =
"start_raise/{id}/{event}")] HttpRequestMessage input,
  string id,
  string @event,
  [OrchestrationClient] DurableOrchestrationClient starter)
{
  await starter.RaiseEventAsync(id, @event, await
input.Content.ReadAsStringAsync());
}
```

Here, you can find an example of waiting for an event:

```
[FunctionName("Orchestration")]
public static async Task<string> Orchestration_Start([OrchestrationTrigger]
DurableOrchestrationContext context)
{
  var @event = await context.WaitForExternalEvent<int>("Approved");
```

```
    if (@event == 1)
    {
        var result = await context.CallActivityAsync<string>(nameof(Activity),
@event);
        return result;
    }

    return "Not Approved";
}
```

The way this works can be described as follows: the first functions allows you to raise a custom event by passing the appropriate parameters. The second function is paused while waiting for the `context.WaitForExternalEvent()` function. If you send an event with the `Approved` type, a function will be resumed and will continue. Additionally, you can pass a payload of an event, which will be passed as a result of `WaitForExternalEvent()`. This method works in the same way as timers and other Durable Functions functions, which are available in `DurableOrchestrationType`—while awaiting, control is returned to the dispatcher and the function itself is deallocated.

Integrating functions with other services

In the last part of this chapter, we will focus a little bit on understanding how Azure Functions integrate with other Azure services. We will take a look at the available triggers and bindings and try to figure out the best use cases for them and how they really work. This section is designed in a way that enables you to explore more by yourself, thanks to a common understanding of how Azure Functions work.

Function file

When you take a look at your `bin` directory, where compiled functions are available, you will find a bit of a different structure than in traditional applications.

Here, you can find my folder from the exercise from this chapter:

bin	21.07.2018 17:54	File folder
Function1	21.07.2018 17:54	File folder
host	21.07.2018 17:53	JSON File
local.settings	21.07.2018 17:53	JSON File

As you can see, it contains the `Function1` directory, which contains one file named `function.json`. Here, you can find its content:

```
{
  "generatedBy": "Microsoft.NET.Sdk.Functions-1.0.14",
  "configurationSource": "attributes",
  "bindings": [
    {
      "type": "httpTrigger",
      "methods": [
        "get",
        "post"
      ],
      "authLevel": "function",
      "name": "req"
    }
  ],
  "disabled": false,
  "scriptFile": "../bin/HandsOnAzure.Function.dll",
  "entryPoint": "HandsOnAzure.Function.Function1.Run"
}
```

It defines some metadata, which is further used by the function's runtime and the `bindings` field, which is a definition of used triggers. If you compare it with a code attribute, you will see that it is quite similar:

```
[FunctionName("Function1")]
public static async Task<HttpResponseMessage> Run(
    [HttpTrigger(AuthorizationLevel.Function, "get", "post", Route = null)]
    HttpRequestMessage req, TraceWriter log)
{
}
```

When you compile your project, a compiler will produce a `function.json` file for each function defined in your code. Here, you can find the output for the event hub trigger:

```json
{
    "generatedBy": "Microsoft.NET.Sdk.Functions-1.0.0.0",
    "configurationSource": "attributes",
    "bindings": [
      {
        "type": "eventHubTrigger",
        "path": "myhub",
        "connection": "EhConnection",
        "name": "myEventHubMessage"
      }
    ],
    "disabled": false,
    "scriptFile": "..\\bin\\FunctionsTest.dll",
    "entryPoint": "FunctionsTest.Hub.Run"
}
```

As you can see, it has the same structure and only the `bindings` field differs, so it reflects another trigger type.

> Note that the content and structure of `function.json` may differ depending on the SDK version used. Do not use it in your application directly to avoid problems that have a lack of backward compatibility.

Input/output bindings

Some bindings are bi-directional, while some can be used only one way. What's more, not every binding can be used as a trigger. An example of both bi-directional and trigger binding is Azure Blob Storage. Here, you can find an example of how it works as a trigger:

```csharp
[FunctionName("BlobTriggerCSharp")]
public static void Run([BlobTrigger("my-blobs/{name}")] Stream myBlob,
string name, TraceWriter log)
{
}
```

Compare it with an example of a function triggered by a queue, but accepting blob as input:

```
[FunctionName("BlobInput")]
public static void BlobInput(
   [QueueTrigger("myqueue-items")] string myQueueItem,
   [Blob("samples-workitems/{queueTrigger}", FileAccess.Read)] Stream
myBlob,
   TraceWriter log)
{
}
```

As you can see, I used the same syntax in both cases besides one thing—I declared FileAccess.Read to tell the runtime that this is not a trigger. Here is another example of output:

```
[FunctionName("ResizeImage")]
public static void ResizeImage_Run(
   [BlobTrigger("sample-images/{name}")] Stream image,
   [Blob("sample-images-sm/{name}", FileAccess.Write)] Stream imageSmall,
   [Blob("sample-images-md/{name}", FileAccess.Write)] Stream imageMedium)
{
   // There goes your code...
}
```

As you can see, the syntax is still similar—the only thing that has changed is the FileAccess value. There are also other possibilities for using the return value of a function. Here, you can find out how to define the result by using an attribute:

```
[FunctionName("QueueTrigger")]
[return: Blob("output-container/{id}")]
public static string QueueTrigger_Run([QueueTrigger("myqueue")] string
input, TraceWriter log)
{
   return "Some string...";
}
```

Custom bindings

While Azure Functions offer a variety of different bindings for many different scenarios, sometimes, you want a custom functionality that is not available. In such cases, it is possible to create a custom binding, which I mentioned earlier in this chapter. To generate it, you need the following things:

- An attribute decorated with the [Binding] attribute
- An implementation of the IBindingProvider interface

- An implementation of the `IBinding` interface
- An implementation of the `IExtensionConfigProvider` interface

By providing all of the preceding implementations, your binding will be automatically fetched by the runtime and enabled. If everything is set correctly, you will be notified of this during runtime start:

```
[24.07.2018 08:31:08] Loaded custom extension 'BotFrameworkConfiguration'
[24.07.2018 08:31:08] Loaded custom extension 'SendGridConfiguration'
[24.07.2018 08:31:08] Loaded custom extension 'EventGridExtensionConfig'
[24.07.2018 08:31:08] Loaded binding extension 'IdentityExtensionConfigProvider' from 'referenced by: Method='LicznikNET
.API.Modules.User.User.UserState', Parameter='identity'.'
[24.07.2018 08:31:08] Loaded binding extension 'DurableTaskExtension' from 'referenced by: Method='LicznikNET.API.Module
s.Location.Location.LocationUpdate_Activity', Parameter='ctx'.'
[24.07.2018 08:31:09] registered EventGrid Endpoint = http://localhost:7071/admin/extensions/EventGridExtensionConfig
[24.07.2018 08:31:09] Generating 48 job function(s)
[24.07.2018 08:31:09] Host lock lease acquired by instance ID '00000000000000000000000016B02F0D'.
```

In the preceding screenshot, you can see that the runtime extracted `IdentityExtensionConfig Provider` from my code, which will be used later when resolving my custom binding.

Summary

In this chapter, you have learned a lot about Azure Functions and how to work with this serverless component. You read about the differences in pricing models, scalability concerns, and basic triggers and bindings. We worked on some simple scenarios regarding monitoring, deploying, and developing this Azure service.

In the following chapters in this book, you will learn even more about serverless services. We will then come back to work even more with functions, as this is one of the most popular Azure components that can be easily integrated with other tools and products.

Questions

1. What is the difference between App Service and the consumption pricing model?
2. What is GB/s?
3. Can you create stateful services with Azure Functions?
4. What is the name of a container that's used for functions?
5. Can you use Python in Azure Functions?

6. Can a binding act both as a trigger and output? Can you provide an example?
7. Why is a function app mode sometimes set as read-only?
8. Can you use the **Application Settings** feature in the same way as in App Services?

Further reading

- Azure Functions overview: https://docs.microsoft.com/en-us/azure/azure-functions/functions-overview
- host.json description: https://docs.microsoft.com/en-us/azure/azure-functions/functions-host-json
- The schema of the functions.json file: http://json.schemastore.org/function
- Triggers and bindings for Azure Functions: https://docs.microsoft.com/en-us/azure/azure-functions/functions-triggers-bindings
- Durable Functions: https://docs.microsoft.com/en-us/azure/azure-functions/durable-functions-overview

8
Integrating Different Components with Logic Apps

Logic Apps are one main enterprise-level integration services and let us automate processes as workflows across the organization. They allow for the simple connection of different services and applications with multiple connectors. Further, by leveraging a serverless model, they reduce costs and shorten the time needed for developing a working solution.

The following topics will be covered in this chapter:

- What Azure Logic Apps is and how it works
- Connectors for Logic Apps
- Creating a Logic App and integrating it with other services
- B2B integration and how works

Technical requirements

To perform exercises from this chapter, you will need the following:

- Visual Studio 2017
- Azure SDK 2.9.1 or later
- Azure Logic Apps for Visual Studio: `https://marketplace.visualstudio.com/items?itemName=VinaySinghMSFT.AzureLogicAppsToolsforVisualStudio-18551#overview`

What is Azure Logic Apps?

Sometimes you need to integrate multiple services and automate tasks such as sending an email, creating a file, or generating a report based on some input data (maybe a database table or a social media feed). If you work with a specific cloud vendor (in this particular case, Microsoft Azure), it could be crucial to be able to rapidly develop workflows that can be versioned and are natively integrated with multiple cloud services, using a tool that does not require learning many different concepts to get started. Such a service is Azure Logic Apps, which you will learn about in this chapter.

Azure Logic Apps – how it works

In the previous chapter, you learned about Azure Functions, which required a trigger to be executed. The situation is similar with Azure Logic Apps—you need to define specific criteria that tell the runtime when a Logic App instance should be executed. During the execution, even more actions are performed:

- Input data is converted so it meets initial requirements
- All conditional flows are executed so one specific execution flow is evaluated
- Temporary variables are assigned values

The following shows an example of a flow that is executed each day and sets a variable that is used to remove outdated blobs:

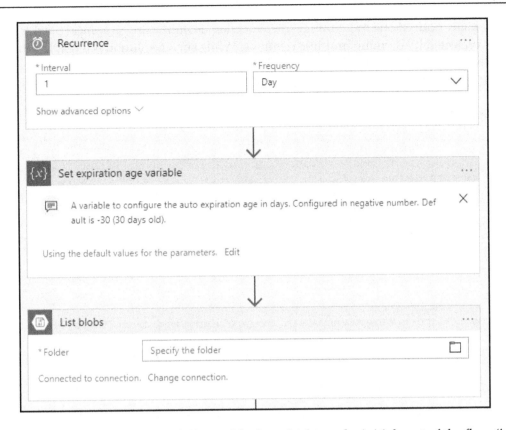

As you can see, it contains three different blocks, which are the initial part of the flow (in fact, the whole workflow is much bigger as it contains a loop and different conditions and actions—we will cover all of these later):

- The first one defines how often an instance of a Logic App should be executed
- The second one defines a variable, which is used by the next steps—it specifies the maximum age of a file in Azure Blob Storage
- The third one feeds the next step (a for each loop) with a list of available blobs within a specific storage account and container

You probably noticed one more thing—the workflow is built using graphical blocks, which can be connected by defining multiple relations. While such a solution is a real handful when creating and modifying Logic Apps, it could be problematic when versioning and developing within a team. Fortunately, each flow is also defined in JSON:

```json
{
    "$connections": {
        "value": {
            "azureblob": {
                "connectionId": "/subscriptions/<subscription-
id>/resourceGroups/handsonazure-
rg/providers/Microsoft.Web/connections/azureblob",
                "connectionName": "azureblob",
                "id": "/subscriptions/<subscription-
id>/providers/Microsoft.Web/locations/westeurope/managedApis/azureblob"
            }
        }
    },
    "definition": {
        "$schema":
"https://schema.management.azure.com/providers/Microsoft.Logic/schemas/2016
-06-01/workflowdefinition.json#",
        "actions": {
            "For_each": {
                "actions": {
                    "Condition": {
                        "actions": {
                            "Delete_blob": {
    (...)
                        }
                    }
                }
            }
        }
    }
}
```

Thanks to such a representation, you can add your Logic Apps to any version control systems (for example, Git or SVN) and modify them when you wish. Additionally, you can automate the creation of different Logic Apps by generating code files on-the-fly.

Azure Logic Apps – advantages

You may wonder what the real use case for Azure Logic Apps is when you have other possibilities available (Azure Functions and custom workflows). If you take a closer look at its features, you will notice the following:

- You do not have to be a cloud developer to develop workflows—even less advanced users (for example, IT professionals, IT admins, and data scientists) can create the one they need without learning much about this particular service
- You do not worry about scaling—as Azure Logic Apps are also a part of serverless services available in Azure, you focus on delivering business value rather than server configuration and capabilities
- In general, you do not have to write code—however, you are not limited to a "codeless" environment as it is possible to host it within Azure Functions and just execute it on demand
- You are able to implement B2B integration, which leverages enterprise standards relating to exchanging messages and communication, such as AS2 or EDIFACT

The following shows the current pricing for Azure Logic Apps:

- Each action costs $0.000025 per execution
- Each connector costs $0.000125 per execution

To fully understand it, we have to describe those two terms:

- **Action**: This is each step executed after a trigger (for example, listing files, calling an API, or setting a variable)
- **Connector**: This is a binding to multiple external services (Azure Service Bus, SFTP, or Twitter), which you will use in your workflows

Note that Azure Logic Apps could be quite expensive when performing complicated workflows very often. In such scenarios, consider using other services (such as Azure Functions), which of course require much more time spent on developing but, on the other hand, offer better pricing.

Connectors for Logic Apps

The main concept of Azure Logic Apps is connectors. Connectors are both actions and triggers that you can use in your workflows to fetch data, transform it, and extend the current capabilities of your applications. Currently, Azure Logic Apps have 200 different connectors available, which allow you to integrate with multiple Azure services (such as Azure API Management or Azure Functions), other systems (OneDrive and Salesforce), and even on-premises systems.

Connector types

In Azure Logic Apps, connectors are divided into two categories:

- **Built-in connectors**: These are designed to work with Azure services and create workflows and are organized around handling application logic and working with data
- **Managed connectors**: These connectors ease integration with other systems and services

Managed connectors are divided into even more detailed groups:

- Managed API connectors
- On-premises connectors
- Integration account connectors
- Enterprise connectors

In this section, we will go through multiple examples of different types of connector so you will be able to understand their use cases and functionality.

Built-in connectors

The following shows examples of built-in connectors that you can use in your Azure Logic Apps:

- **Schedule**: For running Logic Apps on a specific schedule or pausing their executions
- **HTTP**: For communicating with endpoints over the HTTP protocol
- **Request**: For making a Logic App callable from other services or sending responses
- **Batch**: For processing messages in batches

- **Azure Functions**: For running custom code snippets
- **Azure API Management**: For integrating triggers and actions defined by other services
- **Azure App Services**: For calling API apps and web apps
- **Azure Logic Apps**: For calling other Logic Apps

As you can see, we have here more generic connectors (schedule, HTTP, and request) and those specific to a service (such as Azure Functions or Azure App Services). In general, these connectors are the foundation of most Azure Logic Apps—when it comes to creating workflows, we very often require to call an API or perform various other HTTP requests.

Note that each connector has detailed documentation available describing its use cases and how you can develop workflows with it. You can find a link to it in the *Further reading* section in this chapter.

Managed API connectors

When using managed API connectors, you will be able to integrate with services and systems that require configuring a connection; these can be used when executing an instance of a Logic App. The following shows an example of a Logic App in a resource group with an additional resource defined as the API connection:

In the documentation, plenty of different API connectors are described—let's review some examples:

- Azure Service Bus
- SQL Server
- Office 365 Outlook
- Azure Blob Storage
- SFTP
- SharePoint Online

As you can see, with these connectors we have access to a variety of different Azure services and other systems (here, Office 365 and SharePoint), which can be leveraged in your workflows to extend your application's logic.

On-premises connectors

As I described previously, with Azure Logic Apps you are able to also integrate with on-premises services such as different database systems (Oracle, MySQL, and SQL Server), business analytics systems (Teradata), or file systems.

 To access on-premises data, you will have to create a resource called an on-premises data gateway. Instructions about how to do so can be found here: https://docs.microsoft.com/en-us/azure/logic-apps/logic-apps-gateway-connection.

Integration account connectors and enterprise connectors

Azure Logic Apps also lets you build so-called B2B solutions using integration accounts and leveraging a variety of advanced connectors such as XML Transforms and X12 encoding/decoding or even accessing enterprise systems such as the SAP. While, for most users, these capabilities are not that useful (as these are rather advanced topics that most people are not familiar with), being able to build Logic Apps that allow for seamless communication between partners is an interesting functionality. We will cover more about B2B integration within Azure Logic Apps at the end of this chapter.

Creating Logic Apps and integrating services

As Azure Logic Apps is also targeted at non-developers, the process of creating instances and working with them is quite straightforward. In this section of this chapter, you will learn how to work with them in Azure Portal and Visual Studio and how to integrate multiple services and use actions to control a workflow.

Creating Logic Apps in Azure Portal

To create an instance of a Logic App, follow these steps:

1. Click on **+ Create a resource** and search for **Logic App**. When you click on the **Create** button, you will see a simple form that allows you to create a new instance of a Logic App:

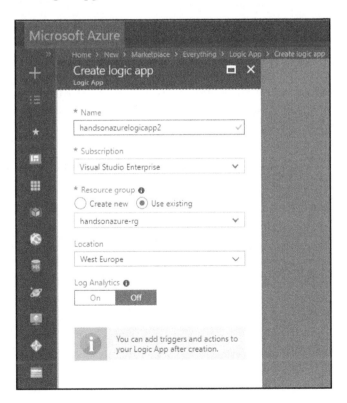

2. In fact, the only extra thing you are able to configure here is enabling Azure Log Analytics. Since this particular service will not be covered in this book, I will skip it in this chapter. When you click on the **OK** button, Azure will start the creation of a new Logic App.

3. When the creation is finished, you can go to the service to check what it initially looks like:

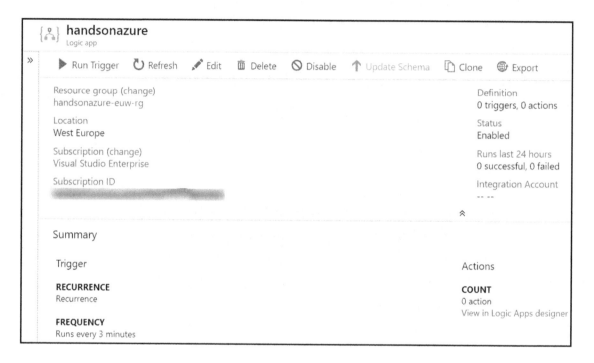

4. Now you can click on the **Logic App Designer** button on the left to access a new blade that enables you to create a brand new workflow. Initially, you will see plenty of different templates available—it is a great start if you are now familiar with this particular service as it displays many different possibilities and configurations that you may achieve using Azure Logic Apps. To get started, in the **Templates** section, select the **Schedule** option in the **Category** drop-down menu and choose **Scheduler - Add message to queue**:

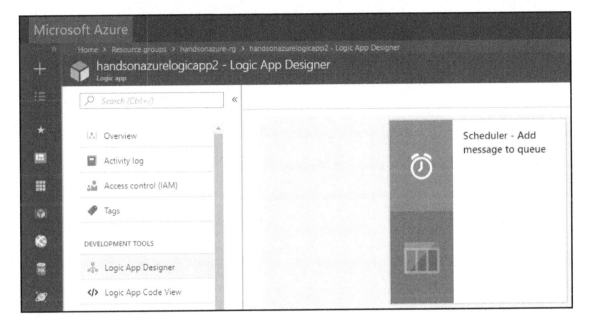

5. When you click on **Use this template**, you will see a designer window where you will be able to finish configuring a workflow. Note that, initially, we do not see all blocks—we have to set all missing configuration values (such as **Queue Name** or **Message**) before we can proceed. Once everything is set up and ready, you can click on **Continue**, which will allow you to work on your workflow:

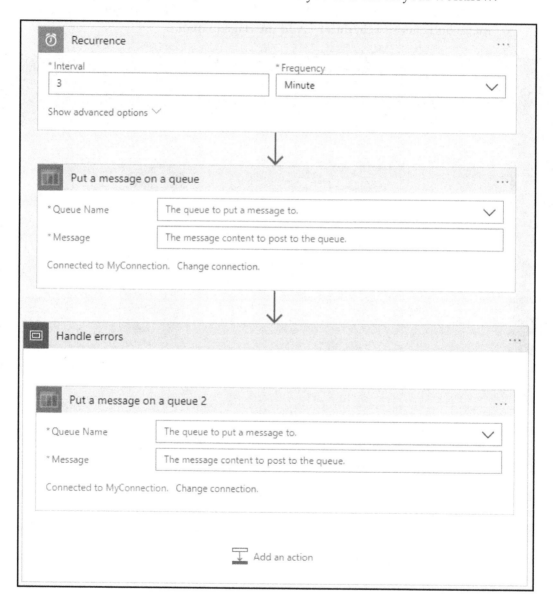

Creating a connection to Azure Queue will require you to create a Storage Account. If you are not familiar with that service, refer to Chapter 11, *Using Azure Storage - Tables, Queues, Files, and Blobs*, about Azure Storage.

6. To finish configuration, you will have to enter all missing values—the queue name and message. Once you do this, you have saved a Logic App and can now try to run it.

 This particular connector does not create a queue if it does not exist. Make sure you have one before starting a Logic App instance. If you do not know how to do so, refer to Chapter 11, *Using Azure Storage - Tables, Queues, Files, and Blobs*, where we discuss Azure Storage features and queues.

If you click on the **Run** button, you will be able to see how the full flow was executed:

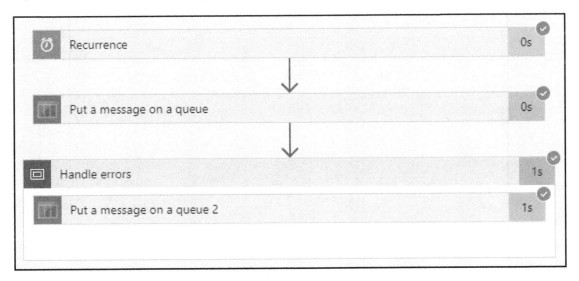

We can compare the preceding execution with a failed one so that you can see the difference between them (such as message content or a dynamic variable created during the execution of a flow). Logic Apps can be debugged really quickly as they provide detailed error messages and directly point you to the place where something is wrong:

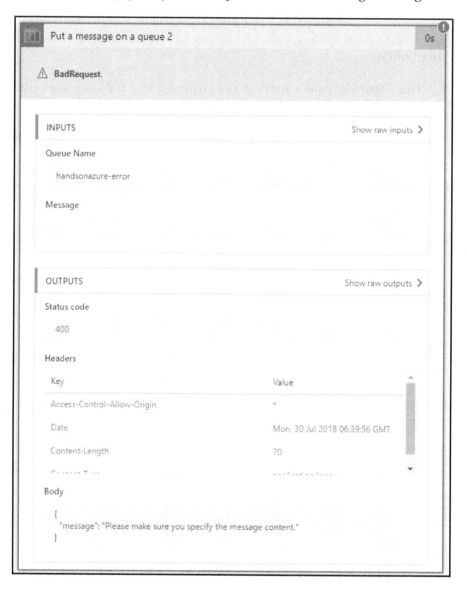

Congratulations, you have created your first Azure Logic App! In the next section, you will see how you can work with it in Visual Studio.

Working with Azure Logic Apps in Visual Studio

While it is perfectly fine to with your Logic Apps using Azure Portal, you do not always want to log in and use its UI. As it is possible to install an extension to Microsoft Visual Studio, which enables you to work with Azure Logic Apps, we will try to check how it work in this chapter:

1. To start working with your Logic Apps in Visual Studio you will have to open the **Cloud Explorer** (**View | Cloud Explorer**) window. It will display a list of available subscriptions and resources within it.

> If the **Cloud Explorer** window appears to be empty, make sure you have the newest version of Visual Studio and the Azure SDK available and you have signed in to your Azure account.

2. Among other types of service, you should be able to find the **Logic Apps** section:

This is the main view and allows you to start working with that particular Azure component. When you click on an instance you are interested in, you will see the additional menu, available below the displayed resources.

You can also right-click on the resource you would like to work with—it will display a menu with available actions.

3. As you can see in the following screenshot, I clicked on **Open with Logic App Editor**, which displays the very same view you saw in the portal:

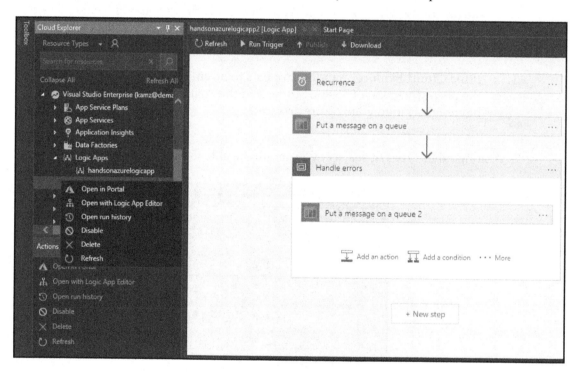

You can work with your Logic App in Visual Studio in the same manner as you would work in Azure Portal. Additionally, you can take a look at its history and disable and delete it.

> When you double-click on an item in the run history, you will get the very same view as in Azure Portal, where you were able to debug a particular invocation. This is very helpful as you can quickly develop and test your Logic Apps and work on other parts of your application without leaving your IDE.

I strongly encourage you to play a little bit with Azure Logic Apps by yourself in Visual Studio as this is a great addition to the whole service, and has the same feeling as the portal.

B2B integration

To a slight extent, we have already covered B2B integration of Azure Logic Apps in this chapter, but I wanted to give you some more information regarding this topic, as this service is not always recognized as an enterprise integration tool. Surprisingly, Azure Logic Apps has many interesting features to offer when it comes to exchanging messages and data between partners and you'll find the relevant details in this section.

Starting B2B integration in Azure Logic Apps

To get started with B2B integration, you will need an **Integration Account**—this is a special container for integration artifacts you will work with. In general, it allows you to store a variety of different items (certificates, schemas, and agreements) in one place, so you can work with them in Azure Logic Apps.

To create such an account, click on the **+ Create a resource** and search for **Integration Account**:

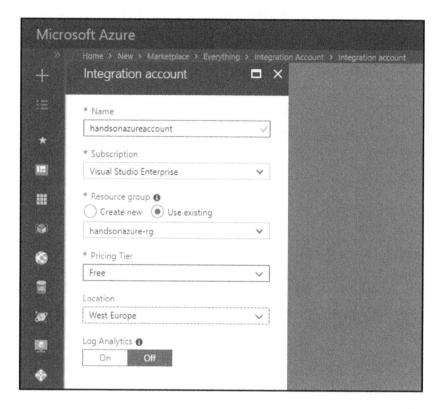

As you can see it offers a simple form where, in fact, the only thing you need to do is select the proper **Pricing Tier**.

The selected tier changes the maximum number of stored artifacts. You can, of course, change it later.

Once you have an integration account instance, you will need to link it with your Logic App. To do so, go to the **Workflow settings** blade in your instance of Azure Logic Apps and search for the **Integration account** section:

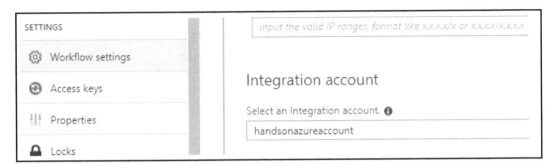

Now you should be able to use connectors, which require an integration account to work.

Normally, if your Logic App has no integration account linked, when you add a step requiring such functionality, you will have to provide a custom name. Once such a connection is available, you will not be asked for additional information again.

In the *Further reading* section of this chapter, you will find additional links that will help you gather more information regarding B2B integration in Azure Logic Apps.

Summary

In this chapter, you have learned about Azure Logic Apps, a simple yet useful service whose use isn't restricted to Azure ninjas. You read about different connectors and multiple ways of working with your Logic Apps—using both Azure Portal (with designed and code editor) and Visual Studio. Additionally, you should know something about B2B integration in that service and how to start it.

In Chapter 9, *Swiss Army Knife - Azure Cosmos DB*, we cover Azure CosmosDB—a serverless database that enables the user to use different DB models in the same service.

Questions

1. What is the pricing model for Azure Logic Apps?
2. Can we use a loop in a Logic App workflow?
3. What is needed to open a Logic App in Visual Studio?
4. How can we debug a particular Logic App execution?
5. Can a Logic App push a message directly to a queue such as Azure Service Bus or Azure Storage Queue?
6. How can we version multiple Logic Apps?

Further reading

For more information you can refer to the following links:

- Azure Logic Apps overview: `https://docs.microsoft.com/en-us/azure/logic-apps/logic-apps-overview`
- Exchanging AS2 messages: `https://docs.microsoft.com/en-us/azure/logic-apps/logic-apps-enterprise-integration-as2`
- Integrating Azure Logic Apps with enterprise solutions: `https://docs.microsoft.com/en-us/azure/logic-apps/logic-apps-enterprise-integration-overview`
- Azure Logic Apps connectors: `https://docs.microsoft.com/en-us/connectors/`

9
Swiss Army Knife - Azure Cosmos DB

When it comes to storage, we often have to store multiple schemas of data using multiple databases. Due to the need for using multiple services, managing our solution becomes cumbersome and requires a lot of skill to do it in the right fashion. Thanks to Azure Cosmos DB, we can both store records using different database models (such as MongoDB, Table Storage, or Gremlin), and pay only for what we agreed on—throughput, latency, availability, and consistency, all thanks to the serverless model.

The following topics will be covered in this chapter:

- What Azure Cosmos DB is, and how it looks compared to other storage systems
- Partitioning, throughput, and consistency
- Different Azure Cosmos DB database models
- Security features

Technical requirements

To perform the exercises in this chapter, you will need the following:

- Microsoft Visual Studio or Visual Studio Code
- Azure subscription

Understanding Cosmos DB

When working with storage, you have probably heard about different kinds; relational databases, NoSQL databases, graph databases, document databases. There are plenty of different models available, with different characteristics, when it comes to storing data. If you need to easily maintain relationships between tables, in most cases you will choose something such as SQL Server. On the other hand, maybe you would like to save each record in the JSON file format, where the best solution would be an instance of MongoDB. While the choice is all yours, the biggest problem is that you need to have a different kind of service to serve the same purpose—storing data. This is where Azure Cosmos DB comes into play. With its multi-model capabilities, flexibility, and scalability it is a great choice for globally distributed and highly responsive applications. In this section, you will learn how to start working with this service and what its main functionalities are.

Creating a Cosmos DB instance in the portal

We will start our journey with Azure CosmosDB by creating it in the Azure portal:

1. When you click on **+ Create a resource** and search for `Azure Cosmos DB`, you will see a simple form that allows you to select the basic features of the service:

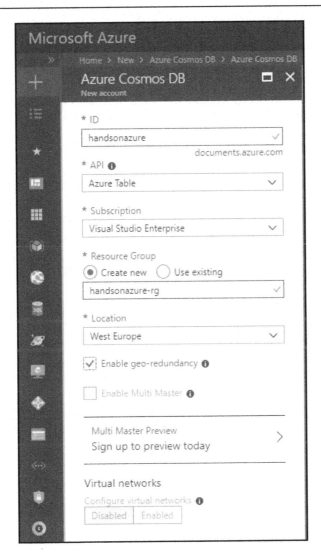

There are, however, some not-so-obvious features, which will require a little bit of explaining:

- **API**: As mentioned earlier, Azure Cosmos DB enables you to use one of a few different APIs during creation. Currently, there are five available APIs: SQL, MongoDB, Cassandra, Azure Table, and Gremlin. Depending on the API selected, you will have different capabilities available (and what is more, different packages will be required for communicating with your database in the application's code).

- **Enable geo-redundancy**: By selecting this option, your data will be distributed between two paired regions (depending on the one you selected in the **Location** drop-down), for example, **West Europe** and **North Europe** or **Central US** and **East US 2**.
- **Enable Multi Master**: This is a new (and currently in preview) feature, where instead of having only a single master, you can have multiple master databases all around the globe. This greatly lowers latency when it comes to reading already saved data (as you do not have to wait for data propagation), and increases consistency and data integrity (as you have the possibility to write data to a master instance in a specific region).
- **Virtual networks**: Depending on the model you choose, you may be able to restrict access to an instance of Azure Cosmos DB by putting it into a specific virtual network and subnet. Currently, this is possible for two database models: SQL and MongoDB.

2. When you are satisfied with all the entered data, you can create it by clicking on the **Create** button. Once your service is created, you can access the **Overview** blade to see how it works initially:

As you can see, it displays a map in the center that tells you how your data is replicated across regions. If you click on the map, you will be able to reconfigure the initial settings. If you click on the **Add new region** button, you will be able to search for a particular one and select it as an additional read region. Alternatively, you can just click on a region icon:

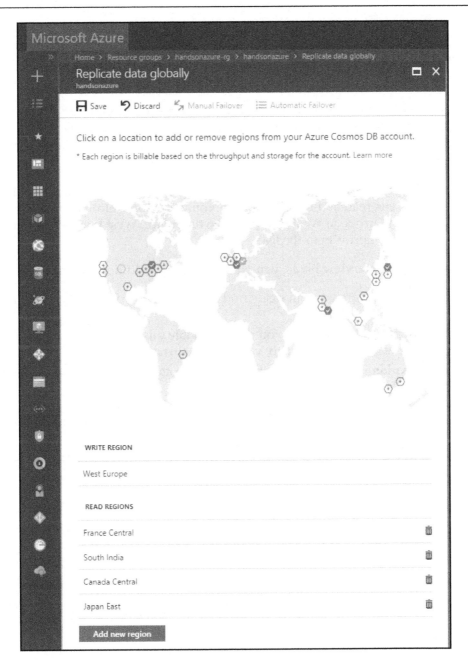

In the current setup, you are unable to add additional write regions. To be able to do so, you have to use the multi-master feature I described previously.

Once you save additional regions, both **Manual Failover** and **Automatic Failover** will become active. The concept for failover is simple—if your write region goes down and becomes unavailable, another available read region can take its place. The only difference is whether you want to perform such failover manually or automatically.

If you opt for automatic failover, you can decide on the order of switching between read and write regions. If you want, for example, to switch from North Europe to West Europe in the first place, West Europe has to be the very first priority in the list.

If you go back to the **Overview** blade, you will notice some additional features:

- **Monitoring**: Here you can easily find all requests to your database and their status.
- **Enable geo-redundancy**: If you did not enable this feature when creating an instance of Azure Cosmos DB, you may do this now.
- **Data Explorer**: By clicking on this button you can easily access an explorer, which allows you to insert and modify data.

Additionally, you can go to the **Quick start** blade, where you will be able to start developing applications using this Azure service:

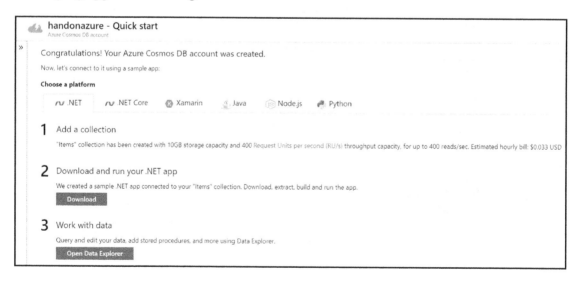

Depending on the selected model of a database, you will have access to different initial configurations. Additionally, as you can see, you have a choice as to whether you would like to use .NET, Node.js, Java, or Python—all these languages can easily integrate with Azure Cosmos DB, making it an even better choice when it comes to creating a multi-platform application.

Using Azure Cosmos DB in Visual Studio

Besides controlling Azure Cosmos DB in the portal, you are able to access it directly in your code and IDE, such as Visual Studio. Like many other services, you can use **Cloud Explorer** to browse all available instances of this database available within your subscription:

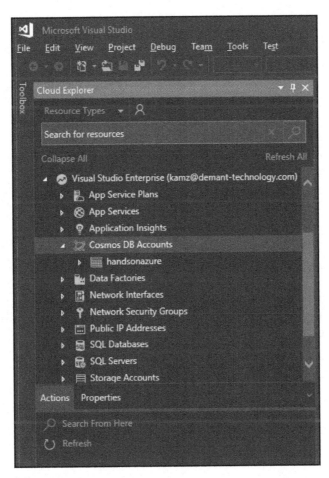

Now let's try to communicate with it from a simple application. While initially an instance of Cosmos DB is empty, we can quickly add a table to it.

 In this section, we will work with the table API in Cosmos DB. If you would like to work with any other type, you will have to consult tutorials in the *Further reading* section.

Consider the following code snippet:

```
using System;
using Microsoft.Azure.CosmosDB.Table;
using Microsoft.Azure.Storage;

namespace HandsOnAzureCosmosDB
{
    internal class Program
    {
        private static void Main()
        {
            // You can get the connection string from the Quick start blade
mentioned previously
            var connectionString = "<connection-string>";
            var storageAccount =
CloudStorageAccount.Parse(connectionString);
            var tableClient = storageAccount.CreateCloudTableClient();

            var reference = tableClient.GetTableReference("handsonazure");
            var result = reference.CreateIfNotExists();

            Console.ReadLine();
        }
    }
}
```

In the preceding code, we are creating an empty table, which should be immediately available within an instance of Cosmos DB. Now if I check **Cloud Explorer** once more, I see that, in fact, it is true:

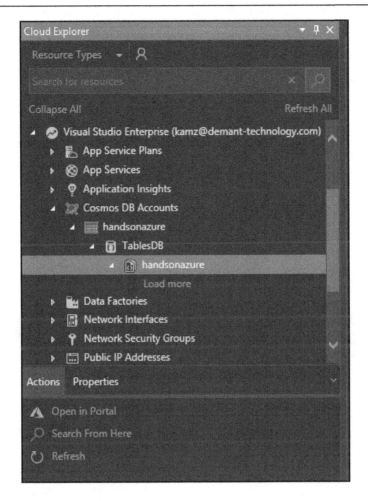

Now we can add a record to it. We slightly modify our code as follows:

```csharp
using System;
using Microsoft.Azure.CosmosDB.Table;
using Microsoft.Azure.Storage;

namespace HandsOnAzureCosmosDB
{
    internal class Program
    {
        private static void Main()
        {
            // You can get the connection string from the Quick start blade
            // mentioned previously
            var connectionString = "<connection-string>";
```

```
            var storageAccount =
CloudStorageAccount.Parse(connectionString);
            var tableClient = storageAccount.CreateCloudTableClient();

            var reference = tableClient.GetTableReference("handsonazure");
            var result = reference.CreateIfNotExists();

            var executionResult =
reference.Execute(TableOperation.Insert(new TableEntity("handsonazure",
Guid.NewGuid().ToString())));
            Console.WriteLine(executionResult.Result);

            Console.ReadLine();
        }
    }
}
```

We now consult **Data Explorer** in the portal to see the difference between Visual Studio and the Azure portal. We should be able to see the entity we have just inserted:

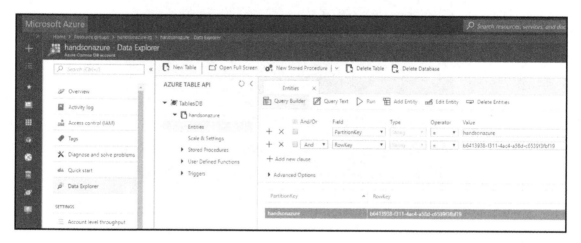

As you can see, all you need to start working with a database with multiple database models, which can be quickly configured for geo-redundancy and scaled across the globe, is just several lines of code.

Pricing in Azure Cosmos DB

Azure Cosmos DB is part of the serverless services available in Azure. This means that the chances of configuring and provisioning servers to run it are either maximally limited or not available. As you probably noticed, we were not able to define how many instances of a service we would like to run (or nodes or clusters). Instead, we have to define throughput for each collection individually:

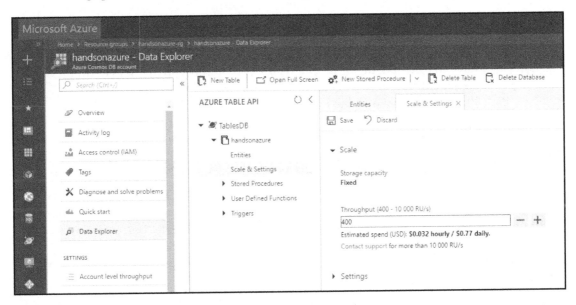

A simple calculator display also estimates the costs of a collection per hour and day. The unit of throughput in Azure Cosmos DB is **request units (RUs)**. During the creation of a container (or a collection—you can use both definitions), you specify also its type—whether it has fixed capacity or unlimited.

 Once the type of collection is defined, you cannot change it later.

By selecting different options, you can select different limits for RUs:

- For fixed, you can select between 400 to 10,000 RUs
- For unlimited, you can go from 1,000 to a maximum of 100,000 RUs

Regarding pricing, you are paying both for the amount of data stored ($0.25 GB/month), and reserved RUs ($.008/hour per every 100 RUs). Having those values, we can quickly calculate the smallest bill possible—it is around $23. Now there is a very important caveat. You are paying per each collection/table/container. That means that, if you have, for example, 20 different tables in your database, you will pay 20 * $23 = $462. In such a scenario, it is sometimes better to model your database in such a way that it will be possible to store all data within a single container.

 While Azure Cosmos DB seems like a quite an expensive service, please do remember that it does many things for you, such as geo-redundancy, multiple read regions, multi-master models, and many more. You always have to calculate the best options for you (and if you are able to do the same with the similar results). To do so, take a look at the Capacity Planner described in the *Further Reading* section.

Partitioning, throughput, and consistency

Now we have learned something about Azure Cosmos DB—how it works and its most common features—we can focus a little bit on three really important topics in this service; partitioning, throughput, and consistency. Those factors are crucial when selecting a database engine to power your application. They directly tell you how it will be performing, how many requests it will be able to handle, and what guarantees apply when it comes to your data integrity.

Partitions in Azure Cosmos DB

Partitioning is directly connected with scaling in Azure Cosmos DB as it allows for load-balancing incoming requests. In fact, there are two different types of partition in this service:

- **Physical**: These are a combination of fixed storage and a variable amount of computing resources. This type of partition is fully managed by Cosmos DB—you cannot directly affect how your data is physically partitioned and how a service handles those partitions. In fact, you are also unaware of how many of those partitions are currently in use. Therefore, you should not design your containers against that specific concept.

- **Logical**: This kind of partition holds data that has the same partition key. Because you are able to define that key (by specifying it in each entity), you are able to control how your data is partitioned.

> Remember that a logical partition has a limit of 10 GB. Additionally, all data for a logical partition has to be stored within one physical partition.

Now you may wonder how partitioning works in Azure Cosmos DB. This can be described in a few steps:

1. Each time a new container is provisioned (and you are providing a number of RUs), Cosmos DB has to provision physical partitions, which will be able to serve the number of requests specified in the number of RUs.
2. It may turn out that the specified amount of RUs exceeds the maximum number of requests per second served by a partition. In that case, Cosmos DB will provision the number of partitions it needs to satisfy your requirements.
3. The next thing to do is to allocate space for partition key hashes. All provisioned partitions have to have the same space allocated (so it is distributed evenly).
4. Now, if after some time any partition reaches its storage limit, it is split into two new partitions, and data is distributed evenly between them.

Of course, the partition key used for partitioning differs for each database model—for a table it is partition key, for SQL it will be a custom path. In general, this operation is slightly different depending on the database type, yet the overall concept remains the same.

> Remember that if your container has only one partition key for all the entities in it, then Cosmos DB will not be able to split a partition. That means that you could hit the maximum of 10 GB per partition and not be able to add any more data.

The best value for the partition key depends solely on your application data specification. In general, you have to choose a value that is quite differential (so partitioning can actually happen). On the other hand, you should not create a unique partition key for each record (while it is possible, it will be quite expensive). There is no one solution to that problem—you always have to analyze each scenario and select what suits you the most.

> In most cases, it is worth including a partition key while filtering data, as it allows for high concurrency.

Throughput in Azure Cosmos DB

In the *Further reading* section, you will find a capacity calculator—a tool that enables you to plan your Cosmos DB instance and estimate the required RUs. As mentoned previously, in this particular service you are not defining the number of instances or clusters. Instead, while creating a container, you have to state your expected throughput for that specific collection (or a set of collections). Thanks to an **Service Level Agreement (SLA)** for Azure Cosmos DB, that value will be guaranteed for you. Additionally, even if you replicate a database to another region, you can expect that problems in one region will not affect others.

 There is one important definition of 1 request unit—it is the processing capacity, that enables you to read a 1 KB entity using, for example, a simple GET request. The same is not true for operations such as inserting or deleting, as those require more computing power to be performed.

If you would like to know exactly how many RUs a specific operation consumes, you have to consult the `x-ms-request-charge` header in a response from a Cosmos DB instance. This will tell you the cost of this operation—of course, you have to remember that it may differ depending on the number of records returned. In the documentation you can find the following table:

Operation	Request unit charge
Create item	~15 RU
Read item	~1 RU
Query item by ID	~2.5 RU

Those are values for executing an operation against an entity 1 KB in size. As you can see, the values are completely different depending on the operation type. You also can see, that it is crucial to carefully check all operations requirements—if you fail to do so, you may face an HTTP 429 response, which tells you that you have exceeded the reserved throughput limits. In such a scenario, you should honor the `x-ms-retry-after-ms` header response, which allows for an easy retry policy.

Consistency in Azure Cosmos DB

Besides different models of a database, Azure Cosmos DB offers also a different level of consistency. You may wonder what consistency is and how it affects your data.

We can define it as follows:

Consistency is a parameter of a database system, which reflects the way a transaction affects data. It defines the rules that are applied when different constraints or/and triggers affect data written to a database.

So basically it tells you what are the guarantees that, if your data becomes affected by a set of operations, it will not be malformed and you will be able to rely on it. The following are the available consistency models in Cosmos DB:

- **STRONG**
- **BOUNDED STATELESS**
- **SESSION**
- **CONSISTENT PREFIX**
- **EVENTUAL**

In the above list, each level below **STRONG** gives you less consistency. This is especially true for **EVENTUAL**, which could be familiar to you thanks to a topic known as eventual consistency. In general, you are setting the default consistency level for your account—then it is possible to override it per each request (of course, if you want to). If you want to know how exactly each consistency level works, please refer to the *Further reading* section. To set a particular level in your Cosmos DB instance, click on the **Default consistency** blade:

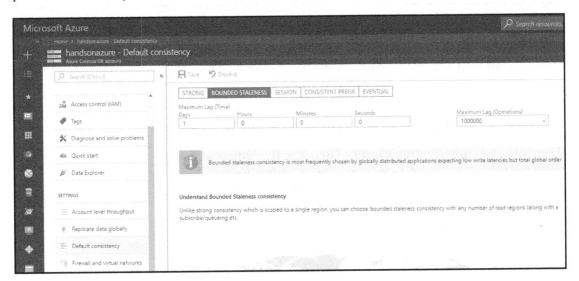

As you can see, it allows you to easily switch to another consistency level depending on your needs. What is more, it displays a nice animation, which describes how reads/writes in multiple regions will work for this particular level. The following screenshot shows the animation for eventual consistency:

In this screenshot, each individual note represents an individual read or write in a particular region. Additionally, on this screen, you are able to set **Maximum Lag (Time)** when the **BOUNDED STALENESS** level is selected.

CosmosDB data models and APIs

As mentioned earlier, Azure Cosmos DB offers five different database models, all sharing the same infrastructure and concepts. This is a great feature, that makes this service really flexible and able to serve multiple different purposes. In this section, I will briefly describe each database model, so you will be able to select one that best serves your purposes.

SQL

If you think about SQL, you probably see a relational database with tables, relations, and stored procedures. When working with **SQL API** in Cosmos DB, in fact you will work with documents that can be queried using the SQL syntax. Let us assume you want to query documents using the following call:

```
SELECT * FROM dbo.Order O WHERE O.AccountNumber = "0000-12-223-12"
```

Here you can find an example of a query written in C#:

```
var order =
  client.CreateDocumentQuery<Order>(collectionLink)
    .Where(so => so.AccountNumber == "0000-12-223-12")
    .AsEnumerable()
    .FirstOrDefault();
```

As you can see, it is all about a simple LINQ query, which allows you to use a specific property to filter data. Because all records in Cosmos DB are stored as JSON documents, you can easily transform them from table to document representations (and possibly denormalize them).

Using document databases is completely different from storing data in relational databases. Always remember to model your data appropriately in line with database capabilities.

MongoDB

As Cosmos DB implements the MongoDB wire protocol, you can easily use all your applications that currently use that document database with new instances of Azure Cosmos DB, without changing anything (besides the connection string, of course). While it cannot mimic MongoDB completely yet (the full list of supported operations can be found in the *Further reading* section), in most cases you will be able to use it seamlessly.
As Cosmos DB has a strict requirement regarding security, you will have to use SSL when communicating with it:

```
mongodb://username:password@host:port/[database]?ssl=true
```

Here you can see a template for a connection string, where `ssl=true` is present—it is required when communicating with this Azure service. What is more, you will not be able to set a communication without authenticating a request.

Graph

Azure Cosmos DB supports Gremlin as a graph database model. If you are not familiar with graph databases, you may think about them as a structure composed of vertices and edges. They can very easily show you relations between different elements of a graph as you can quickly traverse the connections and see that element A knows something about element B indirectly, thanks to element C. To be more specific, Cosmos DB supports a more specific model of a graph database known as a **property graph**. The following is an example query for Gremlin:

```
:>
g.V('thomas.1').out('knows').out('uses').out('runsos').group().by('name').b
y(count())
```

The preceding example is taken from the documentation and literally answers the question: What operating systems do relations of the user of the `thomas.1` ID use?. Graph databases are great for applications such as social media portals or IoT hubs.

Table

While you can use Azure Storage Table for your applications (which will be covered in upcoming chapters), it is possible to also take advantage of Cosmos DB's Table API and consider more advanced scenarios with that service. There are some differences between both services:

- While the current maximum limit for operations in Azure Storage Tables is 20,000 operations/sec, with Cosmos DB you can achieve millions of them
- You cannot initiate failover for Storage Table
- In Cosmos DB, data is indexed on all properties, not only on the partition key and row key
- Different pricing (storage versus throughput)
- Different consistency levels

Developing against Cosmos DB Table API is the same as working with Azure Table Storage. The following is an example of code in C# retrieving entities from a table:

```
CloudStorageAccount storageAccount = CloudStorageAccount.Parse(
    CloudConfigurationManager.GetSetting("StorageConnectionString"));
CloudTableClient tableClient = storageAccount.CreateCloudTableClient();
CloudTable table = tableClient.GetTableReference("people");
TableQuery<CustomerEntity> query = new
TableQuery<CustomerEntity>().Where(TableQuery.GenerateFilterCondition("Part
itionKey", QueryComparisons.Equal, "Smith"));

foreach (CustomerEntity entity in table.ExecuteQuery(query))
{
    Console.WriteLine("{0}, {1}\t{2}\t{3}", entity.PartitionKey,
entity.RowKey,
        entity.Email, entity.PhoneNumber);
}
```

Cassandra

The last available model in Azure Cosmos DB is Cassandra. Cassandra is a scalable, durable, and decentralized database for storing massive amounts of data. Now, if you use it with Cosmos DB, you can focus on development rather than on operations or performance management, and choice of consistency. While currently this model is in preview, you can test it and check what advantages it gives to you. Under the hood, it uses the Cassandra API, so it is possible to use Cassandra Query Language to communicate and interact with data. This model has the same feel as MongoDB—you can use the same tools you used for your current Cassandra instances and should not notice any difference.

Different features of CosmosDB

Azure Cosmos DB has multiple different features that can be used to lower your bills, secure an instance, or integrate with other services. In this section, we will quickly take a look at most of them, so you will fully understand the basics of this service and will be able to progress on your own.

Account level throughput

Instead of defining throughput per each collection, sometimes you would like to set a fixed value for the whole account. This is a great addition if you have many different containers and instead of paying for each individually (as you remember—it was over $20 per month), you can go to **Account level throughput** and set a throughput for the whole account:

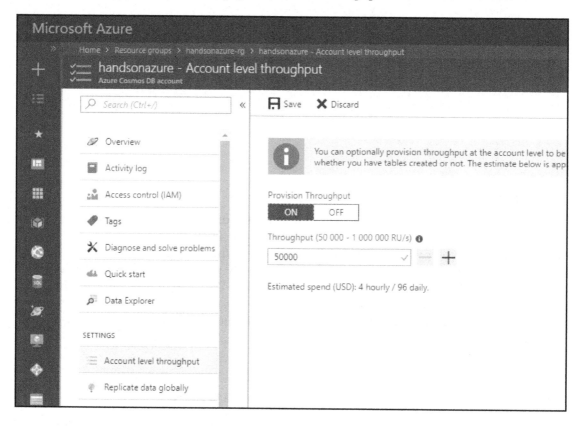

The only limitation of this feature is you can no tables currently in the account. If you enable it, all your requests to all tables will share the same amount of throughput (so you can pay less, but in the case of "greedy" collections you can run out of RUs). The downside of that functionality is that you will pay for the provisioned throughput, whether you have created collections or not.

 Note that the aforementioned feature is available only for the Table API.

Database level throughput

In Azure Cosmos DB it is also possible to provision throughput directly on the database. To do so, you need to select the **Provision throughput** checkbox during database creation:

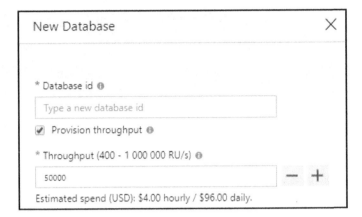

With that feature on, all provisioned RUs will be shared across all collection available for a database.

Firewall and virtual networks

If you configured the virtual network feature during Cosmos DB creation, in this blade you will be able to configure it further. What is more, it is also possible to configure a firewall—so you can restrict access to a specific range of IPs or disallow connections from other Azure data centers. In general, you do not want to have a database that can be accessed by everyone, so if this feature is available, I strongly recommend you use it.

  Note that currently firewalls and VNets are available only for the SQL API and Mongo API. Support for other APIs should be available soon.

Azure Functions

You can easily integrate Azure Cosmos DB with Azure Functions by using the **Add Azure Function** blade:

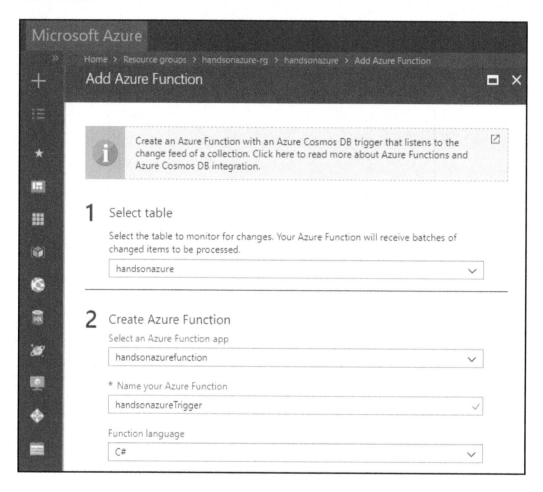

Creating a function from Cosmos DB will add the following code to your Function App:

```
#r "Microsoft.Azure.Documents.Client"

using Microsoft.Azure.Documents;
using System.Collections.Generic;
using System;

public static async Task Run(IReadOnlyList<Document> input, TraceWriter
log)
{
    log.Verbose("Document count " + input.Count);
    log.Verbose("First document Id " + input[0].Id);
}
```

This is CSX code, which we did not cover—however, besides slight changes in syntax, it is pure C#. This function will listen to changes to a collection you selected during creation—it is up to you what it will do next. In general, it is a quick and easy way to integrate these two services. What is more, you can have more than just one Azure Function generated for your collection or table. Now if I add a document, I can see it triggers a function:

```
 Pause  Clear  Copy logs  Expand
2018-08-07T06:01:28  Welcome, you are now connected to log-streaming
service.
2018-08-07T06:01:34.556 [Info] Function started (Id=5fb63ab3-e128-45ad-
b7a8-4ccfdad38c82)
2018-08-07T06:01:34.573 [Verbose] Document count 1
2018-08-07T06:01:34.573 [Verbose] First document Id test_document
2018-08-07T06:01:34.591 [Info] Function completed (Success, Id=5fb63ab3-
e128-45ad-b7a8-4ccfdad38c82, Duration=21ms)
```

Stored procedures

Azure Cosmos DB allows for creating stored procedures that can be executed individually and can hold extra logic, which you do not want to share.

If you go to your collection in **Data Explorer**, you will see the **New Stored Procedure** tab and the ability to create one:

Stored procedures are written in JavaScript—this allows you to easily access the document's schema (as they are all JSON). What is more, they are registered per collection. Here you can find an example of the easiest stored procedure:

```
function sample(prefix) {
    var context = getContext();
    var response = context.getResponse();

    response.setBody("Hello, World");
}
```

User-defined functions and triggers

To extend the query language, you can write your own **user-defined function** (UDF) and in your queries. Note that you cannot use these in Stored Procedures. UDFs are used to extend the SQL query language in Azure Cosmos DB and can be only called from inside queries. Triggers, however, are divided into two categories:

- Pre-triggers
- Post-triggers

Additionally, you can select an operation that this trigger refers to:

- **All**
- **Create**
- **Delete**
- **Replace**

Here you can find an example of a trigger that updates a timestamp in a document before it is created:

```
var context = getContext();
var request = context.getRequest();
var documentToCreate = request.getBody();

if (!("timestamp" in documentToCreate)) {
  var ts = new Date();
  documentToCreate["my timestamp"] = ts.getTime();
}

request.setBody(documentToCreate);
```

Triggers, of course, are also available from **Data Explorer**:

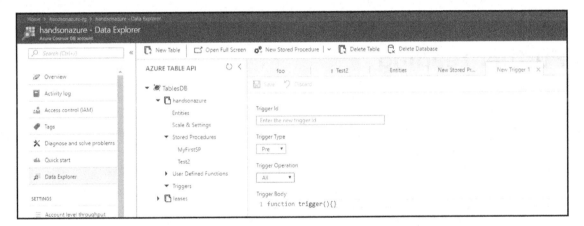

Summary

In this chapter, you have learned about another serverless Azure component named Azure Cosmos DB. You saw multiple database models that this service supports, and also multiple different features, such as geo-redundancy and the ability to easily scale up and introduce new read regions, where data will be replicated. What is more, you are now aware of multiple consistency models and how to change them in the Azure portal.

In the next chapter, you will learn about another hot topic: reactive architecture with Azure Event Grid.

Questions

1. Which APIs does Azure Cosmos DB support currently?
2. Are there any differences between the capabilities of Azure Table Storage and Table API in Cosmos DB?
3. What are the available consistency models?
4. Which consistency model is more consistent—bounded, staleness, or eventual?
5. Is it possible to restrict access to Azure Cosmos DB to only a single IP?
6. Is SQL API the same as SQL Server?
7. What is the reason for using stored procedures?
8. Is it possible to provision throughput in Azure Cosmos DB for the whole account instead of per collection?

Further reading

- Partitioning data in Azure Cosmos DB: https://docs.microsoft.com/en-us/azure/cosmos-db/partition-data
- Capacity planner: https://www.documentdb.com/capacityplanner
- Azure Cosmos DB RUs: https://docs.microsoft.com/en-us/azure/cosmos-db/request-units
- Consistency levels: https://docs.microsoft.com/en-us/azure/cosmos-db/consistency-levels
- Mongo DB support: https://docs.microsoft.com/en-us/azure/cosmos-db/mongodb-feature-support#mongodb-protocol-support
- Graph API and Gremlin: http://tinkerpop.apache.org/docs/current/reference/#intro

10
Reactive Architecture with Event Grid

Azure Event Grid is another cloud component that represents serverless services in Azure. It can be considered an events gateway, able to both make our solution work faster and to reverse control, so our services don't have to wait for others, burning available resources just to be idle. It's also a great routing tool, able to quickly distribute load and multiply it, allowing jobs to be finished faster.

The following topics will be covered in this chapter:

- Azure Event Grid and reactive architecture
- Connecting to other services through Azure Event Grid
- Security features of Azure Event Grid
- Publishing custom events to Azure Event Grid
- Integrating Azure Functions with Azure Event Grid

Technical requirements

To perform exercises from this chapter you will need:

- An Azure subscription
- An IDE compatible with Visual Studio 2017

Azure Event Grid and reactive architecture

When working with multiple services in the cloud, you often need to have a centralized service responsible for routing events to a different endpoint. This makes the exchange of data a piece of cake—you do not have to maintain different URLs of APIs, as you can leverage a common event schema and custom routing configuration based on, for example, event type. In Azure, such a service is called Azure Event Grid—a serverless event gateway, which is one of the newer cloud components available. With a pay-as-you-go pricing model, you can quickly build a reactive architecture that inverts communication between your services and makes them passive. In this chapter, you will learn how to work with Event Grid and integrate it with other Azure components.

Reactive architecture

To get started, let's consider the architecture shown in the following diagram:

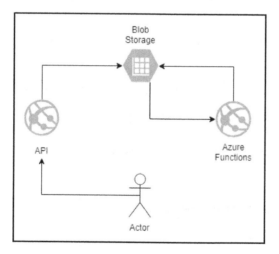

In this diagram, you can see an example flow of uploading, for instance, an image for an avatar from a user. A file is transferred through an **Azure App Service** and put into **Azure Blob Storage**. Then, it is processed by **Azure Functions**. While such a setup is perfectly fine, consider the following disadvantage—to be able to process the image, **Azure Functions** has to be notified about the fact that a new file was uploaded.

Since **Azure Blob Storage** is unable to do so (at least with the functionality available publicly), the only way to achieve that is to pool a storage and somehow maintain processed files. While conceptually, this is not rocket science, you have to bear in mind that, in the cloud, when you use a resource, you pay for the time taken. So basically, in the preceding scenario, you would be paying even if no file was uploaded to the storage, since a trigger in **Azure Functions** (here, a Blob trigger) will have to maintain a state of files available and check at intervals whether something new appeared, so you will often pay for nothing. Now, consider the following change:

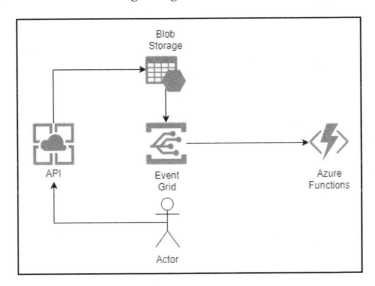

As you can see, I put an **Azure Event Grid** between **Azure Blob Storage** and **Azure Functions**. What has it changed? Well, functions processing a Blob do not have to pool storage to get info about uploaded files. This is possible thanks to version 2 of Azure Storage (you can find a link to a description in *Further reading* section)—it can publish events to **Azure Event Grid** so they can then be forwarded to all subscribers of that particular event type. Thanks to this, **Azure Functions** can remain passive—they will be called by **Azure Event Grid** when needed, so if nothing is uploaded, you will pay nothing. This is, of course, an element of serverless architecture—being able to pay for usage makes such a setup possible.

Remember that you will not be charged if you only use the Consumption plan in Azure Functions. If you have to use an App Service Plan for your functions, you will not be able to save money with the preceding architecture—on the other hand, you will save some compute power, which could be used for other workloads, so reactive architecture concepts will still be valid.

This is what we call **reactive architecture**—a model where your components can remain idle and wait for upcoming requests.

Topics and event subscriptions

There are five main topics when it comes to working with Azure Event Grid:

- Events
- Event handlers
- Event sources
- Topics
- Event subscriptions

In this section, we will go through each of them to build a better understanding of this service.

Event sources

Currently, Azure Event Grid supports the following event sources:

- Azure Blob Storage
- Azure Media Services
- Azure Subscriptions
- Resource Groups
- Azure Event Hubs
- Azure IoT Hub
- Azure Service Bus
- Custom topics
- Container Registry
- Storage **General-purpose v2 (GPv2)**

As you can see, there are plenty of different services integrated and available when working with Event Grid. While we know which event sources we can use, we still have not defined what an event source actually is. Take a look at the following diagram:

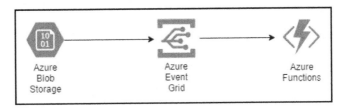

In this scenario, a file uploaded to **Azure Blob Storage** triggers an event, which is then fetched by **Azure Event Grid** and passed further to the consumer. The event source is the origin of an event that was then handled by Event Grid. When working with this service, all event sources have a way to publish an event and communicate with **Azure Event Grid**. There is also one extra event source possible—it is Custom topics. It is possible to publish your own custom events directly to an Event Grid endpoint—we will cover that later in this chapter.

Event handlers

In the previous example, we covered event sources. Let's take a similar scenario:

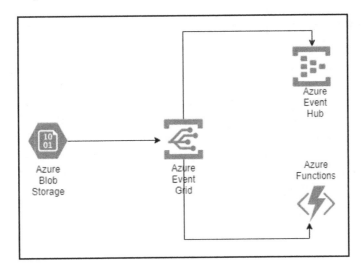

Once more, we have **Azure Blob Storage** as a publisher, but this time, events are forwarded to both **Azure Functions** and **Azure Event Hub**. In that architecture, services presented on the right are event handlers. Here is a list of currently supported services:

- Azure Functions
- Azure Logic Apps
- Azure Automation
- WebHooks
- Azure Queue Storage
- Hybrid Connections
- Azure Event Hubs
- Microsoft Flow

So what actually is an event handler? You can think about it as a processor of an event—based on the configuration, Azure Event Grid will forward events to handlers, where they will be deserialized and analyzed.

 In general, Azure Event Grid uses a common event schema when delivering events to handlers. What is more, it can deliver more than just one event at the time—you have to be prepared for a possible batch of events.

Topics and subscriptions

A topic is a general messaging concept that allows for one-to-many communication. It works with subscriptions in the following way—you publish a message to a topic in a messaging service, and then subscribe to it with your consumers. In Azure Event Grid, you are responsible for creating a topic—that means that you have to publish a custom application that handles communication between publishers and the Event Grid endpoint. You can have a single application, or many of them—this depends on your design and expected throughput. Additionally, you have to configure subscriptions—in the next section, you will see how to do that, and how to set up proper filtering. The general structure could look like this:

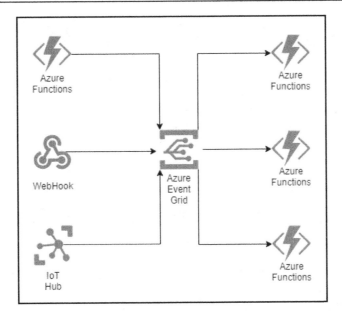

The left side of the preceding diagram represents publishers and a topic (the line between a publisher and **Azure Event Grid**) and subscriptions with handlers. Each line is a different topic and subscription. The whole configuration and routing resides within Event Grid and can be managed there.

 Azure Event Grid takes care of retrying undelivered messages. This can be configured with a custom policy that defines the rules for retrying. Additionally, when a custom topic is used, events have to be published in batches to make it work.

To sum up, we can define both a topic and a subscription as follows:

- **Topic**: A channel between a service and Azure Event Grid, which allows the former to push an event to the Azure service
- **Subscription**: A channel between Azure Event Grid and a service, which is used to retrieve events in the former

Connecting services through Azure Event Grid

Now that you know something about what Azure Event Grid is and how it works, we will try to test it and create a working solution. We will start by creating an instance in Azure Portal and configuring it to accept and route events. You will see also what the schema of an event is and how to leverage it so you can send custom events that will be handled by Event Grid.

Creating Azure Event Grid in Azure Portal

To get started with Azure Event Grid, do the following in Azure Portal:

1. Click on + **Create a resource** and search for `Event Grid`. From the list, select **Event Grid Topic** and click **Create**.
2. You will see a really simple form, where you have to enter the name of an instance of a service:

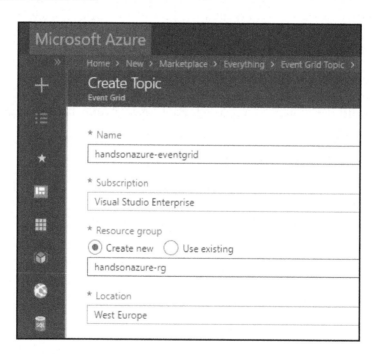

3. When you click **Create** and wait a moment, an instance of a service will be created. Once it is finished, you can go to your resource to see an empty instance:

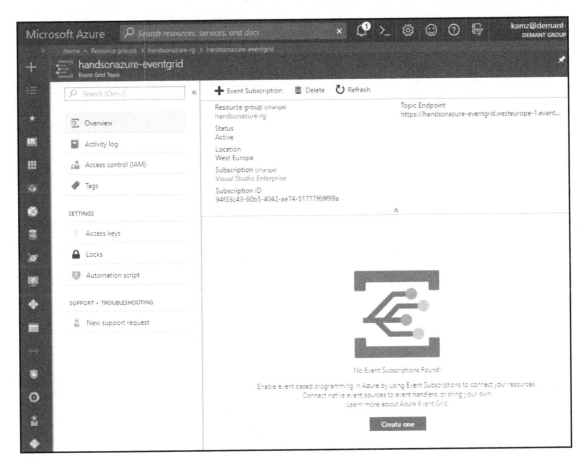

As you can see, there is no subscription created yet. What is more, there is also no topic, which is what would send events to our instance. Before we proceed, let's take a look what we have on the **Overview** blade. Besides the option to create a subscription, there is also one other important thing—**Topic Endpoint**. You will use this to publish events from your custom topics. There is also one important blade—**Access keys**. When you click on it, you will see two keys that can be used to authorize access to Azure Event Grid:

Now let's try to create a topic with a subscription. To do so, we will use the following code snippet:

```
$myEndpoint = "<my-endpoint>"

Set-AzureRmContext -Subscription "<subcription-name>"

New-AzureRmEventGridSubscription `
  -Endpoint $myEndpoint `
  -EventSubscriptionName "<event-subscription-name>"
  -ResourceGroupName "<rg-name>"
```

This PowerShell code should create a Resource Group topic that will push events to an endpoint defined in the $myEndpoint variable. However, if you execute the code, the following error will occur:

```
New-AzureRmEventGridSubscription : Long running operation failed with
status 'Failed'. Additional Info:'The attempt to validate the provided
endpoint <your-endpoint>. For more details, visit
https://aka.ms/esvalidation.'
```

What has happened? Well, it turns out that we cannot create a subscription, because our endpoint is not validated. How can we validate our endpoint so it will be possible to create a subscription? I will explain shortly.

Azure Event Grid security

Besides access tokens, Azure Event Grid also checks whether or not an endpoint is valid and secure. This validation will not happen for the following handler types:

- Azure Logic Apps
- Azure Automation
- Azure Functions when `EventGridTrigger` is used

The rest of the endpoints (and especially those triggered by an HTTP request) have to be validated to be used. Here is how that kind of validation is processed:

1. Firstly, `SubscriptionValidationEvent` is sent to an endpoint containing multiple fields, such as topic, validation code, and others. Additionally, a special `aeg-event-type: SubscriptionValidation` header is sent.
2. Secondly, Event Grid expects a success response containing a validation code that was sent in the request.

Here is an example of a validation event:

```
[{
  "id": "3d178aaf-364c-67b-bq0c-e34519da4eww",
  "topic": "/subscriptions/xxxxxxxx-xxxx-xxxx-xxxx-xxxxxxxxxxxx",
  "subject": "",
  "data": {
    "validationCode": "512d38b6-c7b8-40c8-89fe-f46f9e9622b6",
    "validationUrl": "<validation-url>"
  },
  "eventType": "Microsoft.EventGrid.SubscriptionValidationEvent",
  "eventTime": "2018-08-10T10:20:19.4556811Z",
  "metadataVersion": "1",
  "dataVersion": "1"
}]
```

In this scenario, to validate an endpoint, you would have to return the following response:

```
{
  "validationResponse": "512d38b6-c7b8-40c8-89fe-f46f9e9622b6"
}
```

After that, you should be able to create a subscription.

As you may have noticed, the validation event also contains the `validationUrl` property. It allows you to manually validate a subscription, instead of redeploying code with a proper application logic.

Creating a subscription

Now that you are familiar with endpoint validation topic, we can try to create a subscription once more:

1. To do so, I created a function that is triggered by an HTTP request. I wrote it quickly in CSX, so I did not have to compile and deploy it manually:

```
#r "Newtonsoft.Json"

using System.Net;
using Newtonsoft.Json;

public static async Task<HttpResponseMessage>
Run(HttpRequestMessage req, TraceWriter log)
{
 var @event = JsonConvert.DeserializeObject(await
req.Content.ReadAsStringAsync());
 log.Info(@event.ToString());

 return req.CreateResponse(HttpStatusCode.OK);
}
```

Thanks to the preceding code, I can see that a validation event was sent to an endpoint. Now, depending on the version of toolset you have, you will have the `validationUrl` value in the payload.

2. To leverage this feature, you will have to install the Event Grid extension for Azure CLI 2.0—a link for download can be found in the *Further reading* section. To progress without this feature, we will have to change the code of our function a little bit:

```
#r "Newtonsoft.Json"

using System.Net;
using Newtonsoft.Json;

public static async Task<HttpResponseMessage>
Run(HttpRequestMessage req, TraceWriter log)
{
```

```
var @event =
JsonConvert.DeserializeObject<ValidationEvent[]>(await
req.Content.ReadAsStringAsync())[0];

 return req.CreateResponse(HttpStatusCode.OK, new
{validationResponse = @event.Data.ValidationCode} );
}

public class ValidationEvent {
 public ValidationEventData Data {get;set;}
}

public class ValidationEventData {
 public string ValidationCode {get;set;}
}
```

3. Note that I am deserializing the validation event as `ValidationEvent[]`, so it is actually an array of events. It is important to bear this in mind to avoid possible issues.

If events were sent to an endpoint that wasn't validated, the batch will be divided into two parts, one with a single validation event, and the second one with the actual events.

4. Now, if you execute PowerShell code that failed earlier, you should be able to create a subscription. To check whether it all works correctly, you can run the following command:

   Get-AzureRmEventGridSubscription

5. Here, you can see the result in my case:

```
PS C:\Users\kamz> Get-AzureRmEventGridSubscription

 Name Topic ProvisioningState SubjectBeginsWith SubjectEndsWith
Endpoint
 ---- ----- ----------------- ----------------- ---------------
--------
rg-subscription /subscriptions/<id> Succeeded
https://handsonazure-function.azurewebsites.net/api/HttpTrigger
CSharp1
```

Note that subscriptions created with the API are not visible in the Portal. This should be changed soon, but as long as this issue persists, stick mainly to the **command-line interface (CLI)** for maintaining Azure Event Grid.

6. Now if, for example, you create a resource in the resource group that publishes events to Event Grid, an event similar to the following will occur:

```json
{
    "subject":
"/subscriptions/.../Microsoft.Storage/storageAccounts/handsonaz
ure",
    "eventType": "Microsoft.Resources.ResourceWriteSuccess",
    "eventTime": "2018-08-10T08:51:32.3888833Z",
    "id": "37f85f91-1af9-4ee3-84a6-ee1955c74edc",
    "data": {
      "authorization": {
        "scope": "/subscriptions/.../handsonazure-
rg/providers/Microsoft.Storage/storageAccounts/handsonazure",
        "action": "Microsoft.Storage/storageAccounts/write",
        "evidence": {
          "role": "Subscription Admin"
        }
      },
      "claims": {
        "aud": "https://management.core.windows.net/",
        (...)
    }
  }
}
```

7. It is also possible to create a connection like this without the CLI—if you go to your resource group, you will see the **Events** blade:

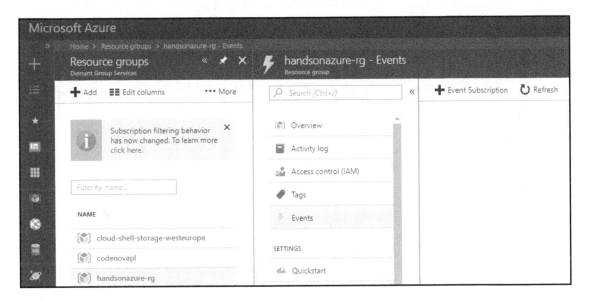

8. When you click on the **+ Event subscription** button, you will see a form that makes the whole process much easier. You can use this form if you prefer configuring services in the Portal, instead of the CLI:

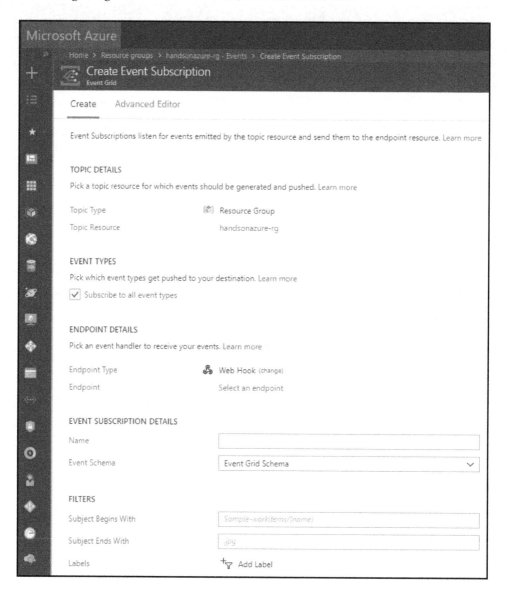

Publishing custom events to Azure Event Grid

So far, we have talked about integrating Azure Event Grid with already built-in publishers and topics, using Resource Group as an example. I mentioned at the beginning of this chapter that this service is capable of handling custom topics, making it a really flexible solution that can act as an event gateway. In this section, we will cover this topic and try to use Event Grid as our router for handling and maintaining the routing of our events.

Event gateway concept

Let's look at the following diagram:

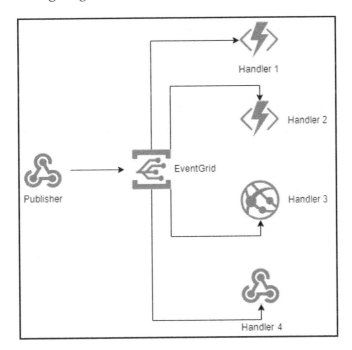

Here, you have a single events producer and four different handlers. Now, if you imagine that **Publisher** publishes only custom events, you can see that Event Grid is able to distribute them among N different handlers (which do not have to be the same type—it can be a mix of any supported handlers available). Of course, this concept can also be used with publishers such as Resource Group, Azure Blob Storage, or Azure Event Hub—personally, I think that it is slightly more useful for custom scenarios. Let's take an example—you are publishing an `OrderCreated` event. With Azure Event Grid, you could now distribute it to different handlers:

- `OrderConfirmation`: For example, for sending a confirmation via a mail message
- `OrderProcessor`: For handling the actual logic of processing an order
- `OrderNotification`: For notifying someone that there is an order that has to be validated

Of course, the preceding steps rely only on your logic—it should, however, give you a hint of what can be done with routing and distributing events using Azure Event Grid.

Handling a custom event

Before we send a custom event, we have to take a look at the Event Grid event schema:

```
[
  {
    "topic": string,
    "subject": string,
    "id": string,
    "eventType": string,
    "eventTime": string,
    "data":{
      object-unique-to-each-publisher
    },
    "dataVersion": string,
    "metadataVersion": string
  }
]
```

As you can see, it is a simple JSON array, containing many different events. Let's describe each field here:

- `topic`: This defines a full path to an event source (for example, Azure Blob Storage).

- `subject`: This defines a path to an event subject (so, in the case of publishing events from a resource group, this could be a full path to an Azure resource, or, in the case of Azure Blob Storage, this would be a Blob path).
- `id`: This is the unique identifier of an event.
- `eventType`: A type of a published event (such as `Microsoft.Resources.ResourceWriteSuccess`).
- `eventTime`: This defines when an event was published using the publisher's UTC time.
- `data`: The payload of an event.
- `dataVersion`: An event schema version defined by the publisher.
- `metadataVersion`: A revision number of event metadata schema version, provided by Event Grid.

Now, if you want to publish an event, you will have to do the following:

- Always use an array of events, even if you are publishing a single one
- Either use an empty topic or use the following syntax, which reflects the fact, that each topic is also an Azure resource `/subscriptions/<subscription-id>/resourceGroups/<resource-group>/providers/Microsoft.EventGrid/topics/<eventgrid-name>`
- Use `aeg-sas-key` or `aeg-sas-token` to authorize a request by providing a key from the **Access keys** blade

Here, you can find an example request:

```
POST /api/events HTTP/1.1
Host: handsonazure-eventgrid.westeurope-1.eventgrid.azure.net
Content-Type: application/json
aeg-sas-key: <sas-key>
Cache-Control: no-cache

[
  {
    "subject": "example",
    "id": "1",
    "eventType": "SectionFinished",
    "eventTime": "2018-08-12T07:41:00.9584103Z",
    "data":{
      "section": 3
    },
    "dataVersion": "1"
  }
]
```

If everything is correct, you should see an HTTP 200 response. Now, you may wonder how you can receive such a request. If you go to your instance of Azure Event Grid and click on the **+ Event Subscription** button, you will see a form where you can create a new subscription:

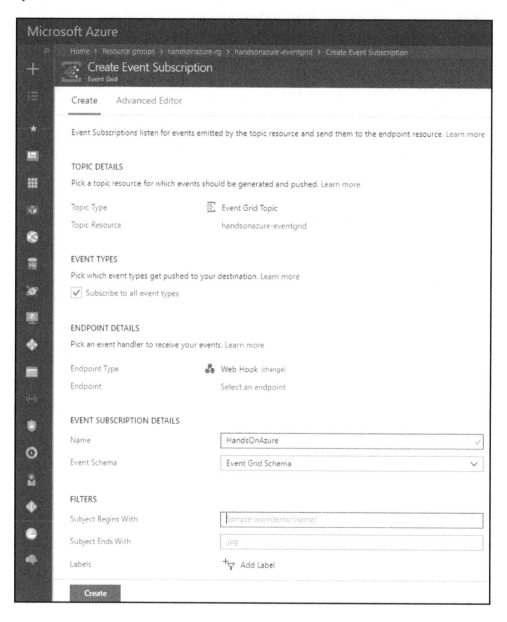

You saw this form before, when we were discussing creating a subscription directly from a resource group. There are, however, some important things to mention:

- **Subscribe to all event types:** You have an option to either route all events types to an endpoint, or just to the ones defined by you (you will be able to enter any event type you wish once you uncheck the checkbox). This is very useful for the proper events routing.
- **Endpoint Type:** You have a choice of different endpoints, including WebHook, Azure Event Hub, and Hybrid Connections.
- **Event Schema:** You can choose to use either Event Grid schema or a more common Cloud Events schema, the latter of which is an open standard specification and can be used to introduce a custom schema for all the components in your system.
- **FILTERS:** You can additionally filter events of a specific type by filtering them with the subject field value.

When you fill all values, click on **Create** to actually create it.

 Remember that an endpoint has to be validated to successfully create a subscription!

Now, if you send an example request, you should be able to receive it in your handler (in my case, Azure Functions):

```
2018-08-12T08:17:25.263 [Info] Function started
(Id=8216a64d-19c5-436f-8cce-69fc49a3cff2)
2018-08-12T08:17:25.404 [Info] [
  {
    "subject": "example",
    "id": "1",
    "eventType": "SectionFinished",
    "eventTime": "2018-08-12T07:41:00.9584103Z",
    "data": {
      "section": 3
    },
    "dataVersion": "1",
    "metadataVersion": "1",
    "topic": "/subscriptions/.../resourceGroups/handsonazure-
rg/providers/Microsoft.EventGrid/topics/handsonazure-eventgrid"
  }
]
2018-08-12T08:17:25.404 [Info] Function completed (Success,
Id=8216a64d-19c5-436f-8cce-69fc49a3cff2, Duration=138ms)
```

You may wonder what will happen if your event handler doesn't return a success response to Azure Event Grid. In that scenario, a retry will be performed.

 Azure Event Grid considers only HTTP 200 and HTTP 202 responses as successful.

By default, Event Grid uses an exponential backoff retry policy. This means that each consecutive retry will be performed with an increased delay between that one, and the next retry. You can customize this behaviour by providing a custom retry policy. A link to that feature can be found in the *Further reading* section.

Integrating Azure Functions with Azure Event Grid

The last thing that we'll cover for Azure Event Grid is integration with Azure Functions. As mentioned earlier, if you use Event Grid to publish events to Azure Functions triggered by an HTTP trigger, you will have to validate an endpoint. This is not the best solution, but fortunately, it is possible to use EventGridTrigger, which allows us to skip the endpoint validation step when configuring services. This topic itself is quite big, so we will not cover each and every problem possible; however, I will point you to the specific parts of the documentation, which will help you understand the topic even better.

EventGridTrigger in Azure Functions

In general, the easiest way to integrate Azure Functions with Azure Event Grid is to use HttpTrigger:

```
[FunctionName("HttpTriggerCSharp")]
public static async Task<HttpResponseMessage> Run(
    [HttpTrigger(AuthorizationLevel.Function, "get", "post", Route =
null)]HttpRequestMessage req,
    TraceWriter log)
{
    (...)
}
```

This is the most generic setup. It provides direct access to a request message and enables you to control its specific parts. There is, however, an alternative to the preceding setup—we can instead use `EventGridTrigger`:

```
[FunctionName("EventGridTriggerCSharp")]
public static void Run([EventGridTrigger]JObject eventGridEvent,
TraceWriter log)
{
    log.Info(eventGridEvent.ToString(Formatting.Indented));
}
```

With `EventGridTrigger` here, you can directly access the payload of a request, which is pretty useful if you are not interested in the remaining part of it. Additionally, you do not have to validate an endpoint. The preceding function can be used a bit differently if you use version 2 of the Azure Functions runtime:

```
[FunctionName("EventGridTest")]
public static void EventGridTest([EventGridTrigger]EventGridEvent
eventGridEvent, TraceWriter log)
{
    log.Info(eventGridEvent.Data.ToString());
}
```

As you can see, instead of binding to `JObject` here, you can access a well defined `EventGridEvent`.

It is possible to use `EventGridEvent` even with version 1 of the Azure Functions runtime. To do so, you have to manually reference `Microsoft.Azure.EventGrid.Models.EventGridEvent` by installing the `Microsoft.Azure.EventGrid` NuGet package.

You can easily create a function triggered by Event Grid using Azure Portal, as follows:

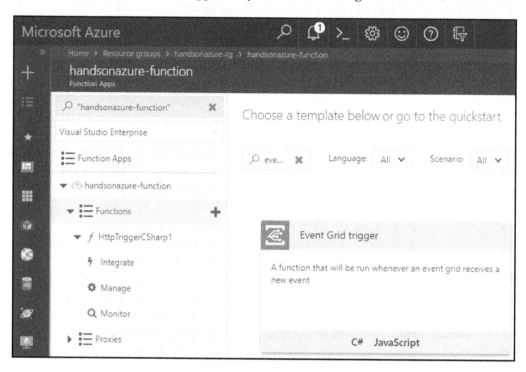

After creating the function, you will see a code snippet from where you can start working on the function. The important thing is to add the Event Grid subscription, which you will have to use to integrate the function with Azure Event Grid:

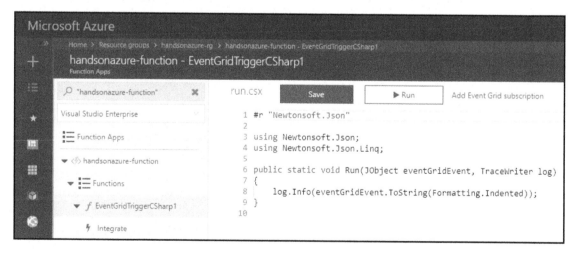

The generated code depends on the runtime version of your Function App—in my example, I used version 1, so I used `JObject` instead of `EventGridEvent`.

When you click on it, you will see a form that you can fill to create a subscription. In fact, it is very similar to the form you saw previously when creating a subscription from within the Event Grid instance:

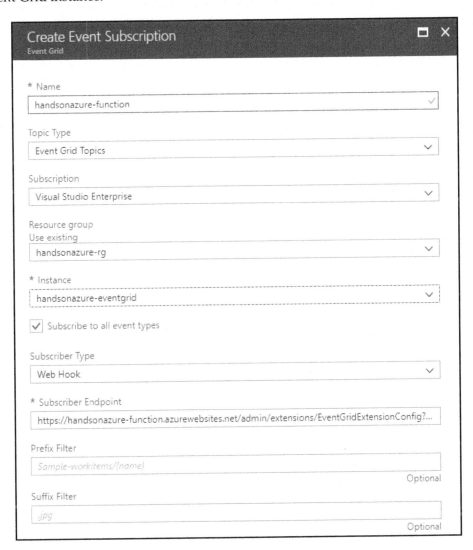

The only difference is that some fields are filled automatically. After creation of a subscription, you can test it by sending, for example, a custom event to Event Grid. What is more, a newly created subscription should be visible on the **Overview** blade of your Azure Event Grid instance:

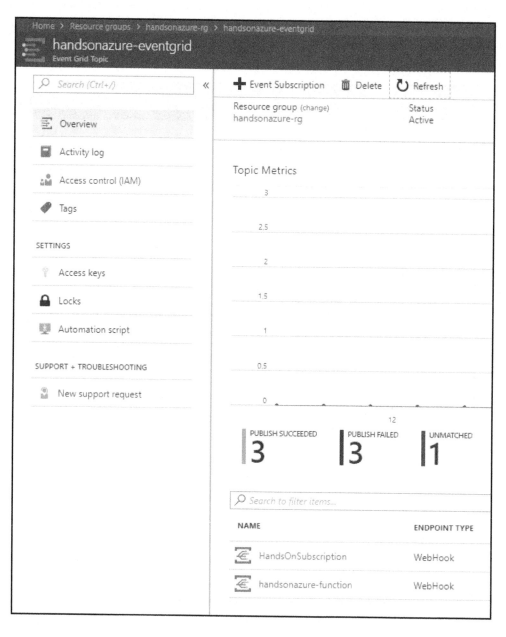

Testing Azure Event Grid and Azure Functions

You are probably thinking about the options for testing Azure Event Grid and Azure Functions locally. In fact, currently, you have two ways of doing this:

- Capturing and resending events to your application
- Using ngrok, available at `https://ngrok.com/`, to forward requests to your local computer

Which of these methods you choose will depend on your capabilities (for example, ngrok exposes your computer's port, so it can be a security concern), so you will have to figure out by yourself what the best option is. Both methods are described in the link mentioned in the *Further reading* section. However, there is one interesting feature of Azure Functions, which can be used to test Event Grid locally. It can be found under the following endpoint:

```
http://localhost:7071/admin/extensions/EventGridExtensionConfig?functionNam
e={functionname}
```

Here you can find an example request:

```
POST /admin/extensions/EventGridExtensionConfig?functionName=Function1
HTTP/1.1
Host: localhost:7071
Content-Type: application/json
aeg-event-type: Notification
Cache-Control: no-cache

[
  {
    "subject": "example",
    "id": "1",
    "eventType": "SectionFinished",
    "eventTime": "2018-08-12T07:41:00.9584103Z",
    "data":{
      "section": 3
    },
    "dataVersion": "1",
  }
]
```

Note one important thing here—you have to set `aeg-event-type` to `Notification`. If you fail to do so, you will receive an `HTTP 400` response. With such a setup, you can emulate how your function will behave when deployed to Azure.

Summary

In this chapter, you learned what reactive architecture is and how to use it with Azure Event Grid. You integrated different event producers with event handlers, and used custom topics to publish custom events. What is more, you now have the knowledge of how to integrate Azure Event Grid with Azure Functions and test it locally.

This chapter ends the second part of the book, which has been on serverless services and architectures. In the next part, we will cover different storage options and messaging and monitoring services, which will broaden your proficiency with Azure even more.

Questions

1. What are the supported event schemas in Azure Event Grid?
2. How can you authorize a request to an Event Grid endpoint when posting a custom event?
3. What has to be returned when validating an endpoint?
4. When will an endpoint not have to be validated?
5. What happens if an endpoint doesn't return a success response?
6. How can you filter events in Azure Event Grid?
7. How can you test Event Grid integration with Azure Functions?

Further reading

- Azure Storage V2 accounts: https://docs.microsoft.com/en-us/azure/storage/common/storage-account-options#general-purpose-v2-accounts
- Azure CLI: https://docs.microsoft.com/en-us/cli/azure/azure-cli-extensions-list?view=azure-cli-latest
- CloudEvents standard specification: https://cloudevents.io/
- Event delivery in Azure Event Grid: https://docs.microsoft.com/en-us/azure/event-grid/manage-event-delivery
- Azure Function Azure Event Grid binding: https://docs.microsoft.com/en-us/azure/azure-functions/functions-bindings-event-grid

Using Azure Storage - Tables, Queues, Files, and Blobs

11

PaaS in Azure is not only about App Services or containers. This particular cloud offers much more, especially when talking about different options for storage, messaging solutions, or monitoring. With services such as Event Hub, Azure Storage, or Application Insights, we're given a complete set of cloud components that offer great flexibility and simplify developing complete, scalable, and easy-to-maintain applications.

The following topics will be covered in this chapter:

- Using Azure Storage solutions
- Storing structured data with Azure Storage Tables
- Implementing fully managed file shares with Azure Storage Files
- Using queues with Azure Storage Queues
- Using Azure Storage Blobs for object storage

Technical requirements

To perform the exercises in this chapter, you will need the following:

- An Azure subscription
- Visual Studio 2017
- Azure Storage Explorer, available at `https://azure.microsoft.com/en-us/features/storage-explorer/`
- Azure Storage Emulator, available at `https://azure.microsoft.com/en-us/downloads/`

Using Azure Storage in a solution

Most applications cannot work without a storage solution. This can be any kind of database—relational, document, file, or graph. Most of them require some skills to be able to configure and start working with them. For now, we have covered one storage solution available in Azure, namely Azure Cosmos DB, which is a serverless database, where the only thing needed was to set a correct throughput value. Of course, Azure offers much more in the way of storage services, of which the most common is Azure Storage. It is a PaaS cloud component (though some define it as serverless, mostly because of a lack of servers) which can be used in four different ways. In this chapter, we will cover all of them, so you will be familiar with their capabilities and features.

Different Azure Storage services

Azure Storage is consists of four different services:

- Table Storage
- Queue Storage
- Blob Storage
- Azure Files

They all serve different purposes and offer different capabilities and limits. While their names are self-explanatory, you will see that each is a completely different service, and though they can be used in connection with each other, they require a different set of skills to be able to do this efficiently, and you need to use best practices. Additionally, Azure Storage offers an additional service called disk storage, which is a feature used by virtual machines. Because of that, it will not be covered in this book. Nonetheless, you can find a link to documentation in the *Further reading* section.

Different types of storage account

Azure Storage offers three different types of storage account:

- **General-purpose Standard**: Supporting tables, blobs, files, and queues, and three different types of blob: block blobs, page blobs, and append blobs
- **General-purpose Premium**: Limited to blobs only, and supporting page blobs
- **Blob storage with hot/cool access tiers**: Limited to blobs only and supporting block blobs and append blobs

You will learn more about different kinds of blob in the next sections. The question, for now, is: what is the difference between the standard and premium accounts—besides pricing of course? You can define them as follows:

- **Standard**: The most common choice with reasonable performance and support for all types of data. These accounts use magnetic disks for storage.
- **Premium**: Accounts with better performance, thanks to the use of SSD disks—recommended for VMs and when you require quick access to data stored on them.

If you would like to compare performance for both types of accounts, here is a comparison for 128 GB disks:

- **Standard**: 500 I/O operations / sec, throughput 50 MB / sec, €3,78 per month
- **Premium**: 500 I/O operations / sec, throughput 100 MB / sec, €15,12 per month

So, as you can see, the **Premium** option offers roughly twice the throughput over **Standard**.

Securing Azure Storage

In general, there are two ways of securing access to your Storage Accounts:

- Azure AD with RBAC
- SAS tokens

Additionally, blobs can be accessed publicly (of course, only if you decide to do so). Depending on your needs, one option or another may cover your requirements—this, of course, depends on the characteristics of your application. The following is the difference between those two methods of securing Azure Storage:

- **RBAC**: This method is used to secure management operations on your accounts. You can restrict access to specific features of a service to only a specific group defined in Azure AD. However, you are unable to use this method to secure a blob or a table (although you can do it indirectly by securing access to an SAS token).
- **SAS tokens**: These are long strings, which store different parameters describing access to a resource. They specify a service type, permissions, and the lifetime of a token, or restrict access to an IP address.

Here is an example of an SAS token:

```
https://myaccount.blob.core.windows.net/securecontainer/blob.txt?sv=2015-04
-05&st=2015-04-29T22%3A18%3A26Z&se=2015-04-30T02%3A23%3A26Z&sr=b&sp=rw&sip=
168.1.5.60-168.1.5.70&spr=https&sig=Z%2FRHIX5Xcg0Mq2rqI3OlWTjEg2tYkboXr1P9Z
UXDtkk%3D
```

As you can see, it restricts access to a `blob.txt` file stored as a blob
in the `securecontainer` container. It defines parameters, such as service version (`sv`),
expiry time (`se`), or the actual signature of a token (`sig`). In general, with SAS tokens, you
are able to restrict access to either an account or a service (and thanks to that also, for
example, to a range of entities in Table Storage).

Replication

When using a cloud, you have to expect that any service can be down at anytime.
Although Azure Storage is considered one of the most durable services (because many
services in Azure rely on it), it is possible that it will face an outage. To mitigate problems
related to such failures, it offers four different kinds of replication:

- **Locally-redundant storage (LRS)**: Three copies of your data within the same
  data center
- **Zone-redundant storage (ZRS)**: Three copies of your data within the same region
- **Geo-redundant storage (GRS)**: Three copies of your data within the same data
  center plus three copies in another region
- **Read-access geo-redundant storage (RA-GRS)**: Three copies of your data within
  the same data center plus three copies in another region with the ability to read
  from that region

When architecting an application using Azure Storage, you have to carefully design its
availability requirements. Depending on your expectations, a different model may suit you
better.

 When using a model that replicates data to another data center (basically
GRS and RA-GRS), take into account the cost of transferring data between
different regions.

You may wonder how durable LRS is compared to other replication models. To define that, you have to understand how data is stored within a single data center. In fact, disks for Azure Storage are installed within racks, which build a bigger concept known as a stamp. Stamps are configured in such a way that they use different power lines and networks, and thanks to such a setup, it is possible to store copies of your data in different fault domains, ensuring that if one fails, the other two will still work. Microsoft states that LRS is designed to provide at least 99.999999999% durability. If that is not enough, you may consider other models.

When using RA-GRS, do not take for granted the ability to easily write to the secondary region if an outage occurs. It is Microsoft's responsibility to initiate a failover (as opposed to, for instance, Azure Cosmos DB, where it was your decision), so **recovery time objective (RTO)** consists of both time for Microsoft to make a decision, and time to change DNS entries to point to another region.

Storing data with Azure Storage Tables

We will start our journey with Azure Storage capabilities by learning something about Table Storage. If you want to store unstructured data with almost limitless capacity and with high demands regarding availability and durability, this service is for you. In this section, you will learn how to start developing applications using Table Storage and the best practices for storing data and achieving the best performance for both writing and reading it. You will also see how to efficiently query it, and what is important when designing services using this Azure Storage capability.

Creating an Azure Storage service

To get started, we have to actually create an instance of Azure Storage. To do so, please following these steps:

1. Go to Azure Portal and click on **+ Create a resource**. Search for `storage account` and click on the **Create** button.

2. You will see a typical form, where you have to configure a new instance of a service. The following is an example of what I chose:

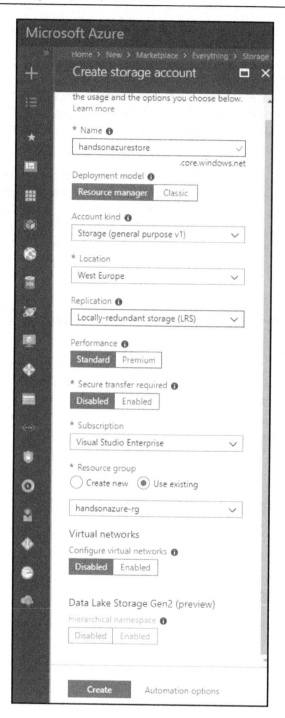

Now I would like to describe some more mystique options available here:

- **Deployment model**: You can select a different deployment model depending on your current requirements. In general, for almost every new storage account, you will select **Resource manager** as the default option. **Classic** mode is designed for legacy deployments, which use classic virtual networks. This choice also limits available options when it comes to selecting **Account kind** and some additional features such as **Performance** tier.

- **Account kind**: You have three options available here (general purpose, V1/V2, and blob). If you would like to use your storage account with multiple capabilities (tables, queues, blobs), select storage. Selecting V2 gives you the possibility to define an access tier (cool or hot), which is directly connected to the frequency of accessing data stored within an account.

- **Secure transfer required**: With Azure Storage it is possible to require a secure connection if this option is enabled. Turn it on for your production workloads, so no-one will be able to access data stored within an account using, for example, HTTP instead of HTTPS.

- **Performance**: It is possible to select either the **Standard** or **Premium** performance tier. As mentioned previously, this impacts hardware used to provision your service with common magnetic disks for the **Standard** tier and SSDs for **Premium**.

- **Virtual networks**: As in many other services, Azure Storage can be provisioned within a virtual network, limiting access to it even more.

When everything is set and ready, you can click on the **Create** button and wait a moment—your account will be created and soon you will be able to start working with it.

Managing Table Storage

When you go to the **Overview** blade, you will see a dashboard with basic information available regarding your account:

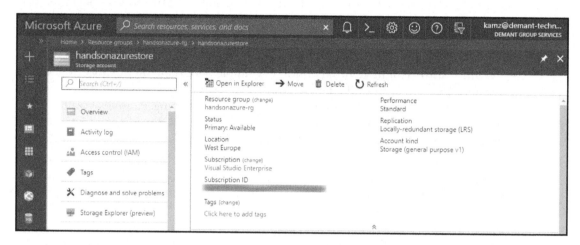

As you can see, it displays the information you defined while creating it, such as location, performance tier, or replication type. Additionally, when you scroll down, you will see the **Monitoring** section, where you can see how the whole service works:

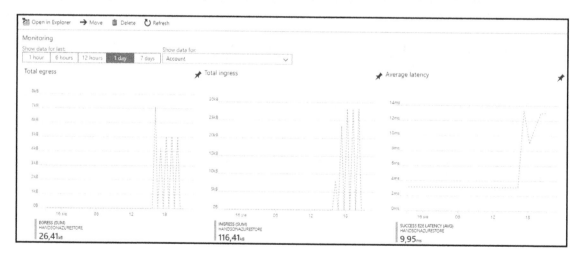

In this section, we are covering Table Storage, so find the **Tables** blade on the left and click on it. Initially, you should see no tables at all—of course, this is something we expected as this instance of a service has been just provisioned. Nonetheless, this is one of the methods to check what is actually stored within an account:

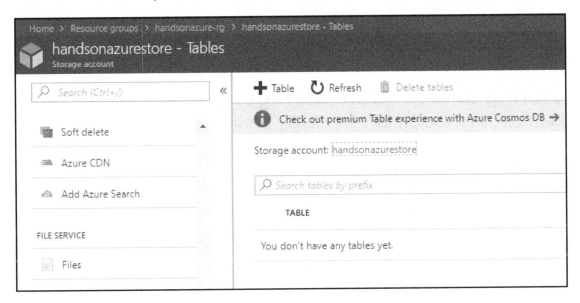

To create a new table, simply click on the **+ Table** button—you will be asked to provide a table name, which is all that is needed to get started. As you probably remember, I described Table Storage as the capability for storing unstructured data. This is the reason why there are no other options for starting with a table—you simply rely on the internal specification of how this service works. The following shows what it looks like when a new container is created:

The preceding screenshot shows an `orders` table and its URL—you may wonder what this URL is all about. As there are multiple ways to manage and use Azure services, Azure Storage allows you to use its capabilities using different methods, such as REST, Powershell, Azure CLI, or Azure Portal. When using SDKs and reading their source code, you could find that they are just wrappers around simple a REST API. This makes this particular service superbly easy to get started and work with on a daily basis. We have talked a little bit about Tables basics—now it is time to describe their schema.

Storing data in Table Storage

Each record in Table Storage has a row structure with multiple columns. Each row has the following base columns:

- `PartitionKey`: Identifier of a partition of a row
- `RowKey`: The row's identifier
- `Timestamp`: This column tells you when a row was recently modified
- `ETag`: Table Storage implements the optimistic concurrency model and uses ETags to control whether an entity should be modified or not

Of course, you are not limited to the columns listed above—you can create any additional columns you want and give each a specified type. However, before we go any further, you have to fully understand the implications of such a design. Here you can find an example of entities stored within a single table:

2018-07-13T11:56:11.108Z

PartitionKey	RowKey	Timestamp	Name	Price	Created	CustomerId	Quantity
Order	16Hbs6gs8s	2018-07-13T11:56:11.108Z			2018-07-13T11:36:11.108Z	customer-001	
16Hbs6gs8s	1	2018-07-13T11:57:17.108Z	Sponge	3.00	2018-07-13T11:36:11.108Z		3

In the preceding example, you data is stored within multiple partitions and though a single table is used, multiple schemas still can work, so there is no need to use additional containers. Additionally, I used a simple pattern, which allows you to introduce 1:n relationship—each order has a unique `RowKey`, which can be used as a partition key for entities related to it (allowing for really easy querying of data).

PartitionKey

Table Storage uses partitions to distribute, load, and handle requests. The number of partition keys within a table impacts the ability to balance them. It is possible to use a single partition per table, but in most cases, this is an invalid approach, which will lower the performance of your storage account. Partition keys are limited to 1 KB in size and have to be unique within a table (so once an entity is assigned a partition key, all others that use the same value will be stored in the same storage). They also have to be strings.

RowKey

Each row key is a unique identifier of a row within a partition (so you can have rows using the same RowKey column value as long they have a different PartitionKey). More importantly, each table is sorted in ascending using values of row keys. This requires a smart design when you need, for example, to read only a selection of the top rows and do not want to provide their row keys (we will cover that later in this chapter). Like PartitionKey, RowKey is also limited to 1 KB and has to be a string.

Timestamp

This column is maintained server-side and is a DateTime value that is changed each time an entity is modified. It is also internally used to provide optimistic concurrency, and cannot be modified. Even if you set it, the value will be ignored.

General rules for entities

Table Storage has some hard limitations when it comes to storing data:

- The maximum number of columns is 255
- The maximum size of an entity is 1 MB
- By default, each entity column is created as a type string—this can be overridden when it is created
- It is not possible to store null as a value—if you do not provide a column value, an entity will be considered as if it does not have it at all

Querying data in Table Storage

To query data in Table Storage, you will need a simple application (it can be a console application) and an SDK for this service. You will also need an instance of Azure Storage—it can be either the one provisioned in Azure, or a local one, if you installed Storage Emulator.

 To get started with Storage Emulator, simply search for an executable (for example, **Start** I type Storage Emulator) and run it. It will initially create a database for storing data and run in the background, so you will not have to worry about accidentally closing it.

To get started, we have to install the WindowsAzure.Storage package using NuGet Package Manager. It has everything that is needed to start working with Azure Storage in .NET. Here you can find an example of code for creating a table:

```
using Microsoft.WindowsAzure.Storage;

namespace TableStorage
{
    internal class Program
    {
        private static void Main()
        {
            var storageAccount = CloudStorageAccount.Parse("<connection-
string>");
            var tableClient = storageAccount.CreateCloudTableClient();
            var table = tableClient.GetTableReference("orders");
            table.CreateIfNotExists();
        }
    }
}
```

We can briefly describe what this code does:

1. It parses a connection string so it can be used in the following methods
2. It creates an instance of CloudTableClientclass, which is the main class for working with Table Storage
3. It gets a reference to a table order, whether it exists or not
4. Finally, it creates an orders table, if does not exist already

You could also use the `Create()` method instead of `CreateIfNotExists()`, although, it could break if a table has been already created.

Now we need to get a connection string, so depending on the storage account you would like to use you either:

- Have to go to Azure Portal, find your storage account, and copy a connection string from **Access keys** blade
- Use the `UseDevelopmentStorage=true` value for connecting with Storage Emulator

When you execute an application, a table should be created without a problem. Now, when we have a table, we would like to actually insert something in it. To do so, you will need the following code:

```
var op = TableOperation.Insert(new DynamicTableEntity("orders",
Guid.NewGuid().ToString(), "*",
    new Dictionary<string, EntityProperty>
    {
      {"Created",
EntityProperty.GeneratePropertyForDateTimeOffset(DateTimeOffset.Now) },
      {"CustomerId",
EntityProperty.GeneratePropertyForString("Customer-001") }
    }));

table.Execute(op);
```

Here we are creating a new `TableOperation`, which accepts one argument that is an instance of `TableEntity`. `TableEntity` is a base class that contains all row properties, and has to be passed to a table (like `PartitionKey` or `RowKey`). Of course, instead of using `DynamicTableEntity`, you can derive from `TableEntity` and introduce a custom entity class.

In the preceding example, we used the `Insert()` operation, which may not be the best choice for concurrent requests. In such a scenario, it is sometimes better to use `InsertOrReplace()` or `InsertOrMerge()`.

The last thing to do is to query a table. To do so in .NET, you will need something like this:

```
var query = new TableQuery();
var result = table.ExecuteQuery(query);

foreach (var entity in result)
{
Console.WriteLine($"{entity.PartitionKey}|{entity.RowKey}|{entity.Timestamp
}|{entity["Created"].DateTimeOffsetValue}|{entity["CustomerId"].StringValue
}");
}
```

We just executed a basic query, which will return all rows from a table. While it works now, it is not the best idea to query all data within a table using such a query—in most cases, you will use something like the following:

```
var query =
  new TableQuery().Where(
    TableQuery.GenerateFilterCondition("PartitionKey",
QueryComparisons.Equal, "orders"));
```

The preceding query will return all rows in a table that have an `orders` partition key. Such queries can be extended as you wish by generating further filter conditions.

 Remember that to achieve the best performance, your queries should include both `PartitionKey` and `RowKey`. Using `PartitionKey` only leads to worse results, but is still acceptable. Using only `RowKey` will result in reading the whole partition anyway. Not using those columns will result in reading the whole table.

You can also check what is stored in a table using Azure Storage Explorer:

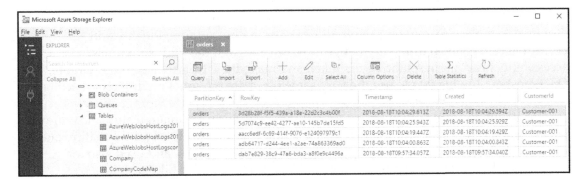

Table API in Azure Cosmos DB

It is possible to leverage the premium offering for Table Storage using Azure Cosmos DB. Using that option has the following advantages:

- Automatic and manual failovers.
- Secondary indexes (the ability to index against all properties inside a row).
- Independent scaling across multiple regions.
- Different consistency levels.
- Dedicated throughput per table.

While failover can be achieved using Table Storage only, the rest of the presented features are available only for Azure Cosmos DB, and can be a great solution when you like the simplicity of this service and still want to challenge it against more complicated scenarios.

Implementing fully managed file shares with Azure Files

When in need of creating a file share, which can be accessed by different people, you often have to either buy some hardware, which will be set up and configured for such functionality, or use third-party solutions, which can be hard to customize, or expensive. With Azure Storage, you can quickly develop a solution that is almost limitless in terms of capacity, offers industry standard protocols, and can be quickly provisioned, and ready to use.

Azure Files concepts

Azure Files has some basic concepts that create the whole picture of a service. In fact, it is designed to replace current on-premise file servers in terms of functionality and performance. The main difference between Azure Files and the "old" solution is accessibility (as you can set the access token and make the URL private). What is more, it is OS-agnostic, allowing you to use the very same file share mounted on different machines using Linux, Windows, or macOS. It, of course, shares other Azure Storage concepts, so you can use it with the same reliability and durability assurance. The main feature of Azure Files is support for the SMB protocol. This is a very common protocol (and a mature one, as it was designed in the mid-1980s) for sharing computer resources, and used also for printers, and other network devices. We could summarize Azure Files as follows:

- **Fully managed**: This is a full cloud service, where you do not have to worry about the OS or its configuration.
- **Durability and resiliency**: With Azure Files you do not have to worry about not having access to data stored and securing your resources against power failures, and other outages.
- **Common dev tools**: Accessing Azure Files is easy, thanks to the system I/O APIs, appropriate SDKs, or even REST APIs.

Working with Azure Files

When you go to Azure Portal and open your Azure Storage instance, you can find the Files blade. It is very similar to the one that will be discussed for Blob Storage. It displays a list of available file shares, as seen in the following screenshot:

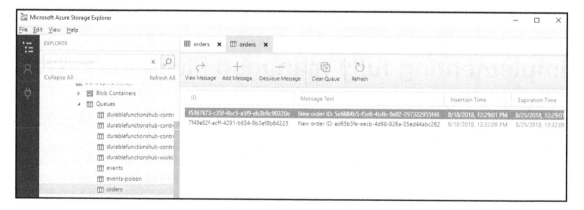

From this screen, you have the ability to create a new one by clicking on the **+ File share** button. The important thing here is the value of the **Quota** field—it determines the maximum capacity of a file share.

> The maximum value for the quota of a file share is 5,120 GB.

To get information about how to connect to a file share, you can click on the **more** button on the right and select **Connect**:

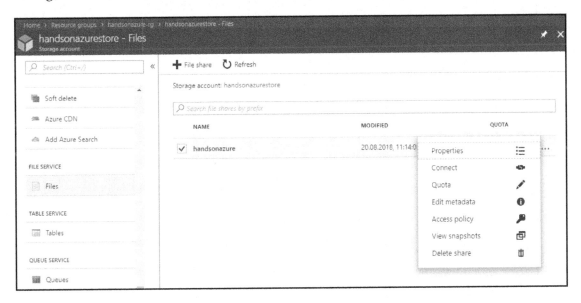

It will display some short instructions about how it is possible to quickly connect from your computer to a specific file share. Here you can find an example of a command for Windows written in PowerShell:

```
$acctKey = ConvertTo-SecureString -String "<key>" -AsPlainText -Force
$credential = New-Object System.Management.Automation.PSCredential -
ArgumentList "Azure\handsonazurestore", $acctKey
New-PSDrive -Name Z -PSProvider FileSystem -Root
"\\handsonazurestore.file.core.windows.net\handsonazure" -Credential
$credential -Persist
```

You can specify the letter of a drive using the `-Name` parameter (in the preceding example it is `Z`).

Mapping a drive is an operation that may require additional permissions—make sure you are running all these commands as an administrator.

Now I can compare the contents of my file share displayed in Azure portal:

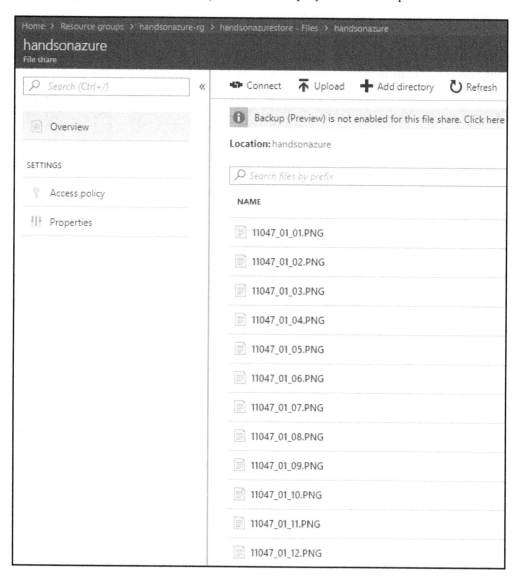

With my mounted disk on a virtual machine:

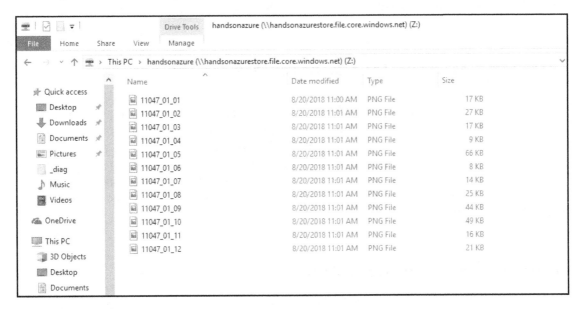

The whole setup took only a few minutes—this is the strength of this service, as normally I would need many hours to set everything up and achieve the same level of portability and reliability. It also gives you unlimited storage capacity—nothing blocks you from attaching multiple Azure Files shares and storing all your files on them.

Blob Storage versus Azure Files

In fact, both Azure Blob Storage and Azure Files have a similar purpose—you create them to store and share files. There are, however, some fundamental differences between them when it comes to use cases, for example:

- If you want to create a common file share space for your company, you will use Azure Files
- If you want to have a space for files uploaded by your users via, for example, your website, you will use Blob Storage
- If you want to have your files completely private, you will use Azure Files
- If you want to configure security on a blob or a containers level, you will use Blob Storage

Both services also have different pricing models (for example, Azure Files is much more expensive when it comes to paying for each GB of data).

Queues in Azure Queue Storage

Azure Storage—besides being a service for storing many different kinds of data—can be used also as a queue. Queue Storage is another capability that allows you to quickly develop a solution that requires a simple queue solution, and additionally is able to store in a queue millions of messages without affecting performance. In this section, you will see how to develop applications using Queue Storage and what is important when using this feature. Additionally, I assume that you already have a storage account. If not, take a look at the **Storing data with Azure Storage Tables** section, where I described the process of creating an account.

Queue Storage features

In general, Queue Storage has two use cases:

- Processing messages asynchronously
- Exchanging communications between different services (Azure Functions, legacy Web roles/Worker roles)

It is a very simple queue solution, which can store and process messages in any format that are limited to 64 KB. The retention time of a message is seven days—after that, it is lost. The capacity of a queue is basically equal to the capacity of your storage account. In general, you should not worry that you will run out of available space. Queue Storage shares many addition features, such as virtual networks, SAS tokens, and many more, with other Azure Storage capabilities. Therefore, we will not reintroduce them in this section.

Developing an application using Queue Storage

For the purpose of presenting Queue Storage, I created two applications:

- Producer
- Consumer

Producer will create and push messages, which will then be consumed by Consumer. Here you can find the code of the `Producer` app:

```
using System;
using Microsoft.WindowsAzure.Storage;
using Microsoft.WindowsAzure.Storage.Queue;

namespace QueueStorage.Producer
{
    internal class Program
    {
        private static void Main()
        {
            var storageAccount =
CloudStorageAccount.Parse("UseDevelopmentStorage=true");
            var queueClient = storageAccount.CreateCloudQueueClient();
            var queue = queueClient.GetQueueReference("orders");
            queue.CreateIfNotExists();

            var message = new CloudQueueMessage($"New order ID:
{Guid.NewGuid()}");
            queue.AddMessage(message);
        }
    }
}
```

And, of course the `Consumer` app:

```
using System;
using Microsoft.WindowsAzure.Storage;

namespace QueueStorage.Consumer
{
    internal class Program
    {
        private static void Main()
        {
            var storageAccount =
CloudStorageAccount.Parse("UseDevelopmentStorage=true");
            var queueClient = storageAccount.CreateCloudQueueClient();
            var queue = queueClient.GetQueueReference("orders");

            var message = queue.GetMessage();
            Console.WriteLine(message.AsString);
            Console.ReadLine();
        }
    }
}
```

When you publish a message to a queue, you can retrieve it at any time—as mentioned previously, you have seven days to fetch it from a queue. Here you can find how a message looks like when stored in a queue:

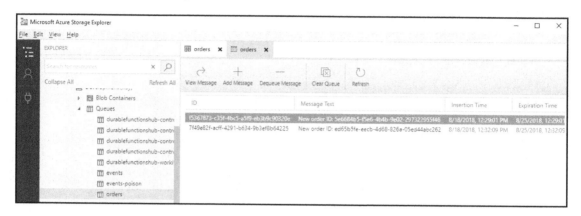

Object storage solution – Azure Storage Blobs

The last capability of Azure Storage is Blob Storage. In the previous sections, we were using this service to store unstructured data using Table Storage, push messages to a queue with Queue Storage, and create file shares, thanks to File Storage. In the last section of this chapter, we will focus on developing solutions that store so-called blobs. You may wonder what exactly a blob is—well, there is no single definition for that. In general. blobs are files of different types, such as text files, images, or audio. You will see how to use them in your applications, how to secure them, and how you can achieve the maximum performance.

Blob Storage concepts

Before we go deeper into the service, you will have to understand the basic concepts of Blob Storage. Here you can find a diagram that clearly defines three main topics:

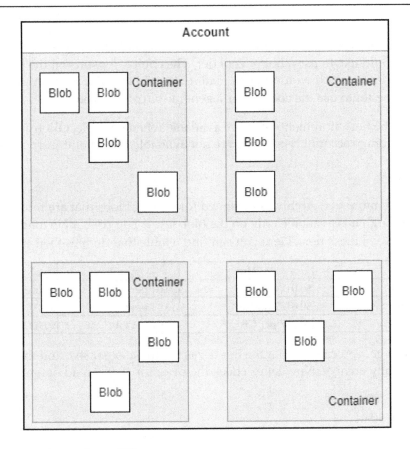

As you can see, we have three different concepts:

- **Account**: Which is basically your Storage Account and stores all data within a Blob Storage.
- **Container**: Which is a logical entity holding an unlimited amount of blobs inside it. An account can have an unlimited amount of containers.
- **Blob**: A file stored within a container.

Additionally, there are three different types of blob:

- **Block blob**: Text or binary data with a maximum size of 4.7 TB. Such a blob is made of smaller blocks.
- **Append blobs**: A more specific type of blob, which is the best for scenarios such as logging data, or storing events or transactional logs. They are optimized for append operations.
- **Page blobs**: Designed for storing VHD files used by VMs.

With the newest version of Storage Accounts (v2), it is possible to use the latest features of this service. One of the most interesting additions is access tiers. Now it is possible to select whether you would like to use a hot or cool tier. The choice depends on the frequency of accessing your data—if you would like to read it often, hot will be the best choice, otherwise, it is better to use the cool tier or a general-purpose account.

> The tiers aforementioned are available when you select Blob as your storage account type. They are not available for general-purpose accounts.

There is also one more tier; Archive—designed for storing blobs that are rarely accessed—although it is available only on the blob level. You probably wonder about the differences between these tiers. Here you can find a table that defines their pricing:

	Hot	Archive	Cool
First 50 TB/month	$0.0184 per GB	$0.01 per GB	$0.002 per GB
Next 450 TB/month	$0.0177 per GB	$0.01 per GB	$0.002 per GB
Over 500 TB/month	$0.017 per GB	$0.01 per GB	$0.002 per GB

In terms of storage, you can see that the hot tier is the most expensive and the rest are much cheaper, especially archive. Now let us check the price for 10,000 read operations:

- **Hot**: $0.004
- **Cool**: $0.01
- **Archive**: $5

Ouch—the difference is huge here! This is why selecting the correct tier is so important—you may end up with a solution that costs many, many dollars, only because you misused the Blob Storage tier.

Inserting data into Blob Storage

Now we will try to actually add something to our Blob Storage. Here you can find a piece of code that allows you to upload a single file to a container:

```
using System;
using Microsoft.WindowsAzure.Storage;

namespace BlobStorage
{
    internal class Program
```

```
    {
        private static void Main()
        {
            var storageAccount =
CloudStorageAccount.Parse("UseDevelopmentStorage=true");
            var cloudBlobClient = storageAccount.CreateCloudBlobClient();
            var container =
cloudBlobClient.GetContainerReference("handsonazure");

            container.CreateIfNotExists();

            var blob = container.GetBlockBlobReference("foo.txt");
            blob.UploadText("This is my first blob!");

            Console.ReadLine();
        }
    }
}
```

As in the previous examples, this one looks pretty similar. You will need to follow these steps:

1. Firstly you have to create an instance of `CloudStorageAccount`
2. Then you need to obtain a reference to a container, and create it if it does not exist
3. Finally, you have to get a reference to a blob, and upload some contents

If I open Azure Storage Explorer, I can see that a new blob was uploaded to a container:

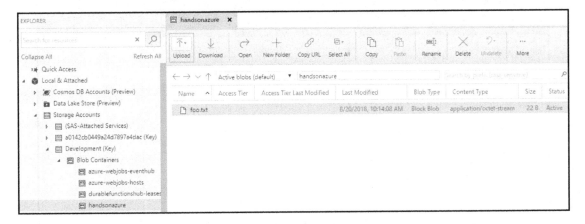

Of course, if I open the file, I will see that it contains the text that I uploaded:

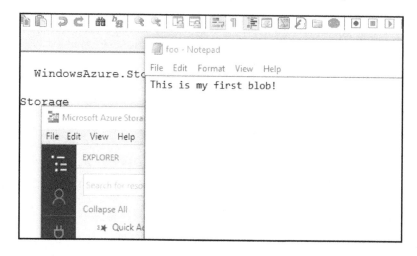

Containers and permissions

It is possible to select a proper access level when it comes to accessing a container stored within Blob Storage. If you go to Azure Portal and open your Azure Storage service, you can find the **Blobs** blade. Inside it, you can click on the **+ Container** button, which will open a small window:

As you can see, besides providing a name for a container, you can select **Public access level**. Currently, you have three different options available:

- **Private**: For no anonymous access
- **Blob**: Anonymous access on a blob level
- **Container**: Anonymous access on a container level

You can click on a container you created to see another screen, where you can manage it. I will use it to actually upload a file to see what other options become available. Here you can find what it will look in the portal when a file is uploaded and I click on it:

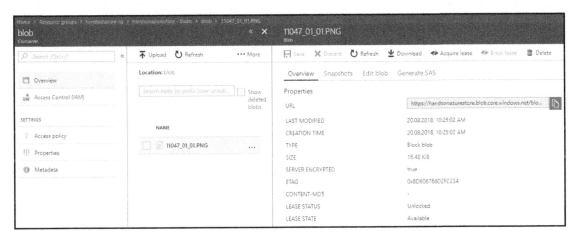

Now I can see additional metadata regarding a file, manage like acquiring leases, or generate an SAS token.

If you want to make a file read-only, click on the **Acquire lease** button—while it will still be possible to change it, such an action will require providing a lease ID.

What is more, there is a **URL** property available, which can be used to access a blob directly, for example, using a browser. Here you can find how it looks like in my case:

```
https://handsonazurestore.blob.core.windows.net/blob/11047_01_01.PNG
```

Now you may wonder what the difference is between **Blob** and **Container** access. To find out, we will use the following code:

```
using System;
using Microsoft.WindowsAzure.Storage.Blob;

namespace BlobStorage
{
    internal class Program
    {
        private static void Main()
        {
            var container = new CloudBlobContainer(new Uri("<container-
uri>"));

            var blobs = container.ListBlobs();

            foreach (var blob in blobs)
            {
                Console.WriteLine(blob.Uri);
            }

            Console.ReadLine();
        }
    }
}
```

I already created two different containers—one with **Blob** access, one with **Container**. If I execute the preceding code for a container with full public access, the following is what I will see:

```
C:\MINE\HandsOnAzure\Chapter11\AzureStorage\BlobStorage\bin\Debug\BlobStorage.exe
https://handsonazurestore.blob.core.windows.net/container/11047_01_01.PNG
```

Now let us run it for a container, which has public access for blobs only:

```
void Main()

er = new CloudBlobContainer(new Uri("https://handsonazurestore.blob.core.windows.net/blob"))
  container.ListBlobs();   blobs = {Microsoft.WindowsAzure.Storage.Core.Util.CommonUtility.<LazyEnumerable>

  blob in blobs)   ⊗ bs = {Microsoft.WindowsAzure.Storage.Core.Util.CommonUtility.<LazyEnumerable>d_0<Mic

.WriteLine(blob.U   Exception Unhandled                                              ⫫  ✕

dLine();              Microsoft.WindowsAzure.Storage.StorageException: 'The remote server
                      returned an error: (404) Not Found.'

                      Inner Exception
                      WebException: The remote server returned an error: (404) Not Found.

                      View Details | Copy Details
                      ▷ Exception Settings
```

As you can see, container-level operations are unavailable when its access level is blob or private. Of course, if you authorize using, for instance, an access key, you will list all blobs within a container, even if it is private. Of course, it is also possible to set a container-level permission directly from your code:

```
using System;
using Microsoft.WindowsAzure.Storage;
using Microsoft.WindowsAzure.Storage.Blob;

namespace BlobStorage
{
    internal class Program
    {
        private static void Main()
        {
            var storageAccount =
CloudStorageAccount.Parse("UseDevelopmentStorage=true");
            var cloudBlobClient = storageAccount.CreateCloudBlobClient();
            var container = cloudBlobClient.GetContainerReference("blob");

container.CreateIfNotExists(BlobContainerPublicAccessType.Blob);

            var blob = container.GetBlockBlobReference("foo.txt");
            blob.UploadText("This is my first blob!");

            Console.ReadLine();
```

```
        }
    }
}
```

Blob Storage: additional features

One of the newest and coolest features of Blob Storage is the **Soft delete** feature. It allows you to perform an operation called a soft delete. What does this mean? In some cases, you may want to delete a file, but have the ability to easily revert the deletion within a fixed time period. In Blob Storage, that option is available via the **Soft delete** blade:

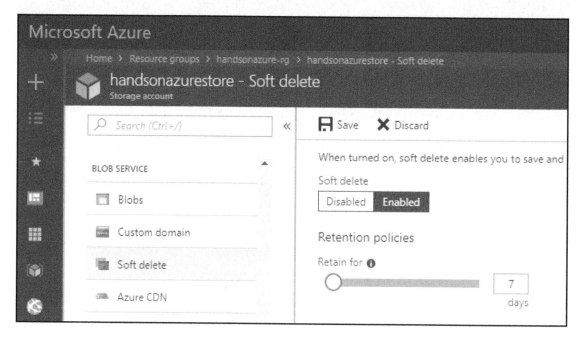

If you turn it on, any deleted blob will still be available within storage (but not for retrieval or modification) for a set number of days. Blob Storage also has two additional features, which can be used with two other Azure services:

- **Azure CDN**: A Content Delivery Network service for serving static content to your customers—we will cover this later in the book.
- **Azure Search**: As already discussed, here you can easily set your Blob Storage as a data source for a search engine.

So as you can see, this is a very flexible and useful Azure Storage capability, which can be used for file storage, as an Azure Search document store, a logs database, and much, much more.

Summary

In this chapter, you have learned some basics regarding one of the most important services in Azure—Azure Storage. We developed a few solutions for Tables, Queues, Files, and Blobs—each enabling you to do different things, from asynchronous message processing to creating file shares. You also read about different redundancy models and how reliable and durable this particular service is. In the *Further reading* section, you will find plenty of additional resources, which will allow you to build even more skills for working with this Azure service, such as Table Storage patterns, performance targets, and a REST API reference. In the following chapters, you will learn something about data processing services, such as Azure Event Hub and Azure Stream Analytics.

Questions

1. What tiers are available during account creation when selecting **Blob** as an account type?
2. What must you include in a query against Table Storage to achieve the maximum performance?
3. What are the available redundancy models for storage accounts?
4. What is the difference between blob and file storage?
5. Can you store binary files using Blob Storage?
6. How long does a message in Queue Storage live before it is removed?
7. What is the maximum size of a message in Queue Storage?
8. What is the maximum size of the `PartitionKey` column value?
9. What concurrency model is implemented in Table Storage?
10. What is the difference between Azure Files storage and on-premise filesystem?

Further reading

- **Disk storage:** https://docs.microsoft.com/en-us/azure/virtual-machines/windows/about-disks-and-vhds
- **SAS token reference:** https://docs.microsoft.com/en-us/azure/storage/common/storage-dotnet-shared-access-signature-part-1
- **ARM vs classic deployment:** https://docs.microsoft.com/en-us/azure/azure-resource-manager/resource-manager-deployment-model
- **Table Storage data model:** https://docs.microsoft.com/en-us/rest/api/storageservices/Understanding-the-Table-Service-Data-Model
- **Blob Storage pricing:** https://azure.microsoft.com/en-us/pricing/details/storage/blobs/
- **File Storage performance targets:** https://docs.microsoft.com/en-us/azure/storage/files/storage-files-scale-targets
- **Guidelines for Table Storage:** https://docs.microsoft.com/en-us/azure/storage/tables/table-storage-design-guidelines

Big Data Pipeline - Azure Event Hub

12

Azure Event Hub is one of the best solutions for introducing an entry point with almost limitless throughput. It's designed for big data workloads and is able to process millions of messages per second. It offers a very simple configuration, and thanks to the available SDK, you can easily adjust it to almost any solution developed in the cloud. It also integrates natively with other Azure components, making creating a whole platform hosted in the cloud a breeze.

The following topics will be covered in this chapter:

- Working efficiently with Azure Event Hub
- Different concepts such as publishers, partitions, throughput units, or consumer groups
- Azure Event Hub security concepts
- Azure Event Hub capture feature

Technical requirements

To perform the exercises in this chapter, you will need the following:

- Microsoft Azure subscription
- Visual Studio 2017

Azure Event Hub service and concepts

Nowadays, we gather more and more data, which has to be aggregated, processed, and stored somewhere. This implies using services that can handle increasing loads, scale to growing demands, and offer the smallest latency available. All these requirements are often mentioned when building so-called big data pipelines—parts of a system designed to process as much data as possible, so it is later accessible by tools such as Hadoop, Spark, ML, AI, and so on. If you are looking for a service in Azure that can handle millions of messages per second, Azure Event Hub is the right choice. In this chapter, you will learn the basics of this Azure component and get familiar with messaging solutions in Azure.

Azure Event Hub concepts

In general, Azure Event Hub is a simple service that is built on top of two concepts:

- Event publishers
- Event processor hosts

Of course, these are not the only topics we will cover here. However, before we proceed, I would like to focus a little bit on the distinction between a publisher and a processor:

- **Publisher**: This is an entity that sends data to an instance of Azure Event Hub. It can use one of the two available protocols (HTTP or AMQP) and is unaware of the current Event Hub capabilities.
- **Processor**: An entity that reads events from Azure Event Hub as they become available. It uses AMQP for communication and relies on additional concepts such as consumer groups and partitions.

The following shows how Azure Event Hub works:

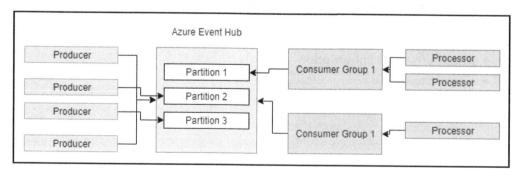

As you can see, there are an additional two concepts mentioned here:

- **Partition**: Each partition is an independent event log that stores data separately. In general, it is Event Hub's responsibility to ensure that each event sharing the same partition key is stored within the same partition in order. Of course, you can set this value by yourself—in such a scenario you have to make sure you are not overloading one specific partition.
- **Consumer group**: If you would like to allow separate processors to consume events separately, you have to use different consumer groups to do so.

As you can see, Azure Event Hub does not use things such as instance topics for distributing data—instead it acts as a single event pipeline that you can read anytime with high throughput. To define this value, Event Hub uses a concept named **throughput units** (**TU**). 1 TU is defined as follows:

- Up to 1 MB/s or 1,000 events for ingress
- Up to 2 MB/s or 4,096 events for egress

Note that Azure Event Hub shares TUs for all consumer groups you are using. If you have 1 TU and 5 consumer groups, the maximum egress will be divided among all consumers (so when all 5 read events at the same time, a maximum of 400 events per second will be available).

If you happen to exceed the available limit, Event Hub will start throttling your requests, finally returning `ServerBusyException`. This is, however, true only for incoming events—for egress you just cannot read more than the current TU value allows.

By default, you cannot have more than 20 TUs per Event Hub namespace. However, this is just a soft limit—you can extend it by contacting Azure support.

Now, let's focus a little bit on partitions. Each hub in Event Hub can have a maximum number of 32 partitions. You may wonder what this implies—in fact, this gives some additional options:

- Because each partition can have a corresponding consumer, by default, you can process messages in parallel using 32 consumers.
- Because you cannot change the number of partitions after the hub's creation, you have to carefully design it at the very beginning.

- Using the maximum number of partitions by default is not always the best option—it should reflect the number of readers you are planning to support. If you choose too many, they will start to race to acquire a lease on a partition.

The following shows globally how data could be stored among different partitions within a hub:

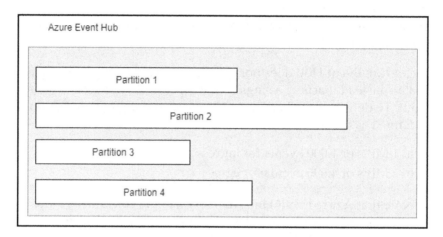

As mentioned earlier, each partition can grow independently—what is more, each one has an individual offset value. What is an offset value? You could think about it as a pointer to some specific point within a log—if it stores events numbered from 1 to 10,000 and you have read 1,000, an offset value will be 1,001. In such a case, it means that a reader should start reading data from the $1,001^{st}$ event.

In fact, offset and consumer groups are connected with each other conceptually—each consumer group has an individual offset value; that is why,by introducing it, you can read all available logs once more.

However, remember that to set an offset, a consumer has to perform a checkpoint. If it fails to do so, the next time it connects, it will read all the data once more. This is very important if you want to avoid processing duplicates—either you have to implement a very durable process for processing events, so you can be sure that a checkpoint will be performed even if something fails, or you need to have a mechanism for detecting duplicates.

If you have to do so, you can easily read previous events by providing the offset value you are interested in when starting a processor.

The last thing to consider for now is Azure Event Hub's retention policy for stored events. By default (or in other words, by using the Basic tier), events can be stored only for 24 hours to be consumed; after that period, they are lost. Of course, it is possible to extend it by using the Standard tier; you will have an option to do so up to a maximum of 7 days from event retention. In general, you should avoid using this service as some kind of a standard queue or cache—its main purpose is to provide functionality for aggregating thousands of messages per second and pushing them further.

Azure Event Hub durability

In many scenarios, Azure Event Hub is one of the main entry points to the system, making it a critical component that should be replicated and highly available. In this particular service, the geo-disaster recovery feature is available when selecting the standard tier and requires you to set up and configure the appropriate environment. To do so, you need to understand the following topics:

- **Alias**: Instead of providing multiple connection strings, you can use an alias to make a connection with a single stable one.
- **Failover**: This is the process of initiating a switch between namespaces.
- **Primary/secondary namespace**: When using the Azure Event Hub geo-disaster recovery feature, you have to define which namespace is the primary and which is the secondary one. The important thing here is that you can send events to both namespaces, but the second one remains passive—that means events from an active namespace are not transferred.

Now, to implement the feature in Event Hub, you can to do two things:

- Monitor your primary namespace to detect any anomalies
- Initiate failover

Of course, if a disaster occurs, you will have to create a new pairing after finishing a failover.

 You have to know the difference between outage, when there are temporary problems within a data center, and a disaster, which often means permanent damage and possible loss of data. The geo-disaster recovery feature is designed for disasters; in the case of an outage, you should implement another way of dealing with it, such as caching data locally.

Working with Azure Event Hub

Now that you are familiar with some basic concepts, we can proceed and start working with a real instance of Azure Event Hub. In this section, you will learn both how to create and access Event Hub in the Azure portal and work with it using its SDK. In fact, using this service is possible both from the portal (as many Azure components seamlessly integrate with it and no additional configuration is required) and by providing custom implementations of consumers that read and process data further.

Creating an Azure Event Hub in the Azure portal

To create an Azure Event Hub, we will start, as in most cases, by clicking on the **+ Create a resource** button. Enter `Event Hub` and select the service from the search results. Here, you can see an example of a configuration of my Event Hub instance:

Let's globally now focus on what we actually have here:

- **Name**: This is the unique name of your Event Hub instance. Note, it has to be unique among all others supported by Azure.
- **Pricing tier**: You can choose between Basic and Standard tiers. In fact, there is also one additional tier – Dedicated, which is, however, available only if you ask for it directly. The difference between Basic and Standard is quite huge in terms of capabilities and throughput; we will cover it in a second.
- **Enable Kafka**: This is a new feature, which allows you to use Azure Event Hub as if it was an **Apache Kafka** instance. Thanks to that, you are able to switch to this Azure service without the need to reconfigure applications communicating with your Kafka instances.
- **Make this namespace zone redundant**: If you wish, you can leverage availability zones for Event Hub and make the whole namespace zone redundant. This improves the availability of your instance of a service with no additional cost (you still have to pay for an additional instance, though). Currently, this feature is enabled for three locations – Central US, East US 2, and France Central.
- **Subscription**: A subscription where an instance will be created.
- **Resource group**: In which RG, an instance of Event Hub, will be created.
- **Location**: In which region Azure Event Hub will be created.
- **Throughput Units**: This setting defines the throughput of the whole namespace. In Azure, each instance of Event Hub shares available TUs between all other hubs in a namespace. You can change the value later, depending on your needs.
- **Enable Auto-Inflate**: Instead of manually scaling the throughput of your namespace, you can enable Auto-Inflate. This feature scales up your namespace automatically as the load grows. Note, however, that it will not scale it down automatically. By enabling it, you can also define the maximum value of TUs, so you will not be charged more than you are supposed to.

 Remember that you are charged for each TU—that means that if you selected the Basic tier and require 10 TUs, you will pay 9.41 EUR * 10 = 94.1 EUR per month!

When you click on the **Create** button, Azure will take care of creating an instance of Azure Event Hub for you.

Working with Azure Event Hub in the portal

The following screenshot shows a brand-new instance of Azure Event Hub:

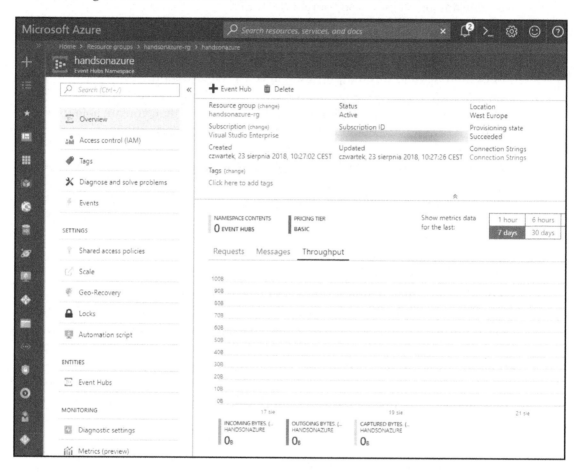

As you can see, it contains some basic info such as metrics, metadata, and access to connection strings. Of course, this is a view of a namespace—we have not created any Event Hub yet. Before we do so, I would like to focus a little on what we have available now. On the left, you can find the **SETTINGS** section, which contains additional features:

- **Shared access policies**: In Azure Event Hub, access policies have two levels—they are assigned either for a namespace or for a hub. With them, you are able to share an access key with a combination of three permissions—Manage, Listen, and Send.
- **Scale**: If you feel that you need more throughput, you can go to this blade and scale a namespace up (or down if you need fewer TUs). From that screen, you can also change the tier – for example, select Standard to be able to use Auto-Inflate.
- **Geo-recovery**: If you have a requirement to make your Event Hub highly available and you selected Standard tier, from this blade you will able to initiate pairing with another region.

Now let's create a hub:

1. Click on the **Event Hubs** blade:

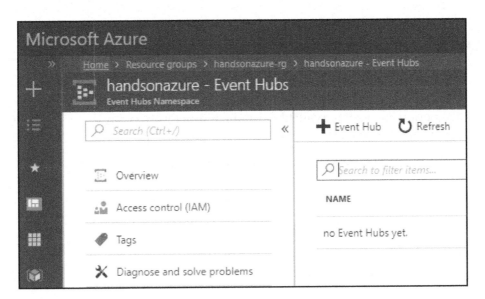

2. Click on the **+ Event Hub** button to see a form that enables you to configure a
   new instance of a hub:

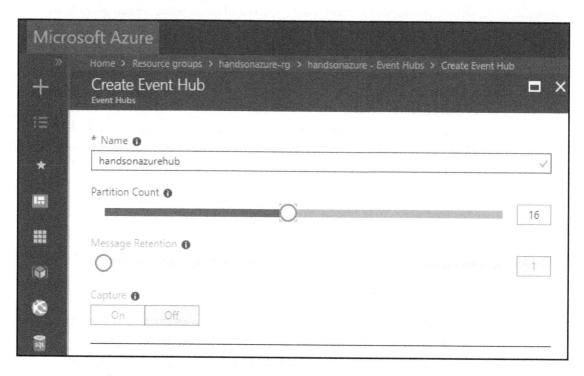

Note that some fields are currently grayed out. This is because I used the
Basic tier for this example; both **Message Retention** (which enables you to extend
the period an event is available to a maximum of seven days) and **Capture** (which
will be described later) are features of the Standard tier.

3. Click on the **Create** button to initiate the creation of a hub.

Once a hub is created, you are able to click on it and access it, as shown:

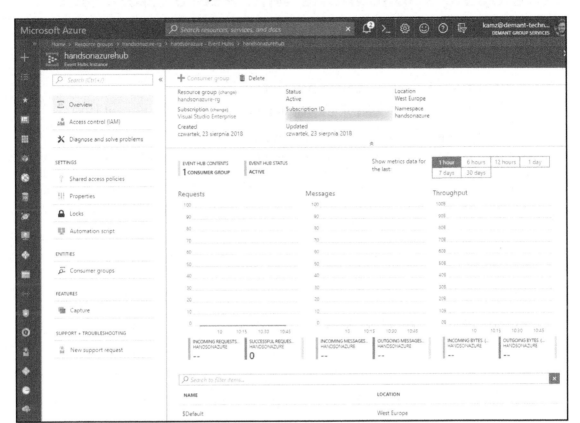

Note that this view is a bit different from the view of a namespace; while it also contains some metadata and metrics, available additional features are limited.

Note that for the Basic tier, consumer groups are also unavailable. With that tier, only the default group—named $Default—can be used.

Developing applications with Azure Event Hub

We created and configured our instance of Azure Event Hub in the Azure portal; now it is time to work with a concept I mentioned at the very beginning—Event Processor Host. In this section, you will learn:

- How to send events to Azure Event Hub
- How to receive events by implementing your own Event Processor Host

Before we start writing some code, however, you have to understand what really underlies such a concept. As opposed to competing consumers, where each consumer uses the same messaging channel, Azure Event Hub uses the idea of an Event Processor Host, which is an intelligent agent able to distribute events between different, partitioned consumers. You may wonder how this idea works when implemented; to get an understanding, here you can see a diagram of the first scenario:

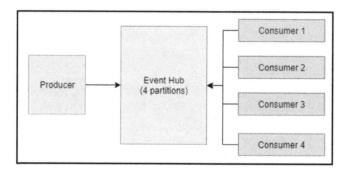

In this diagram, you can see that there is a single **producer** and four different **consumers**. Each consumer implements `IEventProcessor`—an interface that is provided by the SDK and makes receiving events possible. Each **consumer** covers one **partition** and acquires a lease on it. Now let's check another scenario:

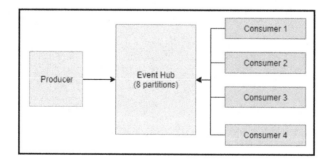

The only change here is the number of **partitions**—now the Event Hub has eight. Event Processor Host makes sure that the load will be distributed equally, each **consumer** will consume two **partitions**. To make things even more complicated, there is a third scenario to consider:

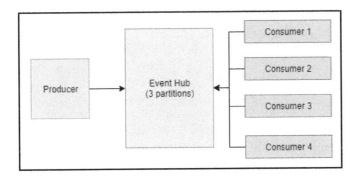

This time, we have more **consumers** than **partitions** available. In that case, you will notice a situation where one **consumer** does not work as there is no **partition** it can process. There is also one more caveat in that scenario; because lease duration (the time during which a partition is attached to a specific **consumer**) is not infinite, at some point currently an idle **consumer** can expropriate others and take control over a partition. Now, when the concept of Event Processor Host is described, we can check how to write some code that can interact with Azure Event Hub. The following code is for an event producer:

```
using System;
using System.Text;
using Microsoft.ServiceBus.Messaging;

namespace HandsOnAzure.Sender
{
    internal class Program
    {
        private const string ConnectionString = "<connection-string>";

        private static void Main()
        {
            var eventHubClient =
EventHubClient.CreateFromConnectionString(ConnectionString);

            try
            {
                var message = Guid.NewGuid().ToString();
                Console.WriteLine("{0} > Sending message: {1}",
DateTime.Now, message);
                eventHubClient.Send(new
```

```
EventData(Encoding.UTF8.GetBytes(message)));
        }
        catch (Exception exception)
        {
            Console.ForegroundColor = ConsoleColor.Red;
            Console.WriteLine("{0} > Exception: {1}", DateTime.Now,
exception.Message);
            Console.ResetColor();
        }

        Console.ReadLine();
    }
}
}
```

To use this code example, you will need a connection string. To get it, I accessed my hub instance, went to the **Shared access policies** blade, and created a new policy with only the **Send** permission:

Now, when I execute my application, I will see that it sends events successfully:

```
23.08.2018 11:20:50 > Sending message: 1a09038b-1aeb-4729-ace0-104f26c7d376
```

We have a producer, now we need a consumer! I created an access policy once more, this time only for **Listen**:

To create a consumer you will need
the `Microsoft.Azure.ServiceBus.EventProcessorHost` NuGet package. Once you install it, you will be able to implement `IEventProcessor` just like this:

```
public class MyFirstEventProcessor : IEventProcessor
{
  private Stopwatch _checkpointStopWatch;

  public Task OpenAsync(PartitionContext context)
  {
    Console.WriteLine("SimpleEventProcessor initialized. Partition: '{0}',
Offset: '{1}'", context.Lease.PartitionId, context.Lease.Offset);
```

```
      _checkpointStopWatch = new Stopwatch();
      _checkpointStopWatch.Start();
      return Task.FromResult<object>(null);
    }

  public async Task ProcessEventsAsync(PartitionContext context,
IEnumerable<EventData> messages)
    {
      foreach (var eventData in messages)
      {
        var data = Encoding.UTF8.GetString(eventData.GetBytes());
        Console.WriteLine($"Message received. Partition:
'{context.Lease.PartitionId}', Data: '{data}'");
      }

      if (_checkpointStopWatch.Elapsed > TimeSpan.FromMinutes(5))
      {
        await context.CheckpointAsync();
        _checkpointStopWatch.Restart();
      }
    }

  public async Task CloseAsync(PartitionContext context, CloseReason
reason)
    {
      Console.WriteLine("Processor Shutting Down. Partition '{0}', Reason:
'{1}'.", context.Lease.PartitionId, reason);

      if (reason == CloseReason.Shutdown)
      {
        await context.CheckpointAsync();
      }
    }
  }
}
```

As you can see, it has three
methods: `OpenAsync`, `ProcessEventsAsync`, and `CloseAsync`. To be able to actually use
such a processor, you have to initiate the whole event processing host:

```
using System;
using Microsoft.ServiceBus.Messaging;

namespace HandsOnAzure.Receiver
{
    internal class Program
    {
        private const string EventHubConnectionString = "<connection-
string>";
```

```
            private const string EventHubName = "<event-hub-name>";
            private const string StorageAccountName = "<storage-account-name>";
            private const string StorageAccountKey = "<storage-account-key>";

            private static void Main()
            {
                var storageConnectionString =
$"DefaultEndpointsProtocol=https;AccountName={StorageAccountName};AccountKe
y={StorageAccountKey}";

                var eventProcessorHostName = Guid.NewGuid().ToString();
                var eventProcessorHost = new
EventProcessorHost(eventProcessorHostName, EventHubName,
EventHubConsumerGroup.DefaultGroupName, EventHubConnectionString,
storageConnectionString);
                Console.WriteLine("Registering EventProcessor...");

                var options = new EventProcessorOptions();
                options.ExceptionReceived += (sender, e) => {
Console.WriteLine(e.Exception); };
eventProcessorHost.RegisterEventProcessorAsync<MyFirstEventProcessor>(optio
ns).Wait();

                Console.WriteLine("Receiving. Press enter key to stop
worker.");
                Console.ReadLine();
                eventProcessorHost.UnregisterEventProcessorAsync().Wait();
            }
        }
    }
```

Now when you run your application, you should be able to see incoming events.

 Note that Event Processor Host requires you to create a Storage Account instance. It uses it to internally manage leases and offsets.

Here, you can see the log coming from my processor:

```
Registering EventProcessor...
Receiving. Press enter key to stop worker.
MyFirstEventProcessor initialized. Partition: '4', Offset: ''
MyFirstEventProcessor initialized. Partition: '9', Offset: ''
MyFirstEventProcessor initialized. Partition: '11', Offset: ''
MyFirstEventProcessor initialized. Partition: '8', Offset: ''
Message received. Partition: '9', Data: '5e0b2a73-
ca9d-418d-8d47-43c7b7feb17e'
```

```
Message received. Partition: '4', Data: '1a09038b-1aeb-4729-
ace0-104f26c7d376'
Message received. Partition: '4', Data: '859cce28-76e1-4a68-8637-
a2349d898e8b'
MyFirstEventProcessor initialized. Partition: '15', Offset: ''
Message received. Partition: '15', Data:
'36f13819-46d6-42c9-8afe-6776264e7aab'
MyFirstEventProcessor initialized. Partition: '1', Offset: ''
MyFirstEventProcessor initialized. Partition: '5', Offset: ''
MyFirstEventProcessor initialized. Partition: '0', Offset: ''
MyFirstEventProcessor initialized. Partition: '7', Offset: ''
MyFirstEventProcessor initialized. Partition: '12', Offset: ''
MyFirstEventProcessor initialized. Partition: '3', Offset: ''
MyFirstEventProcessor initialized. Partition: '14', Offset: ''
MyFirstEventProcessor initialized. Partition: '10', Offset: ''
MyFirstEventProcessor initialized. Partition: '2', Offset: ''
MyFirstEventProcessor initialized. Partition: '6', Offset: ''
MyFirstEventProcessor initialized. Partition: '13', Offset: ''
```

Note how a single receiver handles all 16 partitions I used for this particular hub. Now you can check what happens if I introduce another consumer:

```
Microsoft.ServiceBus.Messaging.ReceiverDisconnectedException: New receiver
with higher epoch of '4' is created hence current receiver with epoch '3'
is getting disconnected. If you are recreating the receiver, make sure a
higher epoch is used.
TrackingId:628871df00003ffd002d0cc25b7fd487_C1655342710_B13,
SystemTracker:handsonazure:eventhub:handsonazurehub~2047|$default,
Timestamp:8/24/2018 9:49:09 AM
    at
Microsoft.ServiceBus.Common.AsyncResult.End[TAsyncResult](IAsyncResult
result)
    at
Microsoft.ServiceBus.Messaging.MessageReceiver.RetryReceiveEventDataAsyncRe
sult.TryReceiveEnd(IAsyncResult r, IEnumerable`1& messages)
    at
Microsoft.ServiceBus.Messaging.MessageReceiver.EndTryReceiveEventData(IAsyn
cResult result, IEnumerable`1& messages)
    at
Microsoft.ServiceBus.Messaging.EventHubReceiver.<ReceiveAsync>b__61_1(IAsyn
cResult result)
    at System.Threading.Tasks.TaskFactory`1.FromAsyncCoreLogic(IAsyncResult
iar, Func`2 endFunction, Action`1 endAction, Task`1 promise, Boolean
requiresSynchronization)
--- End of stack trace from previous location where exception was thrown --
-
    at System.Runtime.CompilerServices.TaskAwaiter.ThrowForNonSuccess(Task
task)
```

```
    at
System.Runtime.CompilerServices.TaskAwaiter.HandleNonSuccessAndDebuggerNoti
fication(Task task)
    at Microsoft.ServiceBus.Common.TaskHelpers.EndAsyncResult(IAsyncResult
asyncResult)
    at
Microsoft.ServiceBus.Messaging.IteratorAsyncResult`1.<>c.<CallTask>b__24_1(
TIteratorAsyncResult thisPtr, IAsyncResult r)
    at
Microsoft.ServiceBus.Messaging.IteratorAsyncResult`1.StepCallback(IAsyncRes
ult result)
Processor Shutting Down. Partition '0', Reason: 'LeaseLost'.
```

As you can see, `Partition 0` has been taken by another receiver, which will start processing events from it:

```
Registering EventProcessor...
Receiving. Press enter key to stop worker.
MyFirstEventProcessor initialized. Partition: '0', Offset: ''
Message received. Partition: '0', Data: '3c3bb090-2e0c-4d06-
ad44-1d0ad4a106a7'
Message received. Partition: '0', Data: '54fed07a-a51e-4f36-8f26-
f2ded2da9faa'
Message received. Partition: '0', Data: '69b8b291-8407-466a-
a2c1-0b33a2ef03ad'
Message received. Partition: '0', Data: 'ec45d759-01bb-41db-ab51-
de469ee5da55'
Message received. Partition: '0', Data: 'fcf41b0e-cd6b-465a-
ac20-100ba13fd6af'
Message received. Partition: '0', Data: '2f05104a-
c4a2-4a8f-8689-957f2dca6c71'
Message received. Partition: '0', Data:
'63d77b4c-584f-4db3-86d0-9f73179ccb9f'
Message received. Partition: '0', Data: '03c70d22-4efa-4bd6-9c5c-
f666c2922931'
Message received. Partition: '0', Data:
'96f4c8be-831c-415c-8aa7-0a5125458f16'
Message received. Partition: '0', Data: 'af2e8a21-d9ce-4256-
a8eb-73483387912c'
Message received. Partition: '0', Data: '73d9f92b-686b-44d1-
b01a-50c0c63426ee'
Message received. Partition: '0', Data: 'bf53ea8f-dd34-405f-
a6a6-0e947ce2473b'
```

It will gradually take control of half of the available partitions until the load is balanced.

Azure Event Hub security

We have covered some topics regarding working with and developing applications using Azure Event Hub – now it is time to learn something more about the security features of this service. In the previous part of this chapter, you used shared access policies, which are the easiest options when you want to restrict access to a hub to some predefined operations (such as listening to events, sending them, or managing Event Hub). Now I will show you something more about the security model and restricting access to the whole namespace by IP filtering.

Event publishers

When creating an Event Hub namespace instance, you had to choose a tier – you could choose between Basic and Standard tier. Besides features such as consumer groups or message retention, Standard tier offers one more thing—the ability to create event publishers. An event publisher acts as a virtual endpoint for sending messages to a hub. In fact, it enhances security by combining an SAS token with the identity of a sender. To generate a token, you have to use the following method:

```
public static string
SharedAccessSignatureTokenProvider.GetSharedAccessSignature(string keyName,
string sharedAccessKey, string resource, TimeSpan tokenTimeToLive)
```

To execute it correctly, you will need:

- **Key name**: the name of an SAS policy
- **Shared access key**: the key generated for a policy
- **Resource**: the URL to a namespace in the following format:
  `sb://<NAMESPACE>.servicebus.windows.net/<EVENT_HUB_NAME>/publis hers/<PUBLISHER_NAME>`
- **Token lifetime**: how long a token will be valid

Remember that PUBLISHER_NAME should be unique for each client.

When you generate a token, it will be in the following format:

```
SharedAccessSignature
sr=%2f%2fZvZExXejq40LO5vmRIikSpWLn9YlKMZ5cwC2Nk83%2bnE%3d.servicebus.window
s.net%2fhandsonazurehub%2fpublishers%2fhandsonazurepublisher&sig=UraqQnVck9
O64h3pd8dcX9KdZZa2rb%2bxfR%2blyod2Ep2Q%3d&se=1535279857&skn=handsonazuresen
d
```

To be able to actually use it, you will have to use `EventHubSender` instead of `EventHubClient`:

```
private static EventHubSender CreateSender()
{
  var publisher = "handsonazurepublisher";
  var token =
SharedAccessSignatureTokenProvider.GetSharedAccessSignature(KeyName,
SASKey,
$"sb://{Namespace}.servicebus.windows.net/{HubName}/publishers/{publisher}"
, TimeSpan.FromHours(24));
  var connectionString =
    ServiceBusConnectionStringBuilder.CreateUsingSharedAccessSignature(
      new Uri($"sb://{Namespace}.servicebus.windows.net"), HubName,
publisher, token);
  var eventHubSender =
EventHubSender.CreateFromConnectionString(connectionString);
  return eventHubSender;
}
```

This is because when using event publishers you can only send events—they cannot be used for other Event Hub operations.

Note that clients, in general, should not be aware of additional features that such generated SAS tokens supply. The most important thing is that they should not be generated by them; instead, you should introduce a service in which they can ask for a full connection string and use it.

Now, when you have control over who or what can access Azure Event Hub, there is one more thing you can do—revoke publisher, so it cannot access a hub anymore. To do so, you will need the following methods:

```
var nsm = NamespaceManager.CreateFromConnectionString(manageString);
nsm.RevokePublisher(eventHubName, publisherId);
```

Once you revoke a publisher, when it tries to send an event, it will receive `PublisherRevokedException`.

IP filters

It is possible to restrict access to Azure Event Hub by introducing IP filters; this feature (as shown next) allows you to secure the whole namespace by knowing which IP addresses should be rejected. By default, the IP filter is empty, that means that Event Hub accepts any connection (so this is equivalent to setting it as approve `0.0.0.0/0` IP address):

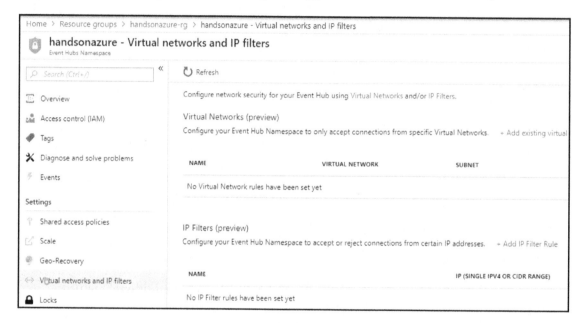

You can easily create a rule by clicking on **+ Add IP Filter Rule:**

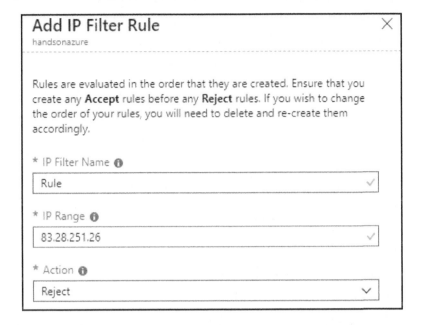

When I restrict access to my computer's IP, I will get the following message when I try to send an event:

```
25.08.2018 13:11:39 > Sending message: 0a7dd971-6600-458c-816d-fbbbee0d81cb
25.08.2018 13:11:40 > Exception: Ip has been prevented to connect to the
endpoint. TrackingId:9421f06c-3a1c-4e4e-8a25-fb76f1cacee6,
SystemTracker:AmqpGatewayProvider, Timestamp:8/25/2018 11:11:36 AM
```

You can choose to either restrict access from some specific IP addresses or allow a particular subset.

Azure Event Hub Capture feature

There is one feature of Azure Event Hub that requires an individual section itself to describe it in depth. It is capture, a functionality which allows you to automatically store events using a predefined storage solution (such as Azure Storage or Azure Data Lake) and process it further. Unfortunately, this particular feature is often misused as its use cases are not so obvious; additionally, the way it works might sometimes be unclear.

How Azure Event Hub Capture works

In common use cases for Event Hub, you need a **producer** and a **consumer** to fetch data and process it. Let's consider the following scenario:

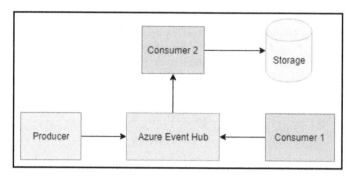

In this scenario, we have two consumers:

- **Consumer 1** for some generic processing
- **Consumer 2** for archiving events

We also introduced **storage** for storing a log of events. As you can see, the downside of that solution is the fact that you need to maintain both consumers—two code bases and two instances. With Event Hub Capture, the scenario we are considering now will change a little bit:

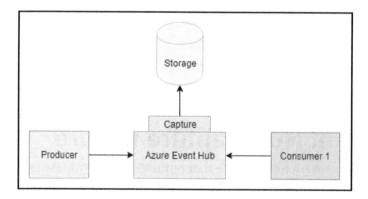

Now we no longer require additional consumers as it will be Event Hub Capture's responsibility to store data. You may wonder how storing data works in that scenario; in general, it is based on a time window which, when it ends, triggers a capture of data.

It can be easily described using an example. Suppose you set your time window to 10 minutes; after that interval, all data which is stored within Azure Event Hub will be captured and stored inside a selected database using **Apache Avro** format.

An important thing is Capture pricing; it costs € 0.085/hour per each throughput unit. It means that if you have Azure Event Hub with 1 TU and Capture enabled, you will pay 80 EUR instead of 18 EUR. With 2 TUs, it will be 160 EUR instead of 37 EUR.

Enabling Event Hub Capture

Event Hub Capture is a feature of an individual Event Hub, not the whole namespace. To enable it, you need to go to your hub and search for the **Capture** blade.

Now, when you enable Capture, you will see a full configuration of the feature, which we will try to understand now:

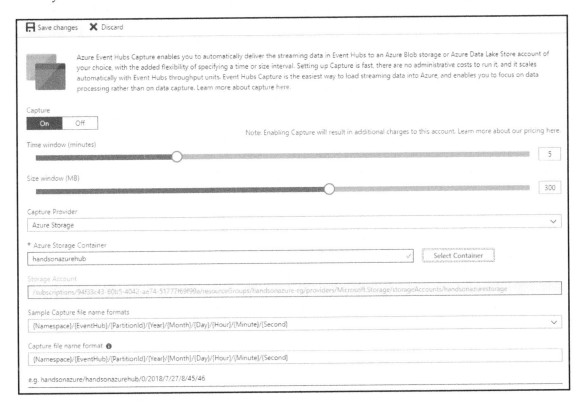

As you can see, it contains the following settings:

- **Time window**: It defines after how many minutes a capture is triggered.
- **Size window**: Alternatively, it is possible to trigger a capture after a window reaches the size limit. Whether it triggers because of time or size depends on which one reaches the limit first.
- **Capture Provider**: You can choose between Azure Storage and Azure Data Lake Store. The choice is yours as it does not imply any additional features or limits.
- **Azure Storage Container/Data Lake Store**: Depending on your choice, you will have to choose a different kind of a container.
- **Capture file name format**: This Event Hub feature has a predefined set of formats for how your files will be stored. Unfortunately, it is impossible to make it fully customizable as it must contain the {Namespace}, {EventHub}, {PartitionId}, {Year}, {Month}, {Day}, {Hour}, {Minute} and {Second} fields.

Once you are satisfied with your choice, you can save the form. After some time, your producers send data; you will see that data from each partition is captured:

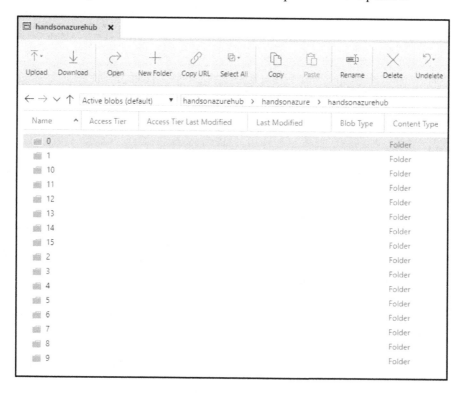

What is more, they contain files with data in the following format:

```
Objavro.codecnullavro.schema{"type":"record","name":"EventData","namespace
":"Microsoft.ServiceBus.Messaging","fields":[{"name":"SequenceNumber","type
":"long"},{"name":"Offset","type":"string"},{"name":"EnqueuedTimeUtc","type
":"string"},{"name":"SystemProperties","type":{"type":"map","values":["long
","double","string","bytes"]}},{"name":"Properties","type":{"type":"map","v
alues":["long","double","string","bytes","null"]}},{"name":"Body","type":["
null","bytes"]}]}
```

This data can be easily converted to JSON:

```
{
  "definitions" : {
    "record:Microsoft.ServiceBus.Messaging.EventData" : {
      "type" : "object",
      "required" : [ "SequenceNumber", "Offset", "EnqueuedTimeUtc",
"SystemProperties", "Properties", "Body" ],
      "additionalProperties" : false,
      "properties" : {
        "SequenceNumber" : {
          "type" : "integer",
          "minimum" : -9223372036854775808,
          "maximum" : 9223372036854775807
        },
        "Offset" : {
          "type" : "string"
        },
        "EnqueuedTimeUtc" : {
          "type" : "string"
        },
        "SystemProperties" : {
          "type" : "object",
          "additionalProperties" : {
            "oneOf" : [ {
              "type" : "integer",
              "minimum" : -9223372036854775808,
              "maximum" : 9223372036854775807
            }, {
              "type" : "number"
            }, {
              "type" : "string"
            }, {
              "type" : "string",
              "pattern" : "^[\u0000-y]*$"
            } ]
          }
        },
```

```
         "Properties" : {
           "type" : "object",
           "additionalProperties" : {
             "oneOf" : [ {
               "type" : "integer",
               "minimum" : -9223372036854775808,
               "maximum" : 9223372036854775807
             }, {
               "type" : "number"
             }, {
               "type" : "string"
             }, {
               "type" : "string",
               "pattern" : "^[\u0000-y]*$"
             }, {
               "type" : "null"
             } ]
           }
         },
         "Body" : {
           "oneOf" : [ {
             "type" : "null"
           }, {
             "type" : "string",
             "pattern" : "^[\u0000-y]*$"
           } ]
         }
       }
     }
   },
   "$ref" : "#/definitions/record:Microsoft.ServiceBus.Messaging.EventData"
 }
```

You will find more about Avro in the *Further reading* section.

Summary

In this chapter, you have learned many things about Azure Event Hub—how it works, what partitions are for, and how to leverage more advanced features such as consumer groups or the Event Hub Capture feature. I strongly encourage you to give it a try and play a little bit with this Azure service as it is a powerful tool for processing thousands of events per second. It is also pretty simple to use and does not require much time to get started.

In the next chapter, you will learn about another service for processing many events, and additionally analyze and transform them in near real time—Azure Stream Analytics.

Questions

1. What are consumer groups for?
2. How many events can be processed in one second using 1 TU?
3. How many partitions should you use for each Event Hub?
4. Are TUs assigned to a namespace or a particular Event Hub?
5. What are the three different permissions you can assign to an access policy?
6. Can an event publisher listen to incoming events using its token?
7. What happens if you have more consumers than partitions?

Further reading

The full documentation on Event Hub disaster recovery of can be found here: `https://docs.microsoft.com/en-us/azure/event-hubs/event-hubs-geo-dr`.

Apache Avro Documentation can be found here: `https://avro.apache.org/`.

13
Real-Time Data Analysis - Azure Stream Analytics

While some Azure components enable us to deliver data to the cloud, in most cases we also need something that is designed for analyzing and querying streamed data. One such service is Azure Stream Analytics, a real-time data analysis tool, which is able to read all messages sent through, for example, Event Hub, and transform, and save them using one of the predefined outputs.

The following topics will be covered in this chapter:

- Working with Azure Stream Analytics
- Available input and output types
- Querying data using the query language
- Ensuring the correct order of incoming data and performing checkpoints or replays

Technical requirements

To perform the exercises in this chapter, you will need:

- Visual Studio 2017 instance
- An Azure subscription
- Azure Stream Analytics tools—https://docs.microsoft.com/en-us/azure/stream-analytics/stream-analytics-tools-for-visual-studio-install

Azure Stream Analytics introduction

In the previous chapter, we discussed Azure Event Hub, which is a solution for receiving and processing thousands of messages per second, by introducing the implementation of event processor hosts. While it is great for workloads such as big data pipelines or IoT scenarios, it is not a solution to everything, especially if you want to avoid hosting VMs. Scaling such architectures can be cumbersome and nonintuitive; this is why there is Azure Stream Analytics, which is an event-processing engine designed for high volumes of data. It fills a gap where other services such as Event Hub or IoT Hub do not perform well (or where to do so they require much more skill and/or more sophisticated architecture), particularly for real-time analytics, anomaly detection, and geospatial analytics. It is an advanced tool for advanced tasks, which will greatly improve your cloud and message-processing skills.

Stream ingestions versus stream analysis

To get started, we will compare two topics:

- **Stream ingestion**: This is a process where you introduce a service/API for receiving messages from your producers. Such a service is designed to ingest data only—it does nothing more (such as transforming or analyzing). To perform any kind of analysis of ingested data, you have to introduce your own processors.
- **Stream analysis**: This is a process where you actually analyze the data. You search for anomalies, duplicates, or malformed data, process it, and push it further to other services for storing, presenting, and triggering other actions.

To make things even clearer, we can take a look at the following diagram:

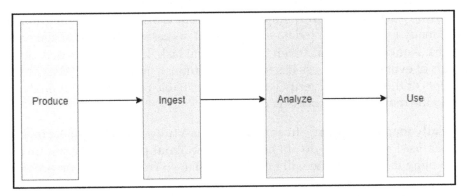

It shows the four steps of data processing:

- **Produce**: Where data is actually produced by different services, devices, and clients
- **Ingest**: This is when the data is consumed from different sources
- **Analyze**: During this step data is analyzed, transformed, and routed to appropriate services and components
- **Use**: Storing, displaying, and processing data further in other services, such as PowerBI, Azure Functions, and many others

While Azure Event Hub or Azure IoT Hub is a part of the ingest step, Azure Stream Analytics is responsible for **analyzing**.

 Note that you are not limited to Azure services when it comes to ingesting data. In such a scenario, you can also use any kind of queue or API, as long as it is capable of processing thousands of events per second.

Azure Stream Analytics concepts

In Azure Stream Analytics, the most important concept is a **stream**. You can think about it as a flow of many events carrying data—they do not necessarily have to be the same or share schema. Analyzing such a stream is not a trivial task. If you have to decode hundreds of thousands of events, the process has to be quick, robust, and reliable. We will discuss the main concepts of this service to verify whether it is capable of acting as our analyzing solution and the main events processor:

- **Fully managed**: Azure Stream Analytics is a fully managed platform as a service(PaaS), so you do not have to worry about provisioning resources and scaling it—the runtime will take care of that, so you can focus on providing optimal queries for data analysis.

- **An SQL-based query language**: To analyze data, Azure Stream Analytics uses an SQL-based query language, which enables developers to build advanced procedures quickly, which extract from a stream exactly what they want. Additionally, you can bring your own extensions such as ML solutions or user-defined aggregates to perform extra calculations, using tools unavailable to the service.

- **Performance**: Azure Stream Analytics is focused on **streaming units (SUs)** instead of some hardcoded values of CPUs or memory. This is because it is designed to provide stable performance and recurrent execution time. What is more, thanks to this concept, you can easily scale your solution to meet your demands.

- **Low cost of ownership**: In Azure Stream Analytics you pay only for what you choose. As pricing depends on the number of SUs per hour, there is no additional cost to be incorporated in the overall payment.

There are also some extra technical concepts (such as input/output types, checkpoints, or replays), which we will cover in the next parts of this chapter. To see the big picture of the whole pipeline using Azure Stream Analytics, please check the following image:

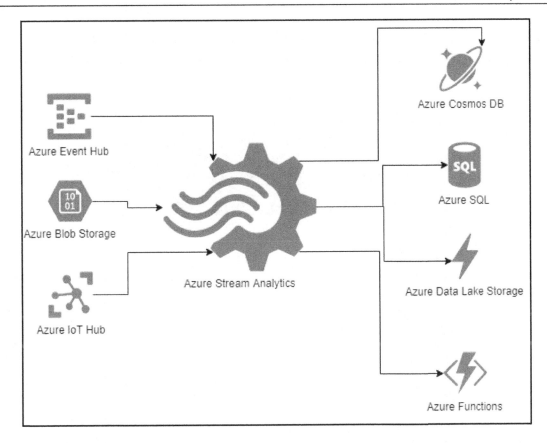

Of course, there could be other references on this picture (additional services, user functions, and analyzers), but for the sake of simplicity, I did not include them.

Input and output types

Azure Stream Analytics offers a seamless integration with some native Azure services, such as Azure Event Hub, Azure IoT Hub, or Azure Blob Storage. Additionally, it can be easily configured to output data to an SQL database, Blob, or Event Azure Data Lake Store. To leverage those possibilities, you will have to define both input and output types, which you are interested in. This allows for data to be easily ingested (in the form of a stream), so a job, which you will write, can work on thousands of events, analyzing and processing them. In this section, you will learn how to get started with Azure Stream Analytics and to define both the inputsand outputs.

Create Azure Stream Analytics in Azure portal

To get started, you will need to create an instance of Azure Stream Analytics. To do so, you have to click on **+ Create a resource** and search for `Stream Analytics job`. This will display a form, where you can enter all the necessary data to create a service:

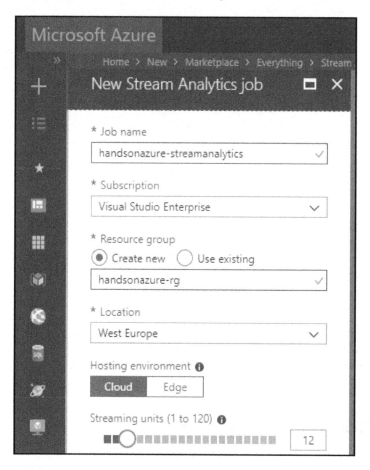

There are two fields, which at first you might overlook:

- **Hosting environment**: Azure Stream Analytics can be hosted in two ways: as a native Azure service or deployed to an on-premise IoT Edge gateway device. IoT Edge is a topic beyond the scope of this book, so the natural choice will be **Cloud**.

- **Streaming units (1 to 120)**: You have to select how many SUs you would like to provision for a job to process your events. The number of required SUs depends on the characteristics of your job, and additionally may vary depending on the input type of your choice. There is a link in the *Further reading* section, which describes in detail how many SUs you may need for your job.

 Remember that you will pay €0.093/hour for each SU you choose, even when it is not working on a job.

Once you click **Create** and open the **Overview** blade, you will see an empty dashboard:

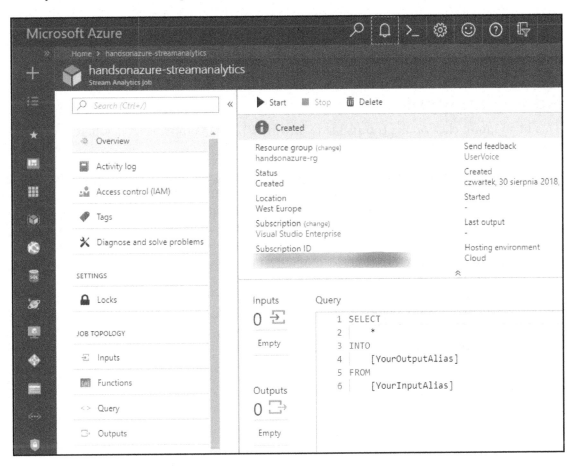

As you can see, both **Inputs** and **Outputs** are empty for now—we have to change this, so we can use them in our query. Both of the features are available on the left, in the **JOB TOPOLOGY** section:

Adding an input

To add an input, click on the **Inputs** blade. It will display an empty screen, where you have two possibilities:

- **+ Add stream input**: Here you can add a link to services that enable you to ingest a stream. Currently available Azure components are Azure Event Hub, Azure IoT Hub, and Azure Blob Storage. The inputs can live (or not) in the same subscription, and such a connection supports compression (so you can pass a compressed stream using, for example, GZip or deflate).
- **+ Add reference input**: Instead of ingesting data from a real-time stream, you can also use Azure Blob Storage and add a reference to it, so you can ingest so-called reference data. In that scenario, Azure Stream Analytics will load the whole data into memory, so it can perform lookups on it. It is an ideal solution for static or slowly changing data, and supports data up to the maximum size of 300 MB

Here you can find an example of configuring **Event Hub** as an input:

Depending on your choices (whether you have an Event Hub in your subscription or not, whether it exists or not), there will be different options available. In the previous example, I configured a new hub (which was nonexistent) to be the source of my data. There are some fields, however, which I would like to cover now:

- **Event Hub consumer group**: If you would like to make Azure Stream Analytics read data from the very beginning, enter a consumer group here. By default, it will use $Default, which is the default consumer group in Azure Event Hub.
- **Event serialization format**: You can choose from JSON, Avro, and CSV. This allows you to deserialize events automatically, based on the used serialization format.
- **Event compression type**: If you are using GZip or Deflate, here you can choose the right option, so the input will be automatically deserialized.

 Note that you need an actual Azure Event Hub namespace to be able to create a hub from Azure Stream Analytics automatically.

After filling all the required fields, you will be able to click on the **Create** button to initialize the creation of a new input. Of course, you can add more than just one input as they will all be available in the input stream, so you will be able to work with the incoming events. Before you start your job, you will need at least one output, which we are about to add now.

Adding an output

To add an output, you have to click on the **Outputs** blade. It is similar to the **Inputs** one, but there are different kinds of output available:

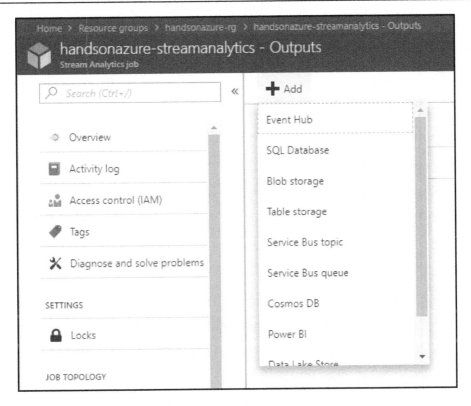

As you can see, there are many different types of output available, which makes Azure Stream Analytics so flexible when it comes to pushing ingested data to different services. We can divide them into different categories:

- **Storage**: SQL database, Blob storage, Table storage, Cosmos DB, and Data Lake Store
- **Reporting**: Power BI
- **Compute**: Azure Functions
- **Messaging**: Event Hub, Service Bus

Depending on the category, you will have different options for what you can do with the processed events:

- **Storage**: Storing data for further operations, archiving, and event log
- **Reporting**: Near real-time reports
- **Compute**: An easy solution for achieving unlimited integration capabilities
- **Messaging**: Pushing events further for different pipelines and systems

Here you can find a configuration for integrating Azure Table storage as an output:

Available fields depend heavily on the selected output type, so I will not focus on them in this chapter. You can find a reference to them in the *Further reading* section.

Azure Stream Analytics query language

The strength of Azure Stream Analytics, besides the rich selection of Azure services that seamlessly integrate with it, lies in its query language, which allows you to analyze an input stream easily and output it to a required service. As it is an SQL-like language, it should be intuitive and easy to learn for most developers using this service. Even if you are not familiar with SQL, the many examples available and its simple syntax should make it easy for you.

Writing a query

In the Azure portal, the query window for Azure Stream Analytics can be found either in the **Overview** or **Query** blade:

In the preceding example, you can see a simple SQL-like query, which performs the following three things:

- Selects data from the input using the given alias
- Chooses the particular columns
- Pushes them into a specific output

You can also click on the **Edit query** link, so you will be routed to the **Query** screen:

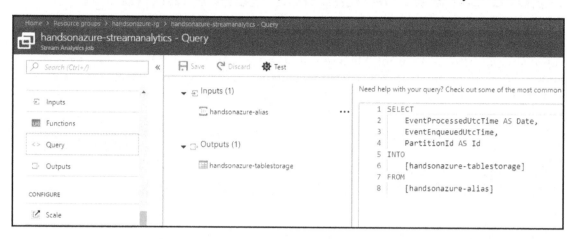

As you can see, to be able to actually work with a query, you will need both an input and an output, as without them you will not be able to save it. In general, a query consists of three elements:

- SELECT: Where you are selecting columns from the input you are interested in
- INTO: Where you are telling the engine which output you are interested in
- FROM: Where you are selecting an input from which data should be fetched

Of course, the preceding statements are not the only ones, which are available—you can use plenty of different options, such as **GROUP BY**, **LIKE**, or **HAVING**. It all depends on the input stream and the schema of incoming data. For some jobs, you may only need to perform a quick transformation and extract the necessary columns; for others, you might require more sophisticated syntax for getting exactly what you want. You will find common query patterns in the link in the *Further reading* section. In the preceding example, in the SELECT part of the query, I have selected three columns, which are available when analyzing Azure Event Hub events. What is more, I used the AS construct to tell the engine to actually rename fields to match those defined in the **Outputs** section. When I run my job, I can see that it actually passes events to my table:

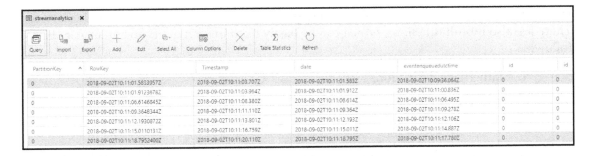

However, there are some problems with the current setup:

- We rely on the Event Hub fields, which might change in the future.
- We are missing the actual data of an event.
- There are duplicated columns.

Let's assume each event has the following structure:

```
{"Id":"165e0206-8198-4f21-8a6d-
ad2041031603","Date":"2018-09-02T12:17:48.3817632+02:00"}
```

Of course, particular data changes over time. We can quickly change the query:

```
SELECT
    PartitionId,
    Id,
    Date
INTO
    [handsonazure-tablestorage]
FROM
    [handsonazure-alias]
```

And adapt the configuration to change the output a little bit:

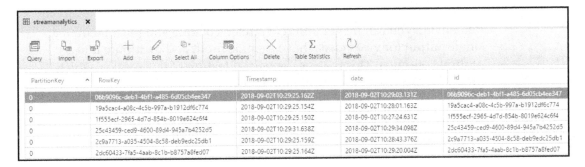

However, the basic constructs are only a few percent of the overall capability of the service. There are also inbuilt functions, which can be easily used in each query to enhance it, as follows:

1. Mathematical functions:

```
SELECT FLOOR(input.x) AS "The FLOOR of the variable x" FROM
input
SELECT SQUARE(input.x) AS "The SQUARE of the variable x" FROM
input
```

2. Aggregate functions:

```
SELECT COUNT(*) FROM Input
SELECT SUM (Income) FROM Input
SELECT AVG (Income) FROM Input
```

3. Analytic functions:

```
SELECT ISFIRST(mi, 10) as first FROM Input
```

4. Geospatial functions:

```
SELECT ST_DISTANCE(input.pos1, input.pos2) FROM input
```

5. String functions:

```
SELECT SUBSTRING (SerialNumber ,1,3 ), FROM Input
```

In addition to these, there are some more such as record functions, date/time functions, conversion, or array functions. The preceding examples are of course not all the available functions. You can find them all in the *Further reading* section. The important thing here is that some functions are deterministic (this means that they always return the same result if the same input values are used), and some are not—this is especially important when handling high loads and trying to avoid possible anomalies.

Remember, you can merge different streams of data and push them to a single output (or vice versa—have a single input and distribute it to multiple outputs). This is a very powerful feature of this service, which makes ingesting and processing data much easier.

Event ordering, checkpoints, and replays

In the previous sections, we covered some basic topics of Azure Stream Analytics: how to configure inputs and outputs, querying data, and using the service. In the last part of this chapter, I will show you its more advanced features such as event ordering, checkpoints, and replays, which ensure that events are processed exactly in a way you would expect. These topics are in fact common subjects in many different messaging solutions, so you will be able to use knowledge from this chapter in your other projects.

Event ordering

There are two concepts of events when it comes to their ordering:

- Application (or event) time
- Arrival time

There is a clear distinction between them:

- **Application time**: This is a timestamp when an event was generated on the client (or application) side. It tells you exactly when it occurred.
- **Arrival time**: This is a system timestamp, which is not present in the original payload. It tells you when an event was received by a service and picked up for processing.

Depending on the input type, arrival time and application time will be different properties (`EventEnqueuedUtcTime` or `EnqueuedTime` for arrival time, whereas application time, in general, will be a generic property). What you have to remember is, depending on the selected scenario, you can process events as they come but out of order, or in order but delayed. This can be easily described using the following event sequence:

1. **Arrival**: `2018-09-02T12:17:49` **Application**: `2018-09-02T12:17:48`
2. **Arrival**: `2018-09-02T12:17:50` **Application**: `2018-09-02T12:17:44`
3. **Arrival**: `2018-09-02T12:17:51` **Application**: `2018-09-02T12:17:46`

If you process events as they come into the stream, they will be processed **out of order**—in fact, they occurred in a different order, so there is a possibility that some data will be outdated. The other option is to sort events by application time; in such a scenario, the process will be delayed, but the order will be preserved.

Whether you need to or not, processing events in order depends on the data schema and characteristics of the processed events. Processing them in order is more time-consuming, but sometimes you just cannot do it the other way.

Azure Stream Analytics has a feature named **Event ordering**, which allows you to make a decision about what to do with events, which are either out of order or outdated:

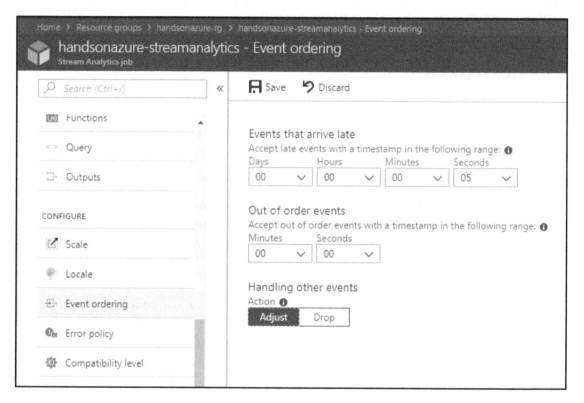

There are two options available:

- **Events that arrive late**: This one allows you to process outdated events (for which the application time does not match the one processed as the last one) within a defined time window.
- **Out of order events**: It is possible that Azure Stream Analytics consider some of your events to be out of order (this situation could happen, for instance, if your senders' clocks are skewed). Here you can set a time window, during which this situation is acceptable).

Additionally, you can define an action, which will be performed if an event either arrived late or was out of order—for **Drop**, it will simply be removed, and if you select **Adjust**, processing will be suspended for some time when such situations occur.

Checkpoints and replays

In fact, Azure Stream Analytics is a stateful service, which is able to track the event-processing progress. This makes it suitable for the following:

- Job recovery
- Stateful query logic
- Different job start modes (now, custom, and when last stopped)

Of course, there is a difference between what is possible after the checkpoint and when a replay is necessary. There are situations when the data stored within a checkpoint is not enough, and the whole replay is required; however, this may differ depending on your query. In fact, it depends on the query parallelization factor and can be described using the following formula:

$$[\textit{The input event rate}] \ x \ [\textit{The gap length}] \ / \ [\textit{Number of processing partitions}]$$

The more processors you have, the faster you can recover when something goes wrong. A good rule of thumb is to introduce more SUs in case your job fails and you have to close the gap quickly.

The important thing to consider when replaying data is the use of window functions in your queries (tumbling, hopping, sliding, or session)—they allow you to process data in different kinds of windows, but complicate the replay mechanism.

Summary

In this chapter, we covered Azure Stream Analytics, a service for processing streams of data in near real time. You have learned what the available inputs and outputs are and how to configure them. What is more, you were able to write your first query, and check how the query language works for analyzing and processing incoming events. If you need a PaaS that can quickly read and transform events and push them to many different Azure services, Azure Stream Analytics is for you.

In the next chapter, we will go through Azure Service Bus, an enterprise-class messaging solution that is in fact the foundation of Azure Event Hub, which we discussed previously.

Questions

1. What is the payment model for Azure Stream Analytics?
2. What is the difference between a stream and the reference output?
3. What is the difference between application and arrival time?
4. Which query construct do you need to select an ID from an input and push it to an output?
5. Can you process different inputs in the same query?
6. When is an event considered out of order?
7. Is it possible to get a substring from a property in a query? If so, which function can be used for that?

Further reading

- Scaling and SUs: https://docs.microsoft.com/en-us/azure/stream-analytics/stream-analytics-streaming-unit-consumption
- Different output types: https://docs.microsoft.com/en-us/azure/stream-analytics/stream-analytics-define-outputs
- Common query patterns: https://docs.microsoft.com/en-us/azure/stream-analytics/stream-analytics-stream-analytics-query-patterns
- Window functions: https://docs.microsoft.com/en-us/azure/stream-analytics/stream-analytics-window-functions

Enterprise Integration - Azure Service Bus

14

Sometimes, to integrate our applications using messaging solutions, we need something more than a simple pipeline, which offers limited capabilities when it comes to distributing data and filtering it. Topics, filters, and many more features are available in Azure Service Bus, an enterprise-level solution designed for providing a reliable, scalable, and efficient way for sending messages to multiple receivers.

The following topics will be covered in this chapter:

- Working with Azure Service Bus
- The fundamentals—queues, topics, and relays
- Securing Azure Service Bus
- The advanced features like geo-replication, sessions, or dead lettering
- Handling outages and disasters

Technical requirements

To perform the exercises in this chapter, you will need:

- Access to a Microsoft Azure subscription
- A Visual Studio 2017 instance
- Visual Studio Code (if you don't have a Visual Studio 2017 instance)

Azure Service Bus fundamentals

You have already learned about other messaging solutions, which allow you to ease communication between your services, and all are characterized by different features. In Azure Event Hub, you were able to process thousands of messages per second, while with Azure Storage Queues you were given a reliable and durable solution, which you could use to work asynchronously on ingested data. In this chapter, we will discuss Azure Service Bus, a multitenant cloud messaging service that introduces advanced concepts like first-in,first-out(FIFO) messaging, dead lettering, or transactions. It is an enterprise-class cloud component able to integrate many different services and applications.

Azure Service Bus versus other messaging services

In the previous chapters, we discussed the following services, which allowed us to process messages:

- Azure Event Hub
- Azure Storage Queue
- Azure Event Grid

They all have similarities, yet they are designed to serve different features and offer different capabilities. We often use the concepts of events and messages alternately. In fact, there is a slight difference between them and understanding this is crucial to be able to use different messaging services successfully:

- **Event**: It carries the information that something happened—the fact that someone or something produced an event does not imply any expectations regarding how an event should be handled. Events, in general, are lightweight information carriers and do not bring the full data to the receiver.

- **Message**: As opposed to an event, when a producer sends a message, it has some expectation about how it will be handled (so there is some kind of a contract between a producer and a consumer). What is more, a message carries the raw data while an event implies that something happened; a message indicates that a component has initialized a communication, which should be handled in the usual way.

Now you can recall what you have learned about, for example, Azure Event Grid or Azure Event Hub—they both have an event in the name, but work in quite different ways:

- **Azure Event Grid**: It is designed to distribute events and react to changes. It delivers only the metadata, and the actual message has to be fetched individually; thus, it can be said, that it distributes events.
- **Azure Event Hub**: It works as a big data pipeline and streams events to other services. Depending on your implementation, it can stream both events and messages.

Now, let's compare Service Bus:

- **Azure Service Bus**: It was created to support critical processes, which have high requirements regarding the order of processing and reliability of the messaging service. You can use it when a message cannot be lost or duplicated. It does not work with the concept of events—instead, it allows you to push the whole data, which can be read by a consumer.

Azure Service Bus and Azure Storage Queues

You may wonder what the difference between Azure Service Bus and Azure Storage Queues is. In fact, they are both messaging solutions, which are reliable, durable, and can handle multiple messages at once. However, looking more closely, you can see they are quite different services, built using different concepts and for a different purpose:

- Azure Storage Queue solutions are forced to poll the queue to receive a message—with Azure Service Bus you can establish a long-polling receive operation via TCP.
- In Azure Storage Queue, you can store messages of up to 64 KB—Azure Service Bus changes that limit to 256 KB.

- Azure Service Bus queues can store less data than Azure Storage Queues—up to 80 GB.
- Azure Service Bus supports consuming batches of messages.
- In Azure Storage Queues, the security model is quite basic—Azure Service Bus supports an RBAC model when it comes to securing queues.
- Azure Storage Queues do not support transactional behaviour.

As you can see, in Azure Service Bus there are many advanced features available, which can be very helpful in applications integrating different systems and applications, and also in third-party ones. Of course, those additional features cost extra as they require a more expensive tier. In Azure Service Bus, you have three tiers:

- **Basic**: Supports queues and scheduled messages only.
- **Standard**: All features are available.
- **Premium**: The maximum message size is extended to 1 MB, and brokered connections are included in the price. This tier also guarantees higher throughput and better performance.

 If you require only the basic functionality (without topics, transactions, or sessions), an Azure Service Bus instance can be even cheaper than using Azure Storage Queues. It all depends on your requirements regarding your system.

Azure Service Bus in Azure portal

To create an instance of the Azure Service Bus, you have to search for the `Service Bus` service in the marketplace. You will see a short form where you fill in the most crucial information, like the name of the service, the pricing tier, and its location:

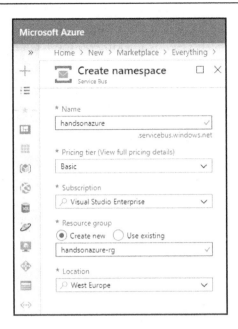

For now, it is all you have to enter—just click on the **Create** button and wait a second until a service is created. The **Overview** blade shows a bit more information, but as you can see, it is very similar to the one you saw when working with Azure Event Hub:

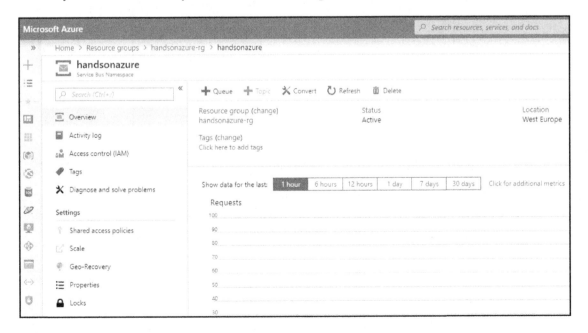

In the preceding screenshot, you see that the **+ Topic** button is grayed out—this is because I selected the basic tier for this exercise. By clicking on the **+ Queue** button, you will be able to create a new queue:

Here things are getting a little bit more complicated:

- **Name**: This is the unique name of a queue.
- **Max queue size**: You can decide the maximum size of a queue (as opposed to a fixed size of 80 GB in Azure Storage Queue).

- **Message time to live**: In Azure Storage Queues, the maximum lifetime of a message was 7 days. Here you can specify the custom lifetime of a message before it is deleted (or moved to a dead letter queue).

- **Lock duration**: When a message is picked up by a consumer, it is locked for a fixed time period to avoid duplicated reads. Here you can customize it (up to a maximum of 5 minutes).

- **Enable duplicate detection**: If you want to ensure the "exactly once" delivery model during a fixed time period, you can enable this option. It enables you to configure a duplicate detection window in which a history of processed messages will be kept.

- **Enable dead lettering on message expiration**: If a message expires, it is automatically deleted. To push it to a dead letter queue instead, enable this option.

- **Enable sessions**: Sessions in Azure Service Bus ensure FIFO message processing. To make sure that the first message pushed to a service is the one to be processed, turn this feature on.

- **Enable partitioning**: This option detaches a queue from a single messaging store, so in fact you are ending with multiple queues. This option ensures that even if a store has an outage, the whole queue or a topic will not go down. There are some limitations, however, regarding this feature—one is that with partitioning you cannot send messages belonging to different sessions in a single transaction. What is more, there is a limit of 100 partitioned queues or topics per namespace.

Partitioned queues and topics are not supported in the premium tier of Azure Service Bus.

This is how a queue looks when partitioning is enabled:

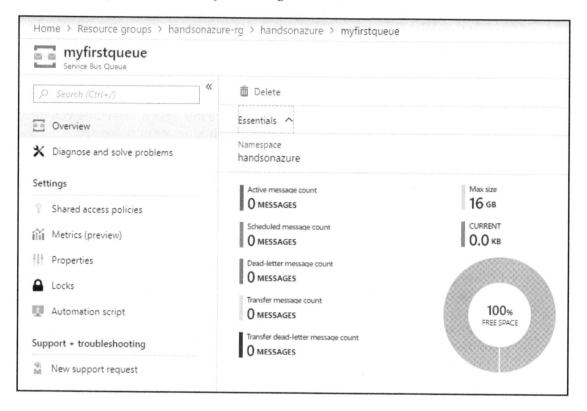

As you can see, the maximum size of a queue is displayed as 16 GB—this is because with partitioning enabled, we are ending with 16 partitions—each hosting a queue of the maximum size of 1 GB.

Because the maximum size of a single queue is set as 5 GB, you can achieve the maximum size of 80 GB by using partitioning. With that feature enabled, the maximum size will be 5 GB * 16 partitions = 80 GB.

Queues, topics, and relays

Azure Service Bus supports three different kinds of entities:

- Queues
- Topics
- Relays

All three give you different options when handling communication.

Queues

A queue is the simplest entity available in the service. You can define it as follows:

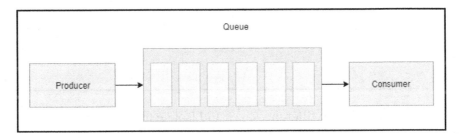

In the preceding sample, you can see that we have the following concepts:

- **Producer**: An application or a service, which pushes a message to a queue
- **Queue**: A container for messages
- **Consumer**: An application or a service, which reads messages from a queue using a pull model

A pull model means that a producer has actually to ask a queue to receive messages. Of course, there can be multiple producers and multiple consumers—this is where the lock duration feature is especially helpful as it ensures that only a single consumer reads a message at any one time.

Topics

Topics are a slightly different model than queues as they allow you to implement a pub/sub communication model. When a queue is a point-to-point communication, topics give you an option to distribute different messages to a different queue:

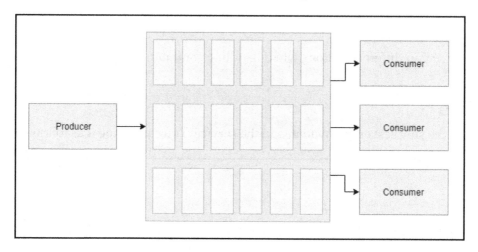

This model makes it possible to filter messages and isolate them, so a consumer reads only those, which they are interested in.

 Remember, topics are not available in the basic tier—you have to use at least the standard tier.

Relays

Both queues and topics are models, which are designed to deliver one-way communication only—a producer sends a message and a receiver reads it. If you want to implement bidirectional communication, you have to use a relay:

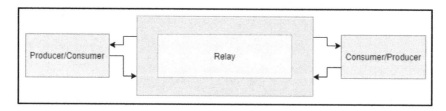

Azure Relay is, in fact, a separate service, and we will not cover it in this chapter. There are, however, many great features, which you may find helpful in your applications:

- It is designed to expose services securely, which are hosted within a corporate network.
- It allows different communication models like one-directional, pub/sub, andtwo-way communication.
- It does not alter the network as a VPN does, making it more stable and scoped to a single application endpoint.

Azure Service Bus design patterns

Azure Service Bus is often a central point of integration for many different cloud services—it can be used in a variety of scenarios, including data integration, broadcasting information, or even bidirectional communication. As the service is rich in different features, you can use it to implement various responsibilities. You can find many examples of design patterns for Azure Service Bus in the *Further reading* section in this chapter.

Developing solutions with Azure Service Bus SDK

There is a rich database of many different examples for working with Azure Service Bus, available on GitHub (you can find a link in the *Further reading* section), so we will cover only the basic ones in this chapter. Here you can find the most simple way to send a message to a queue:

```
using System.Text;
using System.Threading.Tasks;
using Microsoft.Azure.ServiceBus;

namespace HandsOnAzure.ServiceBus
{
    internal class Program
    {
        private static void Main()
        {
            MainAsync().GetAwaiter().GetResult();
        }

        private static async Task MainAsync()
        {
```

```
            var client = new QueueClient("<connection-string>", "<queue-
    name>");
            var message = "This is my message!";

            await client.SendAsync(new
    Message(Encoding.UTF8.GetBytes(message)));
        }
    }
}
```

As you can see, all it requires (at least to get the basic functionality) is to use
a QueueClient instance. If you want to work with a topic, you could
use TopicClient instead:

```
var client = new TopicClient("<connection-string>", "<topic-name>");
```

In fact, all you need is to install the Microsoft.Azure.ServiceBus NuGet package. After
I ran the preceding code three times and checked my queue, this is what I saw in the portal:

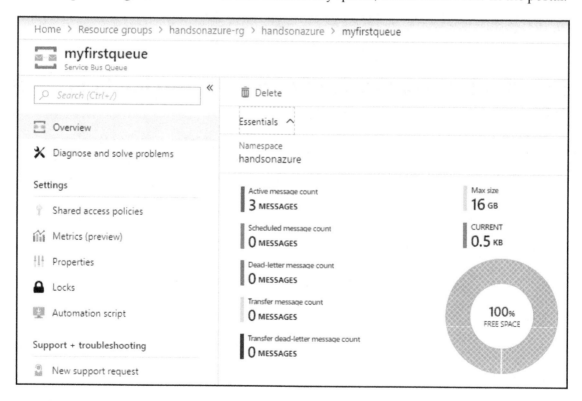

As you can see, there are three active messages. That means that I have successfully published them and they are ready to be pulled. There are many different options for pulling a message—here you can find an example using `PeekAsync`:

```csharp
using System;
using System.Text;
using System.Threading.Tasks;
using Microsoft.Azure.ServiceBus.Core;

namespace HandsOnAzure.ServiceBus.Reader
{
    internal class Program
    {
        private static void Main()
        {
            MainAsync().GetAwaiter().GetResult();

            Console.ReadLine();
        }

        private static async Task MainAsync()
        {
            var receiver =
                new MessageReceiver(
                    "<connection-string>",
                    "<queue-name>");

            while (true)
            {
                var message = await receiver.PeekAsync();
                if(message == null) continue;

                Console.WriteLine($"New message:
[{message.ScheduledEnqueueTimeUtc}]
{Encoding.UTF8.GetString(message.Body)}");
                await Task.Delay(100);
            }
        }
    }
}
```

However, if you only peek messages, you will not create a message store. To actually do that, you have to use `ReceiveAsync`:

```csharp
var message = await receiver.ReceiveAsync();
```

The difference will be visible when you read messages using both methods. `PeekAsync` will not change the state of messages (so they will be still visible as active, even if you set the `ReceiveMode` option to `ReceiveAndDelete`). `ReceiveAsync` will use the value of a `ReceiveMode` option and possibly act as an atomic `CompleteAsync` operation.

> To mark messages as read after using `PeekAsync`, you can use `CompleteAsync`.

We will cover more advanced scenarios later in this chapter.

Azure Service Bus security

As Azure Service Bus is described as an enterprise-level cloud service designed for integrating different services, there are serious expectations regarding the security features it offers. Besides shared access tokens, there are new features in the preview, which allow much more flexible access management.

Managed Service Identity

Managed Service Identity (MSI) is a feature in Azure Cloud, which eases authentication between services, without storing credentials in your code. The whole description can be found in the link in the *Further reading* section. When it comes to using it with Azure Service Bus, there is no additional blade available—what you need is just to find an identity in the access control (IAM) blade:

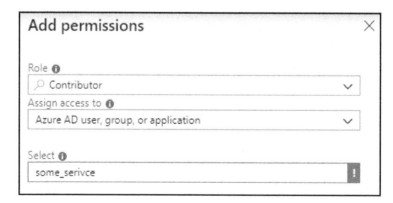

Now, instead of using an SAS token or access policy, you can use the following code:

```
var tokenProvider =
TokenProvider.CreateManagedServiceIdentityTokenProvider();
var sendClient = new
QueueClient($"sb://{namespace}.servicebus.windows.net/", {queue-name},
tokenProvider);
await sendClient.SendAsync(new
Message(Encoding.UTF8.GetBytes(messageInfo.MessageToSend)));
await sendClient.CloseAsync();
```

As you can see, the flow becomes much simpler as you do not have to store credentials or keys, and instead let the provider handle the authentication.

RBAC

In Azure Service Bus, there is also a possibility to leverage roles defined in Azure AD to grant access to a service. The whole feature relies on the assumption that a user will be able to take responsibility for granting access to a Service Bus instance. The first step is exactly the same as with MSI authentication: you have to add a user to a service, so it gains access and can start pushing and receiving messages. The full instructions can be found in the *Further reading* section.

Note that with the ability to tell explicitly how a user or an application can access Azure Service Bus, you are given much better control over how messages are published and received. This a great improvement over Azure Storage Queues, where such features are not available.

There is also a possibility to use RBAC authentication to grant access to a service to another service (if MSI is not available). In that scenario, there will be no interactive login required as it is all handled by Azure AD.

Even if interactive login is required, it is not handled by an application so you can be sure that it will not handle any credentials directly.

Advanced features of Azure Service Bus

We have already covered some of the basics of the Azure Service Bus, like SDK, the most crucial concepts, and security considerations. Now we will focus a little bit on more advanced use cases, like dead lettering, performance, sessions, and transactions. All those topics are crucial when developing a reliable and important service integrating many different applications and systems. Also remember to take a look at the Azure Service Bus examples in the *Further reading* section, as it points to a GitHub repository where you can find many different use cases and concepts when using this service.

Dead lettering

In general, dead lettering means that there are messages in a queue considered as dead (because there was no receiver interested in pulling them) and you have two options to proceed:

- Either delete them permanently
- Push them to an additional queue, named a dead letter queue

In Azure Service Bus, you have two options to push a message to a dead letter queue:

- Set the maximum lifetime of a message—once it expires, it is automatically moved to a dead letter queue
- Use the `DeadLetterAsync` method on `MessageReceiver` as follows:

```
await receiver.DeadLetterAsync("<lock-token>", "<reason>");
```

Here you can find the complete example, and you can find a lock token:

```
while (true)
{
  var message = await receiver.ReceiveAsync();
  if(message == null) continue;

  Console.WriteLine($"New message: [{message.ScheduledEnqueueTimeUtc}]
{Encoding.UTF8.GetString(message.Body)}");

  await receiver.DeadLetterAsync(message.SystemProperties.LockToken,
"HandsOnAzure - test");
  await Task.Delay(100);
}
```

Once you push messages to a dead letter queue, their status will be visible in the portal:

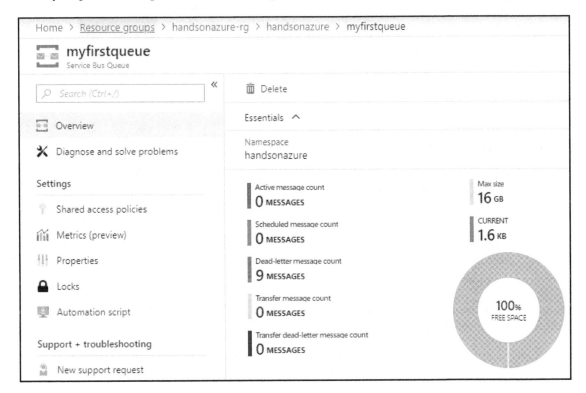

Of course, it is possible to fetch messages from a dead letter queue. To get the name, you can use the following method:

```
var deadLetterQueueName = EntityNameHelper.FormatDeadLetterPath("<entity-
path>");
```

Sessions

In Azure Service Bus, sessions are used to achieve a FIFO guarantee. In general, the service does not control the relationship between messages, so even if in most cases the order is preserved, it is not guaranteed. To put a message to a session, you have to leverage a `SessionId` property:

```
await client.SendAsync(new Message(Encoding.UTF8.GetBytes(message)) {
SessionId = Guid.Empty.ToString() });
```

To handle a session on the receiver side, you have to use
the `RegisterSessionHandler` method on a `QueueClient` instance:

```
var client = new QueueClient("<connection-string>", "<queue-name>");
client.RegisterSessionHandler((session, message, ct) => Task.FromResult(new
SessionHandler()), args => Task.CompletedTask);
```

Additionally, you will have to implement `IMessageSession`.

Transactions

Transactions in Azure Service Bus are a wide topic referring to many different entities,
which you can work with in this service:

- Clients (`QueueClient`, `TopicClient`)
- Messages (by using operations like `Complete`, `Defer`, `Abandon`, and many
  more)
- Sessions (`GetState`/`SetState`)

As you can see, there are no receive operations listed; this is because there is an assumption
that they are atomic by design.

In general, there is a requirement for using
the `ReceiveMode.PeekLock` mode when pulling messages and opening
a transaction scope inside a loop or an `OnMessage` callback.

You can refer to the following code snippet to get a better picture of what we are talking
about in this section:

```
var message = receiver.Receive();
using (scope = new TransactionScope())
{
    var newMessage = // transfer
    sender.Send(newMessage);
    message.Complete();
    scope.Complete();
}
```

In the above example, a processor (which at the same moment is responsible for producing a message) marks a message as complete, while transferring a new message to another queue. The whole model leverages the autoforwarding feature of Azure Service Bus. The following is an example of a topic:

```
var subscription = new SubscriptionDescription(sourceTopic,
subscriptionName);
subscription.ForwardTo = destinationTopic;
namespaceManager.CreateSubscription(subscription);
```

When a transaction is implemented, you can be sure that committing to a queue log will only happen if the whole transaction succeeds; otherwise, there will be simply no trace of the messages that were handled inside it.

Handling outages and disasters

If you make Azure Service Bus the center of your architecture—a service that is responsible for integrating dozens of services and handling the communication—you have to make sure that it is replicated and invulnerable to disasters. There are two topics to consider here: disaster recovery and handling outages. As those terms are completely different concepts, you have both to understand them and be able to implement a solution in case unexpected issues and accidents occur. In the last section of this chapter, you will learn how Azure Service Bus can be made into a durable cloud component, on which you and your applications can rely.

Disaster recovery

When a disaster happens, you may lose a part or all of your data. In general, a disaster is defined as a temporal or permanent loss of the whole service with no guarantees that it will become available again. Such disasters are floods, earthquakes, or fires, just to name a few. Disasters tend to occur in a single region (the probability of disasters occurring in separate regions simultaneously is very small), so in general you need two different data centers to implement disaster recovery (DR).

 Remember, using two different data centers may not be enough if they are close to each other—you have to select two that can satisfy your requirements, but at the same time are as far from each other as possible.

When it comes to implementing DR in Azure Service Bus, the flow is the same as in Azure Event Hub:

- Create the primary region
- Create the secondary region
- Create the pairing
- Define a trigger for failover

In general, to create the pairing, you need the following code snippet:

```
var client = new ServiceBusManagementClient(creds) { SubscriptionId =
subscriptionId };

var namespace2 =
  await client.Namespaces.CreateOrUpdateAsync(
  "<resource-group-name>",
  "<secondary-namespace>",
  new SBNamespace { ... params ... });

ArmDisasterRecovery drStatus =
  await client.DisasterRecoveryConfigs.CreateOrUpdateAsync(
        "<resource-group-name>",
      "<primary-namespace>",
      "<alias>",
      new ArmDisasterRecovery { PartnerNamespace = namespace2.Id })
```

 The preceding sample uses the `Microsoft.Azure.Management.ServiceBus` NuGet package for operating on a namespace.

Once a pairing is configured and created, it is up to you to trigger and initiate a failover. To do so, the following line is all you need:

```
client.DisasterRecoveryConfigs.FailOver("<resource-group-name>",
"<secondary-namespace>", "<alias>");
```

 Note that a failover is initiated against the secondary region—this is crucial as the primary region may not be available at the time of initiating an operation.

Once a failover is finished, you can start handling messages using your secondary region. There is, however, one important thing to remember: in case another outage happens, you want to be able to fail over again. Because of that, it is also very important to set up another secondary namespace (and make the current one your primary) and pair them to be secure again.

Handling outages

While a disaster often means that some part of your data is lost, an outage may be described as a service being temporarily unavailable. This is why once it is resolved, you may want to synchronize both Service Bus namespaces. While this process is automatic, it may take a while. It is stated in the documentation that only 50-100 entities will be transferred per minute. For this reason, you may consider the concept of active/passive replication:

- **Active**: In such an approach, you have two active namespaces, which actively receive messages. Then a receiver always receives both of them—you have to tag them properly with the same unique identifier used to detect duplicates (you can use either the `MessageId` or `Label` property for that).
- **Passive**: Instead of actively using both queues (or topics), you can use the second one only if a message cannot be delivered to the primary namespace. This approach has its caveats, however: it may cause a message delivery delay (or even loss) or duplicates.

Here, you can find an example of passive replication:

```
private async Task SendMessage(BrokeredMessage message1, int maxSendRetries
= 10)
{
  do
  {
    var message2 = message1.Clone();
    try
    {
      await _activeQueueClient.SendAsync(message1);
      return;
    }
    catch
    {
      if (--maxSendRetries <= 0)
      {
        throw;
      }
```

```
        lock (_swapMutex)
        {
          var client = _activeQueueClient;
          _activeQueueClient = _backupQueueClient;
          _backupQueueClient = client;
        }
        message1 = message2.Clone();
      }
    }
    while (true);
}
```

As you can see, it clearly shows how a duplicate of a message is passed to a backup queue. An example of active replication is slightly different:

```
var task1 = primaryQueueClient.SendAsync(m1);
var task2 = secondaryQueueClient.SendAsync(m2);

try
{
  await task1;
}
catch (Exception e)
{
  exceptionCount++;
}

try
{
  await task2;
}
catch (Exception e)
{
  exceptionCount++;
}

if (exceptionCount > 1)
{
  throw new Exception("Send Failure");
}
```

Here we are sending the same message to both namespaces, even if one of them fails. One more thing that should be considered to handle outages is using partitioned senders (though unavailable in the premium tier). When using them, you are safe in case of an outage of a single messaging store, and you can still use other partitions to send and receive data. The following example enables partitioning on a topic:

```
var ns = NamespaceManager.CreateFromConnectionString(myConnectionString);
var td = new TopicDescription(TopicName);
td.EnablePartitioning = true;
ns.CreateTopic(td);
```

Summary

In this short chapter, you learned the basic concepts of Azure Service Bus including queues, topics, SDK, and more advanced features like dead lettering, sessions, and transactions. There are still many things to learn: asynchronous messaging, **Advanced Message Queuing Protocol (AMQP)**, and advanced transaction scenarios. In general, it is a great service for both simple and critical scenarios as it gives you enough flexibility to adjust it to most applications, and at the same time it is quite easy to learn how to get started. Remember, you can use the basic tier for the simplest use cases, which gives you a cheap and reliable solution, a much richer option than Azure Storage Queue. In the next chapter, we will focus on monitoring services with Azure Application Insights.

Questions

1. What is the difference between a queue and a topic?
2. Can you use topics in the basic tier?
3. What is the reason for using a dead letter queue?
4. What are sessions for in Azure Service Bus?
5. What is the maximum size of a queue with partitioning enabled, when a single queue has the maximum size of 1 GB?
6. What is the difference between active and passive replication?
7. How is disaster recovery achieved in Azure Service Bus?

Further reading

- **MSI overview:** https://docs.microsoft.com/pl-pl/azure/active-directory/managed-identities-azure-resources/overview
- **RBAC authentication:** https://docs.microsoft.com/en-us/azure/service-bus-messaging/service-bus-role-based-access-control
- **Service Bus samples:** https://github.com/Azure/azure-service-bus/tree/master/samples/DotNet
- **Azure Service Bus design patterns:** https://msdn.microsoft.com/en-us/magazine/mt845652.aspx

15
Using Application Insights to Monitor Your Applications

Azure is not only about developing an application. Once we have our solution deployed to the cloud, we have to somehow monitor and diagnose it. The Azure Application Insights service offers a complete toolset for maintaining your applications, with SDKs available for multiple languages and platforms, alerts, query language, and integration with many native Azure services. It simplifies logging in to applications and gets rid of multiple sources of truth when it comes to analyzing an issue using data from several places.

The following topics will be covered in this chapter:

- Using the Azure Application Insights service
- Monitoring different platforms
- Using the Analytics module
- Automating Azure Application Insights

Technical requirements

To perform the exercises in this chapter, you will need:

- An Azure subscription
- Visual Studio with the following workloads installed—ASP.NET,web development, and Azure development

Using the Application Insights service

One of the most important features when developing applications (especially hosted in the cloud) is the ability to easily monitor them and detect at an early stage any possible issues and flaws. To do so, you need a whole architecture of loggers, storage, and report tools, which you have to integrate, configure, and maintain daily. This requires an additional set of skills in your team and, of course, takes time—the bigger your application is, the more is required. With Azure Application Insights, all those operations are much simpler: you have a single service and endpoint for logging all required information, and the rest is done for you automatically.

Logging data in the cloud

Let's assume you have the following architecture:

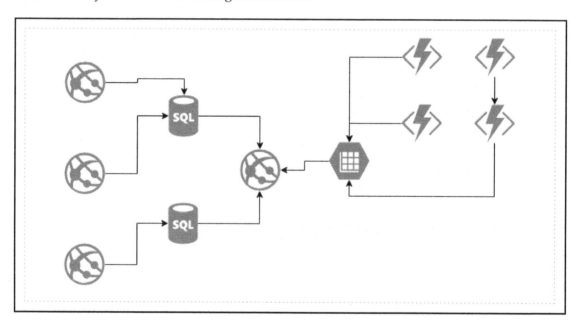

It contains many different web apps, different storage capabilities (such as a SQL database or Azure Storage), and also Azure Functions. If we want to be able to monitor all those services, we will need the following components:

- A tool for saving logs (which is able to use different outputs such as storage or a file, possibly multiplatform)

- Storage able to store gigabytes of log data
- Some kind of dashboard, which will get data from the storage and display it using different filters and parameters

When you take all those into account, you may find the following caveats:

- Storing raw data is not enough as you will need some kind of projections view, which can be quickly fetched and does not require extra transformations or processing.
- You have to find a way to store data that allows users to query at will with different vectors—appending logs may seem great for checking recent records, but for creating an index of dynamic parameters it is not so good.
- You have to implement some kind of data retention—most logs have no use after a fixed time period.
- Performance for both applications and the reporting solution should be repeatable and should not change in time (for example, with the increased amount of data stored).
- Having a dedicated team for issue tracking may not be the best allocation of resources—people with reporting and data analyzing skills are much more valuable when they work on actual business data.

The ideal solution for the preceding problems would be a single component capable of doing everything we mentioned earlier:

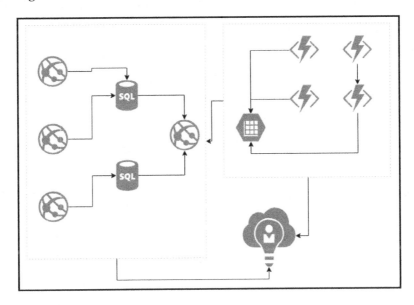

In Azure, such a component is Azure Application Insights, which we will cover in this chapter.

Azure Application Insights fundamentals

Connecting to the Azure Application Insights service can differ depending on your circumstances. In general, you have multiple possibilities when integrating the service:

- Seamless integration within the portal—no additional steps required, you just enable and configure a feature—the rest is already implemented
- Using an appropriate SDK depending on the platform
- Sending telemetry events directly to the service endpoints

Depending on the concept you use, a different configuration will be used:

- For the portal, you need no extra steps as you are already authenticated, and a resource can be selected for example from a drop-down menu.
- For SDK, you need an instrumentation key, which can be found in the portal—we will cover this topic later in this chapter.
- Using REST APIs, there are different options available, such as App ID, key, or OAuth2 flow .

 Note that, depending on the method of logging used, different features and capabilities may be available. This is especially true for sending custom events or custom logging logic—such actions often will require using a dedicated SDK.

Besides some obvious features (such as the ability to log and store information about a request or an exception), Azure Application Insights has many different capabilities implemented:

- **Requests telemetry**: You can automatically gather information regarding the request count, average latency, and failure rates. If using this service, for example, with Azure App Services, you are given full insights into your web application by just implementing the SDK.

- **Dependencies**: Besides general telemetry, in Azure Application Insights you can find information about how your dependencies (such as Azure Table Storage and Azure SQL) perform. This is especially true if you have multiple services integrated and you want to know which one affects the latency the most.

- **Exceptions**: Having information about failed requests or dependencies is one thing, but a detailed dashboard displaying aggregated data about errors is a much more useful thing. In Azure Application Insights, you can easily check which type of error is connected to some specific subset of requests. This gives you a much better understanding of what is going on under the hood in your application and where to start fixing it.

- **User telemetry**: Do you want to know exactly how many users you have? Are you interested in what the flow is when they use your application? In Azure Application Insights, there are additional features that give you information about user and session counts, their behavior, and overall activities.

Of course, I have not listed all the available features—there are even more, such as gathering information regarding AJAX calls, page view, and web performance; performance counters (for VMs), and host diagnostics from Docker. In fact, the availability of a feature also depends on the service you have chosen—a different telemetry is gathered for Azure Functions and for Azure App Services.

 In reality, you can achieve the same level of granularity of your logs with similar charts and diagnostics available in most services. What changes is the level of effort required—the less integration a service has with Azure Application Insights, the more you have to do on your own.

Creating Azure Application Insights in the portal

To create an instance of Azure Application Insights, you have to search for the service in the marketplace.

You will have to fill in the following simple form to proceed:

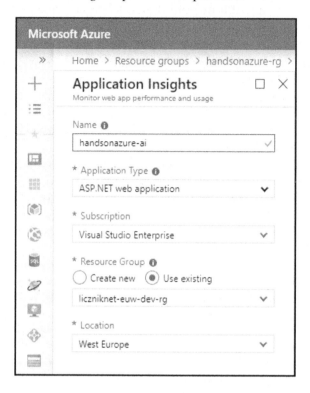

In fact, it contains one field that you probably have not met yet:

- **Application Type**: Depending on your choice (**ASP.NET web application**, **Java**, **App Center**, **Node.js**, or **General**), a different set of charts will be selected. This option does not affect the available features of a service. Rather, it ensures that, for a specific instance, you will see only the information you are most interested in.

The rest of what your instance is capable of depends solely on the services integrated with it and the amount of data sent to it.

> Unlike most Azure services, in Azure Application Insights there is no requirement to have a unique service name for all instances globally—here you just cannot use the same name for multiple services within a service. This is because it does not use a DNS name to work and connect with other applications.

When you click **Create,** it should not take long to provision a new instance of a service, which should look similar to the following:

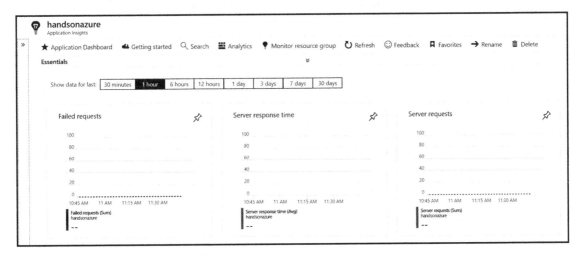

As you can see, there is the **Essentials** section, hidden by default—it contains some common metadata and, what is more important, an instrumentation key— and an identifier, which uniquely identifies your instance of your service. We will use it to actually connect to Azure Application Insights—the rest of the feature will be described later in this chapter.

Monitoring different platforms

The strength of Azure Application Insights is its ability to monitor simultaneously from different platforms. You can choose from ASP.NET pages, Java, Node.JS, or even Python or Ruby (however, there are some languages and frameworks officially supported by Application Insights teams and some are supported by the community). The point is, it is platform-agnostic. When you, in fact, need the implementation of the communication channel, with an instrumentation key you can easily send data to an instance of a service without additional keys and an extended configuration. In this section, we will focus on sending information from different platforms, so you will be able to start integration in your projects easily on your own.

.NET

In .NET applications, the only thing you have to do to get started is to install the latest `Microsoft.ApplicationInsights` package. The easiest way is to use the following code snippet:

```
TelemetryConfiguration.Active.InstrumentationKey = "<instrumentation-key>";
var telemetryClient = new TelemetryClient();
```

This code does two things:

- Sets the current configuration by providing an instrumentation key. It is all that is needed to connect to a service.
- Initializes an instance of `TelemetryClient`—this class is a proxy to a service, which enables you to communicate with it.

Then you can use different methods to log some data:

```
telemetryClient.TrackTrace("Hello World!");
telemetryClient.TrackException(new Exception());
telemetryClient.TrackDependency(new DependencyTelemetry());
```

Of course, there are more methods available—you can find them in the *Further reading* section. In the first snippet, we used the `TelemetryConfiguration` type—in fact, the data stored in the configuration it provides is initially fetched from the `ApplicationInsights.config` file—it can look like this:

```xml
<?xml version="1.0" encoding="utf-8"?>
<ApplicationInsights
xmlns="http://schemas.microsoft.com/ApplicationInsights/2013/Settings">
  <InstrumentationKey>8sad7asd-asd876asf-
jr323jsd-3hshjahj</InstrumentationKey>
  <TelemetryInitializers>
    <Add
Type="Microsoft.ApplicationInsights.DependencyCollector.HttpDependenciesPar
singTelemetryInitializer, Microsoft.AI.DependencyCollector"/>
  </TelemetryInitializers>
  <TelemetryModules>
    <Add
Type="Microsoft.ApplicationInsights.DependencyCollector.DependencyTrackingT
elemetryModule, Microsoft.AI.DependencyCollector">
      <ExcludeComponentCorrelationHttpHeadersOnDomains>
      </ExcludeComponentCorrelationHttpHeadersOnDomains>
      <IncludeDiagnosticSourceActivities>
        <Add>Microsoft.Azure.ServiceBus</Add>
        <Add>Microsoft.Azure.EventHubs</Add>
```

```
        </IncludeDiagnosticSourceActivities>
      </Add>
   </TelemetryModules>
   <TelemetryChannel
 Type="Microsoft.ApplicationInsights.WindowsServer.TelemetryChannel.ServerTe
 lemetryChannel, Microsoft.AI.ServerTelemetryChannel"/>
 </ApplicationInsights>
```

If the file is not present (or it does not contain all values), the configuration will not be correct; in such a scenario, you have to provide it manually.

 Please note, those above instructions are applicable only if you are using .NET framework.

It is worth mentioning here that the setup differs between platforms. We have discussed the most basic (console app) one, but we can use other application types, like Windows desktop applications:

```
public partial class Form1 : Form
{
  private TelemetryClient _telemetryClient = new TelemetryClient();

  private void Form1_Load(object sender, EventArgs e)
  {
    _telemetryClient.InstrumentationKey = "<instrumenation-key>";

    _telemetryClient.Context.User.Id = Environment.UserName;
    _telemetryClient.Context.Session.Id = Guid.NewGuid().ToString();
    _telemetryClient.Context.Device.OperatingSystem =
Environment.OSVersion.ToString();

    _telemetryClient.TrackPageView("Form1");
  }
}
```

Or we can use web apps that have a seamless integration with Azure Application Insights.

Node.js

To start working with Azure Application Insights in Node.js, you will need the following command:

```
npm install applicationinsights
```

It will install an NPM package of Application Insights, which allows working with this service. Here is a full example of the interface of this package:

```
let http = require("http");
let appInsights = require("applicationinsights");

appInsights.setup("<instrumentation-key>");
appInsights.start();
let client = appInsights.defaultClient;

client.trackEvent({name: "my custom event", properties: {customProperty:
"custom property value"}});
client.trackException({exception: new Error("handled exceptions can be
logged with this method")});
client.trackMetric({name: "custom metric", value: 3});
client.trackTrace({message: "trace message"});
client.trackDependency({target:"http://dbname", name:"select customers
proc", data:"SELECT * FROM Customers", duration:231, resultCode:0, success:
true, dependencyTypeName: "ZSQL"});
client.trackRequest({name:"GET /customers",
url:"http://myserver/customers", duration:309, resultCode:200,
success:true});


http.createServer( (req, res) => {
  client.trackNodeHttpRequest({request: req, response: res});
}).listen(1337, "127.0.0.1");

console.log('Server running at http://127.0.0.1:1337/');
```

Try to run the example and check the insights—you will see that first requests are logged:

Azure Functions

Azure Application Insights also offers seamless integration with another Azure service, Azure Functions. There are two ways of enabling integration: either turn it on while creating a service, or manually by providing an instrumentation key in the settings.

The following is a form where this feature can be enabled:

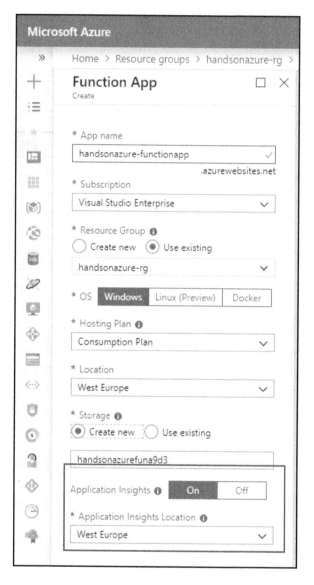

There is, however, one caveat to such a setup: you cannot select an instance of a service if you already have one. To do so, you have to enable integration manually by providing APPINSIGHTS_INSTRUMENTATIONKEY in the settings of the **Function App**.

There is one more option. Instead of providing a key manually, you can click on the **Monitor** tab of any function and then **Configure**. This option will be available if the classic view is not yet enabled.

With integration enabled, you will be able to analyze the executions of all your queries:

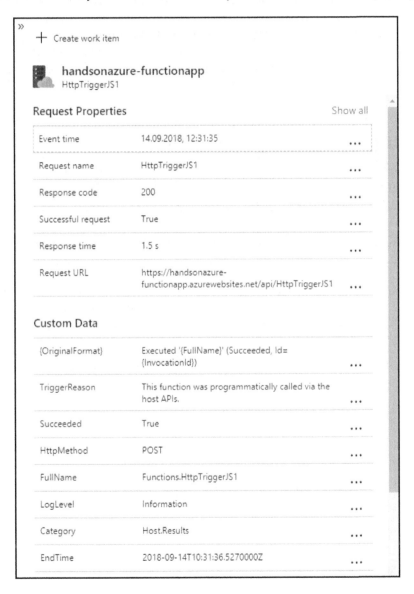

Analytics module

Multiple ways to integrate Azure Application Insights with different services (as well as a custom application) is not the only big feature of this service. Another important and crucial thing is the analytics language available in the Analytics module. It is an interactive query language, which enables you to explore logged data easily, using a simple and intuitive syntax. Another great thing about it is that you do not need any additional tools to get started—once you store traces, exceptions, or requests, it is available out-of-the-box—the only thing you need to do is write a query. In this section, we will cover both the query language and the module, so you can start writing your own queries and discover many different dimensions available in stored logs.

Accessing the Analytics module

Getting started with the Analytics module is really easy. Go to the **Overview** blade of your instance of Azure Application Analytics and click on the **Analytics** button:

It will display another window showing new options, such as the ability to enter a query, use a pre-defined one, or simply explore the different dimensions available:

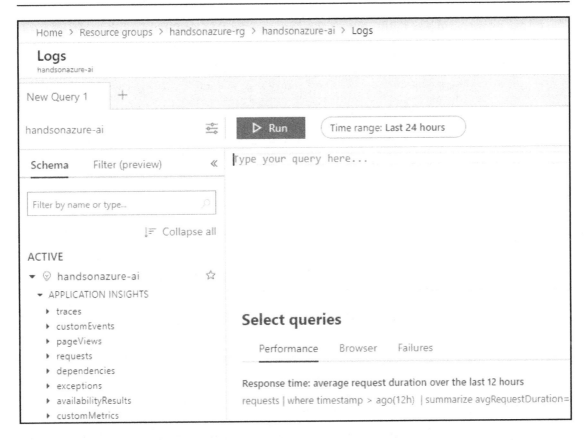

The most important thing here is the query window. It is an interactive feature which enables you to write a query and offers you additional capabilities, such as a syntax validator and suggestions. Let's start with a simple query which displays request counts over the last few days:

```
requests
| summarize totalCount=sum(itemCount) by bin(timestamp, 30m)
| render timechart
```

As you can see, it has three parts:

- `requests`: The dimension you are querying
- `summarize`: A function which defines what you want to get from the dimension
- `render`: An optional function that draws a chart based on the data

Of course, queries can have different structures; you can find one that is a bit more complicated:

```
requests
| summarize RequestsCount=sum(itemCount), AverageDuration=avg(duration),
percentiles(duration, 50, 95, 99) by operation_Name
| order by RequestsCount desc
```

From the preceding example, there will be no chart—instead, it will display a table:

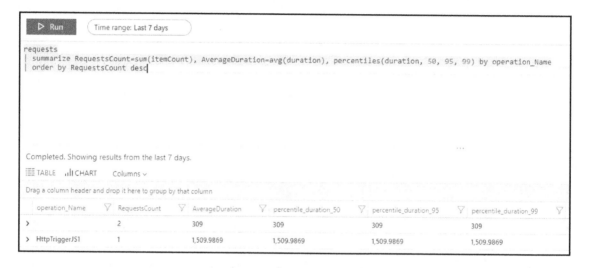

The important thing is the date range for a query as inside it you can just filter data. You have to select which dates you are interested in. To do so, click on the **Time range** button, next to the **Run** button, and choose the right option:

The query language in Azure Application Analytics is very rich as it defines many different functions for different data types and actions (you can use many different window functions, for example, `next()`). The relevant reference can be found in the *Further reading* section.

Additionally, when a query is actioned, you can select an additional filter for it (based on the result), so you can choose specific records:

There is also one other helpful feature of the Analytics module—smart analytics. It is a set of additional functions which extend the analytic capabilities by introducing elements of machine learning in data analysis. Currently, the following functions are available:

- **Autocluster**: A function which automatically divides data into clusters to make it easier to understand.
- **Basket**: This one automatically finds interesting data inside the results of a query.
- **Diffpatterns**: This feature operates on a column that stores true/false data and tries to find patterns corresponding to the differences between them.
- **Timer series**: This function (`make-series`) will convert data into a single row making it possible to analyze the root cause of a problem.
- **Linear regression**: With this function, you will easily find data trends based on the results (whether, for example, the number of exceptions grows or not).
- **Outlier value detection**: This one finds how a value is anomalous in comparison with others.

With these advanced functions, you can greatly improve the analysis of your data. They incorporate many helpful features, making the whole service much more flexible. What is more, you do not have to be a data scientist to actually work on data, find trends, and anomalies.

Application Insights automation

Monitoring is not something you like to spend time on on a daily basis. In fact, the more automated the service is, the better results you can get. It is always easier to let the machine look at different dimensions and find problems based on some preset rules; it will do it quicker and more carefully. In Azure Application Insights, you have many options when it comes to automation: ARM templates, alerts in the portal, or integrating external services (such as Microsoft Flow). In the last section of this chapter, you will learn how to get started with automation and make sure you focus on development, instead of log analysis and service maintenance.

Alerts

An alert is a feature which enables you to be notified when an anomaly occurs. There are plenty of different possibilities when it comes to setting up an alert, starting with an ARM template:

```
{
  "name": "[variables('myFirstAlertName')]",
  "type": "Microsoft.Insights/alertrules",
  "apiVersion": "2014-04-01",
  "location": "[parameters('appLocation')]",
  "dependsOn": [
    "[resourceId('Microsoft.Insights/components',
parameters('myApplicationName'))]"
  ],
  "tags": {
    "[concat('hidden-link:', resourceId('Microsoft.Insights/components',
parameters('myApplicationName')))]": "Resource"
  },
  "properties": {
    "name": "[variables('responseAlertName')]",
    "description": "response time alert",
    "isEnabled": true,
    "condition": {
      "$type":
"Microsoft.WindowsAzure.Management.Monitoring.Alerts.Models.ThresholdRuleCo
ndition, Microsoft.WindowsAzure.Management.Mon.Client",
      "odata.type":
"Microsoft.Azure.Management.Insights.Models.ThresholdRuleCondition",
      "dataSource": {
        "$type":
"Microsoft.WindowsAzure.Management.Monitoring.Alerts.Models.RuleMetricDataS
ource, Microsoft.WindowsAzure.Management.Mon.Client",
        "odata.type":
"Microsoft.Azure.Management.Insights.Models.RuleMetricDataSource",
        "resourceUri": "[resourceId('microsoft.insights/components',
parameters('myApplicationName'))]",
        "metricName": "request.duration"
      },
      "threshold": "[parameters('responseTime')]",
      "windowSize": "PT15M"
    },
    "actions": [{
      "$type":
"Microsoft.WindowsAzure.Management.Monitoring.Alerts.Models.RuleEmailAction
, Microsoft.WindowsAzure.Management.Mon.Client",
      "odata.type":
```

```
"Microsoft.Azure.Management.Insights.Models.RuleEmailAction",
    "sendToServiceOwners": true,
    "customEmails": []
  }]
}
}
```

While initially such an ARM template may be a little bit overwhelming, in fact it contains a fixed set of parameters which can be easily found using Resource Explorer (you can find a link to it in the *Further reading* section). Here you can find out how existing alert rules can be discovered:

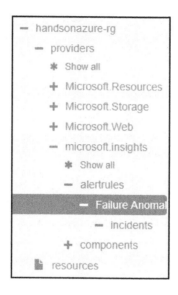

In the preceding screenshot, I displayed the available alert rules inside an Azure Application Insights instance, which I created inside a particular resource group. When you click on it, you will see a full description of the resource inside Azure.

> Resource Explorer is a great tool when you work with ARM templates and search for a reference to a particular resource. It displays all parameters describing a service from the ARM point of view.

Here, you can find the default alert, created when a service is deployed:

```
{
  "id": "/subscriptions/.../resourceGroups/handsonazure-
rg/providers/microsoft.insights/alertrules/Failure Anomalies -
handsonazure-ai",
  "name": "Failure Anomalies - handsonazure-ai",
  "type": "Microsoft.Insights/alertRules",
  "location": "West Europe",
  "properties": {
    "name": "Failure Anomalies - handsonazure-ai",
    "description": "",
    "isEnabled": true,
    "condition": {
      "$type":
"Microsoft.WindowsAzure.Management.Monitoring.Alerts.Models.ThresholdRuleCo
ndition, Microsoft.WindowsAzure.Management.Mon.Client",
      "odata.type":
"Microsoft.Azure.Management.Insights.Models.ThresholdRuleCondition",
      "dataSource": {
        "$type":
"Microsoft.WindowsAzure.Management.Monitoring.Alerts.Models.RuleMetricDataS
ource, Microsoft.WindowsAzure.Management.Mon.Client",
        "odata.type":
"Microsoft.Azure.Management.Insights.Models.RuleMetricDataSource",
        "resourceUri": "/subscriptions/.../resourcegroups/handsonazure-
rg/providers/microsoft.insights/components/handsonazure-ai",
        "resourceLocation": null,
        "metricNamespace": null,
        "metricName": "...",
        "legacyResourceId": null
      },
      "operator": "GreaterThan",
      "threshold": 2,
      "windowSize": "PT1H",
      "timeAggregation": null
    },
    "action": null,
    "lastUpdatedTime": "2018-09-14T12:04:57.6355645Z",
    "provisioningState": "Succeeded",
    "actions": [
      {
        "$type":
"Microsoft.WindowsAzure.Management.Monitoring.Alerts.Models.RuleEmailAction
, Microsoft.WindowsAzure.Management.Mon.Client",
        "odata.type":
"Microsoft.Azure.Management.Insights.Models.RuleEmailAction",
        "sendToServiceOwners": true,
```

```
          "customEmails": []
        }
      ]
    }
}
```

To make things a little bit easier to understand, let's check how to set an alert inside a portal. You can access the **Alerts** blade in the **Configure** section:

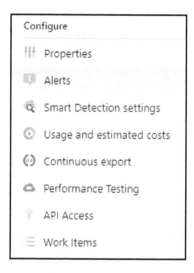

To get started you need to click on the **+ New alert rule** button. What you will see is a detailed wizard, providing a quick way to set up an alert. The most important thing here is the conditions—they define how an alert is triggered:

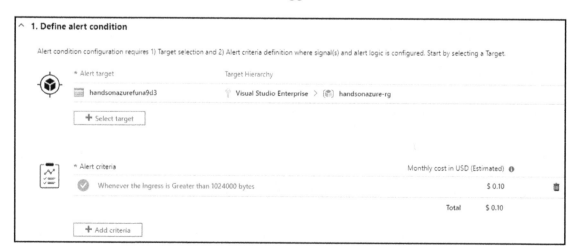

Of course, an alert can have more than only one trigger as it all depends on its characteristics. What is more, the conditions can be quite complex; they can refer to multiple resources and introduce the concept of composite alert rules. The next thing defined here is the alert details—you have to provide some metadata which describes them:

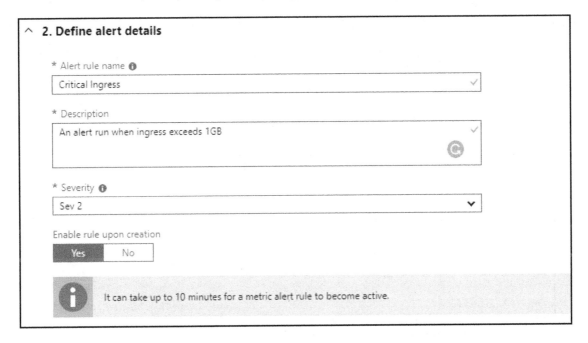

The important thing is the severity of an alert: the higher it is, the more crucial an alert will be. The last part of the wizard is the actual action, and you have multiple options available:

- Email/SMS/Push/Voice
- Azure Function
- LogicApp
- Webhook
- ITSM
- Automation runbook

Some of them require you to already have a service which will handle an alert—you have to select the option that suits your needs the most. When you create an alert, it will be active and visible in the service:

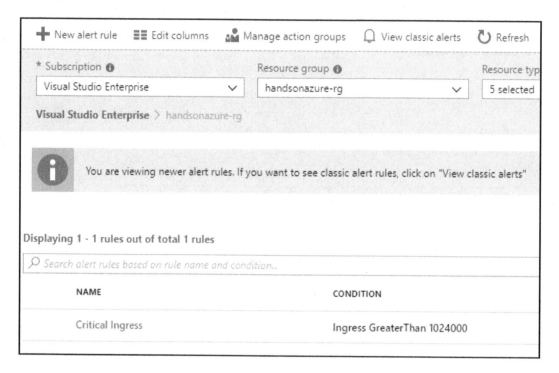

Summary

In this chapter, you learned about a monitoring solution available for Azure: Azure Application Insights. We covered things such as provisioning a resource, creating an alert, and integrating with other services. This Azure component offers many additional features besides those mentioned in the chapter—there are things such as smart detection, continuous export of data, or detailed usage logs. I strongly encourage you to explore it further on your own, as it greatly simplifies monitoring activities and resolving issues. In the next chapter, we will cover the last Azure service within the scope of this book: Azure SQL, which is a PaaS service, being an Azure version of the well-known database engine.

Questions

1. What is needed to identify an Azure Application Insights instance and connect to it?
2. Is it possible to use Azure Application Insights inside a Node.js application?
3. What is the Smart Analytics module?
4. How can you query logs stored inside Azure Application Insights?
5. How can you automate creating alerts in the service?
6. Is it possible to use SMS as an action for a triggered alert?

Further reading

- TelemetryClient reference: `https://docs.microsoft.com/pl-pl/dotnet/api/microsoft.applicationinsights.telemetryclient?view=azure-dotnet`
- Azure log analytics reference: `https://docs.loganalytics.io/index`
- Smart analytics: `https://docs.loganalytics.io/docs/Learn/Tutorials/Smart-Analytics/Understanding-Autocluster`
- Resource Explorer: `https://resources.azure.com/`

16
SQL in Azure - Azure SQL

Microsoft SQL Server is one of the most popular databases and is often the core of many popular applications. Thanks to Azure, we can skip the whole cluster setup, installation, and maintenance by using Azure SQL—a cloud version of SQL Server with the same features available. Thanks to flexible pricing, we can select whichever option we want when it comes to both performance and available features. We don't have to worry about geo-replication and storing backups either—all these functionalities can be easily configured and automated in the cloud.

The following topics will be covered in this chapter:

- Differences between Microsoft SQL Server and Azure SQL
- Working with Azure SQL in the Azure portal
- Security features of Azure SQL
- Scaling and monitor Azure SQL

Technical requirements

To perform the exercises in this chapter, you will need:

- An Azure subscription

Differences between Microsoft SQL Server and Azure SQL

Microsoft SQL Server is a well-known and widely used SQL database server that has gained much popularity and is considered a default choice for many projects ranging from very simple websites to enterprise-class services that handle high load and are considered critical for a business. As cloud technologies gain more and more popularity, the natural consequence of such a situation is the expectation that by moving an application to Azure, it is also possible to move its database. To meet such needs, Microsoft has developed Azure SQL Service—a PaaS version of Microsoft SQL Server that is managed and upgraded by their teams; the only things you are responsible for are configuration and data management. There is also one more offering from Azure called SQL Server VMs, which is one more option for using this database in the cloud. In this section, we will focus on the differences between these two offerings and try to identify different use cases for them.

Azure SQL fundamentals

By using PaaS services in the cloud, you are shifting responsibilities a little bit:

- You are no longer the maintainer of the infrastructure
- You are no longer responsible for different updates when software is considered
- By signing SLA with you, your provider is responsible for making sure that a service is up and running

Instead, you should focus on the following points:

- Properly configuring a service, so it meets your performance targets and legal requirements
- Integrating different services and applications, so they reflect the best practices when it comes to communicating with a service
- Implementing HA/DR scenarios, so an outage or disaster in one region does not impact your systems

By using Microsoft SQL Server, you are fully on your/leased machines, which you have to maintain and monitor. While such a case is valid in many scenarios (as there can be some legal requirements that disallow you from storing data outside your own data center or simply, for some reason, Azure does not provide you with the expected performance you seek), yet in many situations, having a PaaS instance of your SQL database is a big improvement. In fact, you are given a few different options when using this service:

- A single database with isolated resources
- A pooled database in an elastic pool
- Managed instance, which is the closest model when it comes to comparing it with on-premise SQL Server

The important thing to know is that all new features and updates are deployed to SQL databases hosted within Azure. This gives you an advantage in comparison with traditional Microsoft SQL Server, as you are always up to date: you do not have to schedule updates on your servers on your own.

The more servers and databases you have, the more complicated and difficult the process of updating them becomes. Take that into account when comparing these two offerings.

Another crucial thing when talking about Azure SQL is its purchasing model. Currently, you have two options:

- **DTU-based**: A DTU is a mix of computing, memory, and I/O resources that are given to your database
- **vCore-based**: This one simply allows you to select all things on your own (including the number of vCores, the amount of memory, and storage performance)

You may wonder how a DTU reflects the actual hardware; there is a good article that tries to explain these metrics a little bit in the *Further reading* section for this chapter.

In most cases, using DTU as the metric is the better choice—very often it is hard to predict the exact hardware requirements for your application. Use the vCore-based model when you are an advanced SQL server user and know how many cores or memory you really need.

You may wonder, What are the scaling capabilities of Azure SQL Service? While of course you can assign more (or fewer) resources to your database, there are scenarios when this makes things much more complicated (or simply your application has different demands when it comes to database performance, and such a model simply will not work). To cover those situations, you are given the option to use elastic pools. The concept is pretty simple—normally you allocate resources to a single database:

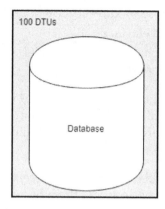

With elastic pools, you change the model a little bit and instead your pool has resources allocated, as follows:

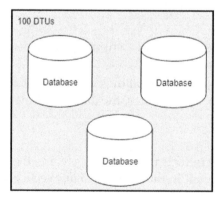

What does that change? Well, this gives you much more flexibility; instead of hosting a huge single database (when it comes to resources allocated), you can easily scale it out, so it can share the load with other instances. What is more, it gives you better control when it comes to costs; you can scale your databases at the same time without the need to control what their individual needs are.

Scaling Azure SQL is an important topic that requires initially much attention—we will come back to it at the end of this chapter.

Besides performance and different scaling capabilities, Azure SQL gives you many additional features that are very important when considering it as storage for your data. Because an application without information stored in a database is, in most cases, useless, availability considerations are also very important here. Fortunately, Azure SQL has implemented many great features that make it a full-fledged storage option:

- **Automatic backups**: In the on-premise world, configuring and managing backups is much more complicated, as it requires you to know the server configuration and find a place to store them. In Azure, things are greatly simplified by integrating automatic backups for Azure Storage for performance and reliability.
- **Geo-replication**: Even if a single region fails, you can still serve data for your customers. With Azure SQL, you can configure a secondary read region that will make sure you can stay online until an outage is resolved.
- **Failover groups**: Instead of implementing failover capabilities and logic on your own, you can rely on what Azure SQL currently provides. This makes creating globally distributed applications much easier as you care only about the configuration and not infrastructure.

To know exactly what is different in Azure SQL in comparison with Microsoft SQL Server, you can refer to the following link : `https://docs.` `microsoft.com/en-us/azure/sql-database/sql-database-features`.

Advanced Azure SQL features

Besides some basic functionalities that ensure Azure SQL is a full version of a relational database on which you can rely and build your system, there are plenty of additional features that make using this service real fun:

- **Automatic monitoring and tuning**: How many times, after using a database for several months, have you ended up with a database full of outdated indexes, procedures, and functions? Azure SQL makes things much easier by actively monitoring how you use and maintain your database and advising you whenever an improvement is possible. I find this feature extremely helpful—nowadays, when development is especially rapid and focused on delivering new values to the market, it is really easy to get lost and lose track of what should be removed from a database. With the service recommendations for dropping indexes, schema improvements, and queries parameterization, I find my storage in much better shape for most of the time.

- **Adaptive query processing**: While this feature is also available for SQL Server, having it in Azure SQL is a great addition to other performance recommendations. Basically, when it is enabled, the server engine tries to find the best execution plan for your queries.

- **Security and compliance features**: It is really important to ensure that the data you store is secure and all vulnerabilities are detected as quickly as possible. In Azure SQL, you are given plenty of additional features that try to analyze your data in terms of sensitivity and compliance. There are in-built tools which search for any kind of anomalies and threats that could affect data integrity or lead to their leak. Additionally, Azure SQL is integrated with the Azure **Active Directory** (**AD**) and allows for **multi-factor authentication** (**MFA**)—this makes things such as auditing and authorization much easier without additional effort.

 The security features for Azure SQL will be described later in this chapter so you have the whole picture of this service's capabilities that matter.

SQL Server on VMs

If you do not want to go full PaaS, you can create a virtual machine with a SQL Server image already in-built. In that option, the performance of the service will rely on the performance of the VM—if you find the database running low on CPU or memory, the only thing you have to do is to scale up the machine. To create a VM in the portal, you have to search for a SQL Server running on an OS of your choice, as follows:

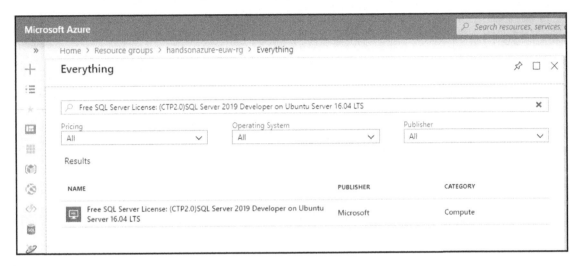

As you can see, there are free SQL Server licenses available and what is more, newer versions can run on Linux machines. Once you select the image you are interested in, you can click on the **Create** button to begin the machine's configuration.

As you can see in the following screenshot, there are many fields which have to be filled in to be able to actually use the service:

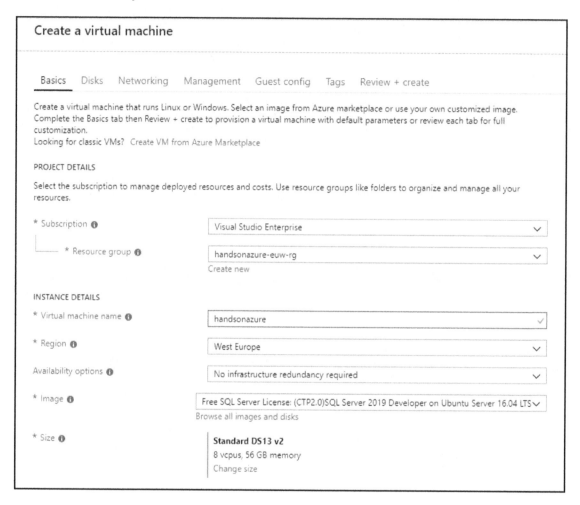

This is, of course, related to the IaaS model of that way of hosting SQL Server inside Azure. The configuration wizard will advise you about the default size of the VM and other parameters required for the machine. Once the configuration is completed, you will be able to connect to it either via RDP or a secured SSH tunnel.

Remember to open the `1433` port if you want to connect to SQL Server remotely.

Creating and configuring Azure SQL

After reading the beginning of this chapter, you should be able to sense how Azure SQL works and what it offers for you. While some theory is always a good thing, it is practice which creates the full picture and allows you to fully understand the topic. In this section, we will focus on creating and configuring Azure SQL in the portal and trying to identify all the afore mentioned features. You will also see how managing this PaaS service is different from the on-premise version, especially when it comes to using its features.

Creating an Azure SQL instance

In the Azure portal, when you search for `Azure SQL`, you will see plenty of different options such as **SQL Database**, **SQL server (logical server),** or **SQL Elastic database pool.** While they all allow you to create a database, the easiest way to get started with the service is to use **SQL Database**—this will require creating a server nonetheless. In the following screenshot, you can find a configuration for my server:

The following shows the configuration for my database:

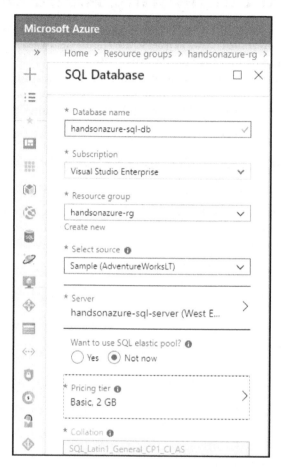

The important thing here is to select the source—you have three options here:

- **Blank database**: In most cases this will be the first option you are interested in
- **Sample**: I used it so I already have data inside my database
- **Backup**: A great option if you want to provision a database from an available backup

For the **Blank database** option, you will also have the possibility to select a collation; in that dropdown, select the option that is correct for your data. We will also focus a little bit on the pricing configuration:

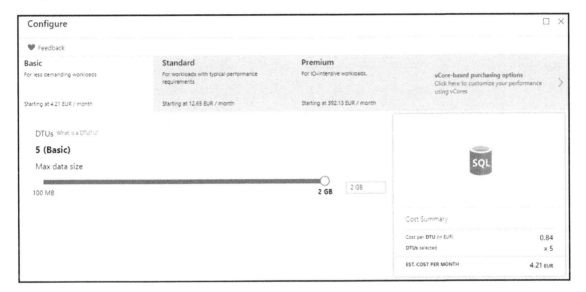

As you can see, when using the DTU model, you have available three different tiers:

- **Basic**: For smaller workloads
- **Standard**: This offers the best balance between cost and performance
- **Premium**: For all workloads which require massive performance capabilities

Depending on the tier, you will be offered either a fixed DTU amount (for **Basic**) or you will have to select the amount you are interested in:

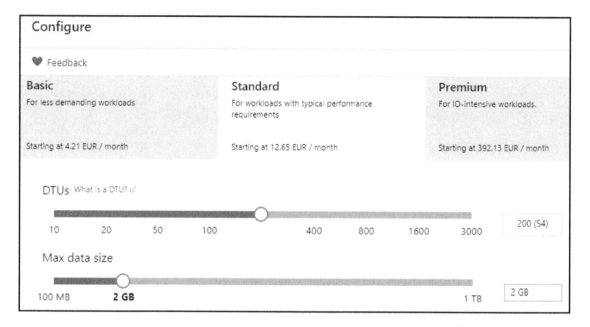

The important thing here is the fact that most of your database costs are resources-allocated—remember to select the biggest database size you can (for example, in the Standard tier and with 400 DTU selected, there is no difference in the pricing between 100 MB and 250 GB).

Of course, you can also switch between a DTU-based model and vCores selection:

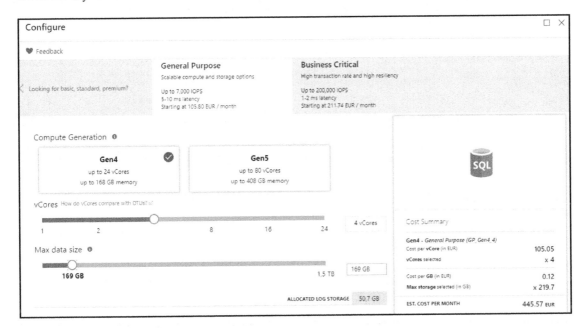

When using vCores, selecting the **Max data size** does affect the pricing. What is more, here you have two different tiers available:

- **General Purpose**: The best choice for most common scenarios without specific needs when it comes to resiliency and traffic
- **Business Critical**: This tier offers better performance and lower latency (and is significantly more expensive)

When you are satisfied with your configuration, you can click on the **Create** button, so the provisioning process will start. When it is finished, you can access your resource by going to the **Overview** blade where basic info is available:

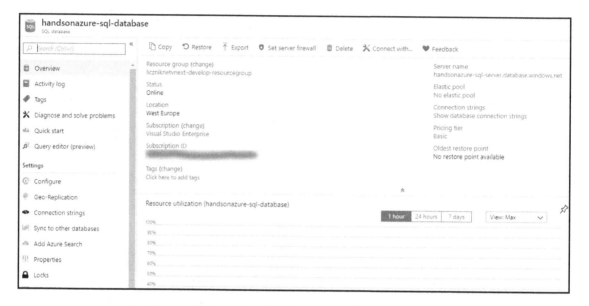

Now we will try to go through most of the features, so you will have a better understanding of how to work with this service.

Azure SQL features in the portal

We will start with the **Configure** blade—when you click on it, you will see that it allows you to set both the tier and the pricing model of your database. This option is especially helpful when you want to improve the performance of your database; you can easily change the amount of DTU or vCores allocated for it, so it can work with queries much quicker.

 As I mentioned before, configuring a single database will work for simpler scenarios, where you can easily monitor it and the performance requirements do not rapidly change. In all other cases, the better option is to use elastic pools.

When you go to the **Geo-Replication** blade, you will see a similar map to the one you saw when testing Azure Cosmos DB:

From this screen, you can quickly create a secondary region, which allows you to perform a failover when you need it. To do so, click on the region you are interested in and that will display the **Create secondary** screen:

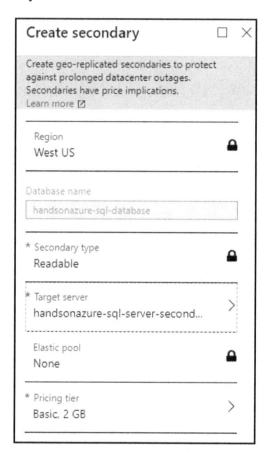

You will have to once more create a server (if there are none already available inside a region) and the pricing tier (which of course can be different for a secondary). Additionally, from this blade, you can enable a failover group for your database—to do so, click on the following panel:

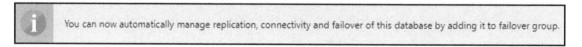

By implementing a failover group, you can introduce an automatic failover for your database:

However, if you want to perform a forced failover, you can click on the secondary database, which will display a screen that allows that operation to be performed:

 Remember that performing a failover can take some time to fully propagate—make sure you are ready for that.

When you proceed to the **Connection strings** blade, you will see a template for a connection string for different environments:

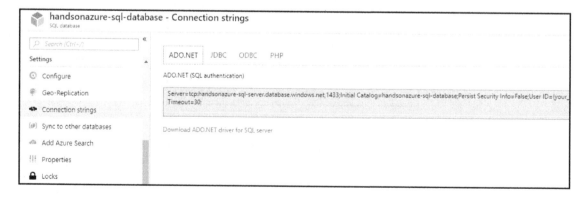

You will also be able to download different drivers for **ADO.NET**, **JDBC**, **ODBC**, or **PHP**.

 Remember that the service presents only a template for your connection string—you will have to set your username and password to make it work.

Currently, we are exploring SQL Database in Azure—let's check exactly what SQL Server looks like currently. You can find it by clicking on the server name on the **Overview** blade. Initially, the screen will look the same, but you will quickly realize that it offers many different features:

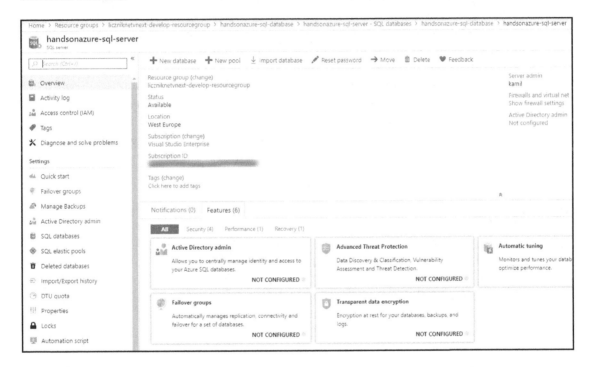

Unfortunately, we will not able to go through all of the features, but I will try to describe most of them for you. When we look at the **Settings** section, we can see the following blades:

- **Failover groups**: As discussed previously, to introduce automatic failover you have to create a failover group. A group consists of a primary and secondary server, which have a defined failover policy and grace period—a setting which defines the time between outage detection and the actual failover.

- **Manage Backups**: To configure backups for your server (for example – enable LTR) you can access this blade. It also displays all available backups.
- **Active Directory admin**: It is possible to set an admin for your server using a user which is defined within your Active Directory users. Of course, you can set more than a single user for that—the trick is to use a group instead of an individual account.
- **SQL databases**: To quickly access a database that is served by this particular server, use this blade.
- **SQL elastic pools**: Similarly to SQL Databases, this blade displays available elastic pools. To create a new pool, go to the **Overview** blade and click on the **+ New pool** button.
- **Deleted databases**: Even if a database is removed from a service, you will still have a chance to restore it. In such a scenario, consult that blade for all databases available to be restored.
- **Import/Export history**: All import and export operations on your databases will be displayed here. This is a great auditing tool, so you will not miss a situation when somebody exported your data without notice.
- **DTU quota**: If you are interested in seeing the quota for DTU/vCores for your server, you can access this blade.

Security

When it comes to Azure SQL features, there are multiple different options you can use to make your solution secure. Things such as firewalls, full operation auditing, and data encryption are the common capabilities of this service and are available even for the Basic tier. In this section, we will focus on learning the afore mentioned capabilities, so your instance is secured and immune to most threats.

Firewall

When browsing your SQL Database, you probably noticed the **Set server firewall** button that is available on the **Overview** blade:

This is the easiest way to set a firewall rule that allows traffic to Azure SQL.

 In Azure SQL, initially all traffic is rejected—you have to whitelist all IPs of computers that should be allowed to communicate with the server.

Before we start configuring the firewall, you have to understand why we really need it. Here is what happens if I try to connect to my server using Microsoft SQL Server Management Studio:

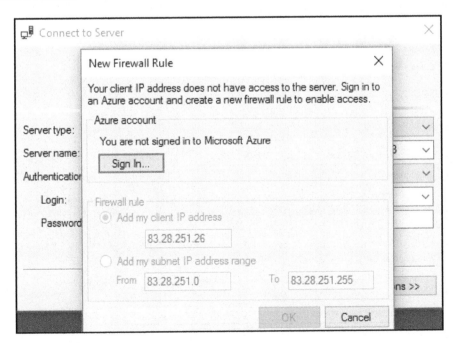

As you can see, it automatically detects that my IP is not whitelisted, hence the server refuses to communicate with me. What we need here is to add a particular IP address, so the communication will be allowed.

In fact, the only machines allowed to communicate by default with Azure SQL are those that are hosted within Azure. If you want to connect to the server from a local computer, you have to set up a firewall rule.

In the portal, you can add the rule by clicking on the **Set server firewall** button—it will display a screen, where you can explicitly set an IP address that should be able to communicate with the server:

From this screen, you can also prevent the Azure service from communicating with your instance of Azure SQL. Additionally, you can add a virtual network here—thanks to that feature, you can create the whole ecosystem with your applications and databases, so they are protected from accessing it with a very strict set of rules.

Advanced Threat Protection

Advanced Threat Protection (**ATP**) is an advanced feature of Azure SQL that by default is not enabled in the service. Currently, it allows for a free trial of 60 days, during which you can test whether this capability is for you. You can enable it using the **Advanced Threat Protection** blade:

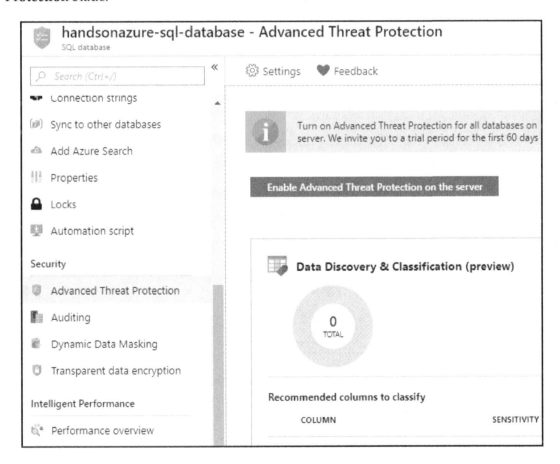

As you can see, it consists of three separate features:

- **Data Discovery & Classification**: For analyzing data in terms of sensitivity and legal classification (for example—GDPR requirements)
- **Vulnerability Assessment**: This checks your database for possible vulnerabilities using the best practices for SQL Server
- **Threat Detection**: A feature which actively monitors your database for suspicious activities and logs them for you

In the following, you can see how Azure SQL classifies example data:

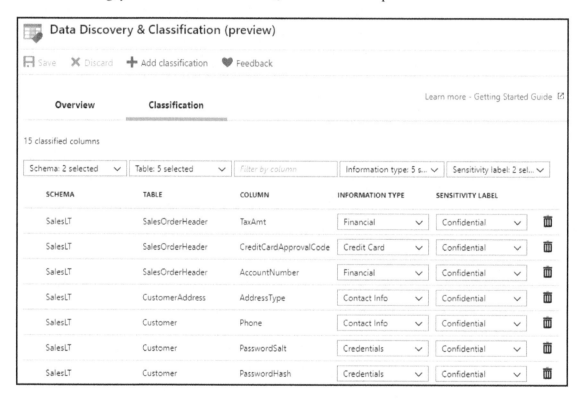

It turns out that it automatically detected the information type and declares its sensitivity label. Then it displays a summary, which gives you the overall picture of the shape of the data stored in a database.

 This feature is a great tool for analyzing big databases for compliance with the new regulations—use it when in doubt as to whether you are storing some sensitive data.

When it comes to **Vulnerability Assesment**, the following are the results of the example scans from my database:

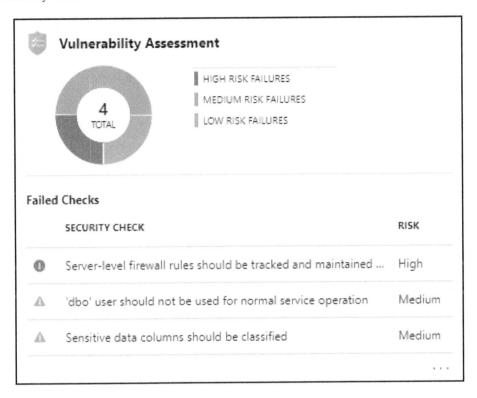

Once a scan is finished, you are given the result of a security check – it checks things such as data classification, whether auditing is enabled, or who can access data. If, for example, you have many users with a wide range of permissions assigned, there will be an alert raised for that. There are almost 50 rules checked during a scan, which is a great addition on top of all other security features.

Even more security guides can be found in the relevant link in the *Further reading* section.

Auditing

If you want to know exactly what happens inside your server, you have to enable auditing:

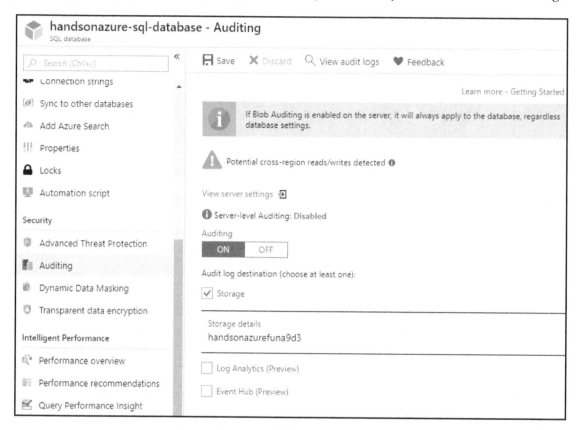

This will log all operations within the selected storage (if, of course, you selected the **Storage** option). Currently, there are three different options for storing auditing logs:

- **Storage**
- **Log Analytics (Preview)**
- **Event Hub (Preview)**

While **Storage** is a little bit of a static option, you can use the remaining two for more dynamic integrations (especially when using Azure Event Hub). Once auditing is enabled, you can see all logged operations as well when you click on the **View audit logs** button:

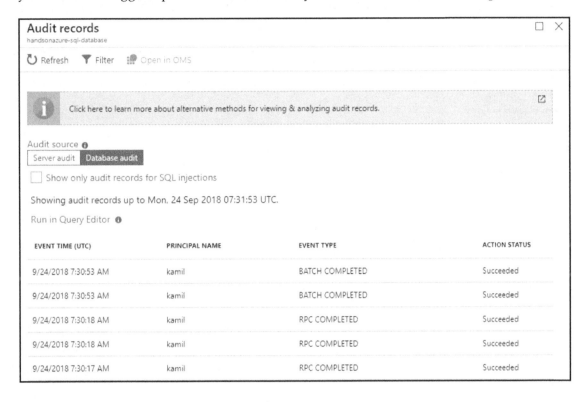

Dynamic Data Masking

Sometimes you want to allow somebody to read data inside a database, yet at the same time you do not want him or her to read more sensitive data (such as birth date, addresses, or surnames). In Azure SQL, there is a feature for that named **Dynamic Data Masking**:

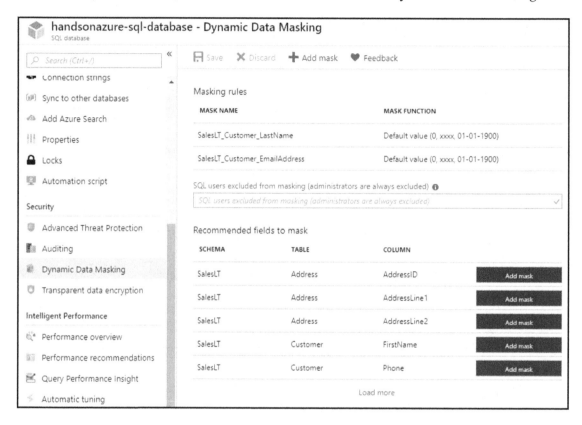

There are two ways to add a mask—either use the recommendation or click on the **+ Add Mask** button to add it manually:

What you will have to do select **Schema**, **Table**, **Column**, and the **Mask field format**—once you configure these and save the rule, users who are not administrators will see the masked values instead. The following shows the values for an admin:

Title	First Name	Middle Name	Last Name	Suffix	Company Name	Sales Person	Email Address
Mr.	Orlando	N.	Gee	NULL	A Bike Store	adventure-works\pamela0	orlando0@adventure-works.com
Mr.	Keith	NULL	Harris	NULL	Progressive Sports	adventure-works\david8	keith0@adventure-works.com
Ms.	Donna	F.	Carreras	NULL	Advanced Bike Components	adventure-works\jillian0	donna0@adventure-works.com
Ms.	Janet	M.	Gates	NULL	Modular Cycle Systems	adventure-works\jillian0	janet1@adventure-works.com
Mr.	Lucy	NULL	Harrington	NULL	Metropolitan Sports Supply	adventure-works\shu0	lucy0@adventure-works.com
Ms.	Rosmarie	J.	Carroll	NULL	Aerobic Exercise Company	adventure-works\linda3	rosmarie0@adventure-works.com
Mr.	Dominic	P.	Gash	NULL	Associated Bikes	adventure-works\shu0	dominic0@adventure-works.com
Ms.	Kathleen	M.	Garza	NULL	Rural Cycle Emporium	adventure-works\josé1	kathleen0@adventure-works.com
Ms.	Katherine	NULL	Harding	NULL	Sharp Bikes	adventure-works\josé1	katherine0@adventure-works.com
Mr.	Johnny	A.	Caprio	Jr.	Bikes and Motorbikes	adventure-works\garrett1	johnny0@adventure-works.com
Mr.	Christopher	R.	Beck	Jr.	Bulk Discount Store	adventure-works\jae0	christopher1@adventure-works.com
Mr.	David	J.	Liu	NULL	Catalog Store	adventure-works\michael9	david20@adventure-works.com
Mr.	John	A.	Beaver	NULL	Center Cycle Shop	adventure-works\pamela0	john8@adventure-works.com
Ms.	Jean	P.	Handley	NULL	Central Discount Store	adventure-works\david8	jean1@adventure-works.com
NULL	Jinghao	NULL	Liu	NULL	Chic Department Stores	adventure-works\jillian0	jinghao1@adventure-works.com
Ms.	Linda	E.	Burnett	NULL	Travel Systems	adventure-works\jillian0	linda4@adventure-works.com

The following shows the values for a user without admin rights:

Title	FirstName	MiddleName	LastName	Suffix	CompanyName	SalesPerson	EmailAddress	Phone
Mr.	Orlando	N.	xxxx	NULL	A Bike Store	adventure-works\pamela0	xxxx	245-555-0173
Mr.	Keith	NULL	xxxx	NULL	Progressive Sports	adventure-works\david8	xxxx	170-555-0127
Ms.	Donna	F.	xxxx	NULL	Advanced Bike Components	adventure-works\jillian0	xxxx	279-555-0130
Ms.	Janet	M.	xxxx	NULL	Modular Cycle Systems	adventure-works\jillian0	xxxx	710-555-0173
Mr.	Lucy	NULL	xxxx	NULL	Metropolitan Sports Supply	adventure-works\shu0	xxxx	828-555-0186
Ms.	Rosmarie	J.	xxxx	NULL	Aerobic Exercise Company	adventure-works\linda3	xxxx	244-555-0112
Mr.	Dominic	P.	xxxx	NULL	Associated Bikes	adventure-works\shu0	xxxx	192-555-0173
Ms.	Kathleen	M.	xxxx	NULL	Rural Cycle Emporium	adventure-works\josé1	xxxx	150-555-0127
Ms.	Katherine	NULL	xxxx	NULL	Sharp Bikes	adventure-works\josé1	xxxx	926-555-0159
Mr.	Johnny	A.	xxxx	Jr.	Bikes and Motorbikes	adventure-works\garrett1	xxxx	112-555-0191
Mr.	Christopher	R.	xxxx	Jr.	Bulk Discount Store	adventure-works\jae0	xxxx	1 (11) 500 555-0132
Mr.	David	J.	xxxx	NULL	Catalog Store	adventure-works\michael9	xxxx	440-555-0132
Mr.	John	A.	xxxx	NULL	Center Cycle Shop	adventure-works\pamela0	xxxx	521-555-0195
Ms.	Jean	P.	xxxx	NULL	Central Discount Store	adventure-works\david8	xxxx	582-555-0113
NULL	Jinghao	NULL	xxxx	NULL	Chic Department Stores	adventure-works\jillian0	xxxx	928-555-0116
Ms.	Linda	E.	xxxx	NULL	Travel Systems	adventure-works\jillian0	xxxx	121-555-0121

As you can see, `LastName` and `Email` are masked for a non-admin user, as planned.

Scaling Azure SQL

The required performance of your database may differ depending on the time and current state of your application. This is when scaling is all-important—you can adjust cost and available resources depending on the needs of your service. In Azure SQL, there are multiple different scenarios that you will consider: whether you use a single database or an elastic pool, whether you need to scale out reads, or whether you need all features available everywhere. In this short section, I will show you how to quickly proceed with your decision and where you can find scaling tools.

Single database

As we mentioned previously, with a single database scaling is really simple—you just need to go to the **Configure** blade and select the new tier you are interested in. You can easily decide whether you need to scale a database up by watching its performance:

If you see constant spikes or simply utilization of the database is becoming dangerously close to the maximum values, it is always a good decision to give it a few more DTUs or other resources.

Remember, you can set alerts when utilization hits upper limits, so there are some ways to automate the process.

Elastic pool

With elastic pool enabled, things change a little bit—instead of operating on, for example, a DTU for a single database, you can select an elastic pool, which introduces a slightly different model of an elastic DTU:

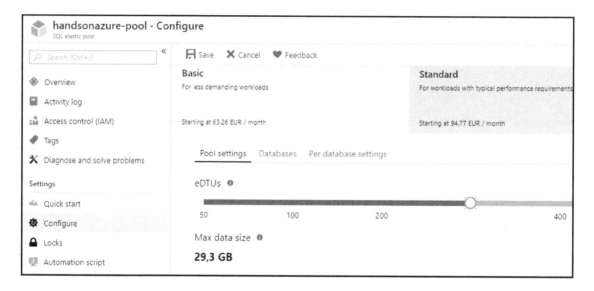

In that model, you scale your database using elastic pool configuration instead. For a single database, you will be able to only change the maximum data size available (which is also limited to the value set by the pool).

Read scale-out

Sometimes you only need to scale reads for your database. Such a situation occurs when you would rather serve content than modify it (for example, you have a very popular portal that is managed from a single place but is served globally). In Azure SQL, there is a possibility to scale out only a part of the service—the one responsible for managing reads for you.

 Note that you need the Premium/Business Critical tier to get this feature working.

To enable read scale-out on your database, you can use the REST API:

```
HTTP PUT
https://management.azure.com/subscriptions/{SubscriptionId}/resourceGroups/
{GroupName}/providers/Microsoft.Sql/servers/{ServerName}/databases/{Databas
eName}?api-version= 2014-04-01-preview

Body:
{
   "properties":
   {
      "readScale":"Enabled"
   }
}
```

Alternatively, you can use PowerShell:

```
Set-AzureRmSqlDatabase –ResourceGroupName <my-resource-group> –ServerName
<my-server> –DatabaseName <my-database> –ReadScale Disabled
```

Sharding

The last way to scale your database is to use sharding. As opposed to elastic pools, by using sharding you allocate individual resources to each of your databases. It is also one of the models for horizontal scaling (so you rather provision another database than scale up your existing one).

 Note that you can use sharding also for elastic pools by using the Elastic Database split-merge tool: https://docs.microsoft.com/en-us/azure/ sql-database/sql-database-elastic-scale-overview-split-and- merge.

In general, you will use sharding if you:

- Have too much data to be able to handle it with an individual instance
- Want to load-balance requests
- Want to geo-distribute your data

The important thing here is the requirement that the data structure for each shard has to be the same. You can find the full documentation on sharding in Azure SQL in the *Further reading* section for this chapter.

Monitoring and tuning

The last item we cover in this chapter will be the monitoring and tuning of Azure SQL. Because databases are often the heart of many applications, it is crucial to have a quick way to diagnose any issues regarding performance or usage, and easily tweak things if needed. Azure SQL uses multiple different features that you can leverage to get insights from your instance.

Monitoring

To monitor your SQL Database, you can use alerts, which should be familiar to you (assuming you have read the previous chapter, `Chapter 15`, *Using Application Insights to Monitor Your Applications*). You can access this functionality by clicking on the **Alerts** blade:

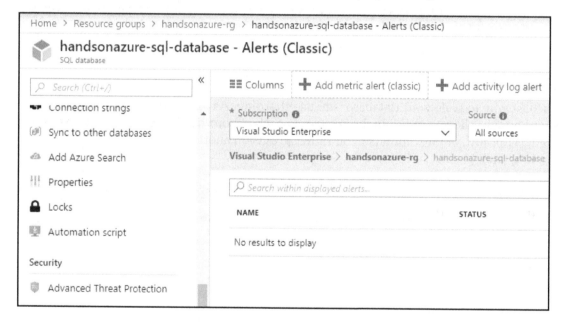

Here you have two types of alert available:

- **Add metric alert (classic)**
- **Add activity log alert**

The way they work is a little bit different—a metric alert is based on values such as CPU percentage, deadlocks, or total database size while an activity log alert is triggered whenever an event occurs. You can use them both simultaneously to cover the following things:

- Insufficient performance (metric)
- Invalid queries (metric)
- Configuration issues (metric)
- Overall service health (metric)
- Incoming maintenance activities (activity log)
- Actual service issues (activity log)
- Service health recommendations (activity log)

Tuning

There is a whole group of features, called **Intelligent Performance**, which allow you to monitor and tune your SQL Database performance:

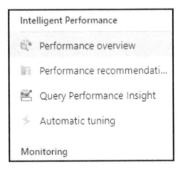

Let's check **Performance recommendations** for now:

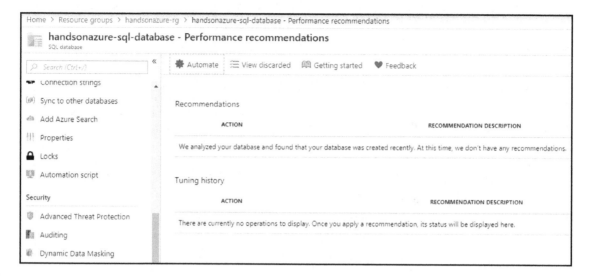

While initially this feature is empty, it displays different recommendations while working with Azure SQL. The important thing here is that we can automate things—just click on the **Automate** button to display another screen where you can select what you are interested in:

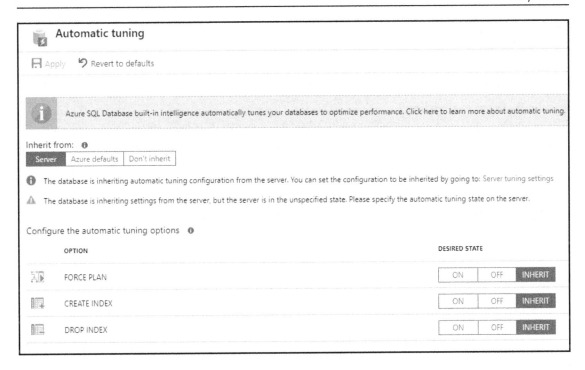

This screen is, in fact, the **Automatic tuning** blade presented earlier. You can use it to automate things such as managing indexes or forcing a query plan.

Summary

Azure SQL is a very complex and extended service that works in a similar way to its on-premise version, Microsoft SQL Server. While being a full PaaS Azure component, it still allows for many advanced operations such as sharding, multi-tenancy, AD integration or failover, and geo-replication. Besides being hosted within a cloud, you can still use it in the same way you would a standalone version of SQL Server. In the next chapter, we will cover the last PaaS service mentioned in this book, which is Azure Data Lake Storage.

Questions

1. What is different in terms of update policy between Azure SQL and Microsoft SQL Server?
2. What is sharding?
3. You created a new SQL Database in Azure SQL, but the server refuses to connect to it. What could be the issue here?
4. What are the two available purchasing models for Azure SQL?
5. What is an elastic pool?
6. What is the difference between DTU and eDTU?
7. How can you mask a particular field in Azure SQL?
8. What audit log destinations are available?

Further reading

- **How to understand DTU:** https://sqlperformance.com/2017/03/azure/what-the-heck-is-a-dtu
- **Performance recommendations:** https://docs.microsoft.com/en-us/azure/sql-database/sql-database-advisor
- **Adaptive query processing:** https://docs.microsoft.com/pl-pl/sql/relational-databases/performance/adaptive-query-processing?view=sql-server-2017
- **Securing SQL Database:** https://docs.microsoft.com/en-us/azure/sql-database/sql-database-security-overview
- **Read scale-out:** https://docs.microsoft.com/en-us/azure/sql-database/sql-database-read-scale-out
- **Sharding:** https://docs.microsoft.com/en-us/azure/sql-database/sql-database-elastic-scale-introduction

Big Data Storage - Azure Data Lake **17**

Sometimes, we have to store unlimited amounts of data. That scenario covers most big data platforms, where having even a soft limit for the maximum capacity could cause problems with the active development and maintenance of our application. Thanks to Azure Data Lake, we have limitless possibilities when it comes to storing both structured and unstructured data, all with an efficient security model and great performance.

The following topics will be covered in this chapter:

- Azure Data Lake Store fundamentals
- Storing data in Azure Data Lake Store
- Security features and concerns
- Best practices for working with Azure Data Lake Store

Technical requirements

To perform the exercises in this chapter, you will need:

- Access to an Azure subscription

Understanding Azure Data Lake Store

When considering your storage solution, you have to take into account the amount of data you want to store. Depending on your answer, you may choose a different option from services available in Azure—Azure Storage, Azure SQL, or Azure Cosmos DB. There is also a variety of databases available as images for VMs (such as Cassandra or MongoDB); the ecosystem is quite rich so everyone can find what they are looking for. The problem arises when you do not have an upper limit for the amount of data stored or, considering the characteristics of today's applications, that amount grows so rapidly that there is no possibility to declare a safe limit, which we will never hit. For those kinds of scenario, there is a separate kind of storage named Data Lakes. They allow you to store data in its natural format, so it does not imply any kind of structure over information stored. In Azure, a solution for that kind of problem is named Azure Data Lake Store; in this chapter, you will learn the basics of this service, which allows you to dive deeper into the service and adjust it to your needs.

Azure Data Lake Store fundamentals

Azure Data Lake Store is called a hyper-scale repository for data for a reason—there is no limit when it comes to storing files. It can have any format, be any size, and store information structured differently. This is also a great model for big data analytics as you can store files in the way that is the best for your processing services (some prefer a small number of big files, some prefer many small files – choose what suits you the most). This is not possible for other storage solutions such as relational, NoSQL, or graph databases, as they always have some restrictions when it comes to saving unstructured data. Let's check an example comparison between Azure Data Lake Store and Azure Storage:

	AZDS	Azure Storage
Limits	No file size/number of files limits	Maximum account capacity of 500 TBs, the maximum size of files
Redundancy	LRS	LRS/ZRS/GRS/RA-GRS
API	WebHDFS	Azure Blob Storage API

The important thing here is the redundancy—for now, the only model which Azure Data Lake Store supports is LRS. That means that, in the event of a disaster, you may lose data stored inside a single data center. To avoid that, you will have to implement your own policy to copy data to a replica. In fact, you have available two models—synchronous replication, as follows:

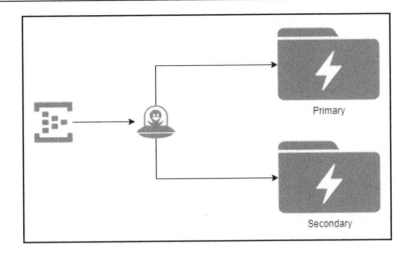

Or you have asynchronous, as follows:

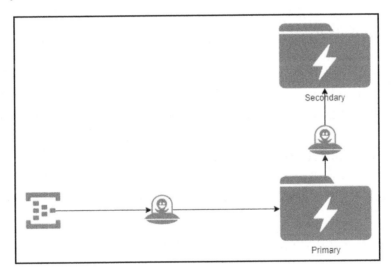

There are some obvious pros and cons of both solutions:

- **Synchronous**: Ensures that a copy of data was saved to a replica, more difficult to handle when considering duplicates, and lower performance.
- **Asynchronous**: Data can be lost (because you will not move data to a replica before a disaster), better performance (because you just save without waiting for replication), and easier to handle.

While replication may look better for Azure Storage, remember that the Azure Data Lake Store filesystem is based on HDFS—this allows for a seamless integration with many OSS tools, such as:

- Apache Hive
- Apache Storm
- Apache Spark
- MapReduce
- Apache Pig
- And many more...!

This gives you a much better ecosystem, tool-wise. If you want to store data inside Azure Data Lake Store and prefer to use HDInsights to perform analysis and transformations over your files, instead of other Azure tools, you can easily connect to your instance and start working on them.

 Note that for now, ADLS supports HDInsight 3.2, 3.4, 3.5, and 3.6 distributions.

When it comes to accessing files stored inside an instance of Azure Data Lake Store, it leverages the POSIX-style permissions model; you basically operate on three different permissions, which can be applied to a file or a folder:

- **Read (R)**: For reading data
- **Write (W)**: For writing data
- **Execute (E)**: Applicable to a folder, used to give read/write permissions in a folder context (such as creating children or listing files)

We will cover more security concepts in the security section.

Creating an Azure Data Lake Store instance

To create an Azure Data Lake Store instance, you will need to search for `Azure Data Lake` in the portal and fill in the following form:

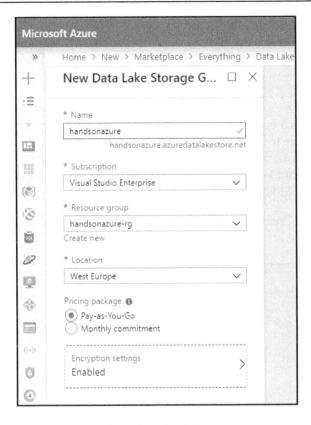

However, you need to take into consideration the following facts:

- **Location**: Currently there are four different locations available—**Central US**, **East US 2**, **North Europe**, and **West Europe**. Do remember that transferring data between DCs costs you extra money, so if you plan to use this service, plan your architecture carefully.
- **Pricing package**: There are two pricing models available—**Pay-as-You-Go** and fixed **Monthly commitment**. They have pros and cons (fixed pricing is in general cheaper but it is not that flexible when your application grows, it is difficult sometimes to plan required capacity ahead), so try to understand as best you can the characteristics of your applications using that service to choose whatever suits you the most.

- **Encryption settings**: By default, encryption of your data is **Enabled** for a new account. While it is possible to disable it, in most cases you will stay with the default settings. What is more, there are two models of encryption—either you let the service manage encryption keys for you, or you provide your own keys (stored inside Azure Key Vault).

Since it is a good idea to rotate encryption keys, you may face the issue when, due to a failure, even redundant copies of your data are inaccessible. While it is possible to recover from backup data, you will need an old key to decrypt it. Because of that, it is advisable to store a copy of old keys in case of unexpected outages.

When you click on the **Create** button, your service will be provisioned—you can access it to see the overview:

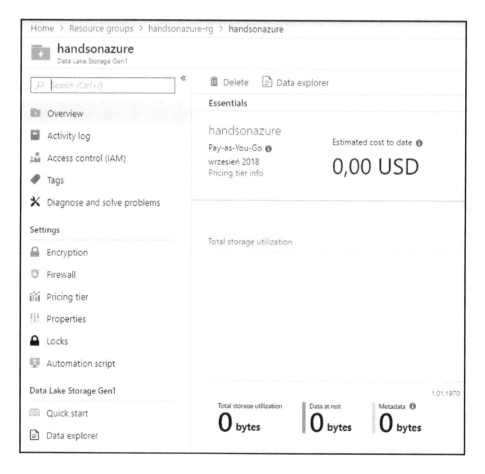

Since it is freshly created, we cannot see different metrics which describe how much data we are storing. What is more, the current cost is 0 USD—this is, of course, something we expected as no file was uploaded to the service. From the UI perspective, there is not much that we can do for now; some additional features such as **Firewall** will be described later in that chapter. Besides the portal, you can also easily access your instance of Azure Data Lake Store by using Microsoft Azure Storage Explorer:

It makes things much easier when you have multiple files and folders and you try to navigate through them.

Storing data in Azure Data Lake Store

Because Azure Data Lake Store is all about storing data, in this section of the chapter you will see how you can store different files, use permissions to restrict access to them, and organize your instance. The important thing to remember here is the fact that you are not limited to using big data tools to store or access data stored within a service—if you manage to communicate with the Azure Data Lake Store protocol, you can easily operate on files using C#, JavaScript, or any other kind of programming language.

Using the Azure portal to navigate

To get started with working with files in the Azure portal, you will have to click on the **Data explorer** button:

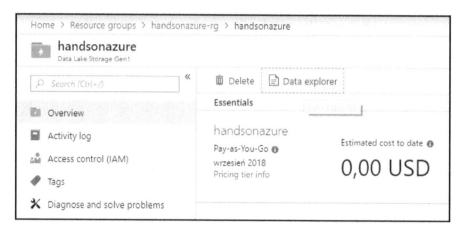

Once you click on it, you will see a new screen, where you are given many different options for creating a folder, uploading files, or changing access properties. While this tool is not the best way to manage thousands of files, it gives you some insight into what is stored and how:

The downside of the UI available in the portal is the fact that it has a tendency to hang, especially if you have hundreds of files. Some options (such as deleting a folder) also tend to fail if you have stored gigabytes of data. In that scenario, it is better to either use PowerShell or custom procedures to perform an operation.

Now we will discuss options available on the UI.

Filter

When you click on the **Filter** button, you will see a screen that tells you what files you are interested in:

It is the easiest way to quickly limit files displayed within a folder, but of course it has some caveats—for example, you cannot use a wildcard to filter only a specific file extension.

To remove a filter, click on the **Reset** button on the **Filter** screen.

New folder

This simple option gives you the possibility to create a new folder:

Note that by default a new folder can be accessed only by you—to make it visible to others (and to allow them to read it), you will have to assign a particular group of users explicitly to it.

Upload

With the **Upload** function, you can upload files directly from your local machine to the cloud:

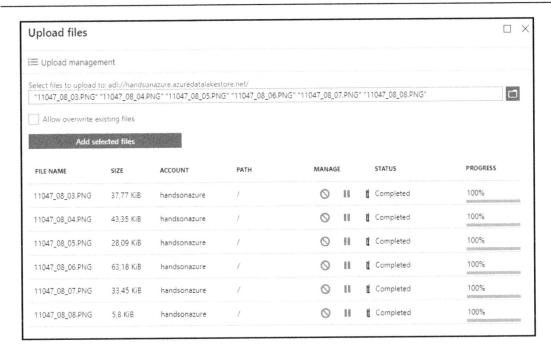

The files you choose will be uploaded to the folder you are currently browsing. There is also the possibility of allowing overwriting existing files; if you decide not to do so and upload a duplicate, you will see the following error:

Access

One of the most important features of Azure Data Lake Store is the ability to fully declare access to a specific resource stored inside it:

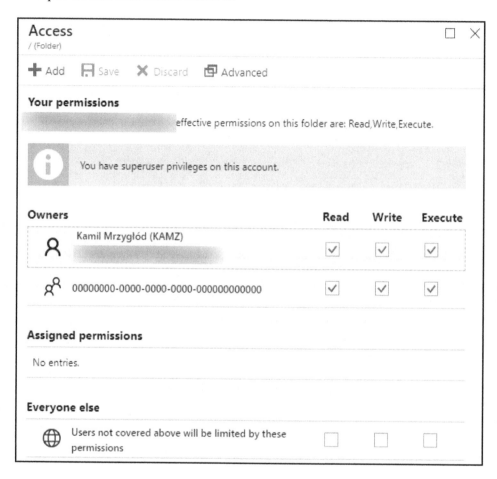

By default, only you can access a file or a folder. To add a new user or a group, you can click on the **+ Add** button:

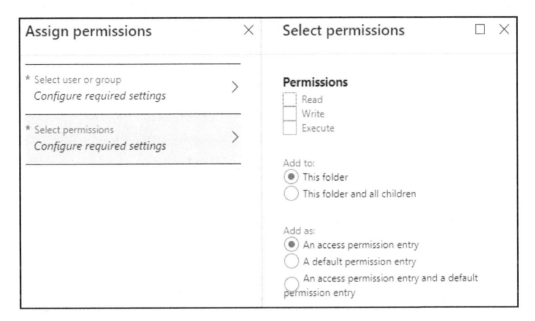

There are important things I would like to cover here:

- **Permissions**: Remember that to grant somebody access to list files inside a folder, you will have to assign two permissions: **Read** and **Execute**. The same applies to creating children inside a folder.
- **Add to**: It is possible to propagate a particular set of permissions, not only to a single folder but also to all folders inside it. This is especially helpful when you can quickly allow somebody to list files and folders inside some parent directory.
- **Add as**: You can add a set of permissions, either as a default permission entry (which will be assigned by default to all other users of a folder) or as an access entry (which specifies how somebody can access it). You can also combine both to speed things up.

Files and folders

Next to each file and folder visible, you can see an icon, which displays a menu with additional options:

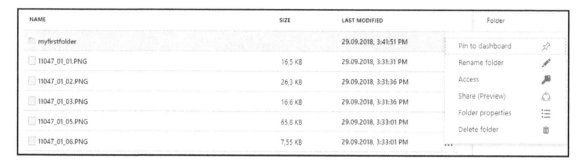

In fact, these are the same options we have just covered—they just apply to a specific folder and file.

Microsoft Azure Storage Explorer

Most of the preceding options can be performed using Microsoft Azure Storage Explorer:

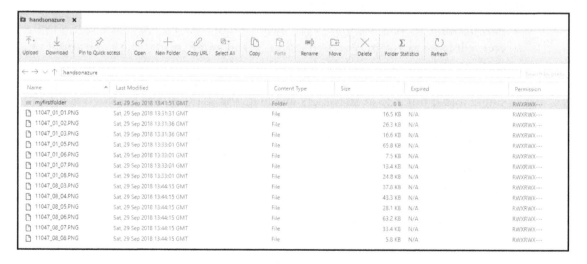

Unfortunately, it does not give you the possibility to assign permissions to files and folders. It is, however, a much better option for browsing stored data—what is more it automatically displays a set of required permissions assigned to an item.

Using SDKs

The most flexible (and the most advanced) option to manage files and your Azure Data Lake Store instance is using an SDK for a language you are using. Currently, there are three different languages officially supported:

- .NET platform
- Java
- Python

There is also the possibility of using a REST API, so basically you can connect with it using any language you want. Here, The following code snippet allows you to connect to the service:

```
var client = AdlsClient.CreateClient("<account-name">, <credentials>);
```

There are two options available when it comes to authenticating to connect to your service:

- End-user authentication
- Service-to-service authentication

Both scenarios are described in detail in the documentation available in the *Further reading* section. Whichever option you choose, you will end up with using a generated OAuth 2.0 token. Here, you can find a simple provider to a service that leverages the described methods and allows you to easily create a new folder and append data to a file:

```
public class DataLakeProvider : IDisposable
{
    private readonly DataLakeStoreFileSystemManagementClient _client;

    public DataLakeProvider(string clientId, string clientSecret)
    {
        var clientCredential = new ClientCredential(clientId,
clientSecret);
        var creds = ApplicationTokenProvider.LoginSilentAsync("domainId",
clientCredential).Result;
        _client = new DataLakeStoreFileSystemManagementClient(creds);
    }

    public Task CreateDirectory(string path)
    {
        return _client.FileSystem.MkdirsAsync("datalakeaccount", path);
    }

    public async Task AppendToFile(string destinationPath, string content)
    {
```

```
        using (var stream = new
MemoryStream(Encoding.UTF8.GetBytes(content)))
        {
            await
_client.FileSystem.ConcurrentAppendAsync("datalakeaccount",
destinationPath, stream, appendMode: AppendModeType.Autocreate);
        }
    }

    public void Dispose()
    {
        _client.Dispose();
    }
}
```

You can read more about writing such a provider in the blog post mentioned in the *Further reading* section.

 The important thing about using SDKs is the ability to abstract many operations and automate them—you can easily delete files recursively or dynamically create them. Such operations are unavailable when using UIs and most serious project developers would rather code stuff than rely on manual file management.

Security

Azure Data Lake Store offers a bit of a different security model than other storage options available for Azure. In fact, it offers you a complex solution that consists of authentication, authorization, network isolation, data protection, and auditing. As it is designed to be the very base of data-driven systems, it has to extend common capabilities when it comes to securing who (or what) and how to access information stored. In this section, we will cover different security features available and describe them in detail, so you are familiar with them and know how to use them.

Authentication and authorization

To authenticate who or what can access data stored, Azure Data Lake Store uses Azure Active Directory to know what the current entity accessing data is. To authorize it, it leverages both **role-based access control (RBAC)**, to secure the resource itself, and POSIX ACL to secure data.

It is important to understand the distinction between these two terms:

- **Authentication**: This determines who or what tries to access a particular resource.
- **Authorization**: This secures a resource by limiting access to it to those who have been assigned a particular set of permissions.

It is important to remember that if you have multiple subscriptions hosting different resources that would like to access Azure Data Lake Store, you have to assign the same Azure AD instance to all of them—if you fail to do so, some will not be able to access data, as only users and services defined within a directory assigned to ADLS can be authenticated and given access to it.

Let's check the difference between the RBAC and POSIX models.

RBAC

RBAC controls who can access an Azure resource. It is a separate set of roles and permissions, that has nothing to do with the data stored. To check this feature, click on the **Access control (IAM)** blade:

On the preceding screen, you can see that I have three different apps (services) and one user assigned to the resource. They also have different roles:

- **Owner**: Full access including determining who can access the resource
- **Contributor**: Full access excluding determining who can access the resource

If you click the **Roles** button, you will see a full list of possible roles for the ADLS:

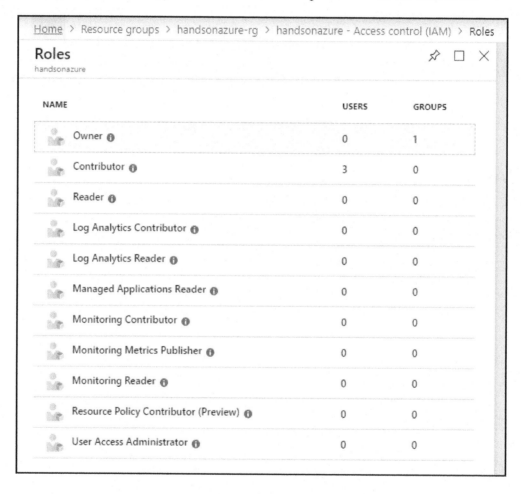

Using the **Access Control (IAM)** blade, you can easily control who can access your instance of Azure Data Lake Store and how—use it any time you want to change permissions or the set of users/services accessing it.

> A good idea is to manage groups rather than individual entities—this allows you to add/remove a user or an entity in one place (Azure AD) instead of browsing resources and their RBAC.

POSIX ACL

As described previously, you can manage access to data stored within your instance of ADLS by providing a set of permissions defined as **Read**, **Write**, and **Execute**. They are the part of the POSIX **access control list (ACL)** that is a feature of Hadoop HDFS, which is the part of the engine of this Azure service. If you have used, for example FTP servers, you probably have worked with filesystem permissions; they were described as numbers or strings containing the letters r, w, x, and the character –. The following is an example:

- -rwx------ is equal to 0700 and declares read, write, and execute permissions only for the owner.
- -rwxrwxrwx is equal to 0777 and declares read, write, and execute permissions for everyone.
- -rw-rw-rw- is equal to 0666 and declares read and write permissions for everyone.

You can find more about the POSIX ACL model in the *Further reading* section.

Network isolation

I mentioned the **Firewall** blade earlier, but we skipped it so you could learn something about it once you are familiar with the service. When you click on the **Firewall** blade, you will see a screen that allows you to specify which IP address can access your instance:

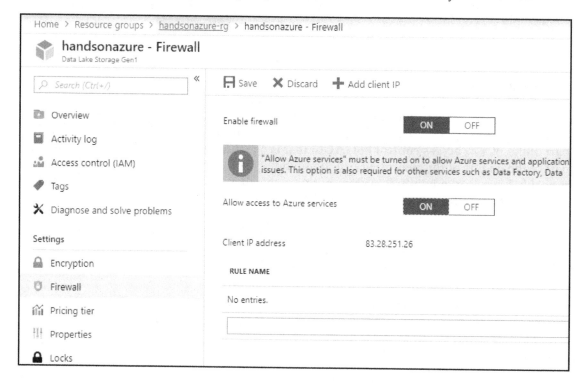

The important thing here is the ability to block other Azure services from accessing your data—this can be helpful if you have requirements that force you to disallow anyone from reading any information stored in ADLS. You can find out more about security features in the link provided in the *Further reading* section.

Best practices

Azure Data Lake Store is a bit different when it comes to accessing data stored and performing read and writes. As this service is designed for storing petabytes of data, it is important to know the best practices for doing so, to avoid problems such as the need to reorganize all files or slow reads/writes. This also includes security features (as discussed earlier), as this is an important part of the whole solution. In this section, we will focus on multiple advice regarding ADLS, so you will use it consciously and leverage the best practices.

Performance

One important feature of many storage solutions is their performance. In general, we expect that our databases will work without a problem whether the load is low or high and a single record is big or small. When it comes to ADLS, you have to take into account the following factors:

- **Parallelism**: As stated in the documentation, it is important to ensure, that you provide a certain level of parallelism when performing reads/writes. The ideal number of threads per one core is defined as 8-12.
- **File size**: While different data analytics solutions may work differently with different file sizes, it is also important to know that ADLS also has an optimal file size to work with. As it is based on HDFS and leverages the POSIX model for permissions, it promotes bigger files (several hundred megabytes) instead of smaller ones to avoid problems with replication, connections, and authentication checks.
- **I/O limits**: While some hard limits when it comes to throughput are not enabled on Azure Data Lake Store, you still can face some problems when your jobs are very demanding, capacity-wise. It is important to remember that even in this service, you can still face some soft limits that can be removed after contacting Azure support. If you face a 429 error, throttling may be the case.
- **Batching**: As in many cases where you face high throughput, it may be beneficial to use batching to lower write operations. In ADLS, the optimal size for a batch is defined as 4 MBs – by performing writes of that size, you can lower the required IOPS and improve the overall performance of the service.

Security

We discussed this topic a little previously, but here we summarize it. When using ADLS and considering its security features (such as authentication, authorization, and access to files), it is important to remember the following things:

- **Prefer groups over users/services**: While, initially, it is easier to assign an individual user to a resource or a folder, you will quickly face problems when the number of people interested in data starts to grow rapidly. This is why it is better to use Azure AD groups to both determine RBAC access to the resource itself and POSIX ACL for files and folders. It also improves the performance of the solution, as it is quicker to check whether an entity belongs to a group than to traverse through a long list of users.
- **The minimum set of permissions**: As in other services, always start with a minimum set of permissions required by someone who accesses your instance of Azure Data Lake Store. Do not assign a **Write** permission to somebody who only reads data, or **Execute** to a service that reads only a single file in a folder.
- **Enable the firewall**: In general, you do not want to allow anyone to access data stored inside ADLS. To secure your solution, so that only a subset of IP addresses can access information, enable the firewall so anyone outside the list will be rejected.

Resiliency

It is crucial to ensure, that your data is stored in a safe manner and will not be lost in the case of any issue inside the DC. As mentioned at the very beginning of this chapter, ADLS does not support geo-redundancy—you have to implement it on your own. To do so, you have to incorporate a tool that will allow you to replicate data in the way you need. There are three different tools mentioned in the documentation—Distcp, Azure Data Factory, and AdlsCopy, but of course, you can use any other tool that can connect to Azure Data Lake Store and integrate with the service.

 When considering DR or HA for Azure Data Lake Store, take into consideration factors such as RPO, inconsistency, and complex data merging problems in the event of performing a failover. Sometimes, it is better to wait for a service to recover instead of switching to the secondary replica.

Data structure

You will choose a different data structure for different use scenarios—for IoT data it will be very granular:

```
{Vector1}/{Vector2}/{Vector3}/{YYYY}/{MM}/{DD}/{HH}/{mm}
```

On the other hand, for storing user data, the structure may be completely different:

```
{AppName}/{UserId}/{YYYY}/{MM}/{DD}
```

It all depends on your current requirements. The data structure is extremely important when you plan to perform an analysis on the files stored—it directly affects the size of files and their number, which can further affect the possible toolset for your activities.

 Another important thing here is the legal requirements—if you use any kind of sensitive data as a folder or a filename, you will have to be able to perform a clean up efficiently if a user tells you that he/she wants to be forgotten or asks for an account to be removed.

Summary

In this chapter, you have learned a bit about Azure Data Lake Store, an Azure service designed to store an almost unlimited amount of data without affecting its structure. We have covered things such as data structure, security features, and best practices, so you should be able to get started on your own and build your very first solution based on this particular Azure component. Bear in mind that what can easily replace Azure Storage for example—it all depends on your requirements and expectations. If you're looking for a more flexible security model, better performance, and better limits, ADLS is for you. This ends this part of the book, which included services for storing data, monitoring services, and performing communication between them. In the next chapter, you will learn more about scaling, performance, and maintainability in Azure.

Questions

1. Which security model is better—managing security groups or individual entities, and why?
2. What is the difference between RBAC and POSIX ACL?
3. What is the maximum size of a file in ADLS?

4. Which data structure is better—a single folder containing thousands of files or a hierarchy of folders containing several files each?
5. Can Azure Data Lake Store be used with any programming language?
6. What is the difference between ADLS and Azure Storage?
7. How do you ensure that your solution based on ADLS is geo-redundant?

Further reading

- **End-user authentication:** https://docs.microsoft.com/en-us/azure/data-lake-store/data-lake-store-end-user-authenticate-net-sdk
- **Service-to-service authentication:** https://docs.microsoft.com/en-us/azure/data-lake-store/data-lake-store-service-to-service-authenticate-net-sdk
- **Writing a Data Lake Store provider:** http://blog.codenova.pl/post/azure-functions-webjobs-and-data-lake-writing-a-custom-extension-2
- **Data Lake Store operations .NET:** https://docs.microsoft.com/en-us/azure/data-lake-store/data-lake-store-data-operations-net-sdk
- **POSIX ACL:** https://hadoop.apache.org/docs/current/hadoop-project-dist/hadoop-hdfs/HdfsPermissionsGuide.html#ACLs_Access_Control_Lists
- **Security overview:** https://docs.microsoft.com/en-us/azure/data-lake-store/data-lake-store-security-overview
- **Best practices:** https://docs.microsoft.com/en-us/azure/data-lake-store/data-lake-store-best-practices

18
Scaling Azure Applications

We cannot talk about reliable and stable applications in the cloud without scaling. While this process may have seemed a bit complicated and cumbersome in models like **Infrastructure as a service (IaaS)** or on-premises, Azure gives many different ways to multiply our applications quickly, and without downtime.

The following topics will be covered in this chapter:

- Autoscaling, scaling up, scaling out
- Scaling Azure App Services
- Scaling Azure Functions
- Scaling Azure Service Fabric

Technical requirements

To perform exercises from this chapter, you will need the following:

- Access to an Azure subscription

Autoscaling, scaling up, scaling out

The cloud is all about scaling—it is one of the most important advantages of such a setup over an on-premises setup. The ability to rapidly adapt to new demands when it comes to incoming traffic, and the flexibility a cloud offers, enables you to create more stable services, which are less prone to unexpected load spikes and insufficient hardware performance. In this chapter, we will focus a little bit on diving deeper into the scaling topic, in order to build a deep understanding of how different services behave in Azure, and how you can ensure that the scaling feature is automated and requires as little attention as possible.

Autoscaling

You can define the autoscaling feature of many services as follows:

Autoscaling is a feature that allows a service, a machine, or an application to automatically scale up or out based on predefined parameters, like CPU utilization, memory used, or artificial factors, like throughput units, or worker utilization.

In general, you can describe autoscaling as follows:

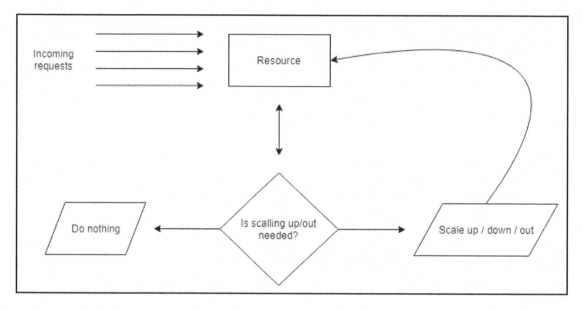

The preceding diagram can be described as follows:

- A resource accepts incoming requests as normal
- Simultaneously there is an entity that monitors a resource—it checks it against the scaling rules and decides whether a scaling operation is required
- An entity takes a decision regarding scaling—it can scale a resource up/down or out, depending on the settings

Of course, besides pros, scaling has its downsides:

- It may render your application unresponsive.
- It requires additional resources for load balancing (if scaling out).

- It takes time, depending on the scaling characteristics. It is, therefore, crucial to plan such action at the design stage.
- In many cases, it causes your solution to be many times more expensive.

How a service scales depends solely on the service itself. Let us look at some examples:

- Azure Event Hub can be scaled manually/automatically (using the auto-inflate feature). You can assign more **Throughput Units (TUs)** to an instance to enable it to accept more messages. Automatic scaling down is not implemented.
- Azure App Services can be scaled both manually and automatically (it depends on the tier you have chosen). You have multiple different parameters available, and scaling down is also performed automatically.
- Azure Cosmos DB relies on the **Request Unit (RU)** units assigned to an instance.
- Azure SQL has different models for scaling—you can either use **Database Transaction Units (DTUs)** or vCores.
- Azure Functions scale automatically using an internal mechanism of workers and the scale controller.
- Azure Storage does not support scaling.

As you can see, there is no single solution for scaling your services in Azure—you have to implement the working solution for each component individually. The rule of thumb is, that the less control over a resource you have, the more automated the scaling will be. While for IaaS scenarios, you have to operate the number of VMs, in **PaaS**, you will end up with virtual cores or other units. Here you can find different cloud models ordered from the left to right in terms of the scaling complexity (where **IaaS** has the most complex model):

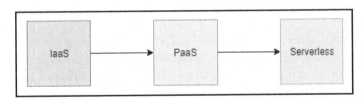

Scaling up and scaling out

There are two different types of scaling (at least when it comes to Azure):

- **Scaling up**: Which upgrades hardware/a tier
- **Scaling out**: Which adds instances of a service

Scaling up can be presented as follows:

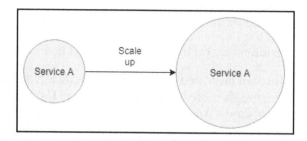

While for comparison, scaling out is described as follows:

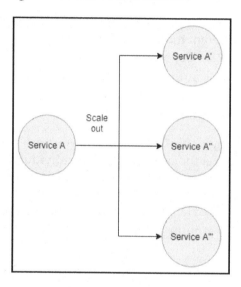

So, in the first scenario (scaling up), you will get a better performance from a single instance, while scaling out will allow you to parallelize your work. The use cases are different in both options and are basically dependent on the workload you are planning to run. These are some examples:

- If your code is sequential and there is no option to multiply it, use scaling up
- If your code requires much compute power in a unit of time rather than dividing it into multiple machines, use scaling up
- If you have a way to load balance your load, use scaling out
- If you are able to perform the same work on multiple machines without a risk of collision, use scaling out

Using scaling out can be compared to multithreading—but of course on a much bigger scale. In fact, the problems are quite the same. If your machine has multiple cores, and they are able to execute your code at the same time, you have to introduce very similar constraints.

> The common problems of scaling out are often caused by the access to the state—whether it is shared via any kind of storage, or distributed amongst many machines. Make sure you are aware of these before using this feature.

In Azure, multiple services scale out/up differently. We will focus on three of them to get a better understanding of the topic.

Scaling Azure App Services

We started our journey through Microsoft Azure by learning some basics of Azure App Services. This is a very common PaaS component, which is widely used amongst many Azure users, both for very simple websites and complex systems requiring high performance and reliability. To make sure that your Web App is always on, or to check if it is under pressure, you have to implement some kind of scaling rules. When it comes to this service, you have two options—either using manual scaling (and implementing some kind of alert, so that you know when such action should happen), or an autoscale feature, which makes things much easier in terms of maintenance. In this section, we will cover and compare both of them.

Manual scaling

Manual scaling is a feature that is available starting from the basic tier—it is not available for free or shared ones. Depending on the actual tier chosen, there will be a different amount of instances that can be used for your App Service.

Here you can find how things look like for the B2 tier:

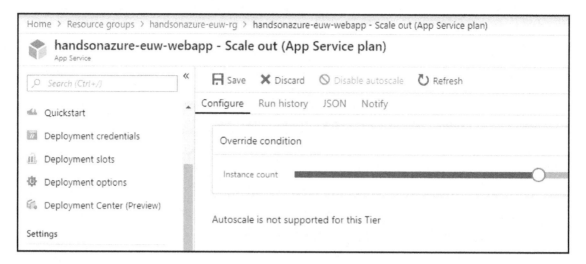

In the preceding configuration, the maximum number of instances available is set to three. However, if I scale up to the standard tier the result is as follows:

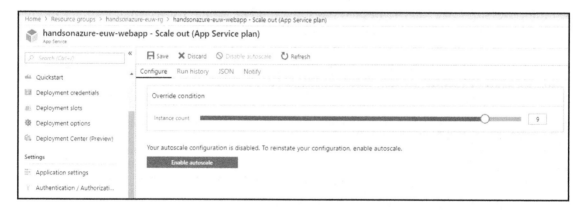

Things look quite different—two features have changed:

1. I can set the **Instance count** to the maximum number of **10**
2. Autoscaling can be enabled

Note that scaling up to the premium tier will allow you to set the maximum number of 20 instances for your App Service.

Autoscaling

While manual scaling can be fine for less demanding websites and systems (as they do not require quick actions when something happens), when your application is, for example, a popular e-commerce shop, you want things to happen quickly, including scaling out. Let us try to enable autoscaling for now—it will display a form that enables you to manage these settings:

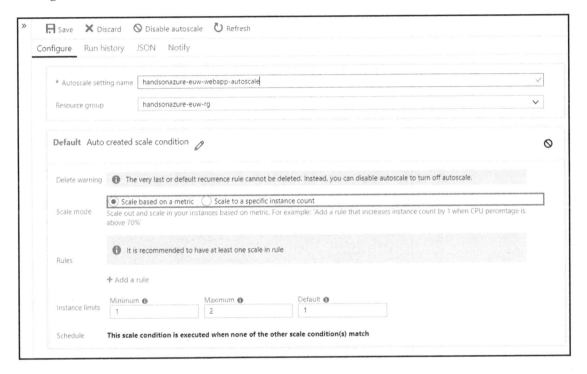

In fact, you have two options here:

1. **Scale based on a metric**: Allows you to select a metric, which will be a trigger for autoscaling
2. **Scale to a specific instance count**: Executed by default (so should be used along with scaling based on a metric)

To configure **scale based on a metric**, you will need a rule. You can add this by clicking on the **+ Add a rule** link. Doing so will display another form (which is far more complex than the current one), where you can select all that is interesting for you:

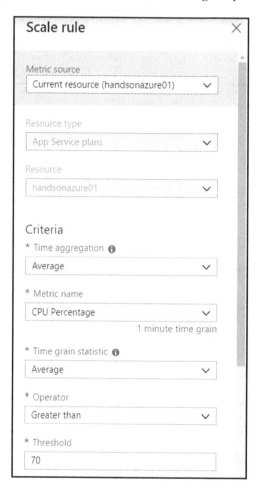

In the preceding screenshot, you can see a rule that will trigger autoscaling when CPU utilization exceeds 70% over a 10 minute period. Once all conditions are met, the runtime will add another instance to the App Service. What is more, if the conditions are true after another 5 minutes (**Cool down (minutes)** period), the scaling out operation will be triggered once more. This will happen as long as the maximum number of instances, which you have set, are hit.

Remember that you can set more than a single rule for your application. What is more, it seems like a good idea to create a decreasing count by rule, which will remove additional instances if the load gets back to normal.

Once your rule is added, you can click **Save** to confirm your changes—now your application will be scaled out anytime a rule is considered active. Before we go further, I would like to show you two more things. You probably noticed two additional sections on the **Scale-out** blade, **JSON** and **Notify**. They give you some additional options when it comes to managing a service:

- **JSON**: This generates a JSON template, which can be used with ARM Templates for automatic provisioning of your resource. It will automatically add scaling rules when a service is created.
- **Notify**: This enables you to automatically send a notification to administrators of the resource in Azure, to notify them when something wrong happens there.

Here you can find a JSON, which was generated for my rules:

```
{
    "location": "West Europe",
    "tags": {
        "$type":
"Microsoft.WindowsAzure.Management.Common.Storage.CasePreservedDictionary,
Microsoft.WindowsAzure.Management.Common.Storage"
    },
    "properties": {
        "name": "handsonazure-euw-webapp-autoscale",
        "enabled": true,
        "targetResourceUri": "/subscriptions/1a2d5d1c-dee5-4deb-
a93a-366cc83feb46/resourceGroups/handsonazure-euw-
rg/providers/Microsoft.Web/serverfarms/handsonazure-euw-appserviceplan",
        "profiles": [
            {
                "name": "Auto created scale condition",
                "capacity": {
                    "minimum": "1",
                    "maximum": "10",
                    "default": "1"
                },
                "rules": [
                    {
                        "scaleAction": {
                            "direction": "Increase",
                            "type": "ChangeCount",
                            "value": "1",
```

```
                               "cooldown": "PT5M"
                    },
                    "metricTrigger": {
                         "metricName": "CpuPercentage",
                         "metricNamespace": "",
                         "metricResourceUri": "/subscriptions/1a2d5d1c-
dee5-4deb-a93a-366cc83feb46/resourceGroups/handsonazure-euw-
rg/providers/Microsoft.Web/serverFarms/handsonazure-euw-appserviceplan",
                         "operator": "GreaterThan",
                         "statistic": "Average",
                         "threshold": 70,
                         "timeAggregation": "Average",
                         "timeGrain": "PT1M",
                         "timeWindow": "PT10M"
                    }
               }
          ]
     }
  ],
  "notifications": [],
  "targetResourceLocation": "West Europe"
},
"id": "/subscriptions/1a2d5d1c-dee5-4deb-
a93a-366cc83feb46/resourceGroups/handsonazure-euw-
rg/providers/microsoft.insights/autoscalesettings/handsonazure-euw-webapp-
autoscale",
"name": "handsonazure-euw-webapp-autoscale",
"type": "Microsoft.Insights/autoscaleSettings"
}
```

Scaling Azure Functions

When using PaaS services, you can configure how your application will behave when CPU utilization hits the maximum allowed value, or the number of requests exceeds the threshold. However, Azure offers services in other models—one of the most interesting is serverless architecture, which abstracts the control even more in favor of easier configuration, minimum maintenance, and ability to focus on delivering a business value.

In this section, you will see the differences between Azure App Services and Azure Functions when it comes to scaling, both from the technical and conceptual point of view.

Scaling serverless applications

When you are using serverless services (such as Azure Functions, Azure Cosmos DB, or Azure Event Grid) you have limited options when it comes to configuring the feature. For example:

- In Azure Functions, you rely on the pricing model (consumption plan vs App Service Plan)
- In Azure Cosmos DB you modify the number of RUs
- In Azure Event Grid you have no way to define how the service will scale

This is all caused by the fact that you do not control the application host—the underlying service engine is completely detached from your application and there is no possibility to directly modify it. What you can do is to control it indirectly, either by changing the number of processing units or via available configuration options, which can be interpreted and applied.

Note that serverless is meant to be a model where you are isolated from the runtime (and, in some cases, even from the cloud vendor). If the lack of control does not play well for you, it is better to try PaaS or IaaS models and services.

Scaling Azure Functions

In Azure Functions, there is no possibility to scale up, at least for the consumption plan. Of course, when using the App Service Plan, you can scale it up and get better hardware, but it does not affect the service itself. Instead it creates more resources to consume. On the other hand, you cannot scale out manually. The only possibility is to let Azure Functions scale automatically. To do so, this service implements the concept of a scale controller. This is an internal feature that constantly monitors how particular workers hosting the Function's runtime behave, and if one of them seems to be overloaded, another machine is added to the set.

Azure Functions scaling behavior is quite sophisticated and only partially described, as it contains parts that are either open sourced, or not available publicly. I will try to describe it in detail in this chapter, so you are aware of the exact algorithm of making a scaling decision.

Before your instance of Azure Functions will make a scaling decision, it will check the following:

1. **Scaling interval**: Scaling only happens after a specific interval has passed.
2. **Current workers number**: If the number of workers (running the function's hosts) exceeds the configured maximum, a decision will be made to remove one from the working set.
3. **Load factor**: If the load factor approaches the maximum value, a new worker will be added. Alternatively, if the load factor drops, one worker will be removed.
4. **Busy worker ratio**: If the number of busy workers exceeds the configured maximum, another worker will be added to the set.
5. **Free workers**: If the number of free workers is greater than the defined maximum, one of them will be removed from the working set.

Defined values for above actions can be found as follows:

```
public const int DefaultMaxWorkers = 100;
public const int DefaultBusyWorkerLoadFactor = 80;
public const double DefaultMaxBusyWorkerRatio = 0.8;
public const int DefaultFreeWorkerLoadFactor = 20;
public const double DefaultMaxFreeWorkerRatio = 0.3;
public static readonly TimeSpan DefaultWorkerUpdateInterval =
TimeSpan.FromSeconds(10);
public static readonly TimeSpan DefaultWorkerPingInterval =
TimeSpan.FromSeconds(300);
public static readonly TimeSpan DefaultScaleCheckInterval =
TimeSpan.FromSeconds(10);
public static readonly TimeSpan DefaultManagerCheckInterval =
TimeSpan.FromSeconds(60);
public static readonly TimeSpan DefaultStaleWorkerCheckInterval =
TimeSpan.FromSeconds(120);
```

 The above values come from the GitHub repository of Azure Functions Host. They may be changed after a while, but if you are interested, take a look at the following project: https://github.com/Azure/azure-functions-host

Additionally, you can control the maximum number of instances by providing
the WEBSITE_MAX_DYNAMIC_APPLICATION_SCALE_OUT value in the **Application
settings** of your Function App:

Application settings

APP SETTING NAME	VALUE
APPINSIGHTS_INSTRUMENTATIONKEY	a366cef1-1189-4dc1-bba2-e681eff4f022
AzureWebJobsStorage	DefaultEndpointsProtocol=https;AccountName=
FUNCTIONS_EXTENSION_VERSION	~2
FUNCTIONS_WORKER_RUNTIME	dotnet
WEBSITE_CONTENTAZUREFILECONNECTIONSTRING	DefaultEndpointsProtocol=https;AccountName=
WEBSITE_CONTENTSHARE	handsonazure-euw-functionappa83c
WEBSITE_NODE_DEFAULT_VERSION	8.11.1
WEBSITE_MAX_DYNAMIC_APPLICATION_SCALE_OUT	3

+ Add new setting

What is more, if you connect the instance of your Function App to an instance of Azure
Application Insights, you will be able to check how many workers it has by checking
the **Live Metrics Stream** feature:

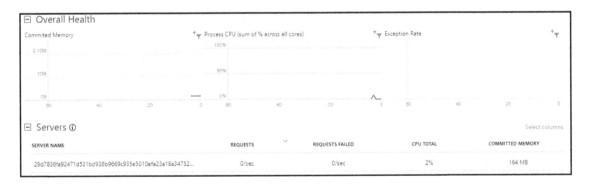

Scaling Azure Service Fabric

We have discussed two different models for scaling by working with two separate Azure
services; Azure App Services and Azure Functions.

They are quite different when it comes to adding new instances or improving hardware performance, in that they introduce multiple concepts, and offer a different level of flexibility. In the last section of this chapter, we will cover one more service, Azure Service Fabric. This particular Azure product behaves in a slightly different manner when it comes to scaling up or out, as it requires you to manage VMs. In addition, a distinct set of skills is necessary to perform this operation seamlessly and in the right fashion.

Scaling a cluster manually

Clusters in Azure Service Fabric can be scaled in two ways:

- **Manually**: By choosing appropriate options in the cluster configuration
- **Programatically**: By using the Azure SDK

In fact, the characteristics of your cluster are selected at the very beginning, when you are choosing node types and their configuration, as shown in the following screenshot:

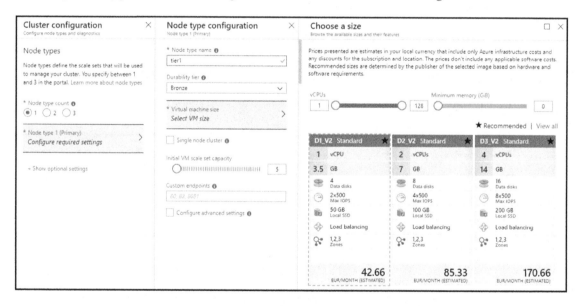

Scaling Azure Service Fabric service is similar to scaling VMs, as it is based on nodes containing an unspecified number of virtual machines, which means you really depend on scale sets.

It is always better to set up a cluster that will handle the planned load than scale it under pressure, especially when you require strict transactional assurances, which may impact scaling time. Take a look at the *Further reading* section, where you will find an article describing efficient cluster planning.

When using scaling with Azure Service Fabric, remember that adding machines to the scale set always takes time. Therefore, consider planning such operations early, so the impact on the current operations will be minimized. To actually scale out your cluster, you have use the **Scaling** feature of the scale set, which was created with it, as shown in the following screenshot:

The other option to perform such operation is to use ARM template with the following snippet:

```
"resources":[
    {
        "type":"Microsoft.Compute/virtualMachineScaleSets",
        "apiVersion":"2017-03-30",
        "name":"[parameters('<scale-set-name>')]",
        "location":"[resourceGroup().location]",
        "sku":{
            "name":"[parameters('<sku>')]",
            "tier":"<tier>",
            "capacity":"[parameters('<capacity>')]"
        }
    }
]
```

By providing the `<capacity>` value, you may easily change the number of virtual machines powering your SF cluster.

Using Azure SDK to scale your cluster

Another option to scale your cluster is to use the Azure compute SDK. You may wonder what are the use cases for that particular feature—all in all, we already have manual/auto-scaling available. However, there are more advanced scenarios, which may be suitable for scaling using your own controller:

- Scaling using a custom metric, which is not available for autoscaling.
- Performing additional operations before scaling can happen.
- Full control over scaling operation in case of critical workloads.

 To get the Azure compute SDK, you have to download the following NuGet package: Microsoft.Azure.Management.Fluent available at: `https://www.nuget.org/packages/Microsoft.Azure.Management.Fluent/`. Similar libraries can be found for other languages (like Java or Python—you can find them in the link in the *Further Reading* section).

To scale out your cluster, you may use the following code snippet:

```
var vmScaleSet = AzureClient.VirtualMachineScaleSets.GetById(ScaleSetId);
var capacity = (int)Math.Min(MaximumNodeCount, vmScaleSet.Capacity + 1);
vmScaleSet.Update().WithCapacity(capacity).Apply();
```

The same can be used for Java:

```
vmScaleSet.update().withCapacity(capacity).apply();
```

As you can see, it is a pretty simple piece of code—you just need to obtain the current scale set ID to get a reference to it, and then change its capacity. In this example, I used a value of 1, but there is nothing that prevents you from using other numbers.

 With the preceding example, you can also scale down your cluster. However, remember that you should not scale down below the cluster's reliability tier. If you do so, you no longer can rely on it and may destabilize it.

If you are using a higher reliability tier than bronze, you do not need to worry about unused machines as they will be automatically removed. Otherwise, you have to do it manually. To do so, you actually have to know which VMs are not currently used. To remove a node that is no longer required, you can use the following operations:

```
await client.ClusterManager.DeactivateNodeAsync(node.NodeName,
NodeDeactivationIntent.RemoveNode);
scaleSet.Update().WithCapacity(capacity).Apply();
await client.ClusterManager.RemoveNodeStateAsync(node.NodeName);
```

They basically do three different things:

1. Deactivate and remove a node from a cluster
2. Decrease a scale set capacity
3. Remove a node state

To find a node to be removed, you have to query a cluster and seek the most recent machine added:

```
using (var client = new FabricClient())
{
    var node = (await client.QueryManager.GetNodeListAsync())
        .Where(n => n.NodeType.Equals(NodeTypeToScale,
StringComparison.OrdinalIgnoreCase))
        .Where(n => n.NodeStatus == System.Fabric.Query.NodeStatus.Up)
        .OrderByDescending(n =>
        {
            var instanceIdIndex = n.NodeName.LastIndexOf("_");
            var instanceIdString = n.NodeName.Substring(instanceIdIndex +
1);
            return int.Parse(instanceIdString);
        })
        .FirstOrDefault();
}
```

 You may wonder why the most recently added machine is selected to be the victim of the scaling operation. This is because work was delegated to it as the result of higher cluster utilization. Originally it was not a part of the set. and once it finished its job, it can be removed.

Summary

In this chapter, we covered the scaling of three completely different services—Azure App Service, Azure Functions, and Azure Service Fabric. You saw how this operation works for different application models—sometimes you scale service instances, VMs, or simply you do not control it and let the runtime do it for you. In fact, scaling services in the cloud is much easier than when using your own servers. You do not have to reconfigure load balancers, firewalls, routers, and servers. When using the scaling feature, always try to automate the process—manual scaling works only for very simple scenarios, and tends to keep your servers underutilized.

In the next two chapters, we will cover two additional Azure services, Azure CDN and Azure Traffic Manager, which help in keeping your applications available, even under heavy load.

Questions

1. What is the difference between scaling up and scaling out?
2. What are the use cases for scaling out?
3. Is scaling up available in serverless services?
4. Does scaling out in Azure App Services affect the pricing of the service?
5. Why can scaling operation be dangerous in Azure Service Fabric?
6. What are the cons of manual scaling?
7. What do you do if you want to automatically scale your Azure App Service when CPU utilization reaches 80%?

Further reading

- Service Fabric cluster planning: `https://docs.microsoft.com/en-us/azure/service-fabric/service-fabric-cluster-capacity`
- Service Fabric cluster scaling: `https://docs.microsoft.com/en-us/azure/service-fabric/service-fabric-cluster-scaling`
- Azure SDKs: `https://docs.microsoft.com/en-us/azure/index#pivot=sdkstoolspanel=sdkstools-all`

19
Serving Static Content Using Azure CDN

Hosting many static files, especially when we're developing a highly popular application, is a serious task, which impacts both the performance of our web service, and overall user experience. If we load images, files, or document too slowly, our customers may choose one of our competitors that provides similar features, but performs better. Thanks to cloud services such as Azure **Content Delivery Network (CDN)**, we're able to handle high-bandwidth content quickly, due to integration with Azure Storage and using components native to Azure.

The following topics will be covered in this chapter:

- CDNs
- Using and configuring Azure CDN
- Optimizing serving static content using Azure CDN
- Developing applications using Azure CDN

Technical requirements

To perform exercises from this chapter, you will need the following:

- An Azure subscription
- Visual Studio 2017

Azure CDN fundamentals

If you are hosting a popular website that contains many static files, you may wonder what is the best way to optimize serving them to your users. When searching for a solution, you have to take into consideration many different factors; HTTP protocol specification, browser capabilities, your server performance, network latencies, and so on. The whole problem is far from being trivial and requires significant resources to be implemented in the right way. To overcome the listed difficulties, the idea of CDNs was developed. CDN stands for content delivery network, and encapsulates the concept of a complex service that takes care of delivering the content to everyone who browses your website. In this chapter, you will learn about Azure CDN, which is an Azure component that is designed to be a fast and reliable solution for all the listed problems.

Working with CDNs

When a user accesses your website, it has to fetch all the static content that is provided for a specific page. This implies the following actions:

- A browser has to request all images, files, and scripts that are required by a web page
- The requests have to be queued, as there is a limit on how many requests to a single domain a browser can perform
- In most cases, a page has to be rendered gradually, as the content is fetched from the server
- A server can throttle requests if it is currently overloaded
- A browser has to respect all implemented caching mechanisms,of course, if your website tells it how to do it

We can describe the whole process as follows:

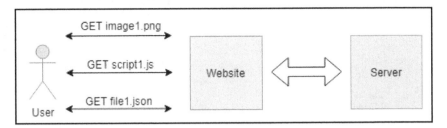

In the preceding scenario, each request from a **user** is routed directly to the **website**. It then connects with the **server** to fetch the data. Of course, we can imagine the situation where files are hosted by separate servers, as demonstrated in the following diagram:

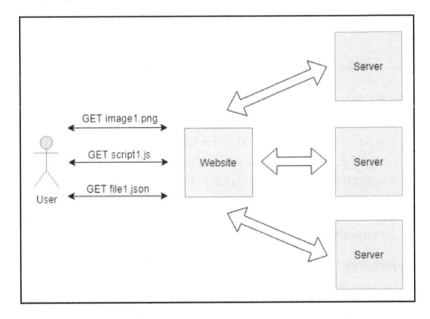

Such an alternative can improve performance a little bit (as servers will be identified using different domain names), but it complicates maintenance and configuration. What is more, such a setup is not the right solution if you struggle with network latencies (as an additional server will not make a difference). While we are discussing different architectures, you are probably starting to imagine one more setup that may make a difference.

A proxy between a **website** and the **servers** that is responsible for proper caching can be easily scaled up and is highly available, as can be seen in the following diagram:

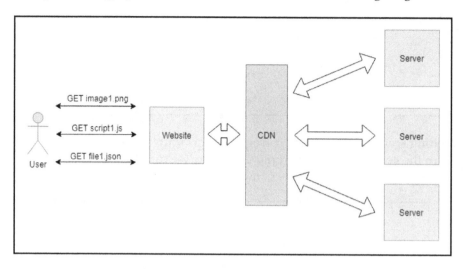

CDNs are exactly the proxy that we are talking about. They provide the following functionalities:

- They can be easily scaled up/out if the load exceeds our expectations
- They can cache requests, so the end servers are not utilized too much
- They respect the cache-control header, so it is easy to provide the **Time-To-Live (TTL)** of a resource
- They improve the responsiveness of your website by serving content to multiple users simultaneously

Later in this chapter, you will learn how to leverage such services by using Azure CDN.

Creating an Azure CDN in the portal

The process of creating an Azure CDN is similar to all the other services that you are working with when reading this book. To get started, you have to click on the **+ Create a resource** button and search for `Azure CDN`. From the search results, you have to choose **CDN**. This will lead you to a form, where you can enter all required information regarding a new service:

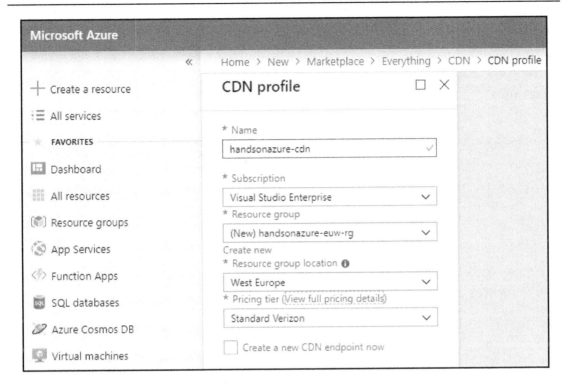

There are two things worth mentioning here:

- **Pricing tier**: Pricing tiers look a little bit different compared with other Azure services, as you no longer have the **Basic**, **Standard**, and **Premium** options to choose from. Here you have to decide which product you will be using—you can select one from the list containing providers such as **Verizon**, **Akamai**, and **Microsoft**. They offer different features, such as dynamic site acceleration, video streaming optimization, and asset pre-loading. The full list can be found in the *Further reading* section for this chapter.

- **Create a new CDN endpoint now**: If you know what your origin (an endpoint that will cache the resources) will be, you can create it right now for the whole service.

To quickly check what is available in the particular pricing tier, you can click on the **View full pricing details** link:

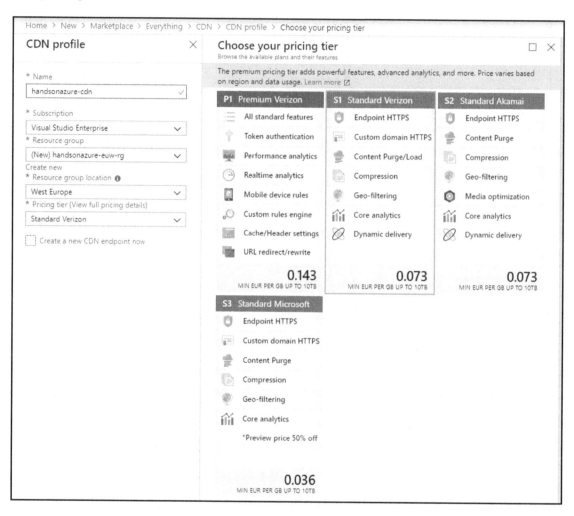

As you can see, you are paying for each GB of outbound data transfer, and depending on the selected provider, the price can differ almost five-fold. When you click on the **Create** button, the service creation process will start. Once it finishes, you can access your very own instance of Azure CDN:

If you decided not to create an endpoint along with the service, you will see a similar screen to mine, with the **Endpoints** section empty. Let us click on the **+ Endpoint** button to actually create one. As mentioned before, an endpoint is the element of a CDN that caches the data and serves it for a particular purpose. In the following, you can find an example setup for my first endpoint:

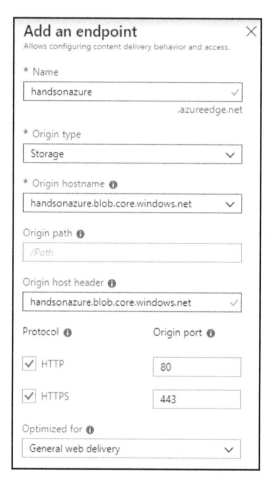

As you can see, I selected **Storage** as the **Origin type**. To be able to do so, you have to actually have an instance of Azure Storage in the same resource group as your CDN. You can also select other available types, such as Cloud Service, Web App, or a custom origin. Once you add an endpoint, you will be able to manage it by clicking on it on the **Overview** tab.

Optimization and caching

CDNs are all about optimizing the content and caching it. In that way, they improve the performance of your website and user experience. In the previous section, you learned a little bit about the concept of Content Delivery Networks and configured your instance of Azure CDN. Now we will try to learn some more advanced features, such as compression, caching rules, and optimization.

Configuring the endpoint

To access the endpoint configuration, you have to click on it on the **Overview** blade:

This will display a new screen, where you can find all information regarding that particular CDN endpoint, such as its hostname, available protocols, and configured rules for content optimization. In fact, the screen looks very similar to the previous one—it just offers some additional options:

Now we will discuss different features available for an endpoint.

Compression

One of the basic features of CDNs is **compression**—they allow you to compress different file types on-the-fly, such as lowering their size and reducing network latency:

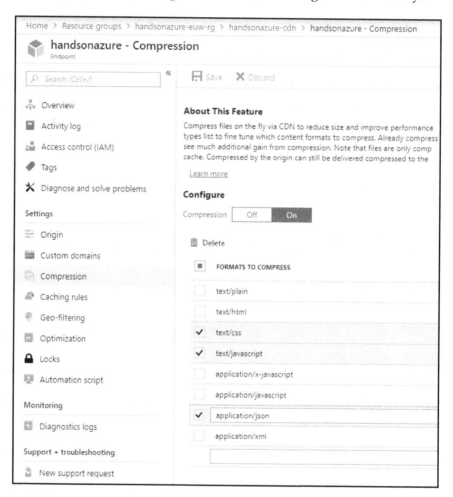

When you enable it, you can select the MIME types you are interested in. You can also add new ones, if you plan to support any.

Remember that a file has to be cached by a CDN to be actually compressed on-the-fly.

Caching rules

By default, CDN caches content based on the Cache-Control header you provide. However, you can explicitly define how it should behave if:

- A header is missing
- A query string is introduced
- A particular match condition matches

Here you can find a basic setup for this feature:

As you can see, it gives you a lot of control over the behavior of the service, especially with the **Custom caching rules**.

Geo-filtering

Sometimes you need to block specific content for specific countries. Such a feature might be problematic without CDN—you have to control programmatically who can access a given image or a file based on the geo-location. With Azure CDN you can enable it within seconds:

On the **Geo-filtering** blade, you can **Configure** different rules blocking or allowing access to a folder or a particular file inside CDN for a particular country.

Developing applications with Azure CDN

Azure CDN itself does not give you anything special—it just caches content and takes responsibility for serving it without delays. The important thing, however, is to know how you can use it in your applications. In Azure, integrating Azure CDN with, for example, Azure App Services, is a piece of cake. It only takes a few mouse clicks to get your CDN working with your existing web applications. In the last section of this chapter, you will see what is required to get the integration set up and ready to improve your website's performance.

Configuring Azure App Service with Azure CDN

To configure Azure App Service to work with your instance of Azure CDN, you will have to find the **Networking** blade. This gives you the ability to enable different web app features, including CDN:

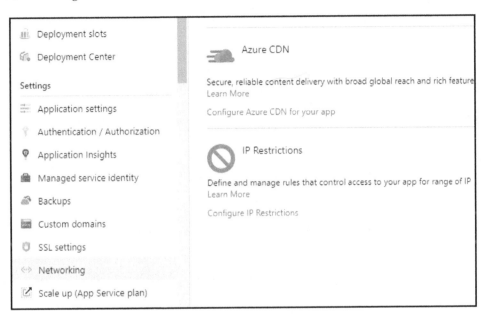

When you click on **Configure Azure CDN for your app**, you will see another screen where you can configure the link between Azure App Service and Azure CDN.

> Azure CDN will automatically start caching static files, which can be found in your site. It is a good idea to publish your application at this moment, so you will not have to wait for the process to end later.

In fact, you have two options to proceed now:

- Use the existing CDN profile (if you performed exercises from the previous section of this chapter, you should have your CDN already created and ready to work)
- Create a brand new profile

In the following, you can find my configuration (I chose an existing endpoint to speed things up):

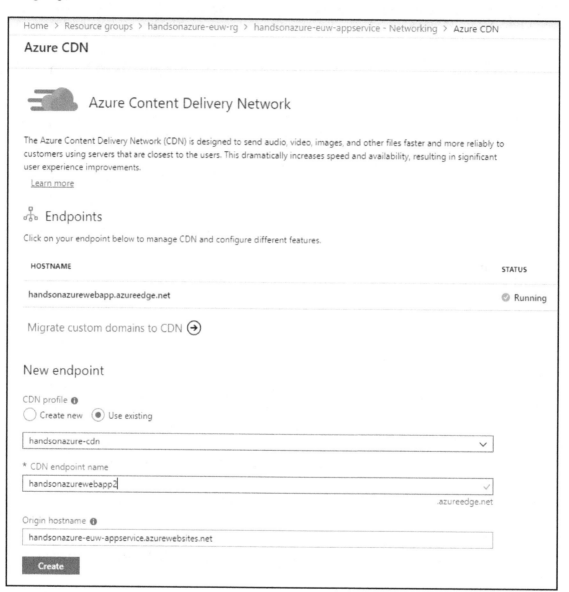

Once your endpoint is created, you can check whether it works. To do so, you can check, for example, the sources for your application as I did:

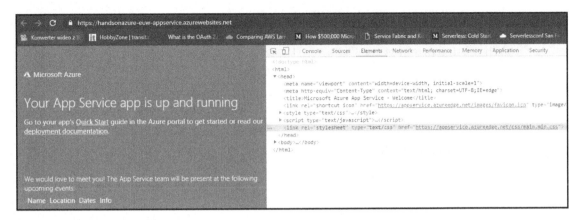

For the purpose of this exercise, I used an example application from the template. As you can see, with the CDN configured, the source of my application is automatically altered—all static content is served using my Azure CDN endpoint instead of my server.

Summary

In this chapter, you learned what CDNs are and how they may help you in achieving better performance and user experience for your web applications. We have configured an Azure CDN instance, and saw how to optimize serving content by compressing it. After reading this chapter, you should be able to filter particular content for particular countries, and be able to develop proper caching rules, so that you can define how your instance will behave.

In the next chapter, which is the last chapter in this book describing Azure services, we will cover one more advanced scenario—distributing load and securing data from outages with Azure Traffic Manager.

Questions

1. What problems does using Azure CDN solve?
2. What are the available CDN providers for Azure CDN?
3. What is the origin of the CDN?
4. How does compression work in Azure CDN?
5. What is the default TTL of content stored within Azure CDN?

Further reading

- CDN features: `https://docs.microsoft.com/en-us/azure/cdn/cdn-features`

20
Distributing Load with Azure Traffic Manager

Sometimes we want to distribute our load depending on the performance of our backends, or maybe route users to different servers while some are under maintenance. This is not an easy task if we don't have a service that will do this seamlessly and quickly. Thanks to **Azure Traffic Manager** we are able to improve the availability of our critical applications, distribute traffic when performing large, complex deployments, or perform maintenance without downtime.

The following topics will be covered in this chapter:

- Using Azure Traffic Manager
- Different routing methods
- Endpoint monitoring

Technical requirements

To perform exercises from this chapter, you will need the following:

- Access to an Azure subscription

Azure Traffic Manager fundamentals

Imagine the following situation—you have an application that has to be served globally. To guarantee the best performance for all your customers worldwide, you provision different instances of your service in different regions (one for North America, one for Europe, and one for Africa). There is one problem, however. You have to explicitly tell your customer to access a specific instance of the application—the one that is closest to its location.

While this is, of course, possible (just give it the right URL), the solution is not ideal. For example, what if your client goes for a holiday and spends the following two weeks in Europe instead of in Africa? To overcome such problems, in Azure you can leverage a service named **Azure Traffic Manager**, which takes care of the proper routing of incoming requests and allows you to implement high availability in your application.

Functions of Azure Traffic Manager

You can think of Azure Traffic Manager as a load balancer that works on the DNS level. To understand the concept, please take a look at the following example. By default, if there is no service such as Azure Traffic Manager, your **customer** uses an endpoint URL to send requests from a **client application** to a **server application**:

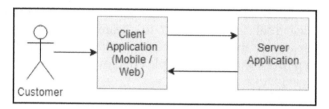

If you want to load-balance incoming requests, you have to introduce another element of an architecture that will take care of routing them to the proper backend (and possibly ensure that they are healthy):

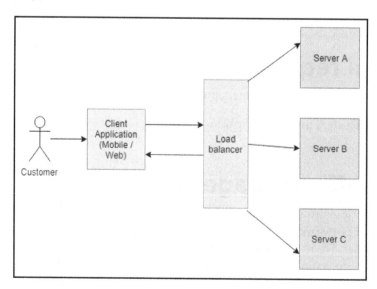

The downside of such a setup is that latency can be introduced. What is more, in that scenario your client connects via a **load balancer** directly, which does not resolve the problem of globally distributing the entry point.

 The preceding example is a common solution when using a reverse proxy, which acts as a gateway to your system.

The described scenario defines a solution, where load balancing is based on distributing traffic based on TCP/UDP, so it is a significantly lower level than DNS. When using Azure Traffic Manager, the flow of a request is completely different:

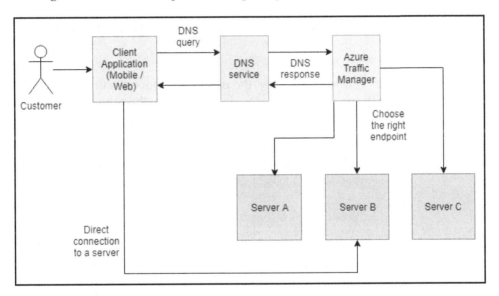

The flow can be described as follows:

1. Send a **DNS query** to a **DNS service** to obtain the address of a server
2. The **DNS service** is configured in such a way that it points to **Azure Traffic Manager**, instead of pointing to a service directly
3. **Azure Traffic Manager** chooses the right endpoint based on the query characteristics and returns a **DNS response** containing the address of the proper server
4. A client receives a **DNS response** and uses it to connect to the right server

In fact, a client has to perform two requests:

- Obtain the URL of a server
- Send the actual request

While it may seem like a bit of an overhead, in reality, the impact is imperceptible.

 Note that the advantage of such a solution is the ability to send requests directly to a server. There is no intermediary service that participates in the communication.

Creating Azure Traffic Manager in the Azure portal

To get started with Azure Traffic Manager in the portal, you have to click on the **+ Create a resource** button and search for `traffic manager`. Then from the search results, select **Traffic Manager profile**. You will see a form, where you have to enter all required fields to be able to create a service:

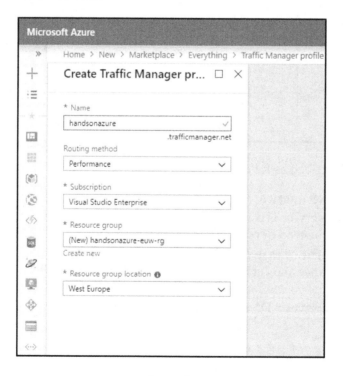

While most of them should be self-explanatory, there is one drop-down that will require our focus, **Routing method**. Here you have six different methods available:

- **Performance**
- **Weighted**
- **Priority**
- **Geographic**
- **MultiValue**
- **Subnet**

Before we describe each and every one, you have to understand what **Routing method** is exactly. Previously I mentioned that Azure Traffic Manager decides to which endpoint a user should be routed. This routing operation may give a different result depending on the selected method. Let's consider the following scenarios:

- Instances of your application are distributed globally, and you want to route a user to the closest one
- Instances of your application offer different performances, and you want to route a user to the one that offers the best user experience
- You have a primary region that handles all the traffic, and you want to route a user to secondary ones in case of an outage or temporary issues
- You want to distribute traffic evenly, or according to set weights
- You want to map user IP addresses to a specific instance

Depending on the chosen scenario, a different **Routing method** should be chosen. Now I will describe them in detail.

Routing method – performance

When using the performance routing method, a user will be routed to the endpoint that is the "closest" one. It is important to remember here, that the "closest" endpoint may not be the one that is the closest geographically, as this method takes into consideration performance, not distance. Let's assume that internally Azure Traffic Manager stores the following information regarding configured endpoints:

Endpoint	Region	Latency
Server A	West Europe	12 ms
Server B	East US 2	67 ms

In the preceding scenario, the endpoint that performs better is **Server A**. When the performance routing method is selected the user will be routed to that server.

 It is important to remember that with the performance method, Azure Traffic Manager checks the latency of a response, taking into consideration the IP address of the DNS server that sent the request. It is not an IP address of a client.

Routing method – weighted

When you want to distribute traffic evenly or based on predefined weights, the weighted routing method is something you are looking for. Using that method, you define weights, which are then taken into consideration when deciding where a request should be routed. Let's take into consideration the following table:

Endpoint	Weight	Status
Server A	100	Online
Server B	100	Degraded
Server A - staging	5	Online

In the preceding example, we have three endpoints, one of which is reporting issues. Although both **Server A** and **Server B** have the same weights, as Server B's status is reported as degraded, it will not be considered as a healthy endpoint, and as a result, a user will not be routed to it. There are two servers left that have different weights. In that situation, Azure Traffic Manager will randomly assign a user to an endpoint with the probability determined by the endpoint's weight. If we imagine that there are 105 requests, 100 of them will be routed to **Server A**, and the rest to the **Server A – staging**.

 A Weighted routing method is a great option for A/B testing, where you randomly route users to the new instance of your application containing new features. If they like them, you can change the weight and route the rest of the traffic to that instance.

Routing method – priority

The priority routing method is the most straightforward as it covers a simple scenario where you have a primary region that hosts your application, and you want to ensure that you can easily fail over to the secondary ones in case something is wrong. Let's consider the following scenario:

Server	Priority	Status
Server A	1	Online
Server A - secondary	2	Online

In the preceding example, all traffic will be routed to Server A for the following reasons:

- Its priority is set to 1
- Its status is considered online

Now something has happened and the primary replica went down:

Server	Priority	Status
Server A	1	Degraded
Server A - Secondary	2	Online

Because Server A is considered unhealthy, all traffic will be routed to the secondary instance until the primary one works again.

> Remember that clients may cache DNS responses, which will extend the period that your endpoint appears unavailable to them.

Routing method – geographic

Sometimes you need to route a user to a specific region, taking into consideration its location. There are multiple reasons to do so, for example:

- Legal requirements
- Content localization
- Serving an application from a server that is the closest one taking distance into consideration

Do remember that a region that is closest to a user may not be the best one regarding network latency. Do not overuse this routing method to achieve the best user experience.

When using the **Geographic** routing method, you assign regions to configured endpoints:

Server	Regions
Server A	France
Server B	Asia
Server C	World

Now to route a user to the proper server, Azure Traffic Manager tries to determine its location by reading the IP address of the source DNS server. It starts from state/province (or country/region if the former is not supported), and ends on the World value.

When using the **Geographic** routing method, Azure Traffic Manager will return an endpoint whether it is healthy or not. It is important to leverage nested profiles, to extend routing methods further, and achieve high availability.

Routing method – MultiValue

The **MultiValue** routing method works a little bit differently from other routing methods, as it allows the return of multiple healthy endpoints, and lets the client choose which one should be used. This scenario covers a situation when on the service side you do not know where to route a user, and simultaneously you want to ensure that a user will be routed to a healthy endpoint.

To make sure that an endpoint can be returned to a user for this routing method, it has to be set as **External** and has an IPv4 or IPv6 address assigned.

Routing method – subnet

The last routing method is the most sophisticated, as it allows you to map specific IP addresses (or a range of IP addresses) to a specific endpoint.

The use cases for that method may vary if, for example:

- You want to block users using a specific ISP
- You want to route users from a corporate network to an internal instance of an application
- You have branded your application and want to route users from different corporate networks to a particular branded instance

 Using the **Subnet** routing method, make sure you have covered all possible IP addresses, as failing to do so will result in a `NODATA` response being returned, resulting in an error being returned to a client.

Once you are satisfied with your choice of a routing method, you can click on the **Create** button to provision a resource in Azure.

Working with Azure Traffic Manager in the Azure Portal

When you access your instance of Azure Traffic Manager, you will see a default screen containing the overview of the service:

As there is currently no endpoint attached to this particular profile, the list of endpoints displayed is empty. Before we add a new one, let's focus a little bit on other service features.

Configuration

When you access the **Configuration** blade, you will see the full configuration of your instance of Azure Traffic Manager:

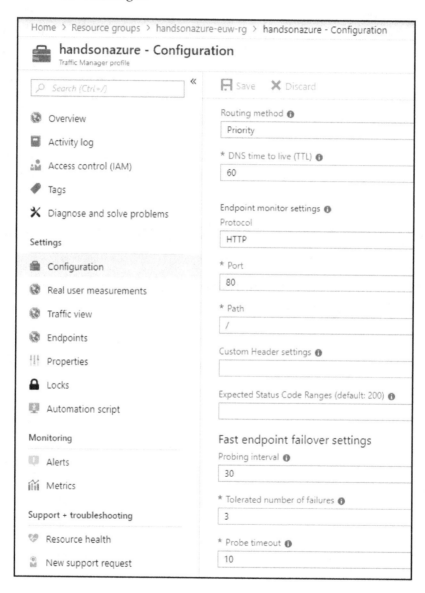

It contains things such as the **Routing method** (by default it displays the one you chose during service creation), **Endpoint monitoring settings**, and **Fast endpoint failover settings**. From this screen, you basically control how Azure Traffic Manager will behave. For instance, let's assume that each of your endpoints has a custom /status endpoint that is designed to work with the service. By default, Azure Traffic Manager checks the default endpoint URL (set here as /), so you will have to change the Path field as follows:

The same goes for expected status codes. If your endpoints can return a range of HTTP status codes, and each of them should be considered as a success, you are able to enter the range in the **Expected Status Code Ranges** field:

You can experiment here with different settings, so they reflect the real scenario you have to cover.

Real user measurements

When using the performance routing method, Azure Traffic Manager checks where DNS requests originate from, and translates the result to an internal table that reflects different network latencies for different end user networks. While this option is perfectly fine for most use cases, sometimes you want to be able to tell Azure Traffic Manager about real latency. With **Real user measurements** features, you are able to inject JavaScript code in to your client endpoints, to send delays to your endpoints directly to this Azure service.

To do so, go to the **Real user measurements** blade and click on the **Generate key** button:

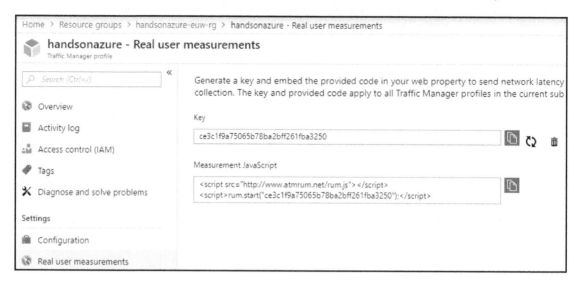

You will see two fields:

- **Key**: Stores the generated key
- **Measurement JavaScript**: Holds the script that should be injected into the client application

Once you use the generated script, it will start sending additional information to your instance of Azure Traffic Manager regarding latencies and client network, which will improve the accuracy of decisions made by the service.

 The accuracy improvement is not instant—Azure Traffic Manager has to gather lots of data from different networks to improve the performance.

Endpoints

The main functionality of Azure Traffic Manager is the ability to configure the endpoints it handles. You can access it through the **Endpoints** blade:

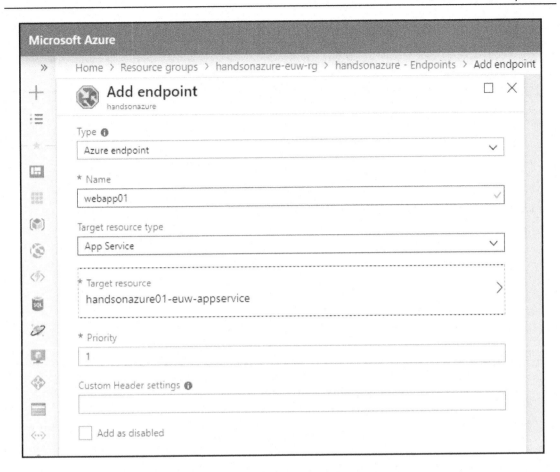

To add an endpoint, you have to enter the following values:

- **Type**: You can choose between an **Azure endpoint**, **External endpoint**, and **Nested endpoint**. The difference impacts the whole form—with **Azure endpoint** you can choose an Azure service, **External endpoint** requires providing a fully qualified domain name or IP, and when you select **Nested endpoint** you can point to another Traffic Manager profile.
- **Name**: Unique name of an endpoint.
- **Target resource type/FQDN or IP/Target resource**: Depending on the **Type** value, you will have to select different values to configure an endpoint.
- **Priority**: Because my routing method is **Priority**, I have to enter the correct value for this particular endpoint. If you select another method, you may find other fields here.

In the following example, I selected an **Azure endpoint** and pointed the configuration to one of my Azure App Services. I performed the operation twice and added two different endpoints to two instances of my application:

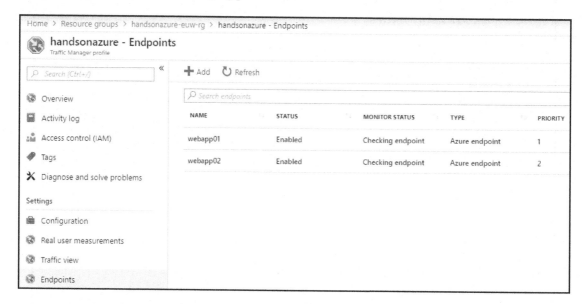

 Remember that you cannot add to a single Azure Traffic Manager profile service domains that point to the same region.

As you can see, right after adding endpoints, their status is displayed as **Checking endpoint**. This means that Azure Traffic Manager tries to gather information regarding their health. If something is wrong, you will see the **Degraded** status:

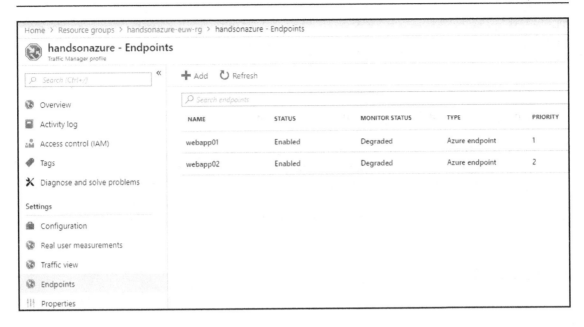

In my case, the problem was an invalid configuration as I set the **Path** field in the **Configuration** blade to/status, which turned out to be an invalid value (in my application, as I implemented that endpoint as /api/status). After correcting the configuration in the primary service, its status was displayed as **Online**:

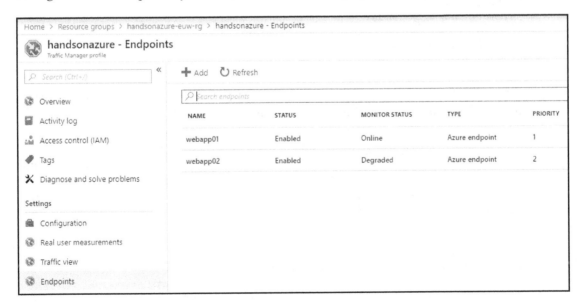

The last thing to configure is the DNS record on your DNS server to point to your instance of Azure Traffic Manager (by using DNS name, which can be found on the **Overview** blade).

Monitoring

Besides routing traffic to a different endpoint, Azure Traffic Manager offers some additional functionalities when it comes to monitoring. Besides the traditional **Metrics** blade, there is an extra feature available called **Traffic view**, which enables you to monitor. What is more, you can use many different built-in mechanisms (like `nslookup` in Windows OS), to check the current configuration of the service.

Nslookup

To use `nslookup`, you have to run the command line in Windows using your administrator account. Once it is loaded, enter the following command:

```
nslookup <Traffic-Manager-DNS-name>
```

After a moment, it should return a result showing the command resolution:

```
DNS request timed out.
    timeout was 2 seconds.
DNS request timed out.
    timeout was 2 seconds.
Non-authoritative answer:
Name: waws-prod-db3-119.cloudapp.net
Address: 40.85.74.227
Aliases: handsonazure.trafficmanager.net
         handsonazure02-eun-appservice.azurewebsites.net
         waws-prod-db3-119.sip.azurewebsites.windows.net
```

As you can see, it points to the second instance of my application (`handsonazure02` hosted within the North Europe region). The reason why I got this response is that my primary endpoint was considered to be downgraded. Once it went back online, I ran the command once more and got a quite different response:

```
Name: waws-prod-am2-229.cloudapp.net
Address: 104.40.250.100
Aliases: handsonazure.trafficmanager.net
         handsonazure01-euw-appservice.azurewebsites.net
         waws-prod-am2-229.sip.azurewebsites.windows.net
```

Now it returned the primary server (as expected, by using the **Priority** routing method).

Remember that you have to wait a fixed amount time before all DNS changes will be propagated. The value can be configured in the **Configuration** blade by changing the **DNS time to live** field.

Traffic view

Traffic view is an additional monitoring feature that enables you to check how the selected routing method works exactly at the DNS level. It gives you extra helpful information like:

- Real latency level
- Volume of traffic
- Users location

Remember that this feature takes up to 24 hours to propagate and gather all necessary information.

By default, the screen for this functionality looks such as the following:

Once the information is gathered, you can leverage a graphical representation of collected data, and better understand the behaviour of the selected routing method (and possibly improve it).

Summary

This was the last chapter in this book and explained the basics of one Azure services, Azure Traffic Manager. You have learned the fundamental concepts of traffic distribution and different routing methods that cover many real use cases, which you may well face in your daily work. Now you should understand how this particular Azure service works and what can be achieved by the proper usage of its features, such as configuration, real user measurements, and monitoring. In the next (and, unfortunately, the last) chapter, I will show you some useful tips and tricks for working with the Azure Portal and different cloud components to improve your skills even further.

Questions

1. What are the supported routing methods in Azure Traffic Manager?
2. How can you use the **Real user measurements** feature?
3. Can you link different Azure Traffic Manager profiles?
4. Is it possible to use an external endpoint?
5. Does a client connect directly to an endpoint returned by Azure Traffic Manager?
6. What is the main difference between a gateway and Azure Traffic Manager?
7. Can Azure Traffic Manager be used to achieve high availability? If so, how?

Further reading

- Disaster recovery with Azure DNS and Traffic Manager: `https://docs.microsoft.com/en-us/azure/networking/disaster-recovery-dns-traffic-manager`
- How it works: `https://docs.microsoft.com/en-us/azure/traffic-manager/traffic-manager-how-it-works`

Tips and Tricks for Azure 21

There's always more than only one way to do a particular thing. This statement is especially true in the Azure ecosystem, where we're given multiple tools and shortcuts when provisioning resources, configuring services, and developing applications. This chapter will show the reader how to enhance productivity even more, and shorten the time needed to deliver a working solution.

The following topics will be covered in this chapter:

- Cloud Shell and the Azure CLI
- Locks on resources
- Proper naming conventions
- Resources in Azure

Technical requirements

To perform exercises from this chapter, you will need the following:

- An Azure subscription
- The Azure CLI, available at https://docs.microsoft.com/en-us/cli/azure/install-azure-cli?view=azure-cli-latest

The Azure CLI and Cloud Shell

Using the Azure portal to perform all actions, such as provisioning a resource, changing its configuration, or finding a particular value, is indeed one of the easiest ways of managing both your subscription and deployed services. However, it may become cumbersome when you have tens or hundreds of different subscriptions, resource groups, and instances. In such scenarios, it is always better to have access to scripts and commands that speed things up and allow for automation, if needed. In this section, we will cover two basic tools available in Azure: the Azure CLI and Cloud Shell, which you can use when just the portal is not enough.

The Azure CLI

The Azure CLI is a cross-platform command-line tool, which you can install locally to manage Azure resources. In general, a command looks like this:

```
$ az [resource] [command] -param1 "Foo" -param2 123
```

For example, you can use the Azure CLI to create a function app like this:

```
$ az functionapp create --name "handsonazureapp" --storage-account
"handsonazurestorage" --consumption-plan-location "westeurope" --resource-
group "myResourceGroup"
```

The instruction for installing the Azure CLI can be found in the *Technical requirements* section. It points to an article that describes the process for multiple different platforms, such as Windows, macOS, and Linux. Once the Azure CLI is installed, open your command line terminal and enter the following command:

```
$ az login
```

After a moment, you should see a result similar to mine, where you are asked to authenticate the Azure CLI locally:

```
$ az login
To sign in, use a web browser to open the page
https://microsoft.com/devicelogin and enter the code DRXXXXXXX to
authenticate.
```

To authenticate the tool, go to the displayed web page and enter the displayed code. If everything is correct, the command will end successfully, and as a result, it will display information about all subscriptions attached to the account. When using the Azure CLI, you do not have to remember all the commands—to find the one you are looking for, you can use the following, which will find all related commands:

```
$ az find -q "query"
```

Let's assume that you want to work with Azure Functions now. To interrogate all the commands related to that service, I can use the following query:

```
$ az find -q function
`az functionapp create`
    Create a function app.
    The function app's name must be able to produce a unique FQDN as
    AppName.azurewebsites.net.

`az functionapp list`
    List function apps.

`az functionapp delete`
    Delete a function app.

`az functionapp stop`
    Stop a function app.

`az functionapp start`
    Start a function app.

`az functionapp restart`
    Restart a function app.

`az functionapp update`
    Update a function app.

`az functionapp`
    Manage function apps.

`az functionapp config`
    Configure a function app.

`az functionapp show`
    Get the details of a function app.
```

As you can see, it is super easy—you can quickly provision new resources without even touching the Azure portal. Here you can find a full example of instruction for creating a function app:

```
$ az storage account create --sku Standard_LRS --kind Storage --resource-
group handsonazure-euw-rg --name handsonazurestorage
$ az functionapp create --name handsonazure-euw-functionapp --storage-
account handsonazurestorage --resource-group handsonazure-euw-rg --
consumption-plan-location westeurope
```

 In the above example, I skipped the process of creating a resource group. If you want to create a new one, just use the `az group create` command.

Cloud Shell

An alternative to using the Azure CLI is a tool named Cloud Shell. You can access it directly within the Azure portal by clicking on the Cloud Shell button:

When you open Cloud Shell, a welcome screen will be displayed at the bottom of the portal, asking you to select a shell you are interested in:

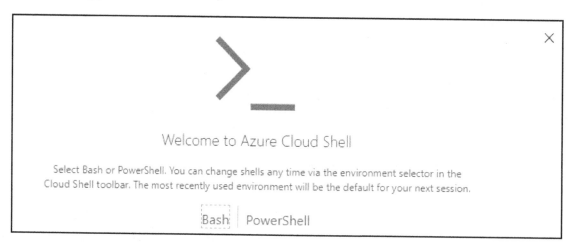

Welcome to Azure Cloud Shell

Select Bash or PowerShell. You can change shells any time via the environment selector in the Cloud Shell toolbar. The most recently used environment will be the default for your next session.

Bash | PowerShell

The choice does not really matter as you can change the selected option anytime. As I personally prefer PowerShell over Bash, the default option in my case is the former.

 Both Bash and PowerShell scripts are aligned with each other when it comes to functionalities. You should select a shell that you prefer to work with.

If this is your first time with Cloud Shell, you will also be asked to mount a storage account that can be used with the feature. Cloud Shell uses it to persist files between your sessions. You have two options here; either you let it create a storage account for you, or you can select particular options by clicking on the **Show advanced settings** button:

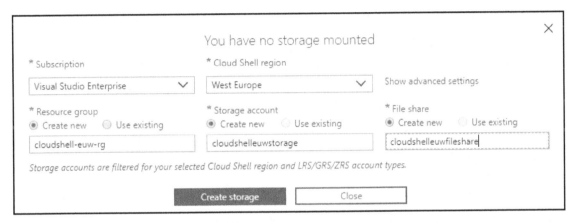

Once everything is configured correctly, Azure will attempt to initialize your Cloud Shell account:

```
Your cloud drive has been created in:

Subscription Id: <subscription-id>
Resource group: cloudshell-euw-rg
Storage account: cloudshelleuwstorage
File share: cloudshelleuwfileshare

Initializing your account for Cloud Shell...\
Requesting a Cloud Shell.Succeeded.
Connecting terminal...

Welcome to Azure Cloud Shell

Type "dir" to see your Azure resources
Type "help" to learn about Cloud Shell
```

```
MOTD: Switch to PowerShell from Bash: pwsh

VERBOSE: Authenticating to Azure ...
VERBOSE: Building your Azure drive ...
Azure:/
PS Azure:\>
```

Using Cloud Shell is similar to browsing a file system. Your Azure resources are presented as directories, which can be accessed by common command-line commands such as `dir` or `cd`. You can select a subscription you would like to work with by entering the following command:

```
PS Azure:\> cd <subscription-name>
```

Then it is easy to browse all resources within it by using the following command:

```
PS Azure:\> cd AllResources
PS Azure:\> dir
```

Note that there is a limit on resources you can access via Cloud Shell—currently you can use it to operate on the following services:

- Resources groups
- Web Apps
- Storage accounts
- Virtual machines

For example, to obtain a connection string for Azure Files, you can use something like this:

```
PS Azure:\> cd StorageAccounts\<storage-account-name>\files
PS Azure:\> dir
```

Of course, inside Cloud Shell, you can use both Azure Powershell commands and the Azure CLI. If you enter the `az` command in the command line, you will see the following result:

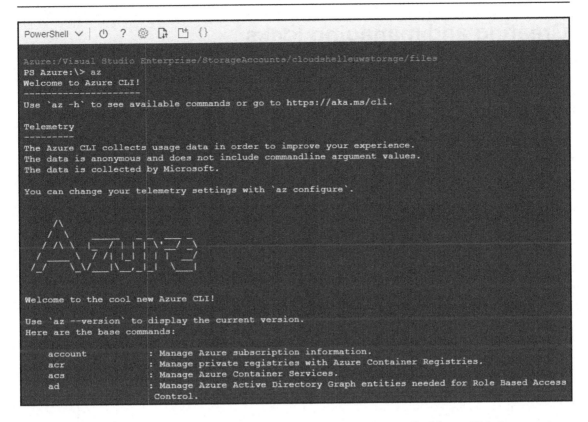

```
PowerShell ∨ | ⏻ ? ⚙ 🗔 🗗 {}

Azure:/Visual Studio Enterprise/StorageAccounts/cloudshelleuwstorage/files
PS Azure:\> az
Welcome to Azure CLI!
----------------------
Use `az -h` to see available commands or go to https://aka.ms/cli.

Telemetry
---------
The Azure CLI collects usage data in order to improve your experience.
The data is anonymous and does not include commandline argument values.
The data is collected by Microsoft.

You can change your telemetry settings with `az configure`.


    /\
   /  \    _____   _   _ _ __ ___
  / /\ \  |_  / | | | | '__/ _ \
 / ____ \  / /| |_| | | |  __/
/_/    \_\/___|\__,_|_|  \___|


Welcome to the cool new Azure CLI!

Use `az --version` to display the current version.
Here are the base commands:

    account       : Manage Azure subscription information.
    acr           : Manage private registries with Azure Container Registries.
    acs           : Manage Azure Container Services.
    ad            : Manage Azure Active Directory Graph entities needed for Role Based Access
                    Control.
```

Basically, all you have learned in the previous section can be applied here. This is a great tool that will enhance your productivity once you get used to using commands instead of browsing the Azure portal.

Locks

Creating and managing Azure resources is much easier when leveraging the various commands available that allow you to work faster and enable you to automate processes. However, when you have hundreds of resources provisioned, mistakes may happen—you can accidentally move, rename, or even delete a resource, which should not even be touched. To prevent such scenarios, it is possible to use locks—a simple feature that stops you from performing a forbidden action. In this section, you will learn how to create them, and use them for your own purposes.

Creating and managing locks

Locks are available on almost every resource available in the Portal. You access them by simply clicking on the **Locks** blade:

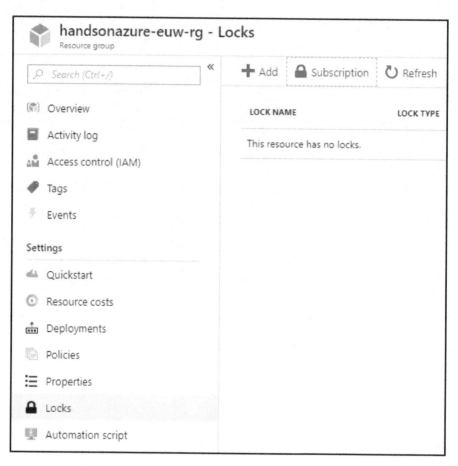

In the preceding example, let's assume that I want to secure my resource group and disallow deleting it. To do so, I have to click on the **+ Add** button and the appropriate lock type:

Now if I try to delete a resource group, I will get the following error:

As you probably noticed, there are two types of lock; delete and read-only.

The read-only lock prevents me from introducing changes to the resource—for a resource group, I cannot, for example, add a new service:

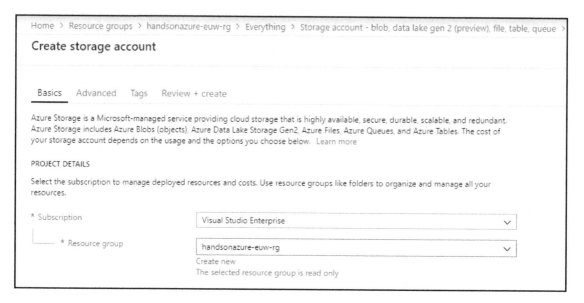

Of course, read-only locks work differently for different resources. If I introduce one to my Azure Storage Account, it will prevent me from making any changes to the service configuration:

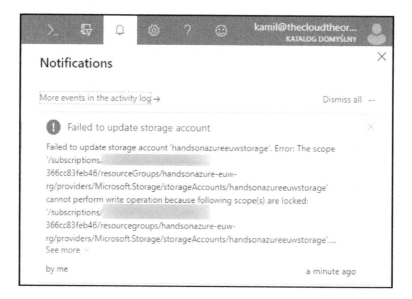

Locks are also Azure resources, meaning that you can manage them by Azure Powershell commands (such as `Get-AzureRmResourceLock`), or ARM templates.

Naming conventions

Governing and managing resources in Azure can become a challenge if you do not introduce a proper naming convention that is simple, intuitive, and easy to follow. In the world of software development, proper naming for services is especially difficult as you have to take into account different regions, environments, and instances. In this section, we will try to discover different concepts for naming conventions, which you will able to apply or adjust to your needs.

Finding the best naming convention

In Azure, you have to consider the following aspects of a resource:

- A region where it is provisioned
- A resource type
- A resource name
- A resource instance type/environment

We will start from a resource group. By default you can name it as follows:

```
MyNewService
newPortal
oldplatform
```

The rule of thumb is to select a name that will be self-explanatory. While selecting a name such as `MyNewService` should be fine, it does not give you the following information:

- Where the resource group is located
- What environment (test/production/staging/and so on) it represents

What is more, if you, for example, list resources inside your subscription, you will not know which resource type `MyNewService` is, without selecting its type. While, of course, commands such as `az group list` give you the full information about a resource, you will need to include an additional field if you want to export only a resource name. In such cases, it would be worth annotating the resource group name with the resource type as follows:

```
MyNewServiceResourceGroup
newPortal-resourceGroup
oldplatform-rg
```

So far so good—the name of the resource looks much better now. Let's now consider adding a location:

```
MyNewResourceResourceGroupEastUS2
newPortal-westEurope-resourceGroup
oldplatform-eun-rg
```

Things look much better now—we immediately know what resource type we are considering and where it is located. With that information it much easier to browse through different services. The last thing that could be added is the environment:

```
MyNewResourceResourceGroupEastUS2Test
newPortal-westEurope-prod-resourceGroup
oldplatform-staging-eun-rg
```

Now the information is complete. Of course, everything depends on your personal setup, as you may decide that all environments are stored inside a single resource group. Even then it is worth including the rest of the data so that you will have cohesive names for all provisioned resources.

 Remember that different Azure resources have different limits when it comes to their names. While Azure App Services may be quite liberated about this, Azure Storage disallows you from using characters other than letters and numbers.

In fact, your requirements for the naming convention will imply what really has to be included in the resource name, for example:

- Whether you deploy resources in different regions
- Whether you use multiple environments for developing your applications
- Whether you use a single resource group for multiple environments

The general rule is to use a convention that you both like, and is flexible enough to cover services deployed to Azure after a few years. The worst thing here is having to change it after some time because it cannot reflect the changes in your business.

Resources in Azure

Microsoft Azure is all about resources—you manage them directly or indirectly, but nonetheless most of what you touch is a resource of some kind. Whether it is a particular service (such as Azure Functions or Azure Traffic Manager), a part of it (such as the application settings available for Azure App Services), or a distinct feature (such as locks, as discussed in this chapter), you can manage all of them using Azure Resource Manager (which is often referred to as Azure RM). In the last section of this chapter, we will discuss how to access properties of Azure resources, so you can use them to investigate the configuration and automate processes, such as deployment or monitoring.

Azure Resource Explorer

The easiest way to access Azure resources is to use **Azure Resource Explorer**. You can access it by going to `https://resources.azure.com/`.

Your default screen will look similar to mine:

To browse your resources, you have to expand nodes available on the left. Initially, you have access to two different node types:

- **providers**: Those are related to a specific Azure service, such as Azure Cosmos DB or Azure Storage
- **subscription**: As a subscription is also an Azure resource, you can browse it using Azure Resource Explorer

These two node types give you access to different kinds of operation; providers are a high-level representation of a specific Azure service, while subscription contains information regarding resources provisioned within it. What is more, it gives you the possibility to directly check the parameters of your resource:

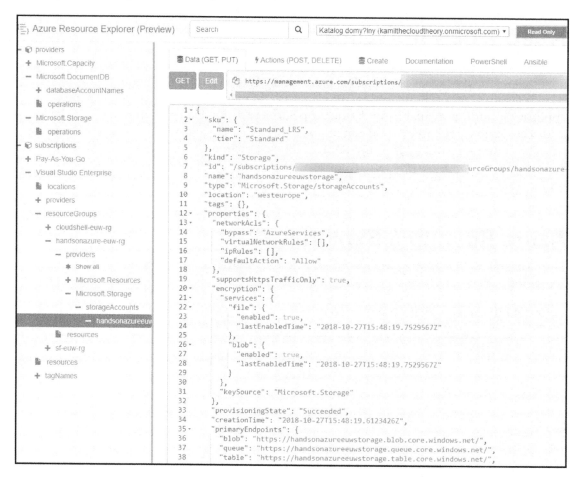

The gathered information can be used to enter the required information in ARM templates. You can always consult them with the visible results from Azure Resource Explorer. This tool allows you to also directly edit the resource parameters (by clicking on the **Edit** button), and generates a PowerShell/Ansible script, which can be used to manage it. In the following, you can find an example of a PowerShell command, generated for my Azure Storage account:

```
# PowerShell equivalent script

# GET handsonazureeuwstorage
Get-AzureRmResource -ResourceGroupName handsonazure-euw-rg -ResourceType
Microsoft.Storage/storageAccounts -ResourceName "handsonazureeuwstorage" -
ApiVersion 2017-10-01

# SET handsonazureeuwstorage
$PropertiesObject = @{
  #Property = value;
}
Set-AzureRmResource -PropertyObject $PropertiesObject -ResourceGroupName
handsonazure-euw-rg -ResourceType Microsoft.Storage/storageAccounts -
ResourceName "handsonazureeuwstorage" -ApiVersion 2017-10-01 -Force

# DELETE handsonazureeuwstorage
Remove-AzureRmResource -ResourceGroupName handsonazure-euw-rg -ResourceType
Microsoft.Storage/storageAccounts -ResourceName "handsonazureeuwstorage" -
ApiVersion 2017-10-01 -Force

# Action ListAccountSas
$ParametersObject = @{
  signedServices = "(String)"
  signedResourceTypes = "(String)"
  signedPermission = "(String)"
  signedIp = "(String)"
  signedProtocol = "(String)"
  signedStart = "(String)"
  signedExpiry = "(String)"
  keyToSign = "(String)"
}

Invoke-AzureRmResourceAction -ResourceGroupName handsonazure-euw-rg -
ResourceType Microsoft.Storage/storageAccounts -ResourceName
handsonazureeuwstorage -Action ListAccountSas -Parameters $ParametersObject
-ApiVersion 2017-10-01 -Force

# Action ListServiceSas
$ParametersObject = @{
  canonicalizedResource = "(String)"
```

```
   signedResource = "(String)"
   signedPermission = "(String)"
   signedIp = "(String)"
   signedProtocol = "(String)"
   signedStart = "(String)"
   signedExpiry = "(String)"
   signedIdentifier = "(String)"
   startPk = "(String)"
   endPk = "(String)"
   startRk = "(String)"
   endRk = "(String)"
   keyToSign = "(String)"
   rscc = "(String)"
   rscd = "(String)"
   rsce = "(String)"
   rscl = "(String)"
   rsct = "(String)"
}

Invoke-AzureRmResourceAction -ResourceGroupName handsonazure-euw-rg -
ResourceType Microsoft.Storage/storageAccounts -ResourceName
handsonazureeuwstorage -Action ListServiceSas -Parameters $ParametersObject
-ApiVersion 2017-10-01 -Force

# Action listKeys
Invoke-AzureRmResourceAction -ResourceGroupName handsonazure-euw-rg -
ResourceType Microsoft.Storage/storageAccounts -ResourceName
handsonazureeuwstorage -Action listKeys -ApiVersion 2017-10-01 -Force

# Action regenerateKey
$ParametersObject = @{
   keyName = "(String)"
}

Invoke-AzureRmResourceAction -ResourceGroupName handsonazure-euw-rg -
ResourceType Microsoft.Storage/storageAccounts -ResourceName
handsonazureeuwstorage -Action regenerateKey -Parameters $ParametersObject
-ApiVersion 2017-10-01 -Force
```

As you can see, you do not have to write such scripts on your own, you can just use Azure Resource Manager, copy them, and potentially adjust them to your needs.

Summary

In this, the last chapter of this book, we covered topics not related to a specific service, but rather extending your current knowledge, and allowing you to become a better user, developer, and architect of solutions based on Microsoft Azure. You have learned how to use the Azure CLI and Cloud Shell to ease management operations, how to leverage locks to secure all fragile resources, and how to read an Azure service configuration. We also discussed the pros for adopting proper naming conventions and how they affect your applications deployed in Azure. This was an exciting journey through the Azure cloud, where you discovered many different PaaS offerings from this particular platform. Azure is a fantastic ecosystem and allows you to build both small web pages and complex, enterprise-level platforms. What is more, it is also incredibly dynamic—this is why I strongly encourage you to take a look at the *Further reading* sections detailed in this book, so you can get more experience with it and become familiar with the more advanced concepts. The important thing here is also to constantly update your knowledge, whether through reading blogs, going to meetups, or conferences, and of course reading articles and books. As cloud computing is one of the major topics in recent years when it comes to software development, it is crucial to become familiar with it and build your skill set, which you can use in your daily work.

Questions

1. What are the two different types of lock for resources in Azure, and how do they work?
2. Can you use the Azure CLI inside Cloud Shell?
3. Where can you obtain detailed information about your provisioned resources in Azure?
4. What pros can a proper naming convention give you?
5. Why does Cloud Shell require the provisioning of a storage account?

Further reading

- Please refer to the Azure blog at `https://azure.microsoft.com/en-us/blog/`.

Assessments

Chapter 1: Azure App Service

1. Yes, App Service and Web App can be used interchangeably.
2. Currently, we have three categories: **Dev/Test**, **Production**, and **Isolated**.
3. Both the **Free** and **Shared** tiers will be blocked after exceeding the computer limit, making the application unavailable for users.
4. Currently, we have five different providers: Azure AD, Facebook, Google, Twitter, and Microsoft Account.
5. Yes, **Premium** tiers are based on new Dv2 machines, which use more powerful CPUs and newer architecture.
6. You have to enable the **Application logging** feature.
7. Unfortunately, you cannot do it; you need at least the **Shared** tier.
8. Yes, you can. App Service Plan can support more than only one App Service.
9. There are three OSes available: **Window**, **Linux**, and **Docker**.
10. No, you cannot—you have to recreate App Service to change the underlying operating system.
11. Where can you find the proper location address? You can use either FTP or FTPS. You can find the location address on the **Overview** blade.
12. User-level credentials will be set for all App Services in all subscriptions you have access to. App-level credentials are created with App Service creation and are attached to it.
13. Scaling up means setting up better servers. Scaling out means setting up more servers.
14. You will pay $50 per instance, so $500 in total.
15. Its purpose is to achieve better reliability and isolation of App Service. It also has higher limits regarding the maximum number of working instances.
16. Yes, it is—using Docker as the operating system.

Chapter 2: Azure WebJobs

1. Yes, it is possible to run WebJobs using the **Free** or **Shared** tier. However, it is not recommended as some jobs require that the **Always On** feature is enabled, which is not possible for the **Free** and **Shared** tiers.
2. We can run a job either continuously or by triggering it manually/on schedule.
3. Yes, you can. In general, WebJobs supports the same programming languages as App Services.
4. You have can we deploy the `run.{extension}` file.
5. If so, how to do that? Yes, you can; it is needed to archive all files as a ZIP package and deploy it.
6. It has to be created as a single instance.
7. Yes, WebJobs share application settings with App Services, which host them.

Chapter 3: Deploying Web Applications as Containers

1. Azure Container Registry is an Azure service, which acts as a Docker private registry that's hosted in the cloud. It is seamlessly integrated with other Azure container services.
2. **Admin login** is a feature that allows you to authenticate in ACR using the registry name as a username and a key as a password.
3. To run containers in App Service, you have to choose **Docker** as the OS.
4. Yes, you can—in fact, there are both possibilities (public/private) available.
5. Yes, you can—there is a specific blade available for scaling your instance.
6. To update an application in AKS cluster and limit downtime, you have to have multiple pods deployed with the same application.
7. You have to create a service principal, which will be used during authentication.

Chapter 4: Distributed Applications and Microservices with Service Fabric

1. **Reliable Actors** implement the Virtual Actor pattern and are designed to distribute load among thousands of stateful services. **Reliable Services** are the patterns in Service Fabric that are used to implement stateful services, which can be multi-threaded and do not have to be scaled to that level.
2. **Stateful services** store the state locally. Stateless services either do not handle the state at all or use an external storage.
3. An interface called `ICommunicationListener`.
4. A node type in SF is the specialized VM scale set that's designed to work on a particular workload.
5. Yes, as they are separate VMSS.
6. Yes, you can.
7. Node-to-node security and client-to-node security.
8. A cluster is the whole instance of Service Fabric—a container for all of the other concepts. An application is a logical container for multiple services, which serve the same purpose. A service is a single unit of work inside an application, which can be scaled according to need. A partition is an identifier that allows you to correctly distribute the load among services. A replica is a particular instance of a VM used to replicate the state or achieve higher durability of services.
9. Five nodes are required to achieve the desired level of resiliency and durability for your cluster and applications hosted within it.
10. The reliability tier is used to set the number of VMs inside a node.

Chapter 5: Using Azure Search

1. An index is a metadata table with documents that are used by Azure Search.
2. The push model is used in applications with low-latency requirements, where your documents are indexed immediately once pushed to the service.
3. Yes, you can define a custom schedule for an indexer.
4. By default, Azure Search uses the Lucene analyzer.
5. Yes, it is possible to use a custom analyzer.
6. A replica is a physical instance of your service hosting an index while the partition is a part of it provisioning particular resources.
7. You have to use the `api-key` header.

Chapter 6: Mobile Notifications with Notification Hub

1. PNS stands for Push Notification Service.
2. Yes, each vendor has its own PNS.
3. The main difference is the patch capability—an installation can be updated after creation, a registration cannot.
4. No, the amount of available devices is different per tier.
5. Depending on your environment, either use Visual Studio or programmatically query the Notification Hub instance.
6. There are many possibilities: either use Azure Portal or Visual Studio or enable **Test send** and send a notification programmatically.
7. Rich content notifications are notifications that contain more than only text (such as an image, for example).

Chapter 7: Serverless and Azure Functions

1. In the Consumption pricing model, you pay for each execution of your functions individually.
2. GB-s is the unit of consumption on Azure Functions; it is gigabytes-per-second and defines how much memory was used in a unit of time.
3. Yes, you can, however it is not the advised model of services.
4. It is called a Function App.
5. There was experimental support for this language in the V1 version of Azure Functions. Currently (in V2), it is not supported.
6. Yes—this is how Azure Storage bindings work.
7. When your Function App is deployed automatically, it is set as read-only to avoid manual changes within the process.
8. Not really—in Azure Function, all settings are available via environmental variables.

Chapter 8: Integrating Different Components with Logic Apps

1. Azure Logic Apps leverage the serverless pricing model where you pay for each execution individually, considering all blocks used for this particular app.
2. Yes, it is possible.
3. You need an extra extension called Azure Logic Apps for Visual Studio.
4. Once the execution is finished, you can access it and see the evaluated values that are used during the execution of the flow.
5. Yes, there is a special connector to work with these services.
6. Azure Logic Apps can be exported to JSON files and stored inside your version control system.

Chapter 9: Swiss Army Knife – CosmosDB

1. Azure Cosmos DB supports SQL, MongoDB, Cassandra, Azure Table, and Gremlin.
2. Yes—in the Azure Cosmos DB Table API, you have almost infinite scaling capabilities, a failover feature, and better performance.
3. Strict, bounded-staleness, session, consistent-prefix, and eventual.
4. Out of those two, bounded staleness is more strict.
5. Yes, by configuring the firewall rules.
6. No, SQL API for Azure Cosmos DB is quite different from the SQL Server.
7. Stored procedures in Azure Cosmos DB are for performing extra logic during your queries.
8. Yes, it is possible.

Chapter 10: Reactive Architecture with Event Grid

1. Currently, it is possible to use either the Event Grid schema or the Cloud Events schema.
2. You have to use either the `aeg-sas-key` or `aeg-sas-token` header.
3. You have to respond with a correct JSON containing validation code.

4. An endpoint does not have to be validated if it is an Azure service.

5. When an event cannot be delivered, the delivery will be retried after a predefined interval.

6. During a subscription creation, you can define filters using the `Subject` field.

7. The Local Azure Functions runtime implements the Event Grid endpoint, which can be used to test your application.

Chapter 11: Using Azure Storage – Tables, Queues, Files, and Blobs

1. Hot and cold—the archive can be selected on a blob level once the account is created.

2. You must include both a Partition Key and a Row Key.

3. The following models are available: LRS, ZRS, GRS, and RA-GRS.

4. File Storage works more like a file share while Blob Storage acts as storage for application and user data. They also have different pricing models.

5. Yes, you can.

6. A message will be available for up to a maximum of 7 days.

7. The maximum size of a message is 64 KBs.

8. The maximum size of the Partition Key is 1 KB.

9. In Table Storage, we work with the optimistic concurrency model.

10. With Azure Files, you can easily scale out your shares by adding additional accounts. When using on-premises shares, you have to buy, install, and configure the hardware before you use it.

Chapter 12: Big Data Pipeline – Azure Event Hub

1. Consumer groups are used to allow for parallel events processing using a different processor, which are unrelated to each other.

2. 1TU allows you to process 1,000 messages per second.

3. It depends on your requirements—the only thing to remember is the fact that you cannot change the number of partitions once the hub is created.

4. TUs are assigned to a namespace and shared by hubs.

5. Send, Listen, and Manage.

6. Yes, it can.

7. Some consumers may lose the lease and become idle.

Chapter 13: Real-Time Data Analysis – Azure Stream Analytics

1. In Azure Stream Analytics, you pay for the **Streaming Units (SUs)**.

2. Stream input lets you digest data directly from a stream. With reference input, you can select a service such as Azure Storage, which will be digested in intervals.

3. Application time is the time when an event was generated. Arrival time tells you when an event was received by the service.

4. SELECT Id INTO [output-alias] FROM [input-alias].

5. Yes, it is possible to work with multiple input values.

6. An event is out of order if you apply event ordering based on the arrival time, which will perturb the actual order of events.

7. Yes, you can—to do so, you have to use the SUBSTRING function.

Chapter 14: Enterprise Integration – Azure Service Bus

1. In queue, once a message is read, it will not be sent to another reader. A topic allows you to implement multiple readers that are focused on the same set of messages.

2. No, you have to use at least the Standard tier to use topics.

3. Dead letter queue is used to avoid blocking your queue by an invalid message.

4. In Azure Service Bus, sessions are used to ensure the FIFO message processing.

5. The maximum size of a queue with partitioning is 80 GBs.

6. In the active replication, you are sending a message to both namespaces. In the passive model, you send a message to the secondary namespace, but only if it can be delivered to the primary one.

7. You have to define the primary and secondary regions, pair them, and define a trigger for failover.

Chapter 15: Using Application Insights to Monitor Your Applications

1. You need an instrumentation key.
2. Yes—Azure Application Insights can be used with a variety of different programming languages.
3. Smart Analytics is a set of functionalities that incorporate machine learning and data analysis to extend the capabilities of Application Insights.
4. You can use the Analytics module to perform queries against collected logs.
5. You can use ARM template to create alerts during a resource provisioning.
6. Yes, this is one of the available options.

Chapter 16: SQL in Azure – Azure SQL

1. Azure SQL is constantly updated and gets the updates faster than Microsoft SQL Server.
2. Sharding is dividing your data and database into smaller chunks, which can be distributed evenly, and handle only their part of the load.
3. By default, the connection is blocked by the firewall—you have to add your IP address to the whitelist.
4. DTU-based and vCore-based.
5. The elastic pool is a model of scaling where instead of having a single database with provisioned throughput, you have a pool, which you can dynamically assign to a set of databases.
6. eDTU is the elastic-DTU that is used with elastic pools.
7. You can use the feature called Dynamic Data Masking.
8. You have three option available: Azure Storage, Azure Log Analytics, and Azure Event Hub.

Chapter 17: Big Data Storage – Azure Data Lake

1. In general, it is easier to manage security groups—in that case, you do not have to add an individual entity each time a new user is granted access.
2. RBAC is based on roles, while POSIX ACL is based on computing the set of permissions based on the actions assigned to a user or a group.
3. There are no file size limits in ADLS.
4. It depends on your requirements—while the particular structure may not affect the performance, file sizes may.
5. Yes, ADLS will work with any language that is able to connect to it.
6. Azure Storage introduces file size limits and capacity limits. It also offers a much simpler security model than Azure Data Lake Storage.
7. You have to implement replication to a secondary region.

Chapter 18: Scaling Azure Applications

1. Scaling out scales your application horizontally (by adding additional instances), while scaling up scales your application vertically (so better hardware is provisioned).
2. In most cases, you scale out rather than scale up. This is because the performance of the hardware is limited and it is easier to add another machine to the set rather than provision a new CPU and memory.
3. Not really—while conceptually it could be possible, serverless services avoid scaling up.
4. Yes—if you scale out Azure App Service, the price for the service will be multiplied by the number of instances currently working.
5. In SF, scaling out is perfectly fine. The dangerous operations are scaling up as it requires you to take your workload from one place and migrate it to another one.
6. Manual scaling can be problematic when the traffic your application handles is dynamic—in that case, you would have to constantly monitor it and scale up/out when required.
7. You can set the auto-scaling feature and declare the CPU trigger for scaling your application.

Chapter 19: Serving Static Content Using Azure CDN

1. Azure CDN is designed to cache to improve the performance of your application while serving static content to multiple users.
2. Currently, Azure CDN supports Verizon, Akamai, and Microsoft.
3. Origin is an endpoint that caches resources.
4. In Azure CDN, the compression feature allows you to compress files on the fly, reducing their size and network latencies.
5. The default TTL for files is set to seven days.

Chapter 20: Distributing Load with Azure Traffic Manager

1. Supported routing methods are Performance, Weighted, Geographic, MultiValue, and Subnet.
2. To use the real user measurement feature, you have to inject a custom script into your website, which will send the updated values for latencies regarding network calls.
3. Of course—in that scenario, you will get a nested profile.
4. Yes, it is possible to use an external endpoint.
5. Once the DNS name is resolved (so that Azure Traffic Manager is pointed to the correct endpoint), a client connects directly with the endpoint.
6. Azure Traffic Manager works on the DNS level, while the gateway is a pattern that enables you to load balance requests, but acts as a single entry to your system.
7. Yes, you can use Azure Traffic Manager to achieve HA—in that scenario, you have to implement a profile, which enables you to failover to other regions if one fails to respond.

Chapter 21: Tips and Tricks for Azure

1. The **Subscription** level locks and **Resource** level locks are available.
2. Of course—Azure CLI is available inside Cloud Shell as part of the service.
3. To get the detailed information, you can access the Resource Explorer application.
4. In general: better resources management, quicker filtering, and easier development.
5. It uses a storage account to persist files between different sessions.

Other Books You May Enjoy

If you enjoyed this book, you may be interested in these other books by Packt:

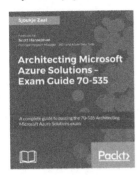

Architecting Microsoft Azure Solutions - Exam Guide 70-535
Sjoukje Zaal

ISBN: 978-1-78899-173-5

- Use Azure Virtual Machines to design effective VM deployments
- Implement architecture styles, like serverless computing and microservices
- Secure your data using different security features and design effective security strategies
- Design Azure storage solutions using various storage features
- Create identity management solutions for your applications and resources
- Architect state-of-the-art solutions using Artificial Intelligence, IoT, and Azure Media Services
- Use different automation solutions that are incorporated in the Azure platform

Implementing Azure Solutions - Second Edition
Florian Klaffenbach et al

ISBN: 978-1-78934-304-5

- Create and manage a Kubernetes cluster in Azure Kubernetes Service (AKS)
- Implement site-to-site VPN and ExpressRoute connections in your environment
- Explore the best practices in building and deploying app services
- Use Telemetry to monitor your Azure Solutions
- Design an Azure IoT solution and learn how to operate in different scenarios
- Implement a Hybrid Azure Design using Azure Stack

Leave a review - let other readers know what you think

Please share your thoughts on this book with others by leaving a review on the site that you bought it from. If you purchased the book from Amazon, please leave us an honest review on this book's Amazon page. This is vital so that other potential readers can see and use your unbiased opinion to make purchasing decisions, we can understand what our customers think about our products, and our authors can see your feedback on the title that they have worked with Packt to create. It will only take a few minutes of your time, but is valuable to other potential customers, our authors, and Packt. Thank you!

Index

.

.NET 412

A

access control list (ACL) 487
Active Directory (AD) 436
Advanced Threat Protection (ATP) 453
AI
  adding, to indexing workload 157
Analytics module
  about 418
  accessing 418, 422
  autocluster 422
  basket 422
  diffpatterns 422
  linear regression 422
  outlier value detection 422
  timer series 422
analyzers
  in Azure Search 150
Apache Lucene
  reference 146, 161
App Service model
  scaling 193
App Service Plans
  development/testing 38
  in production 39
  isolated 40
app-level credentials
  downloading, from Azure Portal 28
  used, for deploying Azure App Service 27
Apple Push Notification Service (APNS) 165
application host 185
Application Insights automation
  alert, using 423, 426, 428
Application Insights

automation 422
  creating, in portal 409
  data, logging 406
  fundamentals 408
  using 406
applications
  developing, with Azure Event Hub 342, 343,
    344, 345, 347
autoscaling 494
Azure Active Directory
  reference 44
Azure App Service
  authentication providers, using 46
  authentication/authorization, configuring 41
  autoscaling 499, 500
  Azure Active Directory, using 42, 45
  Azure Web App, selecting from available
    services 8
  configuring, with CDN 523, 525
  creating 8
  creating, Azure Portal used 8
  creating, Visual Studio Code used 30, 33
  creating, with Visual Studio 15, 18
  deploying 8
  deploying, app-level credentials used 27
  deploying, FTP used 22
  deploying, with user-level credentials 22, 27
  diagnostics 46
  features 37
  manual scaling 497, 498
  Metrics blade 47
  monitoring 46, 48
  Overview blade 47
  plans 37
  scaling 497
  securing 41
  tools, reference 16

Azure CLI
  about 546, 547, 548
  reference 298, 545
Azure Container Instances (ACI)
  about 87
  application, creating 87
  application, deploying 87, 89, 91
  image, pushing to Azure Container Registry
   (ACR) 89
Azure Container Registry (ACR) 76
Azure Data Lake Store
  about 470
  Azure portal, using 476
  best practices 489
  cons 471
  data, storing 475
  fundamentals 470
  instance, creating 472, 475
  Microsoft Azure Storage Explorer 482
  pros 471
  SDKs, using 483
  security 484
Azure Event Grid
  about 383
  and reactive architecture 272
  Azure Functions, integrating with 292
  concepts 274
  creating, in Azure Portal 278, 280
  custom event, handling 288, 292
  custom events, publishing 287
  event handlers 275
  event sources 274
  gateway concept 287
  security 281
  services, connecting through 278
  subscription, creating 282, 286
  topics and subscriptions 276
Azure Event Hub Capture feature
  about 353
  enabling 355, 356
  working 354
Azure Event Hub security
  about 350
  event publishers 350, 351
  IP filters 352

Azure Event Hub
  about 383
  applications, developing 342, 343, 344, 345,
   347
  concepts 332
  consumer group 333
  creating, in Azure portal 336, 337
  durability 335
  partition 333
  processor 332
  publisher 332
  service 332
  throughput units (TU) 333
  working 332
  working with 336, 338, 339, 340
Azure Files
  concepts 314
  features 314
  used, for implementing fully managed file shares
   313
  versus Blob Storage 317
  working with 314, 316
Azure Functions
  about 184, 415
  and Azure Event Grid, testing 297
  bindings 191
  cloud vendor, responsibilities 184
  cloud vendors, comparing 185
  concepts 187
  developing, by local environment configuration
   193
  Event Grid binding, reference 298
  EventGridTrigger 292, 296
  features 205
  function 189
  function app 187
  host.json file, creating 211
  integrating, with Azure Event Grid 292
  monitoring 209
  platform features 205
  pricing model 185, 191
  publish option 212
  reference 224
  scaling 192, 502
  securing 504
  security 207

serverless applications, scaling 503
serverless feature 184
starting with 193, 196
triggers 190
workflow 213
Azure key vaults
reference 111
Azure Kubernetes Service (AKS)
about 73
application, executing 82
application, preparing 74, 76
application, scaling 82
application, updating 82, 86
cluster, scaling 86
container registry 76
Kubernetes cluster 76
problem, solving with authentication 84
working with 74
Azure Logic Apps
about 226
action 229
advantages 229
B2B integration, starting 241
connector 229, 230
creating 233
creating, in Azure Portal 233, 237, 239
functioning 226, 227
services, integrating 233
working with, in Visual Studio 239, 241
Azure Portal
access option 480
Azure Logic Apps, creating 233, 238
files and folders 482
Filter button 477
new folder 478
Upload function 478
used, for creating function 201, 204
used, for navigation 476
using 142
Azure Resource Explorer 557, 559
Azure SDKS
reference 510
Azure Search service
Azure Portal, using 142, 144, 145
creating 141

Azure Service Bus 383
Azure Service Fabric
Azure compute SDK, using for scaling 508, 509
cluster, scaling manually 506, 507
reference 510
scaling 505
Azure SQL
advanced features 436
configuring 439
creating 439
differentiating, with Microsoft SQL Server 432
elastic pool 462
features 444, 448, 450
fundamentals 432, 435
instance, creating 439, 441, 443
monitoring 464
read scale-out 462
reference 435
scaling 460
sharding 463
single database 461
tuning 464, 465, 467
Azure Storage
accounts 300
replication 302
securing 301
securing, RBAC method 301
securing, SAS token method 301
services 300
using, in solution 300
V2 accounts, reference 298
Azure web app
App Service Plan, creating 11, 14
configuring 10
selecting 8
Azure
reference 561

B

B2B integration
starting, in Azure Logic Apps 241, 243
best practices, Azure Data Lake Store
data structure 491
performance, factors 489
resiliency 490

security features *490*
blobs
  append blobs *321*
  block blob *321*
  page blobs *321*
built-in connectors
  Azure API Management *231*
  Azure App Services *231*
  Azure Functions *231*
  Azure Logic Apps *231*
  batch *230*
  HTTP *230*
  request *230*
  schedule *230*

C

capabilities, Application Insights
  dependencies *409*
  exceptions *409*
  requests telemetry *408*
  user telemetry *409*
checkpoints *377, 379*
Cloud Shell *546, 548, 550, 551*
cluster monitoring *138*
cluster security
  about *134*
  client-to-node security *135*
  node-to-node security *134*
clusters
  in SF *133, 134*
  scaling *136*
  scaling, up or down *136*
  security *134*
Cognitive Search
  AI, adding to indexing workload *157*
  configuring *158, 159*
command-line interface (CLI) *284*
connectors, Azure Logic Apps
  account connectors, integrating with enterprise
    connectors *232*
  built-in connectors *230*
  managed connectors *230*
  on-premises connectors *232*
consumer *389*
consumption model

scaling *192*
Container Registry
  about *76*
  Docker image, pushing *77*
containers
  about *107*
  cluster, creating *107, 109*
  deploying *111*
  Docker *107*
  service, packaging *113*
  Windows Server *107*
Content Delivery Network (CDN)
  about *511, 512*
  Azure App Service, configuring *523, 525*
  creating, in portal *514, 517, 518*
  features, reference *526*
  used, for developing applications *522*
  working with *512, 514*
content
  caching *519*
  optimizing *519*
Cosmos DB
  about *246*
  APIs *260*
  consistency *258*
  features *263*
  instance, creating in portal *246, 248, 251*
  partitioning *256*
  partitions *256, 260*
  pricing *255*
  reference *270*
  throughput *256, 258*
  using, in Visual Studio *251, 254*
CosmosDB data models
  Cassandra *263*
  graph *262*
  MongoDB *261*
  SQL *261*
  table *262*
CRON Expression
  reference *55*

D

Data Lake Store operations
  reference *492*

data processing steps
   produce 363
data storage, Table Storage
   about 308
   entities, rules 309
   partition keys 309
   time stamp 309
data, importing
   pull model, using 156
   push model, using 154
Dev/Test App Service Plans
   B1 38
   D1 (Shared) 38
   F1 (Free) 38
direct connection 166
disaster
   handling 399
   recovery 399, 400
Durable Functions
   about 214
   external events 218
   orchestration client 215
   orchestration history 216
   orchestrations and activities 214
   reference 224
   timers 217

E

end-user authentication
   reference 492
endpoint configuration
   accessing 519
   caching rules 521
   compression 520
   geo-filtering 522
event 382
event ordering
   application time 377
   arrival time 377

F

features, CosmosDB
   account level throughput 264
   Azure Functions 266
   database level throughput 265

firewall 265
   stored procedures 267
   user-defined functions and triggers 268
   virtual networks 265
features, Service Bus
   about 396
   dead lettering 396, 397
   sessions 397
   transactions 398, 399
file types
   using, for WebJobs 68
filters
   reference 161
Firebase Cloud Messaging (FCM) 165
full-text search, Azure Search
   linguistic analysis 150
   request, sending 146, 148
function components
   additional bindings 190
   function decorator 190
   trigger 190
function
   compiled function file 219
   creating 198
   creating, Azure Portal used 201, 204
   creating, Visual Studio used 198
   custom bindings 222
   input/output bindings 221
   integrating, with other services 219

G

guest executables 107

H

health monitoring 138

I

index 143
indexing, Azure Search
   about 154
   data, importing 154
IOS push notification
   reference 182
Isolated App Service Plans
   isolated (I1/I2/I3) 41

K

Kubernetes cluster
  about 76
  creating, AKS used 80

L

linguistic analysis, full-text search
  about 150
  analyzers 150, 152
  selecting 153
Live Stream blade 192
load balancer 529
locks
  creating 552, 553
  managing 552, 553
Lucene query operations
  reference 150

M

Managed Service Identity (MSI) 394
manual trigger 204
message 383
microservices
  about 102, 103
  diagnosing 106
  languages and frameworks, using 103
  monitoring 106
  scaling 104
  state, dealing with 105
  updating 104
  well-designed interfaces and protocols, using 105
Microsoft SQL Server
  and Azure SQL, differentiating 432
model-view-controller (MVC) 17
MongoDB 261
monitoring levels
  application monitoring 106
  cluster monitoring 106
  health monitoring 106
  performance monitoring 106
monolith
  versus microservices 102
multi-factor authentication (MFA) 436

N

naming conventions
  about 555
  searching 555
node-to-node security
  certificate security 135
  client-to-node security 135
  Windows security 135
Node.js 414
Node.js Azure WebJob
  deploying, from Visual Studio Code 69
Notification Hub
  application design, challenges 164
  application, registering 171
  available registrations, checking 173
  creating 170
  devices, registering 169
  installation, using 169, 174
  reasons 164
  reference 182
  registration, using 169
  tag 169
  template 169
  using 164
notification
  generic notification 178
  native notification 178
  SDK, using 177
  sending 175

O

operating system
  selecting 34
  working with 33
outages
  active replication 401
  handling 399, 401, 403
  passive replication 401

P

partitions
  about 143
  logical 257
  physical 256

party clusters 120
Platform as a Service (PaaS) 8
Platform Notification Service (PNS) 165
platforms, monitoring
   .NET 412
   about 411
   Azure Functions 415
   Node.js 414
platforms
   application settings, working with 36
   selecting 35
   working with 33
pricing models
   App Service Plan model 191
producer 389
Production App Service Plans
   about 39
   Premium (P1v2) 40
   Standard (S1) 39
property graph 262
pulll model 156
purchasing model
   DTU-based 433
   vCore-based 433
push model 154
push notification architecture
   about 166
   direct connection 166
   queued communication 167
   triggered communication 168

Q

Queue Storage
   features 318
   queues 318
   used, for application development 318
queued communication 167
queues 389

R

RBAC authentication
   reference 404
reactive architecture 272
recovery time objective (RTO) 303
relays 390

reliable actors
   about 107, 124
   client, creating 129
   used, for creating project 125, 127
reliable services 107
replays 377, 379
replica 143
replication
   geo-redundant storage (GRS) 302
   locally-redundant storage (LRS) 302
   read-access geo-redundant storage (RA-GRS)
     302
   zone-redundant storage (ZRS) 302
resources
   Azure Resource Explorer 557, 559, 560
rich content notification
   about 180
   creating 180
   sending 180
role-based access control (RBAC) 485
routing method
   about 531
   geographic 533
   MultiValue 534
   performance 531
   priority 533
   subnet 535
   weighted 532

S

scaling out 493, 495
scaling up 493, 495
search unit (SU) 143
security, Azure Data Lake Store
   authentication 484
   authorization 484
   network isolation 488
   POSIX ACL 487
   RBAC 485
security
   about 450
   Advanced Threat Protection (ATP) 453, 455
   auditing 456
   Dynamic Data Masking 458
   firewall 451

server
  firewall 452
Service Bus SDK
  used, for developing solutions 391, 393
Service Bus security
  about 394
  Managed Service Identity (MSI) 394
  RBAC 395
Service Bus
  and Storage Queues 383
  design patterns 391
  design patterns, reference 404
  fundamentals 382
  queues 389
  relays 389
  topics 389
  using, in Azure portal 384, 387
  versus other messaging services 382
service level agreement (SLA) 38
service-to-service authentication
  reference 492
services
  communication channel, creating 130, 133
  diagnostics 137
  monitoring 137
SF application
  creating 114, 117
  deploying to cloud 119, 122, 124
SF
  clusters 133
  containers 107
  reliable actors 124
  reliable services 107, 114
smart analytics
  reference 429
SQL 261
SQL Server
  executing, on VMs 437, 438
storage accounts, Azure Storage
  blob storage with hot/cool access tiers 300
  general-purpose Premium 300
  general-purpose Standard 300
Storage Blobs
  account 321
  additional features 328

blob 321
Blob Storage 320
  containers 321, 324, 327
  data, inserting 322
  permissions 324, 327
  using 320
storage emulator
  reference 195
Storage General-purpose v2 (GPv2) 275
stream 364
Stream Analytics
  about 362
  concepts 364
  creating, in Azure portal 366
  fully managed 364
  input and output types 365
  input, adding 368, 370
  low cost of ownership 364
  output, adding 370
  performance 364
  query language 373
  query, writing 373, 374, 376
  SQL-based query language 364
stream ingestion
  reference 362
  versus stream analysis 362
streaming units (SUs) 364
subscription 277

T

Tables Storage
  Azure Storage service, creating 303
  data, querying 310, 313
  managing 306, 308
  table API 313
  used, for storing data 303
TelemetryClient
  reference 429
test notification
  in Azure Portal 175
  in SDK 177
  sending 175
topic 277, 390
Traffic Manager
  about 527

configuration 536
creating, in Azure portal 530
endpoints 538, 542
finals 541
functions 528, 529
monitoring 542
Nslookup, using 542
real user measurements 537
traffic view 543
working, in Azure portal 535
triggered communication 168

U

Universal Windows Platform (UWP) 164
user-defined function (UDF) 268

V

Visual Studio Code
Node.js Azure WebJob, deploying 69
used, for creating Azure App Service 30, 33
Visual Studio
Azure Logic Apps, working with 239, 241
Cosmos DB, using 251, 254
used, for creating Azure App Service 15, 16, 20, 21

used, for creating function 198
WebDeploy, configuring 29

W

web app
creating, in container 92, 95
custom application, deploying 96, 98
for containers 92
WebDeploy
configuring, in Visual Studio 29
WebJobs SDK
automatic triggers 64
job, calling manually 63
job, publishing 66
working with 60, 63
WebJobs
application, creating in Visual Studio 52
creating 51
creating, in Azure Portal 52
deploying, from Visual Studio 57, 59
deploying, in Azure Portal 52, 53, 56
file types, using 68
limitations 67
Node.js application, creating as 68
Node.js application, deploying 68
Windows Notification Service (WNS) 165

Made in the USA
Monee, IL
18 December 2019